An Ungovernable People

An Ungovernable People

The English and their law in the seventeenth and eighteenth centuries

Edited by

John Brewer and John Styles

Rutgers University Press
New Brunswick, New Jersey

Published in the USA by
Rutgers University Press

Library of Congress Catalog Card Number 79–67826
ISBN 0–8135–0891–6

First published 1980

Published in Great Britain by
Hutchinson & Co. (Publishers) Ltd

Printed in Great Britain

Contents

Illustrations

Plates (between pages 176 and 177)

A group of 'good fellows' at the alehouse (British Library)

Presentment of the jury for the hundreds of Hinckford and Witham, Essex, October 1644

'Midas; or the Surry Justice' (*Oxford Magazine*, 1768)

'Mr Alderman W——s in his Magisterial Character' (*Oxford Magazine*, 1770)

The area between the Turvin valley and the town of Halifax, from Thomas Jeffrey's map of Yorkshire, 1775 (The Syndics of Cambridge University Library)

A pair of dies for striking counterfeit moidores (Calderdale Museums Service)

The front parade of the King's Bench prison in the early nineteenth century

King's Bench prisoners tossing a bailiff in a blanket

Maps and charts

Preface

An Ungovernable People was conceived during 1976 as a joint enterprise by a group of historians who, Robert Malcolmson apart, had all been based at the University of Cambridge. In so far as the subsequent dispersal of the contributors across four countries has permitted, the undertaking has remained a collaborative one. Although John Brewer and John Styles have shared responsibility for the editorial chores, each contributor has benefited from the advice and criticism of *all* his or her colleagues.

The contributors would like collectively to thank the staffs of the Public Record Office and the British Library, for their assistance, and Claire L'Enfant of Hutchinson, for her enthusiasm, her encouragement and her patience in the face of repeated delays.

Keith Wrightson would like to thank the staffs of the Essex Record Office, the Lancashire Record Office and the Greater London Record Office, for their assistance, the SSRC Cambridge Group for the History of Population and Social Structure, for permission to quote material from their literacy file, and the Vicar of Burnham-on-Crouch, for permission to use the parish register of Burnham.

John Walter would like to thank all those who have helped him in the preparation of his chapter and, in particular, Professor D. C. Coleman and Keith Wrightson. He owes a special debt to the staff of the Essex County Record Office, particularly Nancy Briggs and Arthur Searle. He would also like to acknowledge with thanks the financial support he received while undertaking the research for his chapter as the holder of the Eileen Power Memorial Studentship.

Robert Malcolmson would like to thank several people who assisted him in the preparation of his essay, notably Dorothy Vinter, who generously lent him some of her research notes on Kingswood, John Beattie, Edward Thompson, and John Walsh. He is especially grateful to John Brewer and John Styles for their thorough, constructive and penetrating comments on an earlier draft of his chapter. He is indebted to the Canada Council, for financial assistance, and to the staff of the Bristol Reference Library, for their efficient help with the sources relevant to his research. The map of Kingswood (page 88) was drawn by Roger Wheate.

John Brewer thanks John Styles, Joanna Innes, Susan Hewitt, John Morrill, David Lieberman. Part of the work for this essay was financed by the Social Science Research Council.

John Styles would like to thank the other contributors and, in particular, his fellow editor, for their help and patience while he was ill; Alan Betteridge, the Calderdale Metropolitan District Archivist, for his unfailing interest and assistance; Bill Connor, Leslie Goldthorpe and Estelle Saunders, for various kindnesses; and Earl Fitzwilliam, the Trustees of the Wentworth Woodhouse Estates Co. and the Sheffield City Library for their kind permission to quote from the papers of the Second Marquis of Rockingham in Sheffield City Library. He would also like to acknowledge with thanks the financial support he received during the preparation of his chapter as the holder of Research Fellowships at the Institute of Historical Research and Sidney Sussex College, Cambridge.

Joanna Innes would like to thank Janet Roper, for suggesting the use of the diagrams in the text; John Brewer and John Styles, for their comments; and the staff of the Guildhall Library. She would also like to acknowledge with thanks the financial support she received during the preparation of her chapter from the Social Science Research Council and as the holder of a Gamble Studentship at Newnham College, Cambridge.

A note on dates

Old style dates are reported as given in the primary sources, except that the year is always taken to begin on 1 January.

Introduction

There is but one thing which the people in this country look upon as repugnant to happiness, which is arbitrary power, despotism: and they think that to abolish despotism it is sufficient to establish rules.[1]*

Largely because of the work of recent social historians, the range of permissible questions and the number of legitimate subjects for historical investigation have burgeoned since the second world war. The grand men of the past – kings, nobles, clerics and courtiers – together with the busy-beaver entrepreneur so beloved of historians of economic development, now have to share the historical stage with the peasant, the craftsman and the day labourer. Detailed scrutiny of the venerable institutions – church, monarchy, administration – is, to an increasing degree, accompanied if not replaced by investigations of the family, work and play, poverty, literacy and, most recently, by the examination of crime and the law. Naturally these subjects have not all been tackled in the same way – the fraternity of social historians is already sufficiently large to preclude this – but the best studies have usually avoided treating their subjects in isolation and have used them as a *point d'appui*, as the basis for inquiry into the nature of political, economic and social relationships within a given society. The best social history, in other words, is not the history of society with the questions of politics and power omitted, nor does it confine itself to a single social group or class, as if groups any more than men are 'islands unto themselves'.[2]

An approach that addresses the questions of power and authority and that examines social groups contextually lends itself ideally to the historical study of the workings of the law, and it is the one adopted by the contributors to *An Ungovernable People* The essays address three main questions: what was the nature of authority and how was power exercised in seventeenth- and eighteenth-century England, a

* Notes to each chapter appear in a section beginning on page 311.

society pledged to 'the rule of law'; how were the law and justice perceived by members of different classes and social groups; and in what ways did people organize themselves to be able to take advantage of the law or to avoid its consequences?

These issues are discussed using a case-study approach. Each essay focuses on a particular source of conflict – village regulation, the price and shipment of grain, the construction of turnpike road, the imprisonment of debtors, the circulation of counterfeit coin, and the nature of political authority – and uses the dispute as a means of raising general questions about the nature of 'the law' and of authority.

This book is not a work of legal history: there is no attempt to delineate the changing internal structure of the law during the seventeenth and eighteenth centuries. Such a complex, even unenviable, task we leave to those who specialize in such developments. Equally, the essays do not seek to chart secular trends in types of crime nor to calculate rates of prosecution. A statistical approach of this sort, which necessarily entails lumping together highly disparate crimes and types of law-breaking into general categories, is inappropriate when investigating the chief concerns of this book, namely the workings of the legal process and people's attitudes towards it.[3] Rather, *An Ungovernable People* follows the approach adopted in *Albion's Fatal Tree,*[4] the illuminating and provocative collection of the Warwick University Centre for the Study of Social History, which has been such an important stimulus to the study of law and crime in this period. One of the chief purposes of this book is to build on the pioneering work of Thompson, Hay and Linebaugh by providing a detailed examination of the particular mechanisms of law enforcement, the structures of authority and the institutional diversity of the law. Some of the essays affirm and others raise issues that question the conclusions of *Albion's Fatal Tree,* but all of the contributors hope that their discussion will extend the debate about the indubitably crucial questions of the nature of authority and the rule of law in seventeenth- and eighteenth-century England.

The case-study approach adopted in *Albion's Fatal Tree* and these essays has several virtues. It enables us to examine the strengths and weaknesses of Stuart and Hanoverian authority in the light of particular laws and agencies which regulated specific forms of conduct. The question of the relationship between the legal system, authority and state power in seventeenth- and eighteenth-century England is one of quite extraordinary complexity. On the one hand, the courts were powerful regulatory mechanisms, dealing not only with crime

but numerous aspects of social and economic life. It is no exaggeration to argue that the long arm of the law was the strongest limb of the
body politic. But, on the other hand, law enforcement varied in its
intensity and efficiency: some areas were virtually 'lawless zones'; the
practice of local courts sometimes deviated considerably from the
letter of the law as enacted or interpreted in Westminster; and most
legal officials were rank amateurs who were as much concerned with
the preservation of local harmony as they were with the (often
divisive) business of litigation. In sum, there were considerable
institutional constraints on the exercise of authority through the law.

The absence of a class of legal administrators, the tensions between
centre and locality and the remarkable variations in law enforcement
make it extremely difficult to generalize about either state power or
the exercise of authority. Because they both manifested themselves
primarily through the law, they were mediated by a complex, varied,
almost idiosyncratic process. The disparate ways in which this process or mechanism operated have received relatively little attention
from historians. These essays therefore focus on particular examples
of the ways in which the different institutions and authorities worked
in an attempt to enhance our understanding of the nature of governance in seventeenth- and eighteenth-century England. Just how well
equipped was the Stuart state to deal with the recalcitrant villager and
the enraged grain rioter? How extensive and effective was the authority that opposed the Kingswood colliers' destruction of turnpikes,
the Yorkshiremen's counterfeiting operations, the attempts of debtors
to obtain their liberty and the efforts of radicals to alter the polity?
These questions can be satisfactorily answered only by a careful
examination of the relevant statutes and common law, by scrutiny of
the structures of authority and officialdom and, most significantly, by
the delineation of the judicial process through which action was taken
by those in authority. Only by piecing together these different com-
ponents can we make specific such abstractions as 'state power' and
'the rule of law'.

Our case studies are also very revealing of attitudes towards
authority and the law. They demonstrate the extent to which seven-
teenth- and eighteenth-century Englishmen's conceptions of government were intimately bound up with their actual experience of the
law. This sense of the political nature of the law (and of the legal
nature of politics) was in part a direct consequence of the state's use
of the courts as the chief means of exercising authority and enforcing
regulations. It was in the courtroom or, at least, in the presence of the

justice of the peace and his clerk, that men were most aware of the powers that were wielded over them. Good governance was equated with justice, and the fair dispensation of the law with good government: in this sense 'the rule of law' was no empty phrase.

Indeed, the notion of 'the rule of law' was central to seventeenth- and eighteenth-century Englishmen's understanding of what was both special and laudable about their political system. It was a shibboletn of English politics that English law was the birthright of every citizeh who, unlike many of his European counterparts, was subject not to the whim of a capricious individual but to a set of prescriptions that bound *all* members of the polity.[5] Such a characterization of the English 'rule of law' will not, of course, pass muster as an accurate description of the *modus operandi* of the legal process, but it did serve as an idealization, a potent 'fiction', to use Edmund Morgan's term,[6] which commanded widespread assent from both patricians and plebeians.

The purchase of this ideology of 'the rule of law' had several important consequences, many of which can be observed in these essays. Those in authority were constrained to some extent by their obligation to act in accordance with this ideology. They recognized (and, as Douglas Hay has pointed out, flaunted their recognition)[7] that they should be bound by the laws which they themselves had a duty to enforce and that they were obliged to follow certain defined procedural rules. Because authority derived its legitimacy from the rule of law, 'the law' was used as a standard by which to judge the just exercise of authority. Authorities therefore chose to limit themselves in order to acquire greater effectiveness: they traded unmediated power for legitimacy.

This self-imposed restraint had its effect not only on authority and the perceived obligations of a patrician class, but also helped shape the opinions of the humbler members of society who, for whatever reason, came within the purview of the law. It is, of course, notoriously difficult to capture that most elusive of historical quarries, popular attitudes towards the law. We can recover patrician views with relative ease (though there is a distressing tendency to simplify them). Lawyers' books, legal treatises, assize sermons, justices' diaries, gentlemen's letters and memoirs: they all provide evidence that is readily to hand. But the *menu peuple* wrote little and still less has been preserved. Fortunately, the sorts of conflict discussed in this book often generated evidence that otherwise would not be available to us. Indeed, it is often *only* when conflict occurred that evidence of demotic attitudes survives. The investigations of authority and the depositions of the courts, recorded precisely because there was a dispute, frequently illuminate popular beliefs and conduct which might otherwise be obscured or hidden. Such evidence, however, needs to be handled with care and sensitivity: those who find themselves in court or before a magistrate are as likely to say what is expected of them, or what they think most appropriate in the circumstances (which, after all, might sometimes be a matter of life and death to them), as they are to blurt out the truth or reveal their true feelings. Nevertheless, the conflicts examined in these essays reveal how widespread was popular knowledge of the law and the extent to which people made explicit assumptions which, under 'normal circumstances', they would have been unlikely or reluctant to express openly or publicly. The Kingswood colliers' letter to the turnpike commissioners, the pamphlets objecting to imprisonment for debt or urging popular sovereignty, the depositions and counter-depositions of Yorkshire coiners: these rich and highly informative materials could have been generated only in the context of an acrimonious dispute. Popular views of authority and the law were forged in the crucible of conflict. Inchoate ideas were given shape and definition, private grumblings previously confined to the alehouse or the parlour were shouted in the market-place. Occasionally men and women were led to redefine their relationship not only with other individuals or groups but towards the law itself.

What, then, were these attitudes, and how were they affected by the notion of 'the rule of law'? At first sight the chief *dramatis personae* of these essays – the seventeenth-century villager and grain rioter, the incarcerated debtor, the sturdy Kingswood collier, the Yorkshire counterfeiter and the Hanoverian radical – appear remarkably cavalier in their attitudes towards the law. Time and again our discussion focuses on a conflict between, on the one hand, statute law and its conventional enforcement – the law of those in authority – and, on the other, the people's own notions of justice or of the legitimacy of certain illegal acts. It would seem that the law of patrician society was not the justice of plebeian culture. But it is important to understand the character of the criticism directed at the law and its office-holders, and the nature of the disputes between the humble and those in authority. Criticism of particular pieces of legislation or of the conduct of individual magistrates and court officers – attacks on specific injustices and abuses – were rarely generalized into a critique of authority or the law. On the contrary, magistrates and laws were usually judged according to their degree of conformity to 'the rule of law'. Popular grievances, often vividly expressed in judicial language, took the form either of complaints about authority's failure to execute the letter of the law, or of attacks on the recalcitrance and moral obtuseness of those who, for whatever reason, refused to fulfil the social and moral purposes for which the law had been created. In sum, grievances were more likely to be expressed in terms of authority's dereliction of duty than as an explicit challenge to authority itself.

The notion that all men were under the law therefore provided the ideological framework for most of the disputes discussed in *An Ungovernable People*. This is not to take a consensual view of seventeenth- and eighteenth-century English society. Though patricians and plebeians both used the language of 'the rule of law', their understanding of what we have called its social and moral purposes could differ sharply. All men assumed that the law should work *pro bono publico*, but one man's view of the public good was often regarded by another as a flagrant instance of private interest. Different meanings were attached to the well-worn cliché of 'the rule of law'.

Such differences of interpretation and meaning can be seen in the attitudes adopted by those who challenged authority, and go far towards explaining why popular criticism remained within the parameters of legal debate. The opponents of the magistrate or of a particular law seized (and laid special emphasis) upon certain aspects of the tradition of the rule of law which appeared to justify resistance to office-holders or to legitimate participation or intervention in the legal process. They drew particularly on the assumption that, if all men were subject to the law, then those in authority were *accountable* for their actions – accountable both in law and to the law. In the spheres of both politics and the law this precept was highly controversial. Was it to be narrowly construed to mean simply that legal action could be taken against office-holders who abused their trust, or did it imply, as many plebeians clearly thought, that injured parties could take extra-legal action to secure redress? These essays demonstrate the extent of the belief, sustained even by those who did not necessarily have access to the law, that they were entitled to assert their notion of the common good, and to ensure that it was secured and sustained by the law and those who executed it. It was legitimate to show the magistrate how he ought to enforce the assize of bread or to demonstrate the fundamental illegality of imprisonment for debt by a mass breakout from gaol. Such were particular examples of the belief, exploited and generalized by Wilkite radicals, in the strongly asserted right to *participate* in securing justice.

Though it is not altogether clear whether these participatory assumptions were peculiarly English, there were many features of the English judicial system which served to reinforce them. Office-holders, as we have seen, were never a class apart. Men from all classes, with the notable exception of the labouring poor, contributed to the workings of a citizen judiciary. Often such service was seen as an imposition, but it was also a source of pride for the men of small property who enjoyed the social standing that came with minor parochial office. Moreover, the absence of a legal post was no necessary barrier to involvement in the judicial process. The 'hue and cry', the *posse comitatus*, the use of the pillory, but, above all, trial by jury – 'putting oneself on one's country' – all explicitly required participation in the workings of justice. There were therefore both ideological and institutional aspects of the English judicial system which encouraged the assertion of the popular right to secure the fair and equitable enactment of justice.

It was also the assumption of those who regarded themselves as injured parties that this popular right commanded at least grudging recognition from those in authority. The actions of aggrieved parties were therefore often highly demonstrative: they were designed to draw attention to complaints and to cajole those in power into remedying the situation. They were neither knee-jerk responses to misfortune nor the temper tantrums of a restrained or frustrated child; rather, they were actions deliberately undertaken as part of a *negotiative process* whose outcome, it was hoped, would satisfy both the aggrieved party and the authorities.[8]

The pursuit of redress could take either legal or extra-legal forms, though more often than not the two were combined. Petitioning and litigation went hand in hand with riots, demonstrations and the anonymous letter. These protests were neither indiscriminate nor unconstrained. The level of violence or disorder almost invariably corresponded to the lack of responsiveness of those in authority. When first aired, a grievance was more likely to be taken through accepted legal or political channels; it was only when authorities declined to act that hostilities escalated.

There was an expectation, therefore, that those in authority knew that protests about specific grievances were intended to provoke a remedial response, and not to challenge authority *per se*. Such an assumption was only possible as long as the aggrieved had some faith in authority's willingness to be bound by the law and the ideals it was supposed to embody. Negotiation, of course, was not carried on between equals: those in authority were far more powerful than those seeking redress, even if both parties were in some sense bound by overlapping conceptions of law and justice. Equally, the aggrieved were playing a very dangerous game in which the odds were heavily against them: as discussed in Chapter 2, the breakdown of the negotiative process could have disastrous consequences for those who pursued redress. But the willingness of those resisting innovation (as in the case of the Kingswood colliers and the turnpikes), asserting a traditional right (grain rioters), or challenging a hallowed but legally dubious procedure (imprisonment for debt) to operate within the parameters of the rule of law is truly remarkable.

In examining the negotiative process we have turned from a discussion of attitudes towards the law to the question of the tactics and stratagems employed by those who had contact with the legal process. There were a number of general features of the English judicial system which made it extremely susceptible to exploitation by individuals or groups. First and foremost, the legal process was of a highly discretionary nature. The amateur officials who manned the courts might be active or indolent; their own predilections affected those offences that were winked at and those that were prosecuted with rigour. Constables and justices acted in a pragmatic, *ad hoc* way. The sentence meted out as punishment, the pardon offered the contrite offender: both were very much the gift – to be granted or withheld – of the appropriate officers of the court. Nearly all prosecutions were brought privately: the decision to prosecute, the choice of the court in which the case was tried,[9] the nature of the charge and the statute under which it was brought were largely in the hands of the party who initiated proceedings. The entire legal fabric, from prosecution to punishment, was shot through with discretion. In consequence it was not difficult for office-holders to employ their position for their own private ends (including that of making money from the law), or for citizens to use the law either to legitimate some particular end such as commercial profit or the reformation of manners, or maliciously to prosecute an opponent, enemy or business rival.

This selective, non-bureaucratic operation of the law has recently been emphasized by Douglas Hay in his discussion of the socially discriminatory operation of the eighteenth-century legal process. He shows how a discretionary system, operating in a society where there were gross inequalities of wealth, was highly conducive to manipulation and control by the propertied men who created the substance of the law, overlooked its execution as justices of the peace and were the customary prosecutors in trials for theft. Discretion, Hay argues, facilitated the use of the courts as a 'selective instrument of class justice'.[10] The patrician elite, able to choose whether to prosecute, whether to provide character references for the accused and whether to ask that mercy be extended to the guilty, wielded a veritable sword of Damocles over plebeian Englishmen. Discretion meant that the leaders of society had both the opportunity to be kind *and* the capacity to be malicious. Such a powerful weapon was used to evoke either plebeian gratitude or plebeian fear and to cement the sometimes fragile bonds of deference.

The use of the judicial process as a class tool was, of course, one of its most important functions. The substance of the law served to legitimate existing social arrangements and to facilitate those changes desired by the patrician class of lawmakers. Seemingly impartial legislation was enforced partially and access to the law was restricted to those who could afford to pay legal costs and fees which, in the higher courts of the land, were substantial. *Pace* the fiction of 'the rule of law', justice was not necessarily the perquisite of every Englishman. But this does not mean that we should regard the seventeenth- and eighteenth-century legal process as simply an instrument of an elite, or as serving only a class function. The discretion and voluntaristic nature of the legal system that aided patrician power also enabled others to exploit the law. Indeed, if this had not been the case, if the courts had not provided a forum or an arena open, within limits, to many groups whose purposes cannot be characterized as the exercise of class justice, then the fiction of the rule of law would not have been so potent. When seventeenth- and eighteenth-century Englishmen thought of the law, they thought not only of the criminal law and its preoccupation with theft, but of the common law in its broadest sense and of the body of regulations and equitable practice which oiled the social mechanism and mediated disputes of all kinds, including those that occurred within as well as between classes. Their apprehension of the law was a comprehensive one which embraced the juridical and political aspects of the society and which saw the benefits (inequitably distributed as they were) of such a system. No doubt this helped humbler men to reach a grudging accommodation with the more egregious aspects of the criminal process.

Even though the plebeian and the underdog were invariably disadvantaged when they clashed with those in authority or had recourse to the courts, they knew that they were never merely the passive victims of a process that they were powerless to effect. Seventeenth-century villagers, eighteenth-century debtors, the colliers of Kingswood and the coiners of Halifax, as well as the metropolitan radicals supporting Wilkes, were all prepared to make concerted efforts to exploit, alter or evade the law and to bargain with, bully and bamboozle those in authority. The ideology of the rule of law was invoked to justify the prosecution and policing of officials and the public presentation of grievances; archaic procedures were used to further radical ends; one authority was played off against another; actions were brought to test the legality of particular laws, and extra-legal action was legitimized by appeals to the principles of justice which the law was supposed to embody. The room for manoeuvre may have been limited, but it was exploited to the full.

In examining the workings of authority through the judicial process, the different attitudes towards the law and the tactics employed by litigants and those who confronted authority, *An Ungovernable People* emphasizes a number of paradoxes. In seventeenth- and eighteenth-century England the law was a remarkably potent force. It was the chief means of exercising authority, the main vehicle of state power, an important way of resolving disputes and, because of the extraordinarily widespread acceptance of the notion of the rule of law, a vital means of legitimizing private initiatives. Yet, for all that, the imprimatur of the law conferred only limited power on those who were its beneficiaries. Both the *modus operandi* of the law and the ideology that lay behind it served to constrain authority and to limit those who tried to manipulate the legal process. Moreover, though one of the main functions of the law was to facilitate the (largely local) exercise of authority by a governing class, that was never its sole function or role. The law was not the absolute property of patricians, but a limited multiple-use right available to most Englishmen, apart (a big caveat this) from the labouring poor. Finally, there were both widely shared and sharply differing ideas about the nature of the law in seventeenth- and eighteenth-century England. The fiction of the rule of law commanded remarkable support and was the framework within which most conflict occurred. On the other hand, appeal to this common prescription should not be allowed to conceal the considerable divergences of opinion about what the rule of law entailed. Such differences point to the intense economic, social and political conflicts that underpin the legal activities discussed in these essays.

1 Two concepts of order: justices, constables and jurymen in seventeenth-century England

Keith Wrightson, University of St Andrews

The Justices will set us by the heels
If we do not as we should,
Which if we perform, the townsmen will storm,
Some of them hang's if they could.

The song of James Gyffon, Constable of Albury (1626)[1]

At about midnight on the night of Saturday 14 August 1652, the watchmen of West Leigh, Lancashire, Robert Sweetlove, a twenty-three-year-old husbandman, and Humphrey Whittall, a thirty-five-year-old buttonmaker, were proceeding on their patrol when they heard 'a great noyse' and saw 'a great light' in the house of Nicholas Rannicar, alehousekeeper. They stopped, entered the house and there 'found William Corfe and Robert Bradshaw of Abraham, John Urmeston and Robert Rigbie of Hindley and John Hurst of West Leigh drinkeing healths singinge and swereinge in a most disorderly manner'. Advancing on this company of 'goodfellows', the watchmen 'urged them to depart and to forbeare these their disorderly courses', saying, 'Gentlemen ye know there is an Acte that none shall continue drinkings after Nyne of the Clock in the night and that no Alewife should fill any drinke after that hower.' To this Rigby and Bradshaw replied, 'Wee know there is such an Acte but weele not obey it, for weele drinke as long as wee please', subsequently threatening the watchmen 'that if they would not goe out of the house they would send them out, for they had nothing to doe with them'. The watchmen went their way.[2]

This unremarkable incident serves to introduce some of the themes which I wish to discuss briefly in this paper. For these exchanges reveal nicely a conflict between the concept of order of the governing magistracy of seventeenth-century England as embodied in legislation and the somewhat broader area of behaviour permitted to themselves by a group of villagers. Ensnared at the point where

national legislative prescription and local customary norms inter-
sected were the wretched village officers, the much tried, sorely abused,
essential work-horses of seventeenth-century local administration.

No student of the period is likely to underestimate the ubiquity
and the emotional force of the concept of order in the England of the
Tudors and early Stuarts. Contemporary moralists, administrators
and legislators persistently employed the word in their discussions of
political, social and economic relationships. Humbler and less articulate Englishmen used it no less in their denunciations of inebriate
and foul-mouthed neighbours than did their betters in their sublime
articulations of the structure of the universe. The concept of order
was ubiquitous, but this is not to say that it was monolithic. For the
notion of order embodied in the stacks of regulative statutes passed
by Tudor and early Stuart parliaments should not be identified too
readily with that implicit in the norms and attitudes which governed
social behaviour in the village community. While both had their
origin in a shared concern with the maintenance of social harmony,
order might have markedly different implications in different situations. In particular, the very process of definition and statutory regulation which was involved in the legislative initiative might ultimately
threaten to create new problems of order and obedience at the point
at which precise national legislation came into contact with less
defined local custom.

This simple fact has perhaps been obscured by the tendency among
historians to conduct discussions of the problem of order primarily
at the elevated level of official ideology. The 'order' discussed is that
of conventional moralists and political thinkers, of the preachers of
assize sermons and the writers of preambles to statutes. It is the order
of the 'Homily on Obedience' and of Wentworth's speech to the
Council of the North. This was order as a coherent structure of social
relationships and moral values, as an aspiration towards a condition
of universal harmony which was, as Christopher Hudson preached
to the magistrates of Lancashire in 1632, a glorification of God, the
orderer of all things.[3] Order thus conceived was at once an ideal
arrangement of human institutions, a pattern of authority and an
ultimate scheme of values. It projected a stable and harmonious ideal
of human affairs which eliminated the possibility of rebellion, of
social conflict, of the sins which might stimulate a stern deity to
chastise his disordered people with his judgements of dearth, pesti-
lence and war.

This concept of order as a positive ideal to be achieved and defended was repeatedly elaborated by statesmen and moralists endeavouring to contain the perplexing problems of a fluid social reality within the framework of a uniform and enduring structure of traditional values and social relationships. John Downame, the Jacobean divine, urged his readers to make the establishment of a righteous order

the principal scope of all their actions, using all good means whereby it may be furthered and advanced. As Princes and Magistrates by enacting good lawes and seeing them duely executed. . . . Ministers by leading those which are committed unto their charge in the waies of truth and godlinesse. . . . Finally the people, by yeelding their cheerfull obedience to the godly lawes of Governors and by embracing the sound and profitable doctrine and imitating the Christian and religious examples of their godly teachers.[4]

Arthur Dent, one of the most popular moralists of the early seventeenth century, argued that in a properly ordered Christian commonwealth,

doubtlesse, doubtlesse we should live and see good dayes: all future dangers should be prevented, our peace prolonged, our state established, our king preserved and the Gospel continued. Then should we still enjoy our lives, our goods, our landes, our livings . . . Yea . . . we should eat the good things of the land, spending our days in much comfort, peace and tranquility and leave great blessings unto our children and posterity from age to age, from generation to generation.[5]

Downame and Dent, of course, were both Puritans. As such they were more acutely aware of England's disorders than many of their contemporaries, more intoxicated with the poetry of the Bible in their projection of the imagined future. Yet only their enthusiasm and the consistency of their idealism distinguished their statements from those of England's secular and ecclesiastical governors. The ideal of order was more prosaically but no less firmly embodied in the regulative penal legislation to which the parliaments of the time devoted so much energy. On the one hand were the Acts which defined, codified, elaborated and generalized existing good practice in the ordering of social and economic life. On the other was the series of enactments pushed through by such moral entrepreneurs as the Puritan gentry to regulate the 'common country disorders' of drunkenness, profanity, sabbath-breaking and the like; legislative support was obtained by an appeal to the generalized concept of order.[6]

Some way removed from the notion of order espoused by moralists and legislators, the order of the study and of the debating chamber, lay the complex of attitudes which surrounded the maintenance of harmony not so much between God and man, or even prince and people, as between neighbours in the face-to-face and day-to-day relationships of the village community. Order, as it was conceived of at this most intimate local level, was less a positive aspiration towards a national condition of disciplined social harmony than a negative absence of disruptive conflict locally. One would not wish to sentimentalize the social relationships of a seventeenth-century village into a picture of neighbourly solidarity and harmony. Villages were riddled with petty conflicts and rivalries of interest. But for this very reason order at this level was characterized by an impulse to avoid, or at any rate contain, such conflict, while at the same time allowing a considerably larger area of ambivalent permitted behaviour than was compatible with the nice definitions of moralists and legislators. 'Order' meant little more than conformity to a fairly malleable local custom which was considerably more flexible than statute law. The maintenance of order meant less the enforcement of impersonal regulations than the restraint of conflict among known individuals in a specific local context. It concentrated above all on the dual task of resolving the more poisonous kinds of dissension, while at the same time avoiding if possible the nuisances and expenses which might endanger the precarious livelihood and marginal surplus of a predominantly peasant population.

Thus the inhabitants of a village might take action, formally or informally, against such a 'daily practiser of mischief' as Robert Wilson of Ashwell in Hertfordshire. His neighbours reported him to the justices as one who pilfered their wood and corn, sowed discord among them by his 'perverse humour and bould speech' and was 'ready to lay hould upon any occasion to enter into tumult'. They might draw up an 'order' for their township, as did the inhabitants of Aughton, Lancashire, in 1630, to avoid the expense of bastard children or of squatters who might inflate the poor rates, and to stipulate the contributions for highway repair and poor relief.[7] They might even welcome a new statute which allowed them to proceed firmly against squatters or vagrants. They were less likely to embrace the full panoply of the penal laws. For a vigorous application of the laws could excite conflict within the local community.

Time after time in the later sixteenth and earlier seventeenth centuries the statutory proscription of established local customs resulted in popular reluctance either to accept the law's definition of an offence, or to enforce it where it ran counter to local needs. The

Edwardian Act for the licensing of alehouses, for example, attempted, in the interests of preventing 'hurts and trobles . . . abuses and disorders', to restrict participation in a trade which had been a customary by-employment of the poor since at least the thirteenth century. Enforcement of the Elizabethan Statute of Artificers might threaten, in some localities, to interfere with the unapprenticed participation in trades and manufactures which was of considerable local economic importance.[8] In the case of laws intended to regulate personal conduct, the common people might enjoy a radically different perception of the value of the behaviour proscribed. 'Unlawful gaming' and 'inordinate tippling' in a 'disorderly alehouse' in the eyes of the law might be 'good fellowship and a good means to increase a love amongst neighbours' in the eyes of villagers. Indeed, one moralist of the time actually complained that linguistic conventions among country people restrained their perception of the disorderly nature of many aspects of their behaviour. A man who supported his word with profane oaths (an offence legislated against in 1623 and 1650), might be regarded locally as 'of stout courage'. A frequenter of 'disordered and unlawfull exercises and pastimes' on the sabbath (legislated against in 1625, 1644, 1650 and 1657) might be 'a fine proper and a nimble man' to admiring locals. Pre-marital sexual lapses which did not result in bastard births were 'the tricke of youth'. A man prepared to stand and fight if need be was 'a tall man'.[9] Above all, the tension between the order of the law and that of the neighbourhood was a question of scale. For the very complexity of relationships within small communities made it exceedingly difficult to judge the behaviour of an individual without bringing into play a host of personal considerations. If a widow eked out a living by selling ale unlicensed, why should the neighbourhood be troubled with a prosecution which might foment local resentment? The order of the village community could survive occasional drunkenness, erratic church attendance, profane language, neglect of the licensing and apprenticeship laws. It was more likely to be disturbed by the enforcement of the host of penal laws which might excite new conflicts and drain, in fines, its resources. What really mattered was the maintenance of specific, local, personal relationships, not conformity to impersonal law.

In this situation the vital area became that of enforcement, for the degree of law enforcement was the factor which could determine whether central regulation and local customary practice were to enjoy a precarious co-existence or to come into disruptive conflict,

Mediating between the national legislative ideal and ambivalent local realities was the whole apparatus of Tudor and Stuart local government. Upon its officers was devolved the essential task of balancing out the needs and requirements of both provincial society and the royal government. In the case of secular administration, this problem was solved by the justices of the peace, who adopted what has been called a 'doubly passive' stance.[10] On the one hand they seem rarely to have acted vigorously to enforce penal legislation except when stimulated by direct and unambiguous commands from the Privy Council, by crisis conditions, or by both, as for example in their energetic enforcement of famine regulations in 1622 and 1630–1. On the other hand, their characteristic form of procedure was to require the high constables of the hundreds, into which each county was divided, to order the petty constables and presentment jurymen of the townships and villages to make their 'presentments' of local offenders. The 'stacks of statutes' laid upon the shoulders of the justices of the peace were more lightly borne by passing on both the final responsibility for their enforcement, and the strains which that enforcement entailed, to these humbler local officers. Who were they?

All that can be said of the petty constables and hundredal jurymen of England as a body is that they were ordinary members of their communities, subject to the prejudices, the strengths and weaknesses of their society. Officially, petty constables were elected for the year by the courts leet of their manors and often this practice continued. Elsewhere the leet might merely confirm the nomination of the parish vestry, or the office might pass round the villagers in rotation by 'the ancient custom of Houserow'. The parish representatives who sat on the presentment juries of the hundreds of a county were selected by undersheriffs before each meeting of quarter sessions and were later sworn in at sessions, before making their presentment of offenders from their district.[11] None of these systems of appointment could be guaranteed to supply the 'honest and substantiall', 'fitt and serviceable', men repeatedly demanded by the Privy Council and local justices to fill these vitally important offices. Indeed, in the case of that of petty constable, villagers were notoriously reluctant to accept the onerous responsibility of office if they could avoid it. Not infrequently this job was pushed on to a poor man or given to a paid substitute by the person elected, if he had the means. The township of Gold-hanger, Essex, for example, elected in 1626 one Henry Motte, 'a poore man . . . haveing no estate to live by but only his day labour'. Aspull, Lancashire, chose in 1638 one Thomas Tinckler who had 'little over two acres of ground' and was indebted, having 'a verye small personall estate whereupon to subsist'. When he appealed to the justices and was excused service, his neighbours took their revenge by prosecuting him for taking in an aged widow as a lodger! What could happen is further illustrated by the case in Little Hulme, Lancashire, in 1651 when John Mosse, Christopher Walton and Humphrey Bradshaw were charged with finding a constable in respect of the subdivided holding which they shared. Mosse and Walton held nine acres each, Bradshaw only half an acre. Predictably, the two larger men were able to use their influence to get Bradshaw chosen and an appeal to the justices was necessary before they even consented to share his expenses in office.[12]

How typical such examples were is difficult to assess. We know of these cases only because of successful appeals to the justices of the peace. Probably they were common enough, but it would be unwise to make too sweeping a dismissal of the petty constables as shanghaied village paupers. At least a quarter of the constables of Elizabethan Essex surveyed by Professor Samaha were men of 'considerable substance' and yeomen served commonly enough elsewhere. In the case of presentment jurymen the picture is much clearer. This office carried some prestige and the jurymen's ranks were filled up by village notables, men of yeoman status predominating.[13]

The constant fretting of the authorities about the social standing of local officers derived largely from their association of ignorance and negligence with low social position. Michael Dalton summed up the situation with his opinion that 'constables chosen out of the meaner sort are either ignorant what to do; or dare not do as they should; and are not able to spare the time to execute this office'. All this was fair enough in itself. Illiteracy and ignorance of the law undoubtedly struck against the efficiency desired by the authorities. The justices of Hertfordshire complained in 1657 of the unfitness for their duties of illiterate constables and there are examples enough of the inability of such men to read the warrants and precepts sent down to them. One Wiltshire constable in 1616 had to walk two miles every time he received written instructions in order to have them read to him. One Worcestershire man was sufficiently baffled and impressed by 'a leaf of paper written folded up', handed to him by a servant girl who had 'a purpose to be merry' at his expense, that he thought the hue and cry was raised. As regards legal expertise, even the justices of the period had increasingly to rely on frequently updated textbooks of their duties in order to keep abreast of the law. Few villagers can be expected to have possessed Lambarde's *The duties of constables* or Dalton's *The Country Justice*. The law was a maze to the unwary officer. As Major-General Worsley was to complain in 1655, many constables were 'doubtful of what power they have', for the simple reason that 'the law is very dark'.[14]

Both the illiteracy and legal ignorance of local officers, of course, varied widely. In the Protestation Oath returns of 1642, only 7 per cent of the constables of Somerset were illiterate, a level almost matched by the constables of Dorset. Illiteracy among the constables of Nottinghamshire, Sussex, Warwickshire and Buckinghamshire ran between 50 and 53 per cent, while Cheshire and Westmorland constables had the dubious distinction of being 100 per cent illiterate. In a society in which adult male illiteracy was heavily concentrated in the lower reaches of the social hierarchy, the relative performance of constables doubtless depended on the degree to which they were selected from literate village notables or from the population as a whole. Presentment jurymen, as might be expected given their social composition, did rather well. Of the forty-four jurors from Terling, Essex, who signed or marked their presentments between 1612 and 1687, for example, only six could not sign their names.[15] Knowledge of the law, on the other hand, probably greatly depended on the extent to which justices of the peace informed local men of their duties by either putting detailed 'charges' to them at sessions, or issuing to them 'articles' as guides for presentment. Where this was done, regular service could familiarize constables and jurymen with at least those statutes which the local bench regarded as most significant. Among jurymen or constables selected from a small pool of parish notables such regular service was not uncommon. Where the office of constable passed round a village in rotation it was correspondingly rare.[16]

The qualifications of local men for their key role in the policing of the countryside thus varied. From time to time very able and conscientious men were thrown up. The constable of Hampton Lovell, Worcestershire, in 1634 must have paid close attention to the 'charge', for example. He referred specifically to several Acts of Parliament in making his presentment. Again, the jurymen of West Mersea, Essex, were sufficiently conscious of their duties to upbraid the justices for negligent law enforcement, complaining that this 'doth discorige us to make presentment'.[17] At the other extreme, however, were those petty constables who surpassed in their disorders the very miscreants whom they were charged to keep in order. The substitutes hired to serve as constables in one Lancashire village in 1632 were so drunken that they had to be clapped in the stocks themselves. The constable of Chelmsford in 1628 'withdrewe his watchmen to drinkeinge' and then led them in an affray with the watchmen of neighbouring Moulsham. Some officers might abuse their public office by maliciously prosecuting private enemies or rivals or by otherwise turning their brief authority to private advantage. The constable of one Essex village, for example, took advantage of his period of office in 1625 to run a disorderly alehouse. There he entertained the men of nearby townships day and night, innocently informing the constables of their home parishes that he had impressed them for the king's service![18]

Such examples of negligent, drunken and disorderly constables are easy enough to find in sessions files. They can be introduced as evidence of the unsteady legs upon which magisterial authority too often swayed. But they are scarcely typical of the norm. The majority of constables were no worse, and the majority of jurymen probably somewhat better, than their peers in these respects. Both, however, were placed in the intolerable position of having to enforce against their neighbours penal legislation which must frequently have seemed excessively severe, save in the most extreme cases. As a result, they risked not only the loss of time and money in pursuing prosecutions, but also the likelihood of arousing the antipathy of the neighbourhood, accusations of officiousness and malice and even physical danger. The efficient constable or juryman in the eyes of the law would be very likely to turn every tongue, if not every hand, against himself. The villages of the period contained sufficient elements of conflict to ensure that a high premium was placed by the local community upon the maintenance of harmony. Yet a diligent local officer threatened to provoke conflict and drag it out of the neighbourhood to the judicial bench, thus triggering a chain reaction of enmity which might be stabilized only with difficulty.

Thus one finds a reluctance of village officers to present to the justices offenders other than those who had scandalized, threatened or alienated the greater part of the community; who had stepped outside the moral community as it were. The constables of Tarleton, Lancashire, were not unusual in presenting with alacrity two girls who had had bastard children which were unfiliated 'and thereby likely to be chargeable to this parish'. The parish officers of North Mynes, Hertfordshire, lost patience with the persistent drunkard and 'abuser of his neighbours', Harrington Bickley, who had called two good women whores and a village patriarch an 'ould fatbacked rogue'. The inhabitants of Waltham Cross presented 'our neighbour' John Bowden, who persistently harboured vagrants in his disorderly alehouse 'to the great disquiet of his neighbours so that unlesse hee bee . . . dealt with according to lawe and justice there will bee noe living by him'.[19] The occasional swearer, tippler, unapprenticed artisan or unlicensed aleseller, however, was fairly safe unless a local informer or zealous minister took a hand in securing prosecution.

Formal prosecution in the courts was by no means the only, or even the preferred, method of settling such conflicts as arose within villages. This is not simply to say that many petty offences were tolerated (which they were), but that a preference existed for less formal sanctions which might be kept under the control of the community. Thus the villagers of Myddle in Shropshire preferred the cudgelling of a petty thief to his indictment. One Worcestershire man requested the justices that a thief be simply bound to her good behaviour (a condition which would be judged satisfied or otherwise by local opinion), since 'he would not charge her with felony being so small a matter'. Wherever possible mediation was preferred, though it was not always successful. When Adam Martindale fell out with one of his Cheshire parishioners, 'some interposed for peace between us, but to no purpose'. The result was an affray in which Martindale was badly beaten up, but he still refused to take the matter to court, since he 'took all such courses for pure revenge and would make no use of them'.[20]

This attitude towards the law could be so extended that village officers who presented cases to the courts might find the informal sanctions of village opinion turned against themselves. When the constables of Moulsham, Essex, presented Peter Decort for allowing gaming in his alehouse, they were accused of being 'too busie' and of making the presentment through 'spit[e] or malis'. A rumour was spread that they 'desired an offis' and they were mocked at as 'our worships'. When the constable of Bury found a group of men drinking illegally one night in 1649 and asked whether they knew 'what the lawes were', one showed his dislike of the law by replying that 'he now knew not, they were new modelised and Cromwellysed'. For this shaft of wit he found himself in court, but even there continued to belittle the constable by approaching him 'in a feareinge manner askinge howe his worsship did' and 'calling him knave in open court'. The presentment officers of another Lancashire village who put forward the names of several local recusants were generally maligned as being too 'presyce'.[21]

Gossip and ridicule were a hazard of office. There were others, less subtle. When the constable of one Worcestershire township rushed into a drunkard's house to keep the peace he had the clothes torn off his back for his pains. Another who tried to break up traditional May Games was knocked over by the revellers, who then threatened to break his neck. A Lancashire constable who entered an alehouse to clear it of Welsh vagrants left hurriedly after being attacked with a chopping knife. Some village officers might even find themselves called into court by cunning adversaries and accused of malicious prosecutions, libel, or illegal entry.[22]

Not surprisingly, these circumstances could make village officers extremely wary about presenting those misdemeanours with which they came into contact and complaints of constabular negligence, in particular, were a commonplace of the period. This reluctance to prosecute, however, cannot be adequately explained simply in terms of the personal inadequacy, parsimoniousness, or liability to intimidation of village officers. There is a more positive logic in the studied negligence of some officers, which derived ultimately from the strains of their mediating position between their communities and the law. Robert Fazakerley of West Derby, Lancashire, when charged with the serving of warrants upon several neighbours conscientiously attempted to do so, but only after first advertising the fact in the hope that they would keep out of his way. Another northern officer allowed persons placed in the stocks to escape while he absented himself 'to fetch a locke to sett upon the same stocks'. The constable of Braintree, Essex, performed his duty, while at the same time preserving good relationships, when he removed a drunk from an alehouse, but 'would not give his consent to have him punished according to the lawe but let him gooe paieinge 1s when he should have paid 5s'. Richard Kay of Middleton, Lancashire, neglected to serve a warrant on a man in a bastardy case – one, significantly, in which the pregnant girl was from another parish – 'in regard of their nere neighbourhood and other allyance'.[23]

These and other cases highlight the conflict raised in the mind of the man who was both neighbour and officer of the law. When John King, an Essex villager, stole eight hens in 1636 he was rapidly taken by the constable Thomas Burrowes, but then 'did falle downe on his knees . . . and did desire him that he would not be the meanes to cast him away for a few hennes, for it was the first offence that ever he had donne'. Burrowes, taking it upon himself to act as mediator, talked the matter over with the victim of the theft and having decided that it was the lesser of two evils, released the thief. The constables of Hatfield Peverel refused to execute orders to whip an unlicensed ale-seller too poor to pay his fine, while those of Wethersfield would not serve process on illegal cottagers 'because they are poor'. Some even tried to plead the case of offenders while at the same time presenting them. The juryman who presented Widow Reynolds of Birchanger for unlicensed aleselling included the excuse that she was 'a very poore woman and takes almes'. Similarly, the presentment of Josias Barritt of Prittlewell, who had neglected to perform his work on the high-ways, explained: 'but he is a verie poore man and hath foure small children'. In an extraordinarily tortured presentment, the constable of Worsley, Lancashire in 1651 informed the justices, who were con-ducting a rigorous purge of alehouses, that

We have one in our township by name Jony Horridge who breweth and selleth alehouse continually without licens and therefore I could not omit to present her as a misdoer and likewise Richard Princeton who brewes at some times when god makes him able; who though he be a poore man I could not omit to expres him a misdoer And also John Man who brewes ale some times.

This valiant attempt to distinguish degrees of culpability failed to pass the clerk of the peace. He, in an action which admirably sym-bolizes the distinction between the order of the law and that of the community, struck through the excusing clauses and neatly sub-stituted the simple legal formula of an indictment for unlicensed ale-selling.[24]

These various factors could combine to produce a situation in which, as James I's Privy Council complained to the justices of Essex, the public service might be 'carried soe confusedly or executed soe remisslie as the vulgar sort of people will in tyme gett a custome of disobedience'.[25] A situation might develop in which the local courts contributed little more to the enforcement of the law than the provision of machinery for prosecutions initiated by private persons or common informers. Indeed, this was very probably the norm in many English counties prior to the tightening up of local govern-ment, which was so marked a feature of the late sixteenth and early seventeenth centuries. By the beginning of the reign of Charles I in 1625 it persisted in some counties. In others, the justices of the peace had succeeded in establishing at least an acceptable level of regulative control. The situation obtaining as the 'increase of governance' peaked in the years after 1625 can best be illustrated by comparing the experience of two very different areas: Essex and south Lancashire.

In the early and central decades of the seventeenth century, Essex and south Lancashire might appear to have had little enough in common. Essex was a fertile lowland county, one of the principal grain-producing counties of England. Moreover, it was a home county, deeply influenced in its economy, its religious life and its administration by its proximity to the markets and radical pulpits of London and the seat of government in Westminster. Essex was comparatively wealthy, closely governed and solidly Protestant. South Lancashire, in contrast, was comparatively poor. Economically, the area embraced not only the lowland triangle between Preston, Warrington and Manchester, but also the pastoral economies of the extensive coastal marshlands and of the hill country of the east. Lancashire lay far from the hub of secular and ecclesiastical government, was comparatively laxly administered and was notorious (save for the Puritan cloth towns around Manchester) for its religious conservatism.

This baldly stated contrast, while it was as much a commonplace among contemporaries as it has become among historians, might on further reflection be considered more apparent than real. Within each county there were local variations in economy and social structure, which, together with local differentials in administrative effectiveness and in religious complexion, went far to modify their stereotyped images. Essex had its dark corners. Lancashire had its radical oases. Moreover, while the localism of English society in the seventeenth century was considerable, we must also remember that there were strong elements of social and cultural homogeneity by comparison with the more diverse societies of the great continental kingdoms. Again, within our period there were strongly integrative forces at work within the relatively small compass of the kingdom. Not least among these was the influence of the increasingly aggressive central government, expressed above all through the activities of the justices of the peace. By comparing the experience of south Lancashire and Essex in this respect we can detect both the local variations which existed within the overall national chronology of administrative change and the extent to which similar processes of change were active within the nation at large. How far, then, did the two areas differ in the nature and volume of the business handled by their governors in their courts of quarter sessions?

The short answer would be that they differed to a significant degree, but that these differences were diminishing steadily over time.

Let us look first at the volume of prosecutions handled by the justices of the peace. In seven sample years of court business between 1626 and 1639, the justices of Essex handled an average of some fifty-one cases per 10,000 population per year. The comparable rate for the seven years, 1626–38, in south Lancashire was thirty-three. In seven sample years for the period 1646 to 1658, however, the rate of prosecutions handled in Essex fell to thirty-three, while in south Lancashire it rose to sixty-two. In three final sample years, 1662–6, the Essex rate remained stable at thirty-three, while that of south Lancashire returned to its pre-civil war level at thirty-four per 10,000 population per annum. The courts of Essex were declining from a peak of activity in the reign of Charles I, while those of south Lancashire witnessed an interregnum boom in court business which was not sustained thereafter.[26]

The reasons for these changes and fluctuations become apparent only when we examine the actual composition of the cases handled by the justices. Tables 1 and 2 in the appendix (pages 300–3) give detailed breakdowns of court business in both counties. Their message is quite clear. From 1626 to 1640 the sessions of south Lancashire dealt primarily with cases which I have categorized as 'interpersonal disputes'. These cases of theft, assault, trespass, disseisin (dispossession) and poaching represent disputes within particular localities which had resulted in private prosecutions before the justices. In addition, the justices handled a smaller number of cases categorized as 'obligation enforcement'. These cases involved the prosecution of individuals, or even whole communities, for neglect or abuse of local office and failure to perform their obligations in the maintenance of roads and bridges. They were usually initiated by the justices themselves, by the grand jury, or by surveyors of the highways. Finally, came a trickle of cases classed as 'regulative prosecutions'. This category represents the regulative jurisdiction of the justices of the peace, the sphere of the penal statutes and of public presentment by constables and jurymen. In south Lancashire prior to 1640 it was distinguished by its emptiness. From 1646, however, this pattern changed. From that year through to the early 1650s the justices dealt with massive numbers of regulative prosecutions. Thereafter cases of this nature continued to form the principal element in court business.

In Essex, by way of contrast, substantial numbers of regulative prosecutions initiated by constables and jurymen always made up the most significant element of court business, prosecution of this kind reaching a peak in 1630/31. Close behind came prosecutions relating to obligation enforcement, while cases originating in interpersonal disputes came a poor third. In the sphere of regulative prosecution the courts of Essex performed much more consistently than did those of south Lancashire. Unlicensed and disorderly alehousekeepers and persons neglecting church attendance were much more regularly presented in Essex, these offences alone going far to account for the predominance of regulative business. In addition a number of other offences – the illegal erection of cottages, swearing, drunkenness and breaches of the Statute of Artificers relating to servants and apprentices – were more commonly dealt with in the southern county. In Lancashire the swing towards regulative activity after 1646 can be accounted for largely by a novel concern with such offences and with the activities of unlicensed dealers in the victuals trade.

One might infer from these findings that the courts of south Lancashire prior to 1646 functioned primarily as passive instruments for the settlement of disputes arising in local communities and brought privately to the justices for adjudication. From 1646 their character had changed. They developed new teeth as courts of aggressive regulation. The sessions of Essex, however, functioned throughout the period as a court of regulation and obligation enforcement. The character of the court remained unchanged over time, though the volume of its regulative activity could intensify in certain years.

We have, then, two points of contrast in the enforcement of Tudor and Stuart regulative statutes by these crucial local courts. The one contrast is regional, between Essex and Lancashire; the other, chronological, between periods of normal, or even lax, prosecution and periods of intense activity. Both of these matters turned upon the vital issue of how business was brought to court and most particularly upon the steps taken to secure the co-operation of village officers.

Regionally, one finds that the quarter sessions rolls of Essex contain five distinct types of document relating to the initiation of prosecutions. These include on the one hand the individual indictments initiated by private members of the community and on the other hand public presentments by a grand jury of minor gentry, by surveyors of the highways, by petty constables and by hundredal presentment juries. Individual presentments by petty constables were rare save in certain years. Regulative prosecutions were usually initiated by hundredal jurymen replying to charges or articles put to them directly by the high constables of the hundreds. The sessions of Essex thus employed a procedure by which the presentment of minor offences at a local level was institutionalized, built into the normal functioning of the court. This in itself goes some way towards explaining the high level of regulative prosecution in Essex even in normal years.

In Lancashire, for reasons of geography, four distinct courts of quarter sessions were in operation. The justices of the different hundreds of the county met, every quarter, at Lancaster, Preston, Manchester and alternately Ormskirk or Wigan. The grand juries of these distinct courts were in themselves hundredal juries. These Lancashire hundredal juries, however, consisted, like the Essex grand jury, of minor gentlemen rather than villagers. Distanced as they were from village life, they confined their activities largely to the vetting of indictments initiated by private persons. Presentments by petty constables or other village officers were rarely requested and rarely brought before them. This peculiarity of procedure largely accounts for the predominance of interpersonal disputes and the low level of regulative business in Lancashire courts prior to 1646.

The institution of hundredal juries composed of village notables could thus go far to improve regulative efficiency. Nevertheless, the actual performance of such juries depended a great deal upon both their composition from session to session and the rigour with which they were examined by the high constables. On occasion, for example, juries explained that they could not report on particular parishes 'by reason there is none of the jury'.[27] Alternatively, jurors could be singularly unwilling to present offenders. When the high constable of Barstable hundred, Essex, took the presentments of the representatives of thirty-four parishes in 1573, he learned only that a few archery butts, a ducking stool and a bridge needed repairing and that five singlemen were living out of service. For the rest the jury chorused, 'all well'.[28] Such replies were common enough in Essex before 1600. The chronology of change can be illustrated from the presentments of the half-hundred of Witham and the various hundreds associated with it on presentment juries. Before 1590, the jurors presented only occasional decayed roads and bridges and very occasional neglectors of church attendance. From the early 1590s, however, they were more closely questioned, one presentment of 1592, for example, being prefaced,

As touching the rules given us in charge this day we have duly made enquiry of them and either of them and have not anything at this present worthy of reformation.

This initial unwillingness persisted through the 1590s, but from 1602 the juries began to expand the scope of their presentments. They soon evolved the pattern of prosecution of alehouse offences, non-attendance at church and other misdemeanours which became such a pronounced feature of Essex sessions business by 1625.[29] The motivation of this more co-operative spirit is an issue to which we will return.

Efficient presentment juries could thus go some way towards the establishment of regulative rigour, though the marginal nature of the persons commonly presented – occasional alehouse offenders, persistent neglectors of church, unwelcome inmates and cottagers – suggests that presentments could be so contrived as to cut only selectively into local life. This point may be reinforced when we consider the activities of petty constables in presenting cases to the petty sessions or 'monthly meetings' of justices which, after earlier attempts, were regularly established in the years after 1631. These sessions were intended to bring a closer control over the parishes. Petty constables were required to appear at them and were fined for neglect of their duties. It was an uphill struggle for the justices. In the Bolton and Deane division of Lancashire in 1634 negligent constables in fact formed the main group of offenders punished. By 1637/38, however, the constables had been disciplined into reporting on vagrancy and disorderly alehouses. Examination of the actual business dealt with in other divisions of Lancashire and of Essex in the 1630s, reveals how eager the constables became to report on the repression of vagrants, how relatively unwilling they remained to present other types of offender among their neighbours. Little enthusiasm was to be found for the presentment of the moral offences which preoccupied the justices who presided over the petty sessions of the 1640s and 1650s (see Tables 3–7, pages 304–6).

Whatever the achievements of the justices with presentment juries and petty sessions and whatever the personal activity of unusually severe individual justices out of court, real regulative efficiency of the type which produced massive crops of offenders in Essex in 1629–31 and in Lancashire from 1646 required something more. It required, above all, steps to overcome the unwillingness and inefficiency of petty constables by more closely regulating their appointment and by prosecuting their neglect, while at the same time instituting a more systematic presentment of offenders. In Essex at the time of the dearth crisis and disorders of 1629–31 and in Lancashire under the rule of Puritan justices struggling against both economic crisis and ungodliness after 1646, this is exactly what the justices did. Orders flowed out for the appointment of 'sufficient', and the replacement of 'insufficient' or incompetent, constables. Negligent local officers were hauled before the justices, punished and dismissed. The slack in the whole apparatus of social regulation was vigorously drawn in. Years of peculiar concern with and harassment of the village officers corresponded exactly with those of towering peaks of regulative prosecutions (see Table 8, page 307).

Nor was this all. Attempting to make sure that fit constables were appointed and negligent men prosecuted was less than half the battle for the enforcement of the justices' conception of order. Action was also needed, as a petition of Lancashire Puritans in 1647 pointed out, 'to cause the Constables to execute their office'.[30] This end was achieved by the novel insistence that the petty constables of individual parishes and townships return not simply their occasional verbal or written presentments, but also written replies to specifically enumerated articles of inquiry. Precepts listing the articles were sent out to the high constables of the hundreds and communicated by them to the petty constables. They in turn were obliged to bring in their detailed replies, commonly repeating in these the date of the original order of quarter sessions and following the form of the precepts issued to them in making their presentments.

Articles of inquiry were in themselves no novelty. They had been issued by central governments since at least the 1590s as guides to the justices of the peace.[31] But the enforcement of written answers to such articles by village officers was something new in both Essex and Lancashire in the years concerned. Where it was enforced the results were spectacular. The transformation of the structure of sessions business in south Lancashire, for example, was wholly the result of a series of regulative initiatives of this kind. In 1646 and 1647 the drive was against alehouse offences; in 1648 against the alehouses, failure to attend church, and marketing offences. Later years saw attacks on such offences repeated, while the articles were expanded to include other misdemeanours – taking in inmates or lodgers, for example. In almost every year of the interregnum the constables were sent scurrying about their duties and still the justices were unsatisfied. In 1659 they announced at Manchester a new programme. Fearing 'the encouragement of offenders . . . for want of puting in execucon those good penall Lawes made against them', they ordered the constables to draw up indictments and presentments at their townships' expense against 'all offenders comittinge any misdemeanours . . . and prosecute the same and see the said parties brought to condigne punishment'.[32] The justices wanted order, whatever the cost. Fortunately for the constables the restoration intervened before this new policy bore fruit. Though the justices of the early years of Charles II's reign made some efforts to control the victuals trade, intense constabular activity of the type maintained during the interregnum was not renewed.

In the case of Essex, the peak of regulative activity in 1630/31 was the result of an exactly comparable policy of requiring petty constables to produce their written returns to articles of inquiry. Essex was to see later inquiries into popish recusancy in 1641 and the numbers of alehouses in 1644, but activity on the scale of 1630/31 would appear to have been unique.[33]

The key to effective social regulation in this period was thus the securing of efficient presentment of offenders to the local courts of provincial England. Prosecution of this kind, however, placed the presenting officers, the jurymen and petty constables, in a position of considerable difficulty. Fortunately for them, vigorous action was rarely required of them, though they were put under a mounting pressure throughout the early seventeenth century. Again, on occasion, the reserves of energy which lay dormant in the apparatus of social regulation could be drawn upon to intensify the control exercised by the magistrates over the local communities within their jurisdictions. Such regulative initiatives, however, required an enormous and exhausting effort and placed a considerable strain upon the machinery of local administration. As a result they were rarely undertaken, save in conditions of acute economic crisis or when magistrates were motivated by a peculiar zeal for social discipline and godly reformation.

In Lancashire only such major drives initiated from above could achieve the order desired by the justices of the peace. Where they were less zealous and relaxed their hands, little business came up to them freely from below. In Essex, however, the situation was somewhat different, for the gentler pressure placed on the presentment jurymen produced in the earlier seventeenth century a limited willingness to co-operate more regularly with the magistrates. This co-operation was selective in two senses; it involved only certain parishes and only certain offences. Taking the example of prosecutions for unlicensed aleselling (something of a litmus test in these matters), we find that in the years between 1616 and the great purges of 1630/31, fewer than sixty out of over 400 parishes and hamlets in Essex freely presented offenders on three or more occasions. Again, the offences which Essex jurymen prosecuted with any regularity were highly selective – alehouse offences, failure to attend church, cottaging, taking in unwanted inmates. If we are to understand why some parishes chose to co-operate and why they did so in such a limited way, we must understand the little dynamic of change in the villages which proceeded alongside the greater dynamic of national and provincial administration. Let us look briefly at a single parish: Burnham-on-Crouch.[34]

The parish of Burnham lies on the Crouch Estuary in south-east Essex, sixteen miles from Chelmsford where the courts met. In the mid seventeenth century the parish had a population of about 500, supported by agriculture, rural crafts and fishing. There was no resident gentry family and parish society was led instead by the minister and a dozen yeoman families. Below them came a somewhat larger group of substantial husbandmen and craftsmen and below these families came those of the cottagers, labourers and fishermen who made up almost two-thirds of the population. Though Burnham was prosperous by comparison with many Essex villages, it had considerable poverty. In 1671 some 20 per cent of householders were excused payment of the hearth tax on the grounds of chronic poverty. Many of the labourers, fishermen and cottagers were probably little better off.

The manor of Burnham-with-Mangapp possessed a manor court throughout our period of study. By the early seventeenth century, however, it had come to confine its activities to the registration of land transactions, the appointment of local officers and the regulation of minor nuisances. In the absence of any local forum for conflict resolution, such disputes as arose were either settled informally or taken to quarter sessions and assizes. Over the whole period 1603–62 only six cases, all of theft, are known to have been brought before the assizes, most of the accused being labourers. In the same period, however, at least eighty-nine cases were brought before the justices of the peace in quarter sessions, in addition to which a number of villagers were bound over to keep the peace without any formal prosecution being made.

These Burnham cases involved comparatively few interpersonal disputes. There were scattered cases of theft or assault and from time to time villagers were bound over to keep the peace to one another. The latter seems to have been a favoured form of pre-emptive action, which probably went far to defuse potential violence. Obligation enforcement was also little looked to save in 1641/42, when a number of villagers were presented for failing to maintain the highways. Over three-quarters of the known Burnham cases were concerned with social regulation and were publicly presented. The vast majority of these were prosecutions of alehousekeepers and their disorderly customers, to which can be added a scattering of cases of illegal cottaging, taking inmates, failure to attend church and the misdeeds of servants and apprentices. Two points must be made about these cases. First, they were essentially misdemeanours of the poor or of those who countenanced their offences. Secondly, they differed from the occasional interpersonal disputes in that they were not evenly spread over time. In fact their chronology, when traced, reveals a great deal about the relationships of the villagers both with the authorities and with one another.[35]

Between 1603 and 1620 the villagers of Burnham had little enough to do with the justices. There were only five regulative prosecutions in the whole period and two of these concerned a single man – Robert Sampson, a persistently disorderly alehousekeeper, who was twice prosecuted and subsequently bound over to keep the peace to the yeoman who had secured his presentment. After 1620 there was rather more activity. A group of unlicensed alesellers were presented in 1623/24. In the years 1629 to 1631 the parish was caught up in the regulative drive of the Essex justices. Burnham jurymen duly reported on their disorderly alehouses, while the constables prepared their written presentments. Though replying in the negative to most of the articles, they named a handful of swearers, 'alehouse-haunters' and neglectors of church services. When magisterial pressure relaxed, so too did Burnham presentments. From 1639, however, things began to change. That year saw the beginning of a spate of prosecutions for alehouse disorders which continued into the early 1640s and was consolidated during the county-wide purge of alehouses in 1644. Then, in 1647, came a parish petition to the justices concerning alehouse disorders; there was a further flurry of prosecutions through into the 1650s. Both before and after the purge of 1644 this activity directed against the alehouses was a movement from below. The justices were not at this time showing the kind of aggression shown in 1630/31. What was going on in Burnham?

As we assemble the information available in the whole range of local sources relating to the parish, a clear picture slowly emerges. The initial burst of activity in 1639 turns out to have been provoked by the actions of a yeoman churchwarden, John Hills. Back in February 1638 Hills had presented Harrison Lattilaw, a tavern keeper, and several of his customers to the court of the Archdeacon of Essex for drinking and disorders in church service time. Hills's action was something of a novelty, since previous churchwardens had preferred to confine their attentions largely to sexual offences when making presentments to the 'bawdy courts'. It may have been inspired by a newcomer to Burnham, the curate Anthony Sammes. He was a notable Puritan and was soon to be appointed vicar by the Puritan magnate, the Earl of Warwick (in succession to a man who had been happier on the alebench than in the pulpit). Whether or not Sammes's influence was there, the presentment infuriated Lattilaw. Not long before, in December 1637, Hills had presented him to the archdeacon for fornication with his maidservant. Probably he was guilty. His wife had recently died and he was shortly to marry the girl. But he was lucky. The case was dismissed, though not before he had been obliged to pay fees. Only a month after the dismissal Hills presented him again for this offence in addition to the charge of tolerating disorders in his house in service time.

Three days later Lattilaw retaliated. With splendid irony he prosecuted John Hills before the court of the Bishop of London for drunkenness. In this he was supported by two yeomen, Robert Brown and John Clements. They may have had good reason to dislike John Hills's activity against village disorders. Both were on the point of taking office for the year as constables, and Clements had a personal axe to grind. He had been prosecuted by Hills for failing to attend church. The case against Hills, however, was dismissed. He bided his time, then six months later presented Lattilaw and his now wife for pre-nuptial fornication. This time the girl's obvious pregnancy proved the case to anyone with fingers to count upon and Lattilaw was obliged both to pay fees and to undergo penance before the minister and churchwardens. These included, of course, the triumphant John Hills.

There the matter might have ended had not Lattilaw decided to take the offensive against trade rivals. In July 1639 he and John Botting, a customs officer, brought private indictments in quarter sessions against four villagers for unlicensed aleselling. Two of those prosecuted merely submitted and we hear no more of them. The other two, however, were William Philby and his son Thomas. They were poor men, but were tenants of the manor and had powerful connections among the manorial jurymen. Petitions in their defence were quickly got up, led by John Hills and supported by eight leading inhabitants of the parish. Interestingly, the petitioners did not try to deny the Philbys' offences. Instead they excused them and asked for the remission of their fines. They explained that the Philbys were poor and that William had recently suffered losses at sea. They pleaded that the offences were committed 'ignorantly', from 'forgetfulness', and would not be repeated, adding for good measure that the prosecutions had been brought 'upon neighbours malice', 'out of a malicious and envious mind'. The churchwardens among the petitioners expressed a generous willingness to remit that part of the fines due to the parish and urged the nearest justice 'to be a mediator' for them with the court. Whether or not these revealing petitions were successful is uncertain. What is certain is that John Hills went on to complete the discomfiture of the prosecutors by presenting John Botting to the archdeacon in April 1640 for failing to attend church and running a disorderly house on the sabbath. He secured Botting's conviction and the payment of a fine to the parish poor.

This case sufficiently demonstrates the complexity of the circumstances underlying prosecutions. Here we see also the conflict they could arouse, the crucial role of village notables in either promoting or resisting prosecution and their extremely ambivalent attitude towards the law. Equally striking, however, is the fact that the conflict of loyalties evidenced in this dispute seems soon to have been resolved. From 1641 the parish officers regularly presented unlicensed and disorderly alehousekeepers themselves. They prosecuted both the Philbys, who had repeated their offence, and Harrison Lattilaw. Times had changed. Why?

One influence may have been the fact that the initiation of prosecutions was now firmly back in the hands of the parish notables. The selection of offenders for prosecution was no longer complicated by the cross-currents introduced by the activities of Lattilaw and Botting. Yet this explains only the smoothness of prosecution, not the willingness to undertake it. I have argued elsewhere that the growing readiness to regulate the offences of alehousekeepers in Essex in this period stemmed ultimately from a growing concern to discipline the parish poor.[36] This concern had its economic element in the desire to keep down the poor rates and prevent further impoverishment in a period of economic polarization in rural society. It also had its ideological element, partly in religiously inspired hostility to the 'disorders' of the popular culture, partly in the slow assimilation of leading villagers to the concept of order proclaimed from the judicial bench. Such influences may very well have been at work in Burnham. The problem of poverty was severe enough and the burden of supporting the parish poor fell upon the same parish ratepayers who also served as parish officers. Again, their concern with the alehouses was soon augmented with a new preoccupation with preventing the taking in of inmates and unlicensed cottaging in their parish. Shifts in attitudes may have been accelerated by the influence of Anthony Sammes. He was now actively laying the Puritan foundations of what was to become one of the strongest nonconformist congregations in Essex.

This compounding of concern for the authority of the parish's 'natural' leaders, the disorders of the poor and the reformation of manners was made explicit in the parish petition of 1647. It was written by Sammes and supported by six leading landholders and two humbler men. Four of the petitioners were recent constables, two churchwardens. All were literate. They complained against a number of 'very poore people . . . of very lewde livinge and conversation' who were guilty of enticing

farmers servants and other poore people to tipple . . . whole or most part of publicke fast and other dayes and nights togeather causeing them to spend their tyme and moneyes there and to neglect their Masters service.

This petition suggests a consolidation of attitudes among a group of yeomen in the parish and an element of group conflict within the community of a kind not evident eight years before. Attitudes had clarified. Ground won against the petty disorders of village life since 1640 was being defended. The perception of such behaviour had been modified. If this was indeed the case, then the critical point had been reached when the yeomen of the parish were prepared to give consistent and voluntary support to the enforcement of the law, even though that support might extend no further than the selection for prosecution of those offenders who seemed to threaten their own position as masters, employers, ratepayers and pillars of the church.

The experience of a single small parish cannot be used to prove a general case. But it may be suggestive in the light of the broader national and regional trends discussed in this essay. Above all, it may suggest a process of change which may have been more common, though subject to variations in chronology and local peculiarities of circumstance. The initial unwillingness to make regular prosecutions and the intense conflict which prosecutions could touch off are by now familiar. The manner in which the authorities could on occasion cut down into village life, sharply reminding men of the demands of the law, has been witnessed in both Essex and Lancashire. The role of parish notables as brokers between the demands of their governors and those of their neighbours has been observed. The selective nature of their support when they chose to give it to the magistrates is strongly suggestive of the combination of factors which could stimulate their co-operation.

One would not expect such a process of change to be either uniform or universal. There were more egalitarian local communities in England where there was less chance of open conflict between the interests of a yeoman elite and the labouring poor. There were also villages where conflict continued to be expressed in a rustic vernacular free from the legitimizing rhetoric of sermon or statute. Yet elsewhere, the proponents of change may have remained a relatively powerless minority unable to call the tune in village affairs. As we have seen, the evidence of change belongs to central, precocious, Essex rather than to peripheral, backward, Lancashire. In the north, significant change at the village level may well have awaited another time, different circumstances.

Nor were such processes of change necessarily ongoing. They might be slowed, even reversed. As the seventeenth century closed, the regulative initiative described in this essay was losing force. Governmental pressure upon local magistrates relaxed. Enthusiasm for new standards of order and reformation waned both at the level of the nation and of the parish when it became evident that despite its conservative intentions it might have revolutionary implications. In many counties, presentment juries became inactive and disappeared. Formal presentments, where they were required, became increasingly ritualized and empty. In a sense, the manipulation of the courts for local ends by parish oligarchies may have been less needed. New instruments of parish government – the vestry, the poor laws, the settlement laws – had matured and introduced new possibilities for the entirely local settlement of conflict and disciplining of offenders. The courts could return to their accustomed role in defending the property of the propertied.

Nevertheless, the developments of the earlier seventeenth century, however halting and incomplete, were matters of some significance. It has been suggested here that the village communities of the period between the Armada and the restoration were to some extent moral communities, in the sense that they placed a premium upon good neighbourliness and preferred local opinion to the impersonal values of the larger society. The developments in local government and law enforcement of the earlier seventeenth century may have both furthered and reflected the weakening of this particular form of localism. For however conservative in intention, the pulsating search for order could play its part in the slow assimilation of the village notables of some rural areas to the values of their social superiors and religious mentors. Where this was achieved, they were encouraged to identify their interests with those of the magistracy and to express in action their dissociation from the vernacular tradition of their neighbours.

In January 1629 the ministers and seven leading inhabitants of Stock and Butsbury, Essex, petitioned the justices for the suppression of six out of the eight local alehouses. They praised the 'most excellent lawes' passed by Parliament for the suppression of alehouse disorders. They condemned

the slacknes of inferiour officers and other inhabitants of parishes (where these evills abound) to informe the magistrates of the delinquents that such good lawes might be executed.

In a crescendo of righteous indignation, they denounced the drunkenness and idleness bred among poor men and servants and urged the justices to root out these 'styes for such swyne and cages of these uncleane birds'.[37] Where such language could be used, a wedge had been inserted between the 'better sort' of the parishes and their poorer neighbours far more subtle and significant than their age-old inequalities of wealth. For it affected their perception of their social world. It edged forward the slow processes of national incorporation and cultural differentiation which marked one stage of the evolution of pre-industrial society in England.

2 Grain riots and popular attitudes to the law: Maldon and the crisis of 1629

John Walter, University of Essex

Nothing more slackens the reins of government, and the stability of peace, which is upheld by the reverent awe and respect which the people and subjects give to the Magistrate, than when by injustice and unworthinesse, they bring their persons and authority under contempt and dislike; but that they seem not as *Gods* but *Idols*, which have *eares but heare not, eyes but see not, mouths but speak not* true judgement. Against such Magistrates, people are prone to think it, not only just, but meritorious to rebell.

JOHN GAUDEN, *A Sermon Preached Before the Judges at Chelmsford*[1]

Where laws are settled there are other remedies appointed for the relief . . . of the poor, by complaint to the magistrate without violating the established laws of kingdoms or states.

SIR MATTHEW HALE, *Historia Placitorum Coronae* (1676)[2]

A complex historical reality lies imprisoned within the legal strait-jacket defining the crime of riot. Not surprisingly then, ambiguity still surrounds historians' treatment of popular disorder in early modern England. In the case of the food riot, however, it is perhaps becoming more generally accepted that the pattern of disorder was somewhat different from that suggested by the fear of the authorities, or that posited by a too simple relationship between poverty, harvest failure and a presumed popular inclination to riot.[3] Years of harvest failure in England in this period were not scarred by widespread food riots; disorder was largely confined to the weak points within an as yet immature national marketing structure.[4] Moreover, while there can be no doubting the alarm sometimes shown by the authorities when confronted by the licence of the unruly crowd, their response to riot was more subtle and less clear-cut than might otherwise have been predicted. In their use of the law, the authorities displayed a sensitivity to circumstance and context which casts doubt on some of the more extreme emphases on magisterial helplessness and consequent wrath in the face of popular disorder. The delicacy which could characterize authority's handling of the crowd appears often (but not always) to have reflected the carefully circumscribed actions the rioters allowed themselves. The authoritative stereotype of the food riot as a collective form of theft with violence rarely captured the reality of such disorder. Riot was seldom, if ever, a simple and unpremeditated response to hunger and starvation. As the ultimate political weapon of the poor, the food riot was often the culmination of a preceding exchange between the poor and their governors in which the threat of popular violence had been used (unsuccessfully) to coerce authority into action on their behalf. The tradition of riot was itself a constant point of reference in a more enduring relationship between rulers and ruled.

The complex relationship between the poor and their governors, with the food riot as its epicentre, forms the subject of this essay. Using legal records as a point of entry into the mental world of the seventeenth-century poor, the essay attempts to recover in the evidence of the food riot popular attitudes to the law and the proper exercise of authority in early modern England. It does so within the specific context of a detailed reconstruction of events centring on grain riots in the Essex port of Maldon in the crisis of 1629. The pursuit of these themes within the framework of an examination of riot in its local setting is deliberate. The complex meaning of the resort to riot can come only with a knowledge of the context of disorder. Narrowing the focus makes possible the identification and use of a wider range of sources to provide that context. Equally important, it also provides an opportunity to redress the balance of the immediate legal record of riot and restore to those otherwise anonymous faces in the crowd a less partial, if still fragmentary, history than that imposed upon them by the authorities.

The disorder at Maldon has acquired a certain notoriety. S. R. Gardiner was perhaps its first historian.[5] Only a handful of historians have referred to it since. Their references have, in the main, been incidental and their understanding of the disorder rather confused. It is, therefore, perhaps advisable to begin by identifying the springs of this confusion and establishing, albeit briefly, the sequence of events at Maldon in 1629. There were, in fact, two distinct riots there in that year. In March a crowd of over 100 women with their children boarded a Flemish ship and forced its crew to fill their caps and aprons with grain from the ship's hold; in May, a much larger crowd, this time dominated by 200 to 300 unemployed clothworkers, again attacked boats taking on grain there. While the March rioters escaped scot-free, the second riot ended with the execution of several of the rioters.[6] Those drawing on Maldon's example appear not to have realized that there was more than one outbreak of disorder or, more seriously, to have taken all the evidence to refer to one riot only, that in May.[7] By conflating the riots they have obscured the vital fact that it is the repetition of disorder that helps to explain a more gruesome conclusion than the authorities' usual response to food riots. For Maldon in 1629 appears to provide the only example in early seventeenth-century England of a food riot that ended on the gallows. Events there therefore form an excellent focus for a local study of riot. The two riots, each eliciting a very different response, together provide an example of the full range of the complex interplay between crowd and authority in early modern England.

Industrial depression was one of the nastier nightmares that ruffled the shaky composure of England's rulers. Where it coincided (as it so often did) with dearth, it provided one of the most testing of challenges to the relationship between the poor and their governors. This was the background to disorder in Essex in 1629. A trade slump in European markets had had a disastrous impact on the cloth industry which dominated much of the county's economy. Its effects were evidently beginning to be felt very early in the year; they were soon to get very much worse.[8] In addition, the plight of thousands of clothworkers denied their only means of subsistence and of the poor generally within the county was aggravated by an increase in the price of their basic foodstuff. Poor weather at the start of the year signalled a bad harvest and prices locally were apparently beginning to rise.[9] An already fragile situation was further exacerbated by the extensive taking up of grain within the county by English and foreign merchants for export to European markets.[10]

It was this last activity that excited most popular comment. Merchants servicing an overseas market were barely tolerated at the best of times by the poor. In the conditions of 1629 they were particularly unwelcome. The merchants competed on unequal terms with the poor for what grain was available, sweeping local markets of their stocks and pushing up prices in the process. In a situation of near-shortage, their large-scale purchases may well have had a decisive impact in driving up prices in the markets in which they operated. This was to be a running grievance within Essex for much of 1629.

It led to disorder at the very beginning of the year. Towards the end of January, there was a flurry of riots in the south of the county in which rioters attempted to put a stop to the movement of grain out of the county. Bands of men and women, armed with pitchforks and pikestaves, had seized grain destined for export along the Thames. Openly 'swearinge they neither cared for pettye highe Constables or Justices of Peace', they had proceeded to impound the grain. The rioters intended, apparently, to enforce a policy of *taxation populaire* (selling the grain at their own popularly determined price) once their own needs had been met. In an attempt to forestall any further movement of grain they gave out threats 'to kill the farmors, or anye other factors yt wear imployed to buye or sell any Corne'. As if to underline these threats, they were reported to be trying to hire muskets.[11]

Clearly, the rioters were trying to play on the fears of their betters. In this they were successful. The local justice, in advising the central government of these disorders, expressed a fear that they would spread. There was, he informed the Privy Council, a need for speedy action to preserve the peace of the country. His letter passed on the threats of the rioters, doubtless amplifying them in the process. Its tone can be taken as the archetypal response of the early modern authorities to popular disorder: alarm, a ready willingness to believe the wilder rumours that deliberately accompanied the crowd's appearance, and fear that it presaged further, more threatening, disorder.[12] If the rioters had as yet failed to act out the roles accorded them in the nightmares of the ruling class, it was only a matter of time before they would do so. The central government's response to this information comes then as something of a surprise. It was prepared to leave the handling of the affair to a small group of local justices. Although its letter was couched in the conventional, shocked language of a government confronted by those upon whom a century and more of instruction in the sinfulness of disorder seems to have had so little effect, the Privy Council contented itself with calling upon the justices, 'to punish the offenders for their misdemeanors according to the quality of their offences as the lawes and statutes and the duties of your place doe require'. They were to be careful to suppress any further disorders 'in their beginnings'. But, at the same time, while stressing the legality of the movement of grain – to allies of the king, by licence and at prices under those set by statute – the government was at pains to publicize that it had issued instructions to the ports to stay further shipments upon first notice of the increase in prices.[13]

Riot and response fell into a familiar pattern. While calling for the punishment of the riot, the government was careful to respond (and to be seen to respond) to the popular grievances that had prompted disorder. Prosecution of the rioters was not actively pursued. Despite the murderous threats and open expressions of contempt for local social and administrative hierarchies, there remains little, if any, evidence that the justices risked local order by pressing on with the discovery and punishment of the rioters.[14]

The January riots provide both an example of the conventional pattern of disorder and the immediate background to the first riot at Maldon. The movement of grain out of the county was clearly exacerbating a local shortage and exciting popular comment. Consequently, the activities of foreign merchants at local ports were ill-received by the poor, the more so since they were popularly held to be flouting the laws designed to cope with a situation of impending dearth. For there is evidence to suggest that there was among the poor at Maldon, as elsewhere, a general awareness and even detailed knowledge of the body of law and administrative practice prescribed by the government to control the marketing of grain. Operating in an essentially oral public culture and faced with the possible recalcitrance and corruption of a sketchy bureaucracy, the early modern government was forced to devote a good deal of energy to getting its measures known. Central to this effort was a use of the law and the law courts. The formal but extremely public devices of proclamation, judicial charge and articles of inquiry to special juries were all clearly intended to publicize the law's provisions.[15] As inhabitants of borough, market-town and port, the poor at Maldon were likely to have been especially receptive to this form of tutelage. The borough records confirm that the town's inhabitants were kept regularly informed by proclamation of government directives regulating the grain trade. In addition to the regular example of control of the market by the borough's courts of leet and quarter sessions, they had had direct experience of the detailed programme initiated by the central government in previous years of dearth.[16] As a port, Maldon also provided a constant reminder of government policy in the proceedings of the vice-admiralty court there. Meeting several times a year, its jury of local men had to answer to prescribed articles of presentment at the heart of which lay questions concerning the illegal export of grain.[17] Any of these courts might require the active assistance of Maldon's humbler inhabitants as minor officials or members of juries. Popular knowledge of the law could come then through active participation in its enforcement. For example, while the records of the vice-admiralty court do not appear to survive for the period preceding the disorder at Maldon, in the 1630s at least one of the rioters' husbands was a regular member of its jury.[18]

There was, therefore, an informed popular expectancy as to what action the authorities should take to curb the activities of Dutch and Flemish merchants when they appeared at Maldon and began buying up grain. This was to be disappointed by the seeming reluctance or inability of those in authority to protect local markets. For despite the warning of the January riots, the outflow of grain was allowed to continue. The government's claim that it had issued general instructions restraining the export of grain needs to be treated with caution. No proclamation was issued banning its export until early May. Letters appear to have been sent to the ports, but it is a commonplace, given the state of early modern administration, that it was one thing to issue a ban, quite another to secure its enforcement. Corruption was rife at the ports. At the centre, the issue of a ban could have ulterior motives – special licences to export prohibited commodities were part of the spoils of court patronage.[19] The registers of the Privy Council reveal that it itself continued to license extensive shipments of grain by English and foreign merchants to allies of the king. It was not until towards the end of March that even this licensed export of grain began to dry up. Provincial authorities who did attempt to enforce a ban on the export of grain by reference to the new restraining order seem to have had their actions, on appeal, repeatedly overruled by the central government.[20] For the moment, political considerations shouldered aside any concern for the poor.

It was undoubtedly this situation of magisterial inactivity that first prompted Maldon's poor to take action. On 23 March, the magistrates at Colchester, Essex's leading port, informed the Lord Treasurer of the disruptive activities of one Lucas Jacobs in the town's market. Jacobs, a leading Dutch corn factor, had been licensed to make extensive purchases of grain in East Anglia. In support of their plea for a ban on his activities, Colchester's magistrates stressed the popular discontent these purchases were causing: 'a greate number of poore people are here verie unrulie by reason much Corne haue benn transported from hence', they warned the Lord Treasurer.[21] Popular discontent was equally marked at Maldon.[22] There too the appearance of foreign merchants excited hostile comment. In the absence of action by the town's authorities, rumours circulated about the precise nature of the merchants' cargoes and helped to heighten popular suspicions. Philip Ewers, a Maldon sailor, was reported to have complained to a gathering of local inhabitants that 'the owners of the said vessells were dunkirk[er]s and ... (that Corne was shipped) yt was pittie they were suffred to lye there', a sentiment echoed by other sailors in the crowd.[23] Ewers's speech was deliberately inflammatory – to label the merchants Dunkirkers (they were either Dutch or Flemish) was calculated to increase popular antagonism towards them[24] – and contained a clear invitation to his audience to take action on their grievances. It met a ready response. On the same day that Colchester's magistrates were writing to the Lord Treasurer about the threat of disorder there, the poor at Maldon took it upon themselves to put a stop to the unwelcome and seemingly unrestrained activities of foreign merchants (among them Lucas Jacobs) in their market.

On Monday, 23 March, a crowd of women, animated by the speeches of Ewers and the other sailors, gathered in the streets of Maldon. (Coming two days after the town's Saturday market, the timing of their action perhaps suggests that post-market grumbles and sabbath-tide discussion preceded the decision to riot.) The crowd processed through the town, calling other women out of their houses to join them as they went. They brushed aside the efforts of the town's magistrates to stop them and, with their children in tow, made for a place known as Burrow Hills. Here they were joined by women from the adjacent village of Heybridge, from the clothing township of Witham and off the nearby Totham Heath. Burrow Hills was a deep-water channel just outside Maldon, frequently used by ships to take on cargoes in preference to the town's hythe; there lay the object of the crowd's attention – several Dutch and Flemish ships taking on grain. The rioters now formed a formidable crowd, some 100 to 140 strong. An unknown number of rioters boarded one of the ships and forced its Flemish crew to fill the aprons and bonnets of women and children in the crowd with small quantities of grain from the ship's cargo of rye.[25] The evidence does not reveal how the riot ended.

As the response to Philip Ewers's attack on the authorities' inactivity suggests, it was undoubtedly this failure to act that impelled the poor to riot. The statements of those rioters who were later apprehended almost unanimously reflect popular impatience with the authorities for failing to prevent the export of grain at the expense of the local market. They drew their examiners' attention (as the riot itself had intended) to the provocative contrast between the nearby grain-laden ships about to sail and the lack of grain in their own market. All but one of the rioters examined linked this offensive juxtaposition of want and plenty with their own poverty as the explanation for their presence in the crowd. Margaret Williams, for example, went to Burrow Hills, 'amongst others of her owne accord', 'Corne being deare and . . . being carried awaie . . . and she being a poore woeman'; while Ann Spearman went 'because she cold not have Corne in the m[ar]kett & [because] certaine fflemishe shipps . . . [lay] at Burrow Hills . . . there to receiue in Corne to carry beyond sea (for transportacion).'[26]

Despite the authorities' insistence (in accordance with elitist preconceptions about the nature of popular political activity) upon discovering the *primum mobile* of the riot, there was amongst those examined a general stress on the crowd's solidarity. The women of the neighbourhood had called on each other to join together. Their mobilization was as much the product of a shared sense of moral outrage as of any prior co-ordination. They had acted as a crowd in the face of their governors' passivity to enforce that law whose explicit justification by the government had been, 'to avoyde the just offence of the inferyour sort, which cannot but be greeved to see such corrupcions in the better sorte suffered without restraint.'[27] 'The Crie of the Country and hir owne want' was one rioter's crisp retort to the question of who had incited her to riot.[28]

Though the claim of poverty might be expected after riot as a necessary mitigating plea in the delicate relationship between crowd and authority, it would seem to have been a genuine statement of the problems facing the rioters at Maldon. Totham Heath was the classic locus of the squatters' settlement in marginal agricultural areas, whose freedom from the discipline of landlord, church and state so alarmed men of property in the seventeenth century. Witham was dominated by the cloth industry: 2000 inhabitants in and around the town were said to draw their living from it. The presence of a contingent of women from Witham in the crowd almost certainly reflects the impact of the trade depression there. Their involvement presages the role their menfolk were to play in the second riot.[29]

Poverty was perhaps less marked at Maldon itself. A rigorous control on in-migration had ensured that the town was not haunted by the numerous poor that scarred other towns in the period. It had little direct involvement with the cloth industry.[30] Nevertheless, although we know the names of only a handful of rioters, painstaking research suggests that for all of them poverty was something more than a necessary fiction in the aftermath of riot. All but one of these rioters came from the poorest of the town's parishes, St Mary's, which was described in the previous year as 'much ouer-charged with poore'.[31]

All were some-time members of that inclusive, penumbral body, the urban poor. Elizabeth Sturgeon, who described herself to her examiners as 'being in pou[er]tie and wanting victuall for her Children', was married to a labourer too poor to be allowed to stand surety for his wife or to figure much at all in the extant records of the borough.[32] Another rioter, Ann Spearman, was the wife of a fisherman. Though described as a cottager in a 1622 listing distinguishing between householders, cottagers and labourers, there is evidence elsewhere of his dependence on occasional day-labour to maintain even this precarious position – without, it would seem, great success. When, in 1633, now described as a labourer, he was fined five shillings for being drunk, the constables reported that he had insufficient goods on which to levy the fine.[33]

Others hovered on the edge of poverty. Dorothy Berry was married to a recent immigrant to Maldon whose varying occupations over time (shepherd, labourer, fisherman) and by-employments (aleselling and victualling, both of which got him into frequent trouble with the authorities) suggest the nature of their precarious existence.[34] Margaret Williams was a widow who had remarried. Her husband was also an immigrant. A leatherworker, he too ended up in that peculiar preserve of the poor, as an aleseller, attempting to supplement his income from an urban craft notorious for its poverty.[35]

The fortunes of Ann Carter, the one rioter not to plead poverty when examined, perhaps provide the best illustration of this group's uneasy balance between sufficiency and want. Her husband, John Carter, was a butcher who by 1629 showed little sign of the wealth attributed to this often prosperous urban trade. To judge by the lists of butchers entering and failing to enter recognizances against Lent, he appears to have moved out of the trade (at least on his own account?) for several years shortly after his marriage to Ann in 1620. But during this time he held land in the town and continued to be described elsewhere as a butcher of Maldon.[36] By 1627 he and his wife had at least two servants, and in 1628 John Carter again appeared among those entering Lenten recognizances. In 1629 he took his place for the first time in the mutual pledging among his fellow butchers that provided their recognizances against Lent.[37] Although the evidence suggests a rise and fall in the Carters' fortunes, there was probably an underlying decline. In 1624 they had transferred their rights in a holding in Maldon, which was then sublet to a local yeoman for a period of four years, he having to give them a penny yearly should they demand it. In 1628 John Carter was being presented to the town's courts as a common alehouse haunter. By mid 1629, one of their servants had left and the other, having had her wages cut by one-third the previous year, had only been taken on again in 1629 for a short period and at no specified wage. By the latter half of the year, John was himself without a residence. He was being presented before the courts as a lodger and harried for his failure to attend church. Shortly thereafter, his name again disappeared from the lists of Maldon butchers.[38]

Where, then, it is possible to get behind the formal and fossilizing descriptions accorded those brought before the law, we can glimpse the tenuous existence of those from whose ranks the crowd was recruited. The picture is one of poverty, not necessarily of overwhelming poverty, but of a constant struggle against the uncertainties and instability of the early modern economy. An understanding of this group's struggle for subsistence and sensitivity to changes in the price of basic foodstuffs helps to explain their hostility to those merchants whose purchases defied popular norms and prompted a local crisis. Clearly, such a crisis, however temporary and localized, could threaten to have a drastic impact on their ability to subsist.

Evidence about members of the crowd derived from sources independent of the immediate legal record of riot may have more to tell us. It may help to explain not only the presence of individuals in the crowd but also the selection of those against whom the authorities chose to take action. Only a handful of the rioters ended up before the magistrates. With the possible exception of Ann Carter (who was suspected by the authorities to have had a hand in the organization of the riot), the legal record gives little indication why this group should have been the only ones singled out. It does not suggest that they played a particularly prominent part in the riot. But from their fragmentary biographies it is possible to put forward a tentative explanation for their unwelcome prominence in its aftermath. For what emerges is that the women (and their husbands) already enjoyed a certain notoriety from being often in trouble with the town's magistracy. They were, in fact, a thorn in the side of authority.

Their frequent appearances before Maldon's magistrates were to some extent part and parcel of their poverty. There were a whole range of generally petty offences for which they found themselves pestered and presented: attempting to keep animals in the town's streets and other infringements of its by-laws, frequent failure to perform compulsory work on the highways and to fulfil other obligations, unlawful aleselling, drunkenness and absence from church.[39]

There were, however, more serious incidents. Ann Spearman's husband, for example, appeared before the authorities on at least three separate occasions for assault and violence. In 1617 he had been called to answer for the death of his apprentice. The corporation had previously scotched Spearman's attempt to dismiss him. Again indicted for assault at the quarter sessions following the March riot, he was joined later in the year by his wife to answer for their combined attack on a local husbandman, his wife and son-in-law in the channel of the port. Since we have only a note of these incidents, we have no way of knowing whether they formed a sequel to the riot.[40]

This range of offences was not, of course, peculiar to the rioters and their husbands. But what does seem to distinguish at least some of them is that they were marked by a particular antipathy to the exercise of authority. This is perhaps to be explained by the marginal political position experienced by the rioters and their husbands. In step with a fashionable tendency towards oligarchy, power and the spoils of office had been concentrated in the grasp of a small ruling group in Maldon towards the end of the previous century, a process which then had occasioned a good deal of popular animosity.[41] None of the rioters' husbands was apparently a freeman of the borough. They were, therefore, neither eligible for membership of the corporation nor allowed even a limited say in its election. None apparently had been chosen to serve in any of the town's minor offices. It was only as 'decenners', unfree members of the tithing from which the leet jury was selected, that they participated in the government of the town; and then, to judge from incomplete lists, their appearances were few and sometimes reluctant.[42] Their wives were, of course, in a formally even more marginal position. This group experienced authority not through participation in its exercise, but through the unwelcome interference of those officials with whom they lived cheek-by-jowl in a town of little more than 1000 inhabitants.[43] Their enforced political inactivity, when coupled with the irritating attention of the corporation's officials, perhaps helps to explain the undercurrent of resentment glimpsed in several of the rioters' lives.

This irksome relationship with authority is probably best seen in the examples of Dorothy Berry and Ann Carter. In the year of the riot, Dorothy Berry (whose husband was repeatedly in trouble in 1629) appeared several times before the authorities for a range of offences. The most frequent was drunkenness. She had been indicted for being drunk at the Easter quarter sessions and sentenced to sit in the stocks for six hours. New stocks may well have been provided for the occasion but, if so, they failed as a deterrent. When, in July, a constable attempted to serve a warrant citing her now two previous convictions for drunkenness, he had little luck. Dorothy Berry displayed her contempt for the magistrates' authority by informing him that 'she wold bring her dogg for one of her suerties and her Catt for the other'.[44]

Ann Carter, the suspected leader of the riot, had a similar, if longer and better-documented, relationship with authority. In 1622 she had been presented at quarter sessions for having launched a verbal assault on one of the town's two chief magistrates, 'calling him bloud sucker and . . . many other unseemely tearmes'. She was again in trouble with authority the following year. When the same hapless bailiff tried to question her about her absence from church, she contemptuously informed him, 'that yf he woold prouid[e] wone to doe hir worke shee would goe', adding 'that she searued god as well as he' – a statement which again landed her in court. In 1624 it was the turn of one of the sergeants at mace to experience in more direct form her contempt for authority. He had been attempting to arrest John Carter when Ann had intervened and, stroking him 'uppon the hed wth a great cudgell divers times', rescued her husband.[45]

It is not surprising, therefore, that members of this group should be found expressing hostility towards the authorities, especially when they found themselves being dragged before the courts for offences which were scarcely thought of as such by them and their neighbours. That shortly before the riot Ann Carter and Dorothy Berry were among a group of inhabitants being prosecuted for a relatively minor infringement of the town's marketing regulations – they had bought up fish before they were cried – while Dutch and Flemish merchants seemingly escaped such attention, can hardly have increased their respect for authority.[46] Perhaps, then, the information provided by these fragmentary biographies of the rioters helps to explain the readiness with which they entered or led the riot, and, possibly, why it should be they (and they alone) who ended up before the authorities. It may well be, though it would be difficult to prove, that for at least several of them it was their earlier conflict with authority and the visibility this brought them, as much as any part in the riot, which determined their selection. Ann Carter's past relationship with Maldon's magistrates certainly helps to explain her presence in this and the later riot; perhaps it also cast her for the role she was chosen to play in the judicial aftermath following the May disorder.

If we return to the riot and examine the authorities' response to the appearance of the crowd, then we can attempt to establish their attitude to the food riot. We know that they tried to prevent the crowd from assembling, but thereafter the evidence is scanty. It is not recorded whether it was action on their part that brought the riot to an end. Not until just over a month later is there evidence of action being taken against members of the crowd. If, however, the authorities were slow to move against the rioters, the crowd's action quickly prompted the sort of response it seemed designed to achieve. Immediately following the riot, Maldon's magistrates ordered a search to be made of the ships' cargoes 'for Corne' and 'to se whethe she were laden with chees butter or baken as it was Reported'. The next day the port searchers, accompanied by the constables and a sergeant at mace, hired boats and searched both Dutch and Flemish ships.[47] On 6 April, the full corporation of bailiffs, aldermen and headburgesses held an extraordinary meeting. At this it was decided, after a vote, that 'the Corne p[ro]vided by Mr. Jacobs the marchant now lyeing within the Burrow shall be bought at Convenient price if yt maybe had for or poore and so to make stay of yt from transportinge'. Most members of the corporation agreed to contribute to the cost of the grain's purchase out of their own pockets: the bailiffs and aldermen were to pay fifty shillings, and the headburgesses twenty shillings, apiece.[48]

While the willingness of Maldon's rulers to purchase the grain at their own expense confirms their anxiety to placate the crowd, the fortnight's delay between search and vote suggests perhaps that in the interval they had tried other (and less costly) ways of preventing the grain's shipment. It is possible that having searched the ships, the corporation wrote to the Lord Treasurer, the minister responsible for regulating the export of grain. They certainly sent one of the sergeants at mace to him with a letter whose precise date in 1629 is unknown. Although no copy of this letter is to be found, it evidently concerned 'the staye of the transportac[i]on of Corne'.[49] Perhaps the corporation had hoped that the Lord Treasurer, in accordance with his own restraining order of late January, would order the foreign merchants to dispose of the grain locally. If, as seems likely, the Mr Jacobs referred to in the vote of 6 April was the Lucas Jacobs whose activities had disrupted Colchester's market, then they were likely to have been disappointed. Jacobs was a Dutch merchant resident in England and one of the leading exporters of grain in the period. His name appears regularly in the registers of the Privy Council. In the previous autumn he had been licensed to export over 2000 lasts of grain, mostly to northern Europe. As the report from Colchester would suggest, a purchase of this size undoubtedly created problems in Essex (which with Norfolk and Sussex appears to have formed the provisioning area for the purchase). In fact, Colchester's efforts were apparently only one of a number of attempts made locally to put a stop to Jacobs's activities. But Jacobs, who seems to have steered pretty close to the wind in his dealings, had friends in high places: in the following year the personal intervention of the Dutch ambassador secured his release from a charge of exporting double the amount of grain specified in his licence. In February 1629 the Privy Council had overruled attempts to restrain Jacobs and called upon local authorities to allow him to ship grain.[50]

If, in such a context, the crowd's actions conformed to essentially unwritten and informal conventions mutually accepted by the crowd and authority – in other words, if they were carefully circumscribed, did not question the local power structure and were directed against an intrusive and generally disliked presence – then they were not altogether unwelcome to the *local* authorities. In the face of the central government's subordination of local interests to its own ill-informed definition of priorities, the appearance of the crowd provided the local authorities with the necessary proof of the seriousness of the situation. It gave them the most effective means of urging a change of policy upon a government for whom the maintenance of order remained the key desideratum.

This unconscious coalition between the poor and authority locally may help to explain the apparent lethargy with which the Maldon authorities pursued the apprehension and punishment of such action. The fact that the riot fell between quarter sessions in the town cannot be taken to explain this delay. The corporation was quick to hold a special meeting to consider the rioters' grievances; it was not until after the next quarter sessions (held on 20 April) that they began to move against the rioters, although several had then been before the court for other offences. Though we lack direct proof, it is tempting to see in this timing evidence that the corporation's action had been prompted either by advice from the county magistracy – the quarter sessions for the county, at which several Maldon officials were present, had met on 16 April – or by instruction from the central government.[51]

It was on 25 April that Maldon's magistrates took their first recorded action against the rioters: they issued a warrant for the appearance before them for questioning of Ann Carter and her husband. Ann Carter appeared two days later. She was examined and released the same day, after admitting to having been a member of the boarding party. Her examiners suspected that it was she who had arranged for the women of Witham to be present at Burrow Hills, but this she denied.[52] On 30 April warrants were issued for the appearance of the other four women on whom the magistrates chose to concentrate their investigations – Dorothy Berry, Ann Spearman, Elizabeth Sturgeon and Margaret Williams. They too were examined and released after confessing their presence in the crowd.[53] Over the next few days all five women were required to enter recognizances for their future appearance. Significantly, the sum demanded as surety for several of the rioters (Ann Carter among them) was set at twice that normally demanded within the borough; and the authorities showed that they expected the sureties to be able to raise this sum by striking out the name of one of the rioters' husbands before the recognizance's completion on the grounds of his poverty.[54]

At this stage, then, it would appear that the town's magistrates were concerned to minimize tensions locally by the familiar use of the recognizance and not to exacerbate the situation by a rigorous prosecution of the riot. Only a handful of rioters had been plucked out of the original large crowd and they, with one exception, were to appear at the next quarter sessions for the borough, some month and more away in late June. In effect, the *threat* of punishment was being used to discipline the rioters.

The one exception was Ann Spearman. According to her original recognizance she was not bound over to appear at the next quarter sessions but 'at such day time and place as shall be appointed unto her by the Lords of his Ma:ts Counsell'.[55] This would tend to lend weight to the idea that the central government had been informed of the riot and that the belated prosecution of the rioters was at its prompting. The evidence, however, does not suggest why Ann Spearman should have been singled out for exemplary punishment. Perhaps she played a greater role within the riot than that for which we have evidence, but in the end it was Ann Carter, and not Ann Spearman, who became the sacrificial lamb, and this for her part in the second riot. There is no evidence that Ann Spearman ever appeared before the Privy Council. Instead, she appeared with her fellow rioters at quarter sessions on 29 June.[56]

Thereafter, despite the second riot in late May, the Maldon authorities' response became even more formal and perfunctory. No action was taken against the women by the court. Once more, they were bound over to appear at the following quarter sessions. This time only their husbands were required as surety, and even the husband previously excluded on grounds of poverty was now admitted. At the October sessions, the husbands of two of the women appeared and were dismissed, one rioter defaulted, and nothing was entered against the fourth, Dorothy Berry, although she was still living within the borough. No further action was taken against these last two.[57]

This slow unfolding of events forms a pattern which is itself a revealing commentary on the attitude of authority locally to the food riot. Although there is no evidence that Maldon had a particular tradition of riot which might have accustomed its governors to the appearance of the crowd, its rulers do not appear to have been especially alarmed by the incident.[58] Their first and immediate response was to take steps to remove the grievance that had prompted popular action. Only later (and, if the interpretation of the timing is right, only under some external pressure) did they investigate the riot itself. Even then, they confined their attention to a handful of rioters and in the end never brought even these to stand trial.

If the leniency with which the urban authorities treated the rioters reflects a certain confidence in their own position, it was certainly made easier by a possibly deliberate policy on the part of the poor in the riot. That it should be the *women* of Maldon and the nearby villages who staffed the crowd is not in itself surprising. Women were present in almost every food riot in the period and some riots were exclusively feminine affairs. As the group most involved in the round of face-to-face marketing, they were especially sensitive to price movements and abuses in the market-place.[59] As the social group most intimately connected with the everyday life of the community, they were through the network of the neighbourhood in an excellent position to gauge popular feelings and able to give voice to these in effective collective action. In this respect, Maldon is only to be distinguished by the size of the feminine presence: it was by far the largest crowd of women rioters to appear in a food riot in the period.

Maldon's example suggests, however, that the presence of women in the crowd was perhaps more deliberate than these explanations would suppose. They may well have felt that the sexual division of labour gave them special licence, as provisioners of their families, to notify authority of its failings in this crucial area of their lives.[60] They were probably more aware of the licence afforded them by their ambivalent legal status at the margins of the law's competence. Their presence in the crowd (and that of their children, another group to the fore in the riots of the period) again highlights the extent to which popular culture was penetrated by a knowledge of the law. For the legal position of women rioters was very unclear in the early seventeenth century. Lambarde, author of the standard textbook of the early seventeenth-century magistracy, informed his readers that

> if a number of women (or children under the age of discretion) do flocke together for their own cause, this is none assembly punishable by these statutes, unless a man of discretion moued them to assemble for the doing of some unlawfull act,

an opinion echoed by Dalton, that other justices' vade-mecum.[61]

In the riots of the period, women actively demonstrated their awareness of the uncertainties of the law. They consciously exploited the ambiguities of their position within the political culture and explored the freedom of action this brought them. In rioting, they were able to turn their marginal relationship to the structure of power within the community (of which their legal dependence was only one aspect) to their temporary advantage, since their intervention, if short-lived, was less likely to threaten the underlying relationship between the poor and their governors. The role of the women and children at Maldon, then, parallels the deliberate use elsewhere of their ambiguous socio-legal status to articulate the community's sense of grievance. If the rioters there did not openly voice the common claim made by their defiant sisters in contemporary enclosure riots 'that women were lawlesse, and not subject to the lawes of the realme as men are but might . . . offend without drede or punishment of law', doubtless some such reasoning helps to explain their exclusively feminine gathering.[62] This was the logic behind the sequence of events in which the equally discontented (but ultimately passive) sailors restricted their participation to mobilizing the women of the community to riot.

There is, therefore, little that separates the first riot at Maldon from other riots springing from comparable grievances elsewhere in the period. While it serves to emphasize the potential specificity of local crisis, its background was a widely shared one in which the authorities were felt to be failing in their self-proclaimed duty towards the poor and defenceless by not enforcing those laws designed to protect them. Either Maldon's market was empty because of large-scale purchases by foreign merchants or because, as was increasingly the case, merchants and vendors had bypassed its market altogether.[63]

Either action was equally likely to have antagonized the local populace, jealously guarding what it saw as its prior claim on grain within the local market and deeply suspicious of any tendency which threatened this lifeline of the urban poor. That it was foreign merchants who were exporting the grain doubtless heightened the sense of popular grievance. Xenophobia was a not infrequent element in the popular disorder of the period and it probably contributed to the decision to riot at Maldon: according to the Venetian ambassador there was in the spring of 1629 a widespread murmur against the Dutch who feared 'some general massacre'.[64] But it was popular awareness that the merchants' activities contravened the necessary laws for dealing with a situation of threatened hunger and the definition of priorities in the marketing of grain these upheld, that informed and helped to legitimize the crowd's actions. In the face of the authorities' apparent unwillingness to enforce those laws on whose necessity they repeatedly and publicly insisted, the poor took it upon themselves to enforce a body of law which emphasized abuses in the marketing of grain as the real cause of dearth and hinted at bureaucratic inactivity and self-interest as the cause of its persistence.

In the short term the Maldon disturbance, as with other food riots in the period, could be said to have achieved its aims. Forcing the Flemish sailors to distribute grain amongst the women and children in the crowd probably satisfied the craving for popular justice. It certainly drew the attention of the authorities to their failings and set in motion the necessary exercise of authority designed to remove grievances which the crowd, by its own actions, could never hope to redress. Grain was kept within the local economy and purchased for distribution to the poor. The central government was alerted to the dangerous situation built up by the continued licensing of grain shipments and official permission to export grain was withdrawn. The restraint on grain exports imposed at the end of January had not stopped the government granting at least forty-three export licences over the next two months; only two such licences were issued in the two months following the riot.[65] This response by authority was absolutely essential to the crowd who could only hope to drive off the purchasers of grain at the risk of also scaring away the provisioners of their market. In the long term, the riot's success lay in its reminding the authorities of the crowd's slumbering existence, encouraging them to take action when either the harvest failed or trade became anything dead.[66]

While the authorities displayed a certain energy in attempting to remove popular grievances, they contented themselves with a token show of action against the rioters. This tolerance was in part the product of a feminine crowd's ability to exploit ambiguities in the enforcement of laws that mirrored popular norms and gave scope for popular initiative. But the muted magisterial reaction, one of negotiation and conciliation, was undoubtedly an implicit recognition of the imperatives of unrelieved poverty.

Had matters so remained, then there would have been little to distinguish events at Maldon from the general pattern of popular disorder elsewhere. The exchange between the crowd and the authorities, marked by an absence of violence and by studied restraint, belonged to a tradition observable both long before and long after this particular incident. But the repetition of disorder in May moves Maldon outside this tradition. Instead of a return to the expected pattern of relationships between governors and governed – an exchange of deference and subordination for good governance – Maldon witnessed the unusual spectacle of a second, larger outbreak of disorder on the exact site of the earlier riot.

In the period between the two riots the economic situation of the county deteriorated rapidly. The problem was essentially one of deepening depression within the textile industry which dominated the economy of north-east Essex. War had damaged overseas markets and created a major slump in textile exports. At home, the dissolution of Parliament and the conflict between the Crown and its opponents over the contentious issue of the legality of customs impositions contributed to the loss of confidence in the mercantile community. An over-expanded domestic industry, dominated by small employers for whom credit and an ability to turn over capital quickly was essential, and whose work-force formed a large, near-landless rural proletariat, was scarcely in a position to weather the storm.[67]

A report drawn up sometime in the spring of 1629 – *A Breife declarat[i]on Concerning the state of the Manufacture of Woolls in the Countie of Essex* – revealed the full extent of the crisis.[68] There were twelve to fourteen townships, besides a host of smaller centres, heavily engaged in the manufacture of cloth. A depressingly similar picture emerged for each of the centres mentioned in the report. For example, at Colchester, the leading cloth town where 20,000 in and around the town were said to depend on the industry, there had been an alarming slump in production: the weekly production of one type of cloth alone had fallen from 400 to 50 pieces in the previous five to six weeks. In other centres, the production of cloth was anywhere between one-fifth and one-third of what it had been. Much cloth remained unsold. At Coggeshall, where production had used to run at 100 pieces a week, 1500 cloths were unsold. Since spring was normally the peak period for cloth sales, this lack of buyers was particularly alarming. Bulging warehouses spelt disaster for the numerous small employers who depended on credit and a weekly sale to finance their operations. If the example of Bocking, one of the leading cloth centres, is typical, then it would appear that the depression really began to bite towards the end of March. The town's clothiers had met at the beginning of February and agreed to provide work for their workmen and all the unemployed until Lady Day (25 March). But by that date they found themselves no longer able to guarantee employment. From Witham it was reported that the clothiers 'bee afraid to goe home beinge not able to pay theire workmen or to sett them any more att worke'.[69]

With little or no land, few savings and no hopes of alternative employment, it was the clothworkers who bore the brunt of the crisis. Still wrestling with the legacy of an earlier crisis in 1623, they were ill-equipped to cope with the events of 1629. Few were able to draw support from the type of dual economy that flourished in other areas of rural industrialization. Many had long since lost what little economic independence their occupation might have offered and were dependent on a wage paid them by the clothier. This, 'but smale in the best tymes', had been progressively cut in response to the problems affecting the industry for much of the 1620s and kept low by the fresh supply of labour drafted in during spasmodic spurts of over-optimistic expansion. As the report on the state of the industry concluded of the clothworkers:

theire pouertie is exceedinge greate, and lamentable is the beinge of all this Multitude of people which liue by these Manufactures, few or none that Can subsist unlesse they bee paied their wages once a weeke, and many of them that Cannot liue unlesse they bee paied euery night, many hundreds of them hauinge no bedds to lye in, nor foode, but from hand to mouth to mainteyne them selues their wiues and Children.

By early April, the Venetian ambassador was predicting the thousand mischiefs that might follow the threat of starvation amongst the unemployed clothworkers.[70]

The records this crisis occasioned make it possible to follow its impact blow by blow and to reconstruct the process of response and counter-response between the poor and the authorities which ended in further riot. The poor's first move was to petition authority. A divisional meeting of justices at Bocking in the heartland of the cloth district attracted petitioning clothworkers at the beginning of April. When, later in the month, the county's magistrates met for the Easter quarter sessions at Chelmsford, they found themselves immediately confronted by a large and unruly crowd of some 200 clothworkers who had tramped to the county seat. These presented the justices with a petition in the name of the weavers of Bocking and Braintree detailing the clothworkers' distress, 'with [as the justices informed the government] too many wordes, and outcryes followinge us from place to place, and moueing us for Com:isseration and urginge present answere, being unwillinge allmost to giue anie space of tyme to Consider what was to bee done for them'. The clothworkers would not allow the justices to proceed with the business of the court until they had assured them that they would inform the central government of their distress and agreed to send some of their number to confer with the clothiers and leading townsmen about possible means of relief.[71]

The county authorities lost little time in informing the central government of these developments, the justices writing to the Privy Council the following day, 17 April.[72] Their letter stressed the fragile situation within the county and their own helplessness when confronted by a crisis whose roots lay outside their jurisdiction. 'Itt is to be feared', the justices informed the council, that 'without speedie reliefe some thinge may happen which may disturbe the Peace of the Countrie.' Their promises to the clothworkers had done some good, but 'there was expressed by diuers of them, soe much distrust that noe Care would bee taken for them in tyme, As wee are of opinion, that our persuasions to settle them in quiett and order Could not prevaile Longe' unless something could be done to answer their needs and complaints. If the justices disliked the manner of the weavers' disorderly petitioning, they emphasized that their complaints were not without just cause. Their own letter was an attempt to manipulate the threat of disorder to persuade the central government of the need to intervene to prevent 'the eminent mischiefe which may happen by these poore people and the Inhabitants of many other Clothinge townes pinched with like want and famine'. Thus it ended with the ominous observation that the clothworkers 'will not longe be quiett, unlesse they haue meanes provided to relieue themselues and families with victualls and other necessaries'. Reports from individual cloth-ing townships underscored the reality of this threat. From Coggeshall ('beinge a very poore towne and unruly') it was reported 'as Certaine the multitudes of the poorer sort must starue, or use unlawfull meanes to support themselues, if pr[e]sent reliefe bee not afforded'.[73]

The message contained in the reports and petitions coming in from the county was not lost on the government at the centre. The govern-ment's response was quickly forthcoming but sadly inadequate. Only two days after the tumultuous petitioning, the Privy Council wrote to the ministers and churchwardens of Bocking and Braintree, the centres of the petitioning, stressing the care being taken by the king for the cloth trade and blaming the war abroad for the depression. In an attempt to communicate directly with the discontented cloth-workers, it ordered that the letter be read in the churches of the district the next day, a Sunday.[74] A week or so later the council wrote to the justices, ordering them to spread the cost of relieving the clothworkers by rating the parishes bordering on the clothing townships. When the justices informed the government that since all parishes were equally interested in the cloth industry, this policy would 'insteade of appeasinge the disorders now on foote, in some few of the greate Clothinge townes . . . thereby infinitely encrease . . . Complaintes' throughout the region, the council wrote again. This time it suggested, unrealistically, the provision of alternative employment and ordered the justices to rate the whole county for the relief of those for whom no such work was forthcoming.[75]

At the same time, the central government countered the justices' use of the threat of popular violence by emphasizing *local* respon-sibility for the maintenance of order. Thus the council's letter of 5 May, while reiterating the personal steps taken by the king in negotiating with the merchants to take up the unsold cloth, ended with this pointed counter-threat:

For as the execucion of the lawes and maintenance of the poore are intrusted to you and other subordinate Ministers, so if you shall be found remiss . . . his Majestie will require and take a strict account thereof from you as those from whome he expecteth . . . a dilligent care of the pre.serveing of the peace and quiett of the Country.[76]

In addition to its emphasis on the king's solicitude for the suffer-ings of his subjects and local responsibility for the county's good governance, the government's correspondence with the Essex autho-rities contained yet another theme. This was an elaboration of ideas

which were commonplace in propertied circles: idleness was the real
cause of poverty, vagrants the real agents of disorder. In its letter
of 29 April, the Privy Council, having perfunctorily ordered the
justices to spread the burden of poor relief, moved swiftly on to
inform them:

> we must seriously recomend unto you the reformacion of a greate abuse,
> which we understand is committed by some persons who sorte themselves
> amongst those Clothworkers that are readiest to trouble you with theire
> often Complaints and doe clamour for wante of worke, though they have
> noe ymployment in the trade of Clothing nor would apply themselves to
> labour or take paines if they should be sett on worke.

Despite the justices' diplomatic response to these instructions – they
had, they informed the government, taken steps to punish vagrants,
'which as yet doe not fully appeare unto us' – in its very next letter the
council again emphasized the threat from those who 'upon this
pretence [of unemployment] doe take occasion to assosiate themselves in a disorderly and tumultuous manner, and so unlawfully
wander abroad in great and unusuall numbers, which may prove of
ill consequence and example if speedie redress be not taken therein'.
This harping on what it chose to believe were the real causes of disorder remained an element within the government's response to the
crisis right up to the outbreak of the rioting. It surfaced again during
the trial of the rioters. Totally inappropriate to the real situation, it
casts doubt on the central government's ability to appreciate the true
seriousness of the crisis.[77]

Disappointed that the promises of the government had so far produced little effective relief, the clothworkers stepped up their petitioning of authority. They addressed the king directly and, under the
licence afforded by petitioning, made a more conscious use of the
threat of violence in an attempt to coerce authority into action. The
weavers of Bocking and Braintree again took the lead in making the
clothworkers' grievances known. In a petition at the beginning of
May, they informed the king that they were 'growen into that extremi-
tie, that they are enforced to sell theire bedds from under them to buy
bread for themselues and families and are faine to lye in strawe'.
Unless some course was taken for their present relief, they and their
families were 'like to perish, for in this declyninge tyme they are not
able to subsist any Longer'. Petitioning the justices had brought
'gratious answere' from the king. This had put them in great hope
and comfort that their wants and necessities should be supplied. But

since that time they 'in hope haue susteyned themselues and families with soe smale a portion of bread as is hardlie to keepe lyfe and soule together . . . [that] findinge noethinge done, they thinke theire miseries are not Creditted'. Against this background of the authorities' continuing failure to implement a policy of effective relief, the clothworkers openly hinted at the threat of popular violence that it made all the more likely. The weavers ended their petition with the fervent wish that 'they may not starue in tyme of plentie . . . but liue to doe your Ma:tyes seruice according to their duties', but this did not stop them from warning the king (as loyal subjects) that had not the lord lieutenant, the Earl of Warwick, appeased them, 'many wretched people would have gathered together in a Mutinie and haue beene with your Ma:tye for they said words would not fill the belly nor Cloth the backe'.[78]

This petition was the signal for another round of correspondence between central and local government. The renewed exchange revealed the effects of the depression still to be spreading. On 15 May, the county authorities informed the government that they had met that day to implement its latest orders, but had found no parish within the clothing hundreds able to relieve any other. The effects of the depression had spilled over into other areas, and the justices' efforts to tax the whole county were met by widespread reluctance to contribute successfully hiding behind legalist objections. Under the guise of keeping the government informed, the county authorities reasserted its primary responsibility for removing the causes of the crisis. Once again they raised the spectre of violence in an attempt to persuade the government of this, concluding 'with all wee hold itt our duties truely to enforme your lordships that wee Cannot possible[y] hope for any quiett amongst the poore people in our Country' without a speedy resumption of cloth sales.[79]

The government's response to this information revealed the full bankruptcy of the king's efforts. On 17 May, it issued a sententious proclamation for the due execution of the laws for setting the poor on work, advised the justices that the whole county could legally be taxed for this purpose, and initiated another round of local administrative action to prepare for this. Parish officials were to report on the state of their parish to the nearest justice, justices at their divisional meetings were to report to quarter sessions, and the assize judges were to oversee the whole operation, reporting directly to the Privy Council.[80] None of these elaborate administrative procedures really got to grips with the central structural problem – depression in the cloth industry. The king might bully and browbeat the merchants to take up the cloth, but in response to the causes of the crisis the government could only reiterate royal concern to end the depression. Thus the letter of 22 May informing the county of the new measures ended with the by now familiar refrain that 'such hath bin his Majesties care and personall paines taken to remove theis impediments that of late have bin to trade, and to open a free vent to the commodities of your Country, that yourselves will shortly see the fruits of it to your comforts.'[81] On the same day a crowd of 200 to 300 inhabitants from the clothing townships of Bocking, Braintree and Witham, their credulousness exhausted, rioted at Burrow Hills.

Although clothworkers were at the heart of the crowd, Maldon's second riot was directed against the same highly visible and traditional grievance as its first.[82] Grain was again being loaded at Burrow Hills. It was this which drew the clothworkers to the coast. Angered by the apparent breach of the recently renewed ban on the export of grain, the crowd proceeded to administer a rough form of popular justice. They boarded a ship taking on grain, assaulted the crew and took away a quantity of its cargo of grain. The ship was forced to put to sea. Another group of rioters broke open a house (possibly a storehouse for grain waiting to be shipped) and carried off more grain. In a parody of the criminal law's sanctions, the crowd assaulted the leading merchant, a Mr Gamble, and forced him to purchase his freedom by the payment of a twenty pound 'fine'. By the time the sheriff and a fellow justice had arrived on the scene with an *ad hoc* body of such horse and neighbours as they could readily assemble, they found the crowd, its objectives secured, beginning to disperse. According to a later report, the crowd's rump greeted their belated arrival with a display of insolence 'intollerable both in speech and action'. All these representatives of authority could do was to examine those the crowd's victims pointed out to them as leading actors, have them committed to custody at Maldon and give orders for a strong watch to be kept.[83]

That the clothworkers formed the main contingent within the crowd should come as no surprise. Their action in Essex in 1629 continued a specific tradition within the county of the clothworkers as a source of disorder, and reflected the response of fellow workers in other areas, in other years, to equally desperate conditions. Nor is the preponderance of rioters from Bocking and Braintree altogether unexpected. Both towns had a history as centres of unrest, distress was particularly acute there, and disorder had long been predicted from their unruly poor.[84] The size of their presence, however, suggests that these two townships may well have taken the lead in mobilizing the crowd. Although little is known of the organization of the weavers' trade, they would appear to have had wardens who were resident there. It was the weavers of these townships who had been to the fore in putting the clothworkers' grievances before both justices and king. Perhaps they carried their leadership of the weavers' cause into the riot. A note in the Maldon chamberlains' accounts refers to the riot as 'the disorderly rysinge of the Brayntree & Bocking men'.[85]

Despite the clothworkers' obvious grounds for appearing in the riot, there is evidence that some prior organization from another quarter went into securing their presence. For whatever her part in the earlier riot, Ann Carter seems to have played a leading role in the making of the May disorder. According to a report of her subsequent trial, she had made a tour of the clothing townships to drum up support and had had letters sent out in which she styled herself 'captain'.[86] Unable to write herself, she had employed a local baker, John Gardner, to act as her secretary.[87] (Unfortunately a copyist's omission robs us of the knowledge of over what collective this clearly pseudonymous title – 'Captain of . . .' – assumed command.) Captain Carter may well have carried her leadership into the actual riot. In an attempt to mobilize the town's inhabitants, which apparently met with little success, she had offered to place herself at the head of a contingent from Maldon. 'Come, my brave lads of Maldon, I will be your leader for we will not starve', she is reported to have cried.[88] If true, it was entirely characteristic of this remarkable virago.

In the aftermath of the riot it was claimed that the crowd's victims, ambiguously described as 'Certaine Marchants of the North', were shipping the grain to Hull and had entered bonds not to transport it overseas. This may well have been the case, although the source for this claim was a member of the special court set up to punish the riot, who consistently attempted to deny the rioters any grounds for their action.[89] But despite the alleged bonds and the proclamation of 2 May banning the export of grain, the poor had no great cause for confidence. There were few customs officials in the outports. As men who had purchased their office, these scattered officials were often less concerned with enforcing the law than with securing a profitable return on their investment by conniving at its evasion. The taking of bonds was often an integral part of this evasion.[90] By late May, however, whether or not the grain was being exported under colour of a fraudulent bond was beside the point. As far as the distressed clothworkers were concerned, grain was being removed from the local economy at a time when prices were rising and government proclamations received in Maldon[91] (and doubtless elsewhere in the county) were stressing the threat of dearth. Grain exports compounded already acute conditions in the heavily populated, grain-deficient economy of the north-east of the county. In so doing, they tended to confirm the government's prophecies of impending shortage. Here, then, was an aspect of the crisis where man was not helpless in the face of economic forces barely understood. Dearth was a familiar phenomenon, its supposed causes widely understood, the necessary counter-measures commonly accepted. Those in authority should prevent the outflow of grain. If not, then the poor would.[92] On this aspect of policing the grain trade, therefore, the consensus between government and people broke down. While the government was concerned to ensure the supply of the poor *within the context of a national economy*, the rioters' actions (and Ann Carter's bold assertion) underlined the essentially local dimension of their own economy.

The rioters' action should not have surprised the government. There had been more than sufficient portents of disorder. Riots in January and March had been followed by frequent warnings from justices, township officials, clothiers and the clothworkers themselves. Towards the end of April, the movement of grain through Colchester, the largest textile centre in the county, had, as its authorities predicted almost a month before, occasioned disorder. If the exact form of this riot by a crowd of weavers and their wives remains obscure, in its composition and in its objectives it presaged the May riot.[93] Yet despite an acute awareness of the threat of disorder, neither local authorities nor members of the central government (for all its emphasis on the king's solicitous care for the clothworkers) had shown themselves able to solve a crisis whose origins lay beyond their respective jurisdictions. Nor, more importantly, had they shown themselves capable of alleviating the grinding poverty this crisis had created. For industrial depression presented a twofold challenge to the basic assumptions of a still essentially Elizabethan poor law. It spawned unemployment on a scale which the individual parish was not really designed to encounter, let alone solve. At the same time, it eroded the economic base of the local community on which the insupportable burden of relieving such poverty was to be placed. If past assessments of the effectiveness of the early modern poor law have been too harsh, recent revisionism has perhaps failed to take sufficient account of that law's abysmal failure to cope with the poverty produced by industrial depression.

'Nothing is more agreeable to the true Rules of Charitie and policie, then the relieuing of the truely indigent and impotent poore, and the setting on worke of those who are able to labour', ran the preamble to the proclamation of 17 May. But as the clothworkers had boldly informed the king (under cover of reporting what others were supposedly saying), 'words would not fill the belly nor Cloth the backe'.[94] This was the nub of the crisis. The inability of those in authority (for all their promises) to relieve the poor threatened the implicit contract between rulers and ruled. For the deference and subordination of the poor were not a reflection of some divinely ordained cosmos; they were in part conditional upon rulers fulfilling the self-proclaimed obligations of their office which helped to legitimize their authority, namely, administering justice and protecting and relieving the poor. The clothworkers had strained to its limit the poor's right to petition in order to urge their governors to act. Some, in a move ill-received, had even flocked up to court in an attempt to make their plight personally known to the king.[95] As the riot was to confirm, petitioning was one side of a relationship between the poor and their governors which could guarantee social order, but which could only be effective if it met with a response from those in authority. In other crises in the period, petitioning authority had secured responses that had upheld this relationship and pre-empted riot.[96] But in the case of Essex in 1629, conditions required greater decisiveness from the authorities in implementing a policy of relief if disorder was to be avoided. The depression in the cloth trade that had produced such concentrated poverty effectively sabotaged any chance of a realizable poor relief scheme. In fact, on this occasion, the government's attempt to implement measures which had previously proved successful in preventing disorder was perhaps counter-productive. While yet another ban on the export of grain offered little prospect of immediate relief for a group whose problem was not so much high prices *per se* but the lack of the wherewithal to purchase grain, it did draw attention to a grievance the government was powerless to stop completely.

Although the government could not help but have been aware of the threat of disorder, indeed, had even used it to badger local authorities, the second riot did shock and alarm it. Of itself, it was far more serious than the previous riot, especially since it differed significantly from the usual pattern of such disorder. Its size was particularly menacing. The crowd of 200 to 300 rioters was much larger than any other operating in the food riots of the period, and it had shown an unwelcome ability to co-ordinate its support over a wide area. Whereas grain rioters frequently contented themselves with staying the grain seized, some of the May rioters had taken away a considerable quantity. Property had been openly challenged. In defiance of the general tradition of riot, a section of the crowd had broken into a house and taken yet more grain. Above all, in rioting a second time the rioters had rejected the canons of behaviour – contrition and renewed subordination – expected to follow riot.

But whatever its disturbing peculiarities, it was the implications of the second riot that invested it with real menace. There was the alarming possibility that the riot might be only the first in a series of incidents involving angry clothworkers. 'Rumors are . . . much spread of an intention to assemble greater numbers speedily, that the Countrie begineth to bee in greate feares', reported the justices who had suppressed the riot.[97] There was also the threat that any future disorder might not be confined to such relatively marginal matters as the movement of grain but might adopt more alarming forms of insubordination. Some attempt had already been made to redirect the crowd's attention. A St Osyth's man, Francis Cousen, committed to Colchester gaol for 'stayinge of corne by the waterside', was also charged with 'animatinge of poore people to the nomber of sixe or seaven score to the Earle of Rivers' house [not far from Maldon] sayinge there was gold & silver enough'.[98] At a time when the political situation at the centre was still tense, the disorder could all too readily be seen to have political overtones. The respect shown the Earl of Warwick for his handling of the crisis and the earlier harping on hopes of parliamentary redress in a county already known for its political opposition must have been unwelcome to a government momentarily uncertain of its future.[99] The rioters' flouting of the king's personal efforts on their behalf scarcely provided an auspicious beginning to the period of 'personal rule'. Even the government's attempted implementation of its religious policy within the county was encountering opposition from godly clothworkers.[100]

In Essex, therefore, the second Maldon riot was both a microcosm of, and focus for, the tensions building up in the country in 1629. In language not normally used in ruling circles to talk of grain riots, the government spoke of the riot as a 'crime being of so high a nature and of so dangerous consequence that it amounteth to little less than a Rebellion'.[101] It was the crisis – at once economic, social and political – which prompted this uncharacteristic description of the food riot, as much as the nature of the riot itself, which necessitated firm action by the central government. Once the situation had reached the point of open disorder, the government had little to lose and possibly much to gain by a rigorous proscription of riot. If it was unable to prevent disorder by swift remedial action, it could at least use the weight of the law to enforce order. The central government therefore took a more immediate interest in the suppression and punishment of the May riot than was usually the case in incidents of food rioting.

The government's first concern was to prevent further disorder. On the day following the riot, the Privy Council fired off almost identical letters to the lord lieutenants, to their deputies and to the justices, ordering them to co-operate in mounting a strong guard of horse and foot at Burrow Hills to be ready on any occasion. The council apologized for this slighting of the normal hierarchy of county government, justifying its action by the need for urgency the crisis imposed. At the same time, it informed the county authorities that a special commission of oyer and terminer was to be sent into the county to punish the riot. Significantly, this decision to set up a special court to try the rioters must have been taken immediately upon notice of the disorder. In a postscript to its correspondence with the county, the council emphasized that it expected that 'an exemplarie punishment be inflicted upon the principall offenders for the conservation of the publique peace and the deterring of others to committ the like hereafter.'[102] The government clearly intended to use the trial of the rioters to demonstrate the limits of the permissible behaviour allowed the poor. In doing so, it acted with uncharacteristic vigour. The commission of oyer and terminer was issued just four days after the riot, on 26 May.[103] Thereafter, this large and formidable body – it was headed by the Earl of Warwick, the most powerful figure in the county, and included among its twenty-three members both assize judges, several other lawyers and most of the leading gentry in the county – moved swiftly to punish the rioters. Maldon's magistrates had issued warrants for the appearance of Ann Carter and her secretary, John Gardner, on 25 May. Two days later, they, together with the other rioters committed to Maldon after the riot, were escorted to Chelmsford under a strong guard. On the 29th, only a week after the riot, the commission sat to execute justice there. On the 30th, it hanged four of the rioters.[104]

Although no formal record of the court's proceedings appears to have survived, we do have a report of the trial in a letter written by a member of the commission. What is most immediately striking in this account by Sir Thomas Fanshawe is the fact that, as in the case of the first riot, very few of the rioters – only eight of the reported 200 to 300 – ended up in court. None the less, this handful was sufficient for the government's purpose. In one indictment, four men apprehended coming away from the riot were charged with taking away fifteen quarters of rye, and Ann Carter was indicted with them as an accessory before the fact. All were found guilty. The men, Fanshawe reported, 'Could not read' and, together with Ann Carter (whose sex denied her the use of the escape clause offered by benefit of clergy) were sentenced to be hanged. In a further indictment, two tilemakers were charged with breaking into a house in the daytime and taking six quarters of rye. John Gardner was indicted with them in a piece of judicial symmetry as an accessory for his office of secretary to Captain Carter. This group was more fortunate. The tilemakers were found guilty of taking the grain, but not of breaking into the house, 'and soe had the fauor of the Courte for a Psalme of Mercy'. Gardner, despite being indicted (according to Fanshawe) 'upon a full euidence', was acquitted by the jury. One of the four men sentenced to be hanged was reprieved (and later broke gaol), but no such leniency was extended to the other rioters. Sentence was carried out against Ann Carter and her companions without delay.[105]

Although we lack a full report, Fanshawe's account hints at a careful management of the rioters' trial. There seems to have been some attempt to deny that the rioters had had grounds for rioting. Sir Thomas made much of the fact that all the prisoners, both at the bar and after their reprieve, had confessed that they were in work at the time of the riot. While emphasis was placed on the legality of the movement of grain, he himself claimed, improbably, that the price of corn was 'at wonderful easie Rates'. All this minimized the embarrassing real causes of the disorder or, in Fanshawe's words, 'did much honour the proceedinge[s]'. The trial was clearly intended to provide a convincing demonstration of the government's ability to prosecute and punish disorder. This the court's swift reprisals ensured. As Fanshawe observed, 'this Justice hath soe terrified them as that wee are satisfied they will finde worke enough rather then runn to outrage againe'. But, at the same time, the court had been careful to temper rigorous enforcement of the law with a judicious display of merciful justice. Although the rioters' convictions were richly deserved – 'the insolencies of these people . . . were [so] intollerable both in speech and action . . ., the perticulers are not to bee Comprehended within the bounds of an ordinarie letter', choked Sir

Thomas – a show of mercy was allowed to soften (and, of course, by contrast heighten) judicial wrath. Three prisoners were reprieved upon favour after conviction, and one was allowed to be acquitted by his peers, despite the evidence against him. 'Thus was Justice and Mercie mingled alike by the Judges and the Jury', was Sir Thomas's satisfied comment on this careful staging of the proceedings. Doubtless both were accompanied by a visual display of judicial might and punctuated by the moralizing of sermon and judicial charge to point up their meaning for the people, a similar process probably being repeated at the place of execution the following day.[106]

In concluding his account of the trial, Fanshawe was able to report (with evident satisfaction) that 'the better sort of people were much pleased with the Justices, beinge before that tyme much dismaied with the insolencie of these people, . . . the proceedinges are much Justified by the Countrie and *exceedingly approued* by the Lordes here aboue' (my italics).[107] There is evidence to suggest that they were less well received among the poor. Two weeks after the executions, James Brownsward, a Maldon fisherman and acquaintance of the Carters, meeting with a draper of Witham who had been a member of the trial jury, spat in his face that 'Witham men were bloodsuckers, and that hee would spend xxli: but that hee would be revenged of some of the Jury'. In Maldon itself, the professed ignorance of a local jury summoned to discover what goods Ann Carter held – as an attainted person her belongings were now forfeit to the Crown – suggests a certain lack of popular sympathy for the commission's 'justice'.[108]

None the less, the attitude informing Fanshawe's report showed the authorities' awareness of the need for such severe action. As he himself observed, 'itt was a remedie applied with all opportunitie, for wee finde that there was a generall inclination for all who pretended pouerty to rise to do mischiefe'.[109] Despite probable unpopularity, the commission's actions effectively demonstrated the government's ability (for all the limitations too frequently stressed) to meet, where necessary, the threat of popular 'violence' head-on. Its ability to do so was made easier by the lack of opposition after the catharsis of riot. For despite evidence of a continuing undercurrent of opposition, we are presented with the paradox of a crowd which, whatever its original belief in the legitimacy of its actions, was prepared to accept authority's redefinition of the situation. No attempt was made to rescue the rioters arrested, no demonstration reportedly greeted their trial and execution. In the exercise of its legal powers (so ample, if so little used) the government was able to reinforce its definition of the boundaries to the initiative permitted the poor: petitioning was acceptable (at a distance); an open challenge to the authority of their governors was not. A measure of the government's success is provided by the marked change in the manner of the poor's petitioning. In a petition to the midsummer quarter sessions, the weavers of Bocking and Braintree were careful to dissociate themselves from the use of violence to obtain their ends:

many of our poore brethren haue runn beyond Compasse by violatinge his Ma:tys Lawes, and haue suffered therefore, which wee the wardens are much grieued for that they fell to such a Course, for wee always persuaded the Contrary, and that they would take a Legall course in all humble and obedient manner, the which wee are persuaded that they [now] will, for they are very sorrowful for that which is done.

While still complaining of the unreformed abuses within the cloth industry, the weavers put great stress on their desire to make their grievances known 'by a legall and honest course'.[110] The change in tone from their petition of early May, with its conscious use of the threat of violence and talk of words not filling the belly, provides ample testimony of the changed situation following the government's severe enforcement of the law. Contrition had been secured, a show of deference regained.

Although the threat of further reprisals was allowed to linger within the county – the commission was adjourned, to meet again in early June if necessary – the government was quick to recognize that punitive action was not by itself sufficient to restore the bonds of obedience and subordination, however skilful the mingling of justice and mercy. The trial had temporarily eclipsed the problem of provision for the poor, but the commission, before adjourning, threw its weighty authority behind enforcement of the government's most recent relief measures. It issued copies of the proclamation for the relief of the poor and the Privy Council's letter of 22 May, and ordered a full return to be made of each parish's condition so that effective action on a county basis could be taken at the next quarter sessions.[111] When, by the midsummer sessions, tensions had shifted to the clothworkers' relations with their employers, the authorities were quick to respond to the weavers' grievances. A committee of justices, headed by the Earl of Warwick, was instructed to call the clothiers before them, and orders meeting the clothworkers' complaints were issued at the following quarter sessions.[112] At the centre, the Privy Council continued to oversee the county's administrators and chivvy them into ensuring that all efforts were made to relieve the poor. The legacy of this renewed concern for the poor was to be seen in the county's response to the more general crisis of the following year. Making unprecedented use of the full range of the county's administration, Essex's magistrates achieved a remarkable degree of regulative control. They controlled the movement of grain and curbed abuses in its marketing. Extra grain was imported and sold to the poor at prices which were sometimes well below those in the market-place. Special care was taken to see Maldon and the clothing towns well supplied. Those with adequate resources were taxed more heavily to support the greatly increased number of poor. The county authorities acted vigorously, often in advance of prompting from the central government, anticipating the programme initiated nationally by the Book of Orders.[113]

The legacy of riot was, then, double-edged. It brought not just a restoration of the bonds of order but also an increased responsiveness to the demands of the poor. Long after the event, the disorder of 1629 served as a testimony to the reality of the threat posed by the poor. As such, it was employed by all groups within county society in an attempt to secure the response they wanted. When, for example, the weavers sought the aid of the justices later in the year in checking the abuses of their employers, they professed themselves unable to live 'without using unlawfull meanes to serue our necessities'. Though they were quick to add the saving clause that they were unwilling to do so, the point had been made and taken.[114] Action followed. When the justices found their efforts to regulate the clothiers thwarted by the assize judges, they in their turn informed them of the weavers' discontent, reminded them of the earlier disorder, cited the government's instructions to prevent any repetition of riot, and ended with the veiled threat that 'if some what bee not presently done wee shall not bee able to keepe these poore people in quiett'.[115]

The memory of 1629 became part of the currency of political discourse within the county community. When, by the spring of 1631, the renewed crisis was at its peak, the county returned to the threat of disorder in an attempt to secure intervention by the central government. One justice almost certainly had 1629 in mind when he supported his plea for an effective ban on grain exports with the observation that there was a suspicion of secret exports, 'w:ch if it should be, and goe on, it would in all probabillyte, breed miserable distractions in the Countye and K:om'.[116] When depression revisited the cloth industry in the later 1630s, the memory of 1629 was still there to be tapped by the poor. One clothworker in a petition for relief managed to remind the justices of Burrow Hills: 'I never took noe lewed course for to rong any man nor yet Rune about the Country as others have done as it is well knowne that some went for Corne to the sea sid[e] and took it by violen[ce]', he informed them. By stressing his former loyalty, he was able in the same breath to revive the spectre of popular violence, closing his petition with the ominous observation that 'it is hard to starue Job saieth, since for skin and all that a man hath he will giue for his life'.[117] His audience was well primed. As one gentleman observed, 'I thinke itt fitt that wee should doe, that w:ch belongeth to us and is fitt to be done for the p:venting of so great a mischeife as the want of worke, to so many poor p:sons may p:duce.' A commission was issued to investigate the clothworkers' complaints.[117]

Maldon, then, has the advantage of having been the scene of two large and comparatively well-documented riots which provide a sharp contrast in both the full range of crowd behaviour and magisterial response. As a case study, it enables us to examine in some detail the early seventeenth-century food riot and to see reflected in its form popular attitudes to the law and the proper exercise of authority. Riot was seldom simply a form of immediate self-help on the part of the poor. The crowd's appearance was not designed to end its grievance unilaterally, but to do so by securing (or coercing) the necessary exercise of authority. By publicly confronting authority with its failings, the crowd attempted (more often than not success-fully) to recall their governors to their self-proclaimed duty of pro-tecting the poor. In so doing, the poor displayed a perhaps surprising knowledge of the law and an often acute awareness of its uses. The courts of law (notably quarter sessions) provided a quasi-legitimate forum for the expression of popular grievances. Where petitioning failed and riot followed, knowledge of the law could be used to reinforce popular norms and to offer a sense of legitimacy to the actions of a crowd bent on enforcing these in the face of magisterial inactivity. An awareness of the law not only helped to license popular initiative; it also formed and fashioned its expression. There was a conscious mimicry of administrative practice by the crowd within the riot.

The example of Maldon also enables us to penetrate the rhetoric of authority and to examine the nature of the magisterial response to disorder. Far from being one of proscription and punishment (as might be suggested by their fear of disorder), the authorities' reaction was often one which implied a recognition of the legitimacy of the complaint, if not the manner of its making. Characteristically, as in the first Maldon riot, the central government accorded the local authorities considerable autonomy in handling the aftermath of riot. This they did with a certain delicacy, not seeking to exacerbate tensions by a rigorous prosecution of the riot but carefully responding to the grievances of the crowd. By contrast, the second riot – however much it may have conformed to the tradition of riot in the object of its attentions and in its sense of legitimacy – provoked a very different response. The size of its disorderly crowd, the attack on property and the repetition of disorder at a time of crisis, all allow us to see another, harsher, face of authority, one which hitherto perhaps has not received sufficient recognition from historians of the period. For though there were limits to the law, in the case of the food riot these lay less in the law's scope than in its enforcement. And whilst acknowledging the oft-stressed limitations on authority in dealing with such disorder – the relative spontaneity of riot, the lack of a police force or standing army – it is important to emphasize that at least some of these limitations were self-imposed. They found their force in the authorities' realization that the best way of handling disorder was not necessarily to be found in a rigorous enforcement of the law against riot. But the second Maldon riot, openly challenging authority and carrying within it the seeds of further disorder at a time of particular stress for both county and central government, revealed the latent strength of the law. It prompted an effective demonstration of the law's ability, when necessary, to meet a persistent challenge to authority (particularly from a crowd whose actions appear to have broken the tacit understanding between themselves and the authorities) with decisive action and exemplary punishment.

This ability to define what constituted acceptable popular action through the exercise of law was of crucial importance to the government's maintenance of social order. It is clear from the tradition of riot that a knowledge of the criminal law's scope and of the government's ability to exact the penalties it prescribed was firmly located within the popular consciousness, alongside an awareness of other laws more beneficial to the poor. If in this period grain riots did not generally conform to the government's stereotype of collective theft with violence nor spill over into a conscious attack on the social and

political order, this was in part at least because popular awareness of
the law of property was already sufficient to suggest that any such
direct challenge would invite savage retaliation.

Knowledge of the law legitimized action. It also suggested caution.
For example, Kentish rioters who had taken the precaution of con-
sulting an attorney's clerk at Canterbury in the dearth of 1596 about
the legality of their plan to stay grain had been told that they might
'soe they tooke noe weapon in hande nor did take any of it awaye' –
advice they were careful to heed when executing their design.[118]
Similarly, rioters in Norwich in 1532 who enforced a policy of *taxation populaire* in the town's market-place – setting their own price on
grain they had brought into the market and supervising its sale – were
careful not to pocket the proceeds of their sale. They surrendered
them to a local official, and when he, having second thoughts,
returned the money to the rioters, they went to considerable lengths
to return it to the owner of the confiscated grain. They did so because
they knew, as one of them put it, that 'iff she had put it in her purse
it shuld have ben stolen'. An awareness of the sanctions of the criminal law was burned into the collective memory. Three to four years
earlier a riot against the export of grain from Yarmouth, Norwich's
coastal port, had got out of hand and ended in the execution of some
of the rioters.[119]

The law, then, served as a pivot for the relationship between rulers
and ruled in early modern England. Their differing responses to the
threat to the social order (for the poor, the threat from dearth and
depression, for the authorities, their outcome in the feared disorder)
were articulated around competing definitions of the uses and enforcement of the law. In the ambiguity of its definition and the flexibility
of its enforcement, the law gave scope for popular initiative while
simultaneously limiting its 'legitimate' expression. If, therefore, the
food riot demonstrated the early modern government's well-known
inability to control the economic order, it also provided an opportunity for authority to redress the balance with a convincing demonstration of its ability to defend the social order. But, it is important
to remember, it was only able to do so in early seventeenth-century
England because conflict prompted by more persistent social and
economic tensions came to be resolved within the framework of the
law, in an active and sometimes violent argument over the interpretation, intent and enforcement, but not (generally or collectively
at least until the 1640s) the validity of existing laws.[120] Why this
should be so demands further investigation. Perhaps part of the

answer is to be found in the fact that disorder also renewed the tradition of riot. It reminded the authorities of the crowd's existence and re-emphasized their need to maintain the submission and obedience of the poor (but not inarticulate) by a return to a more active pursuit of measures designed to meet popular grievances. It is perhaps significant that the widespread grain riots prompted by the crisis of 1630–1 were noticeable by their absence in a previously troubled, but now actively governed Essex.

3 'A set of ungovernable people': the Kingswood colliers in the eighteenth century

Robert W. Malcolmson, Queen's University, Canada

The exercise of established authority in eighteenth-century England was not only subtle and complex, it was also very uneven in its impact and effectiveness. In some parts of the country authority was un-challenged and securely enforced; in other areas the exercise of authority was tenuous, uncertain and often ineffectual. Everywhere some men had the legal right, reinforced by economic strength, to rule over other men, but the actual effectiveness of such authority in any particular place depended on a multiplicity of local circum-stances. In one type of community – perhaps a small market-town or a dominant squire's parish – we detect evidence of firm social disci-pline, outward deference and quiescence; in other places we uncover a social reality of dissent, frequent social conflict and plebeian inde-pendence. Perhaps for some localities the image of a hierarchical social order, smoothly functioning and almost universally accepted – an image which some historians have espoused – is accurate enough; however, for other localities – the eastern parts of London, some fen-land communities, numerous industrial towns and villages, many recent settlements in forests and on wastelands – this image is patently inadequate. For in many parts of England the formal institutions of power were neither deeply rooted nor widely respected; the popula-tions of these places were partly withdrawn from, and sometimes resistant to, the exercise of 'lawful' authority. These, in short, were areas which had not been fully colonized by the nobility and gentry: official authority was weak, plebeian independence was prominent and relatively unconstrained. It is the intention of this essay to investi-gate these limits of authority with special reference to one particular area, the Forest (or Chase) of Kingswood in Gloucestershire.

Although popular 'lawlessness' in the eighteenth century occurred in many different localities and involved a variety of occupational groups, it is clear that some types of locality were more prone to dis-turbances than others, and that some groups of labouring people were especially inclined to challenge certain actions of authority, often by rising *en masse* to defend what they saw as their interests. Throughout the country at large forest regions appear to have been particularly notorious for their unruliness: by common repute they were thought to be among the most lawless parts of seventeenth- and eighteenth-century England. In the forests of the country, whether wooded or not, settled arable agriculture had not taken root; consequently, although the game of the forests was protected by law, there had been no economic basis for gentlemen, farmers, and ecclesiastics to impose their characteristic imprints of permanence – manor houses, substantial farmsteads, churches – on local society. The exercise of parochial authority – in the form of resident gentlemen and prosperous tenant farmers, church discipline, a manorial court, a select vestry – was either non-existent or very weakly felt. The forest-dwellers, as a result, were relatively unconstrained by the immediate presence of institutional authority, and they were only minimally involved in any relations of clientage with members of the governing class. They subsisted by a variety of (often makeshift) devices and were able to fashion their own distinctive modes of existence, and their culture and conduct were often sharply in conflict with the imperatives of the established order around them. In the seventeenth century forest areas were noted for their religious nonconformity, frequent unruliness, and general disrespect for established authority.[1] In the next century some of them became centres of serious social disorders, most of which stemmed from the efforts of royal officials and large landlords to impose more effective controls on the forests' inhabitants and to appropriate the forests' resources for their own exclusive uses. The turbulence in the forests of south-east England, and the tensions which arose over the competing claims to the use of game and common land in Cannock Chase, have been fully documented in recent studies.[2] Other forests exhibited similar signs of lawlessness – as seen by the lawmakers. Cranborne Chase in Dorset, for example, was noted in the eighteenth century for its social disorders; deer-stealing was common, smugglers sought refuge in the woods, and the local inhabitants were said to be given to 'all kinds of vice, profligacy, and immorality' and to have contracted 'habits of idleness and become pests of society'.[3] Thieves were often reported to be working out of some forest area, waylaying travellers and sometimes terrorizing the residents of neighbouring villages. The Forest of Selwood, near Frome in Somerset, was said in the late eighteenth century to 'have been, within the memory of man, the notorious asylum of a desperate clan of banditti, whose depredations were a terror to the surrounding parishes. One of their evil practices, and which perhaps was far from being the worst, was that of coining money'.[4] Similarly, Arthur Young complained of the 'morals' of the people dwelling in and around Wychwood Forest in Oxfordshire:

The vicinity is filled with poachers, deer-stealers, thieves, and pilferers of every kind: offences of almost every description abound so much, that the offenders are a terror to all quiet and well-disposed persons; and Oxford gaol would be uninhabited, were it not for this fertile source of crimes.[5]

Just as forest regions had acquired a clear notoriety, so men of certain occupations had become noted for their lack of deference and their independent habits, and among these the coal-miners of England were probably the most prominent. Colliers are well represented in the documentation concerning popular protests, ranging from the numerous accounts of industrial disputes in Durham and Northumberland to the bulky files of evidence which relate to years of food riots. On these latter occasions colliers frequently played leading roles in trying to force the local magistrates to ensure 'just' prices, or in taking over the market-place, or in compelling farmers to bring provisions to market, or in preventing the export of grain from their own localities. An inspection of the evidence bearing on the widespread price disturbances in 1740 and 1756–7, for instance, leaves little doubt as to the prominence of colliers as well-disciplined activists in the cause of 'redressing' popular grievances. The citizens of market-towns and even large provincial cities anxiously feared their arrival at times of dearth, and the local authorities probably felt less secure in dealing with aggrieved colliers than with any other group of discontented people. From almost all parts of the country where coal was dug – Somerset, the Forest of Dean, Wales, the West Midlands, Tyneside – there are frequent reports of popular disturbances involving miners (and the tinners of Cornwall might justifiably be added to the list). Miners had a strong sense of corporate identity and were able to mobilize their forces for collective actions with particular effectiveness. They lived in communities which were culturally and sometimes physically isolated; they lived apart from other men – partly cut off from ordinary life by the blackness of their skin, the mysteriousness of their underground places of work, the peculiarities of their manners – and they depended very much on their own resources, sharing a distinctive and dangerous working environment. Their distance from others helped to draw them closely together;

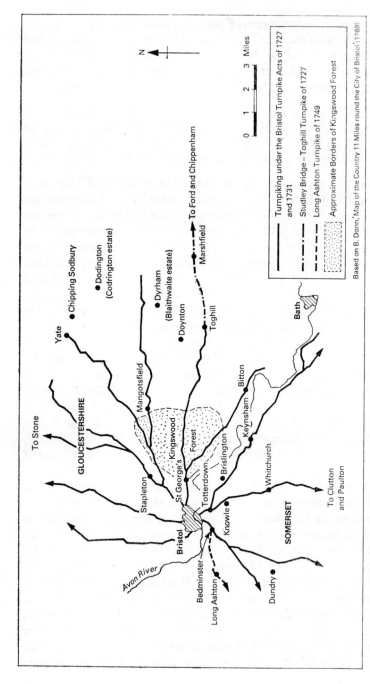

Kingswood and its region in the mid eighteenth century

Key:
— Turnpiking under the Bristol Turnpike Acts of 1727 and 1731
—·—·— Studley Bridge – Toghill Turnpike of 1727
— — — Long Ashton Turnpike of 1749
⬚ Approximate Borders of Kingswood Forest

0 1 2 3 Miles

Based on B. Donn, 'Map of the Country 11 Miles round the City of Bristol' (1769)

N

GLOUCESTERSHIRE

SOMERSET

Yate
Chipping Sodbury
Dodington (Codrington estate)
Dyrham (Blaithwaite estate)
Doynton
Marshfield
To Ford and Chippenham
Toghill
Mangotsfield
Bath
Bitton
Keynsham
Kingswood Forest
Brislington
Stapleton
St George's
Totterdown
Whitchurch
Bristol
Knowle
To Stone
Avon River
Bedminster
Long Ashton
Dundry
To Clutton and Paulton

their social solidarities were highly developed, they were well disciplined and they were resolute. When they had grievances the colliers of England were a force to be reckoned with.

Both of these themes – the unruliness of forests and the corporate solidarity of miners – come together in this essay, for Kingswood Chase, a partly deforested region just east of Bristol which was occupied principally by colliers, was certainly one of the most unmanageable areas of eighteenth-century England. Kingswood, indeed, gained a reputation for independence and rebelliousness which few other areas could match. John Wesley, who first came in contact with Kingswood in March 1739, wrote in November of that year of the notoriety of the district's colliers: 'Few persons have lived long in the West of England who have not heard of the colliers of Kingswood: a people famous, from the beginning hitherto, for neither fearing God nor regarding man.'[6] The reputation seems to have been justly earned. During the reign of George II the colliers were involved in numerous incidents of popular protest; on several occasions the city of Bristol was thrown into turmoil by their interventions; and as a result of their disposition for collective action, troops and the local authorities were often kept busy in the defence of the law, though they usually refrained from entering Kingswood itself. The colliers' well-known disrespect for official authority was a frequent source of anxiety – sometimes even terror – over a period of at least three decades. The Kingswood colliers may well have been the most rebellious group of labouring men in the country between the 1720s and the 1750s. In fact, a student of popular protest during the early Hanoverian decades has concluded that they were 'the rioters par excellence of the period' – 'the most prominent rioters in the country over the period 1714–54'.[7]

Kingswood Chase, covering some 3400 acres, included parts of four parishes directly to the east of Bristol: St Philip and Jacob (later to become the parish of St George), Bitton, Stapleton, and Mangotsfield. The whole Kingswood area, as well as several parishes immediately to the north, east, and south of the forest, abounded in coal, much of which was readily obtainable at or near the surface of the ground. The city of Bristol was almost entirely dependent on the region for its supply of fuel, both for domestic and industrial uses; the local industries included copper and brass works, distilleries, glass-houses and sugar refineries, all large consumers of coal. The control of the chase was for many years a matter of dispute between the Crown and the large local landowners; these manorial lords gradually appropriated most of the forest (and especially its mineral resources) for their own use and successfully resisted the claims which various officials and patentees of the Crown attempted to exercise. The undiscriminating designation of the area by contemporaries – it was sometimes called a chase, sometimes a forest – was a reflection, perhaps, of the erosion of any clear sense of a special royal presence. By the end of the seventeenth century almost all of the deer were gone, much of the wood had been destroyed and the royal rights were in practice defunct.[8] During the early eighteenth century the forest was divided into four main private 'liberties', each controlled by a powerful family: the Chesters, the Berkeleys, the Newtons, and the Players.[9] The profits from their mineral 'rights' were reputedly very substantial, and thanks in part to this wealth, two of the lords, Norborne Berkeley (1717–70) and Thomas Chester (1696–1763), served for long periods as MPs for Gloucestershire. The actual coal-workings were leased out to master colliers, sometimes known as the 'adventurers of the coal mines'. A few of these men were substantial entrepreneurs, many were small, and some of them worked in part-nerships; these adventurers had charge of hiring the labour required for their pits. About seventy pits were being operated in the later seventeenth century,[10] and most of these coal-workings were organized on a relatively small scale. The lords normally received around one-eighth to one-fifth of the value of the coal which was raised.[11]

In the early modern period the uncultivated forests and wastelands of England were among the principal centres of immigration and rapid population growth, and Kingswood certainly conformed to this pattern. Migrants were attracted to the chase by the easy availa-bility of land (they often took it by straightforward encroachment), by *de facto* common rights for their animals and by the possibility of industrial employment. By the late seventeenth century a large num-ber of cottages had been erected in Kingswood: around 300 would seem to be a reasonable estimate, though one source suggests almost 500. The majority of Kingswood's inhabitants probably depended directly on the coal-workings for their living, either as actual miners or as 'horsedrivers' – that is, as drivers of the horses that carried coal to Bristol. (The roads east of Bristol were heavily used for the carriage of coal: in 1698, when passing through Kingswood, that indefati-gable traveller, Celia Fiennes, 'was met with a great many horses passing and returning loaden with coals dug just thereabout'.)[12] One observer in 1672 reported that Kingswood contained a 'multitude of coal pits, and was stuffed with cottagers and alehouses, and overlaid with horses for carrying coal' to Bristol; in 1743 a report to the French government referred to 'le nombre prodigieux de gens qui travaillent aux mines de charbons dans ses terres aux environs de Bristol'.[13] According to a useful, though somewhat incomplete, survey of the chase in 1691, Kingswood's population included 111 colliers and 65 horsedrivers, and this is almost certainly an understatement; in the same year one observer put the number of colliers at 500, probably an exaggerated figure.[14] At least 100 cattle and more than 500 horses were kept in the forest, all of which could be conveniently pastured on the wasteland or in suitable enclosures.[15] In 1722 it was reported by a local resident that 'the cottages multiply greatly every year in Kingswood',[16] and there is no doubt that the population was growing very rapidly in the area. By the end of the eighteenth century it was said that the colliers' houses were so numerous 'that Kingswood has from the neighbouring hills the appearance of being one vast, rural suburb of Bristol'.[17]

This, then, is the basic social background to our study of Kingswood: but what about its reputed unruliness? There were already complaints about the character of Kingswood's squatter-inhabitants shortly after the Restoration. It was said in 1667 that large numbers of cottagers were settling in the chase 'without leave . . . and generally live there without government or conformity in idleness and dissoluteness', and that they were not 'responsible to any Civil officer or Minister for their behaviour or Religion'. (There was no church in the forest until the 1750s, and the impact of civil parochial controls seems to have been extremely weak.) The people of Kingswood, according to these representations, were 'of all persuasions living in a lawless manner, almost every Cottage selling Ale without Lycence & keeping what rule they please and never going to Church & in pilfering and stealing'. As a result of these depredations it was said that the main road between Bath and Bristol 'is become very insecure to Travellers and so are ye goods and houses to the adjacent Inhabitants'.[18] Here, it seems, was a group of men very much withdrawn from the normal means of social discipline. Established authority was likely to be significantly limited in the ways in which it could deal with such people.

The looseness of social discipline in Kingswood probably accounts for the area's apparent attractiveness as a haven for a variety of criminals. Forest regions tended to provide the cover of obscurity because their topography, and the inhabitants' faces, habits and social relations, were not well known to gentlemen and the established authorities; and such obscurity – physical and social – must have been an active encouragement to those who perceived the rewards of living outside the law. 'Criminality' in Kingswood is only documented in a fragmentary way, but the evidence that exists is worth reporting. Poaching had long been common in the area and, until the deer disappeared, guns and hunting dogs were kept, along with ferrets, nets, and snares; sheep-stealing may also have been practised.[19] There are passing references to robberies, two of which suggest the existence of an organized criminal community in Kingswood. In April 1738 a collier who was awaiting execution for horse-stealing, and who confessed to stealing thirty-three horses, revealed the activities of a gang of thieves working out of Kingswood; he also declared that there were 'several Coiners among the Colliers', exposing two of them by name. Numerous Kingswood coiners, according to this report, had been discovered and prosecuted a few years earlier, though some had succeeded in avoiding arrest.[20] In early 1749, when two Kingswood colliers were committed to prison for various robberies, it was said that around thirty other colliers were 'concern'd in divers other Burglaries and Felonies . . ., several of whom have absconded from their Dwellings'. This 'gang' was referred to again a few months later.[21] Two Kingswood colliers were executed for highway robbery in March 1741; and in April 1750 a man who had several warrants against him, and who was briefly apprehended in Bristol, was described as 'the noted Thom. Summers of Kingswood'.[22] Kingswood was conveniently situated, not only for the robbery both of the neighbouring estates and of the travellers who were obliged to pass through the chase on their journeys to and from Bistol, but also for the sort of crime which depended on the existence of a nearby, populous and wealthy city – and Bristol was virtually on its doorstep. In the late eighteenth and early nineteenth centuries parts of Kingswood were notorious for the organized criminality, and special measures had to be taken to deal with the problem.[23]

We have, then, some preliminary evidence which suggests that Kingswood was, to a considerable degree, a territory that was beyond the effective control of the local authorities in both Bristol and southeast Gloucestershire. The law could not be fully enforced in the chase, and the colliers were often able to behave more or less as they pleased, sometimes in opposition to 'lawful authority', and with little fear of punitive retribution. In 1729 a condemned man was ordered to be executed in Bath and his body hung in chains outside the city; but the colliers, for reasons which are not revealed, 'rose in a Body & swore he [would] never be hang'd there; whereupon he was conveyed to Wells and there executed in the most private Manner'.[24] Official interventions in Kingswood were infrequent, and when one such intervention did succeed it was a matter for public comment. In July 1739 a sheriff's execution was levied 'upon one William Hains of Kingswood, without the least Obstruction. This may be deem'd a great Favour, no Officer having within the Memory of the oldest Man Living, been able to effect an Undertaking of this Nature in so peaceable a Manner'.[25] The early Methodist preachers, who began their evangelizing mission in Kingswood in 1739, were unanimous in viewing the colliers as a 'neglected' people, withdrawn from any civilizing influences, and thus especially suitable for spiritual ministrations. In 1714 the colliers were condemned by one (admittedly partisan) observer as 'filthy Ruffians'; and around the same time some gentlemen in the area were talking of setting up a school in Kingswood 'for the educating of the barbarous people there',[26] though there is no evidence that any institutions with such socializing intentions came to be established in the chase before the late 1730s. By the mid 1720s it seems that the colliers had already acquired a reputation for a strong sense of corporate identity and effective collective action, for in the winter of 1726–7, at a time when there were serious industrial disturbances in the Wiltshire woollen towns, it was reported that some of the riotous weavers had been sent 'to invite the Kingswood Colliers to their assistance'.[27] The colliers must have already engaged in some actions which had allowed them to gain such a reputation, though because of the thinness of the evidence we have no clear picture of their conduct during the early years of the eighteenth century. All we know is that they led a food riot in Bristol in May 1709, a year of very high grain prices; and that they were accused of being actively involved, in the Tory interest, in a political riot in 1714 (and perhaps in one or two other politically inspired disorders in Bristol during the last years of Anne's reign).[28] It is only with the accession of George II in 1727 that the evidence on the colliers becomes fairly abundant, and it is this evidence which allows us to examine the nature of their relations with the established authorities, and the patterns of interaction between those entrusted with enforcing the law and a body of men who had their own ideas about the law, its legitimacy, and how it should operate.

A prolonged period of often intense conflict between the colliers and the established authorities began in 1727 with the passage of two

Acts that affected the roads leading east from Bristol. In late February two petitions were presented to the House of Commons, one from the corporation and merchants of Bristol concerning the roads leading out of their city, and one from some gentlemen in the Chippenham area concerning that part of the London to Bristol road which ran between Studley Bridge in Wiltshire and Toghill in Doynton, Gloucestershire, leading directly to Bristol through Kingswood. Both petitions complained of the bad condition of the local roads and pointed to the need for special measures to keep them in better repair.[29] The result, as expected, was two turnpike Acts, both of which received royal assent on 24 April. The Bristol Act (13 Geo. I c. 12) allowed tolls to be levied on twelve roads leading out of Bristol, six of which ran through or near the coalfields to the east of the city. Every horse or mule was liable to a toll of one penny, though animals carrying coals were to pay only a half-penny apiece; the Studley Bridge–Toghill Act (13 Geo. I c. 13) allowed no such reduced rate for carriers of coal. Each Act appointed a large number of trustees to manage the affairs of their respective turnpikes, presumably in an effort to mobilize as much support as possible for the new enterprises: the Bristol Act named 146 individuals, the Studley Bridge–Toghill Act, 62; almost all of the trustees were gentlemen of substance in their own localities.

The colliers of the Bristol region wasted no time in demonstrating their opposition to these new impositions. On the first day for the collection of the tolls, 26 June, the colliers of Kingswood, along with some from Brislington in Somerset, another mining community just south-west of Kingswood,

assembled in a Body, and pulled down 4 of [the turnpikes] . . .; some of which they set on Fire, and some they threw into the River: That at Totterdown, in the Bath Road, being erected again, they went the next Day to view it, and finding it not done to their Minds, demolisht it again the second time, and swear, they'll bring no Coal into the City, nor suffer any Turnpikes in their Roads till they are exempted from paying Toll.[30]

The rioters were estimated to number about a thousand by one report, 'some hundreds' by the mayor of Bristol. They continued to destroy the turnpike gates during the following week, letting it be known that they would allow none to stand. On one occasion, to demonstrate their determination and sense of grievance, and presumably hoping to intimidate the authorities, the Kingswood colliers marched through Bristol 'with Clubs and Staves in a noisy manner'; according to Bristol's mayor they 'Committed no violence here Tho I am perswaded had any opposition been made the Consequence would have been fatal'. They usurped the prerogatives of the turnpike authorities and imposed their own levies on travellers, treating some of them 'rudely' and 'insolently'. In response to their refusal to deliver coal to Bristol, the city government felt obliged to send to Wales for special supplies. The Kingswood colliers, said the mayor, 'are a set of ungovernable people violent in their way, and regardless of Consequences'. On 4 July troops were sent in pursuit of some colliers who had just cut down a gate and four prisoners were taken. The colliers, who were regarded by many Bristolians as 'desperate Fellows', threatened to come and pull down the gaol where the prisoners were held; there was talk of the citizens arming in their own defence, a picket guard was posted at the guildhall and patrols were dispatched to watch the borders of Kingswood.[31]

By mid July the colliers were in a more subdued temper, largely because no attempt was being made to reconstruct the turnpikes near to Bristol, and deliveries of coal to the city were resumed. Some of the gates further afield were still standing, but later in July and early in August several of these were also destroyed, including at least two on the road leading from Toghill through Marshfield to Chippenham, erected under the Act of 13 Geo. I c. 13. Some of the rioters were disguised, 'being dress'd in Women's Cloaths and high crown'd Hats'.[32] It was rumoured in October that the Bristol turnpike commissioners were intending to set up eleven new gates in place of those destroyed, but there is no evidence that these plans were ever realized. In May 1728 it was said that at Marshfield the turnpike gate had been cut down at least half a dozen times and that 'now they are obliged to hire Six or Seven Soldiers at a time, to guard the said Turnpike Day and Night; which is a great Expence'.[33]

How can one account for this vehement popular hostility to turnpikes? On one level the colliers were clearly acting to resist a new and unpopular form of taxation. It was reported that they 'thought themselves aggrieved by being made to pay the Turnpikes, being excused in other Places; and their Cry is, K. George and no Turnpike'.[34] They must have been aware, then, of the more attractive provisions in some other Acts: the Bath Turnpike Act of 1708, for instance, specifically exempted the carriage of coal from paying tolls (6 Anne c. 42 section 17). But there was more to the colliers' grievances than simple dislike of a new tax. Indeed, one gets a reasonably clear idea of the broader context of their resentment from a document which was sent to the Bristol Trust, entitled 'The Colliers Letter to the Turn-pike', dated 3 July 1727 from Kingswood and signed 'We Colliers of Kings-Wood'. First, they complained about the power given to the trustees by 13 Geo. I c. 12 to remove furze and heath from any common lands, for road repairs, without paying for them. The concern here was for the preservation of their commons and the sustenance derived from them: furze bushes, for instance, might be useful, not only for firing, but also for pasturage and shelter for livestock. Indeed, much later, in October 1776, when Arthur Young was travelling through the Forest of Dean, another Gloucestershire forest in which coal was dug, he noted that 'the colliers in winter get young furze, chop it in a trough, and give it to their horses with great success'.[35] Second, the Kingswood colliers alleged that the bad condition of the roads was partly a consequence of various forms of abuse of these roads by the local landowners, most of whom were now turnpike trustees, and their tenants. (The poor state of the English roads at this time resulted in part from the increase of wheeled traffic – that is, traffic mostly of and for wealthy people; and turnpikes were particularly intended to better facilitate wheeled travel and transport, an objective which would have meant little to the colliers, whose main concern was the carriage of coal by horse.) Third, and perhaps most important, the colliers complained that these poor road conditions were a consequence of the failure of the magistrates to enforce the existing laws for repairing the roads; these men of substance were accused, in short, of having neglected to act *properly* in accordance with the authority and responsibility which was vested in them as justices. As the colliers' letter put it, 'by the Omission of your Duty, and your Carelessnes and Over sight, you have lost your Honourable Magistracy, and brought your self under the reproach of a Turnpike'. The supposed 'necessity' for imposing road tolls was felt, then, to stem from the previous failure of the authorities to behave responsibly; and the so-called 'riots' in which the colliers had been involved were represented as forms of corrective action, conduct which was intended to set things right: the colliers likened their actions to efforts to put out a fire which had been 'wilfully kindled' by others.[36]

There was a strong sense in all this that the colliers regarded the initiatives of the turnpike promoters as patently illegitimate and dishonourable, and their own reactions to these initiatives as entirely proper and reasonable. They may have objected to the fact that the Bristol Act specifically stated that all persons who had been previously chargeable for the repair of the roads now to be turnpiked would remain liable for such costs and duties in the future: in short, while new burdens were being introduced, old ones were continued. Moreover, turnpike trusts normally involved the transference of some of the costs of road repairs and upkeep from the landowners (who were assessed for highway rates) to the road users, and this was unlikely to please working people who were as heavily implicated in road transport as were the Kingswood colliers and coal-carriers. (Pedestrians were seldom, if ever, liable for road tolls, and this helps to explain the absence of popular opposition to turnpikes in many parts of the country.) The colliers certainly thought poorly of the motives of those whom they addressed, in the singular, as 'Mr. Turnpike'. They recited a short verse apropos the recent interest in turnpikes:

Now Turnpikes are grown mutch in Fashion
The hardest Tax in all our Nation –
For where Wine & Women & Stock-jobbing past,
The Turnpike must help us at Last –

The turnpike Act they saw as 'a thing Clandestinely purchas'd' and the trustees as men needing pointed instruction as to their social duties.

So Mr. Turnpike, we most humbly beg you, when you Purches another Act of Parliament against the Colliers, not to put any Lattin in it; one thing more we would desire of you, that you would lay out all the Money that you have got by the Turnpike – in Catichismas, which you may have for two pence a peice, and give one to every one of those whose name are quoted between the 8th and 13 pages of your Act [i.e., the trustees], and by that they may Learn to do their Duty in that State of Life unto the which it shall please God to call them.

This sense of the illegitimacy of turnpike tolls may have supported the belief which was attributed to them by one witness, who said that their 'pretence' for destroying turnpikes was 'that there was no Act of Parliament for Turnpikes in those Parts, for that the King had not set his Hand to it'.[37] The king, the defender of justice and moral authority, could not (in some eyes) have sanctioned such acts against his people. The colliers were not rebelling against authority *per se*. In fact, they may have regarded themselves as perfectly loyal Englishmen, for they concluded their letter by acknowledging that 'we remain our Gracious King's Subjects untill Death'. Their complaint was against authority that had not fulfilled the people's expectations of it, and which needed to be reminded of its duties.

The local authorities, as one would expect, did not take kindly to these popular interventions in the cosy world of oligarchical rule. On 30 September 1727 a letter was sent to the Duke of Newcastle, signed by eight Gloucestershire gentlemen, at least seven of whom were turnpike trustees, complaining of 'the Violent Outrages of several licencious Persons (particularly our Coleworkers) who have held unwarrantable Assemblies and committed great Riots and Disorders in pulling down the Turnpikes which at no small Expence were Erected on the Roads leading from Bristol', and seeking advice on how to handle the situation and deter such 'disorders' in the future.[38] Little headway was made in apprehending or punishing any of the rebellious colliers, as these correspondents admitted. The prisoners who were tried at the 1727 summer assizes in Gloucester were acquitted, and subsequent and apparently determined efforts by the Bristol authorities to prosecute some of the colliers were unsuccessful. This failure cost the corporation almost £125 in legal expenses.[39] The commissioners of the Studley Bridge–Toghill turnpike offered a reward of ten guineas in September 1727 for the discovery of those responsible for destroying their gate at Marshfield, but there is no evidence that anyone was ever apprehended.[40] One problem facing the authorities was that it was unclear, at least to some gentlemen, under what statute such hostile acts against turnpikes could be successfully prosecuted. The Act of 13 Geo. I c. 13 included a clause providing for a fine of ten shillings for the destruction of toll-bars, though the Bristol Act included no such provision. As a result of this uncertainty and the concern about the lack of a serious deterrent, on 9 May 1728 the Studley Bridge–Toghill trustees petitioned Parliament for a law which would provide a more effective punishment for the destruction of turnpikes.[41] The result, less than three weeks later, was an Act (1 Geo. II c. 19) which allowed, for the first offence, a gaol sentence of three months and a public whipping, and for the second offence, transportation for seven years. This statute was a direct result of the events around Bristol in the previous summer.

The other direct result of the colliers' actions was an amendment to the Bristol turnpike Act. Little, if any, progress was made in repairing the roads leading out of Bristol, partly because of (as the formula for such things would have it) the 'many Difficulties, Doubts, and Inconveniences that . . . did arise'.[42] The new Act which was obtained in 1731 (4 Geo. II c. 22) introduced some administrative changes in the management of the trust's roads, intended to allow the gentry more effective control over the turnpikes which ran through their own localities; and it included a clause which exempted animals bearing coal from paying tolls. One (though only one) of the colliers' grievances, then, had been satisfied, though the toll on coal remained in force on the road from Chippenham through Marshfield which met the Bristol turnpike at Toghill, just east of Kingswood.

Armed with this new Act, in late June 1731 the trustees began to erect toll-gates again on the roads leading out of Bristol. The colliers, however, along with some of 'the country people', took immediate action to oppose these new initiatives and destroy some of the gates, several of which were quickly reconstructed, but just as quickly cut down again. On 30 June, while a party of colliers was destroying a turnpike set up in Dyrham, at the end of one of the turnpiked roads, they were attacked by a private posse led by William Blaithwaite, the principal landowner in Dyrham (and also a justice of the peace and turnpike trustee), who took four of the rioters prisoners. The next day, however, before the prisoners could be conducted to gaol, 'a great Body of Colliers' laid siege to Blaithwaite's house, threatening to destroy it if 'their Brethren' were not released. Blaithwaite 'was forced to permit a Rescue', and he found it prudent to refresh his visitors with several casks of ale. Some of the colliers (said to number some 400) then travelled eastward to Marshfield and Chippenham and destroyed more gates; and though Blaithwaite and another justice and turnpike trustee, Sir William Codrington of nearby Dodington (he also owned land in Marshfield), tried to stop them by reading the Riot Act, 'they went on in the most impudent Defiance to Authority'. There were reports of other popular 'outrages': on 15 July the London Post was stopped for several hours and 'used in a rough Manner by the Colliers'; and it was said that several turnpike commissioners had received threatening letters.[43] The local authorities in south-east Gloucestershire were much concerned about the weakness of their position (Codrington, for instance, in explaining the difficulties in ensuring public order in this area, noted that justices 'are but few on this side of the County nor indeede could wee have more for want of Gentlemen'), 'the Insolencies of the Rioters', and their inability to protect the turnpikes without the assistance of troops. 'The License these Rioters have Taken', wrote Codrington and Blaithwaite to the secretary of state on 22 September 1731, 'makes it difficult to execute any Process or warrant of the Law at present.'[44]

Several features of these disturbances in 1731 deserve to be emphasized. First, the colliers appear to have concentrated their attacks, not on the turnpike gates near Bristol and Kingswood itself, where the exemption on coal unquestionably applied, but on those to the east and north-east of Kingswood, where a toll *may* still have been levied on the carriage of coal. There was no exemption for coal on the turn-pike through Marshfield and Chippenham, where gates had been destroyed; and at Dyrham and Yate, which had experienced similar disturbances, there may also have been tolls on coal, for the gates were at or beyond the terminal points of two of the turnpiked roads from Bristol, and it is not at all clear that the exemption would have applied at these places. Another Gloucestershire turnpike Act, for instance, which applied to a large area north of Kingswood and included within its rather vague frame of reference a road or roads 'leading to or near' Chipping Sodbury, and for which Codrington was also a trustee, allowed no exemption for the carriage of coal (12 Geo. I c. 24). These facts, partly circumstantial, may account for the selectivity in the colliers' direct actions, and their apparent in-attention to those gates where it is certain that no coals were being taxed. Second, it is noteworthy that the two justices who were most active in contending with the colliers on this occasion both had sub-stantial estates in the neighbourhood east of Kingswood, and both were likely to benefit from the improvement of the roads running near their properties. Third, it appears that the military assistance which was rendered by the central government to the Bristol region was concentrated in the city itself and was not extended to the troubled county jurisdictions to the east, despite the urgent entreaties of the Gloucestershire magistrates. Perhaps this was a reflection of the superior political clout of Bristol's city corporation, which was controlled by the Whigs, certainly a not-negligible consideration during this period of Walpole's ascendancy. At any rate, with no troops available to protect the toll-gates east of Kingswood, the local authorities remained unable to enforce the law. No prosecutions resulted from the summer's disorders.

Confronted with this unhappy situation, the local gentlemen looked for relief through an extension of the 1728 statute concerning the penalties for destroying turnpikes. In March 1732 three petitions to this effect were received by the Commons, one from the trustees of the Studley Bridge–Toghill turnpike, one from the justices and gentlemen in the two hundreds east and north-east of Kingswood which had experienced the disorders of the previous summer, and one from the trustees of the Hereford turnpike Act, who had been faced with similar manifestations of popular revolt. The petitioners complained of these recent 'outrages' and the inadequate deterrents which were provided by the existing laws.[45] The result of their initiatives was an Act, 5 Geo. II c. 33, which allowed a person convicted of destroying turnpikes to be transported for seven years. This new and more severe law, it was hoped, would discourage future attacks on turnpikes. When the Kingswood colliers let it be known that they had 'enter'd into Articles not to suffer any Turnpikes to be erected', the *Gloucester Journal* of 30 May 1732 pointed to the risk they would now be taking, and hoped that, given the new statute, 'they will alter their Resolution'.

Newly armed at law, on 31 August 1732 the trustees of the Studley Bridge–Toghill turnpike ordered that two toll-gates be erected on their road between Marshfield and Chippenham. The consequence was that two weeks later, on 16 September,

a Party of Bristol Colliers, arm'd with Axes and Hatchets, came up from Kingswood, and cut down the Turnpike at Ford in Wiltshire, without any Opposition: Notice thereof was given to Mr. Holland at Chippenham . . ., Representative in Parliament for that Borough, and that they were coming on to destroy the Turnpike which stood about two Miles from that Town, on the Bristol Road; Mr. Holland, with two other Gentlemen and Servants, immediately mounted their Horses to go and defend it; but before they came thither the Colliers had cut down the Gate, and were proceeding to demolish the Walls on each Side, and the Turnpike-House: The Gentlemen required 'em to surrender, or they would fire on them; the Colliers swore they would die first, and attack'd them with Stones very smartly: The Return they met with was a Discharge of small Shot amongst them, which made 'em take to their Heels and run away across the Fields; but they were soon pursued, and three of them taken Prisoners. The next Morning they were sent away under a strong Guard to Salisbury Jail.

The turnpike trustees wasted no time in reasserting their authority, for two days after this disturbance they met again to authorize the reconstruction of the demolished gates. The taking of the three prisoners caused considerable agitation among the colliers, for a little later it was reported that they were holding frequent meetings to determine how to release 'their brethren', and that they were threatening to pull down the house of Rogers Holland and set fire to the town of Chippenham.[46]

This incident at Chippenham brought the colliers into a direct confrontation with one of the west of England's most energetic proponents of turnpikes and a prominent local supporter of Walpole's government. Rogers Holland, born in 1701, served as MP for Chippenham between 1727 and 1737; except for the excise bill, he voted with the administration in all recorded divisions during this decade.[47] He was perhaps more actively involved in the promotion of turnpike trusts than any other man in the Bristol–Chippenham region. In the winter of 1727, before his election to Parliament, he gave evidence in favour of the establishment of a turnpike between Studley Bridge and Toghill; and he was later named as a trustee for both the Bristol and the Studley Bridge–Toghill turnpikes. In May 1728, when the Commons was considering the need for specific penalties for the destruction of turnpikes (the petitioners were the Studley Bridge–Toghill trustees, of whom Holland was one), he took the leading role in seeing the bill through Parliament; he helped to prepare the bill, reported from the committees, and carried the bill to the Lords. In 1732, when a harsher law was sought concerning the destruction of turnpikes, Holland was again the leading figure in preparing an appropriate bill and superintending its passage through Parliament.[48] He was present at both of the Studley Bridge–Toghill Trust's meetings in the late summer of 1732 which ordered the erection of toll-gates. Here, then, was a man who had been actively engaged in promoting turnpikes and in trying to secure them against popular attack. He was unlikely to feel much sympathy for the Kingswood colliers.

In the winter of 1733 strenuous efforts were made to secure convictions of the three imprisoned colliers. This determination was undoubtedly reinforced by one further hostile act against established authority, for in February Holland was sent an anonymous threatening lettter warning him not to proceed against the three prisoners. As an active government supporter Holland could expect to get material assistance from the highest authorities: a reward of £200 was offered by the king for evidence leading to the conviction of those involved in making these threats, and a few days after the receipt of the letter it was announced that the rioters would be prosecuted at the Crown's expense. At the Salisbury assizes in March two of the colliers were convicted and sentenced to transportation, presumably under the Act of the previous year (5 Geo. II c. 33).[49] Rogers Holland was much encouraged by these convictions, and in a letter written a few days after the trial to one Thomas Haynes (in Bristol), a fellow trustee of the Bristol turnpike Act, he suggested that 'We must now resort to Turnpikes again, if we will amend our ways, & I cannot but suppose that they will stand now, if you set them up in the middle of Kingswood.' A little later he received some further evidence which led him to suppose that the colliers might behave more submissively in the future. On 14 April he wrote to the same correspondent that

Last Night Stock [one of Holland's tenants] sent me a Petition from the Kingswood Colliers to the King, imploring pardon for their two convicted Brethren, with above 200 Names to it. As soon as I am able I will lay it before the Secretary of State, but I don't know what Effect it will have, however they promise in their Petition to oppose any Attempt for destroying Turnpikes for the future (if ever made). Sure the Gentlemen about you may make a very good use of this if you think proper, & I should be glad to hear that they did.[50]

Here was a clear statement of one influential man's expectations of what the criminal law, when properly used, could achieve in terms of popular quiescence. The colliers' petition, unfortunately, does not seem to survive, and there is no indication as to what effect it had, and no record of the deliberations which it may have caused among men of power. The lack of any evidence of a pardon suggests that the sentences were probably carried out.

Rogers Holland's hopes for a full restoration of law and order, and a tranquil life for the friends of the turnpikes, were clearly premature. During the following two years turnpike agitation in the Bristol area certainly subsided, and a few of the toll-gates remained securely in place; but there were renewed disturbances in the summer of 1735, some of which probably involved the colliers, and Sir William Codrington was again writing to the secretary of state, providing some details on the disorders and complaining about the government's lack of support for the local authorities. The turnpike commissioners, he said, 'are all determind never to act any more if the Government will not support them & if the Laws are to be broke through by such a set of villins without being made an example of. God knows where it may end'. Some troops were ordered to be sent to the area as requested.[51] By 1735, however, the centre for turnpike disturbances in England was no longer around Bristol: it had shifted northwards to Herefordshire, and largely as a result of these disorders there was a final extension of the law concerning the destruction of turnpikes, an Act of 8 Geo. II c. 20 (1735), which allowed the penalty of death for a first offence. This Act, yet another addition to the swelling list of capital crimes in England, was passed quickly and after little debate.

In the Bristol area the efforts to construct turnpikes had already been seriously frustrated; their promoters may have become dispirited, for there is no evidence that much was done through the

1730s to revive the turnpike schemes. At the end of the decade most of the roads running east from Bristol were in much the same condition as they had been in the 1720s, as several observers attested. Because of the confusion and uncertainties associated with the Bristol turnpikes, it was difficult for the trustees to borrow capital for road repairs on the security of their tolls. The two main roads between Bristol and Bath certainly remained unturnpiked, at least partly because of the colliers' opposition: as Ralph Allen of Bath said in 1739 with reference to one of these roads, 'the Colliers have pulled down, and do constantly pull down, any Turnpikes that have been at any time erected'.[52] A decade later it was said that 'several thousand pounds' had been spent in erecting the Bristol turnpikes, but that because of the risings against them the two Acts of Parliament had been rendered largely ineffectual.[53] In early 1738 there had been further talk of re-erecting the turnpikes, and rumours circulated that they would be guarded by troops, but the talk came to nothing. It seems as well that efforts were being made to have a regiment of soldiers quartered in the Kingswood area 'in order to reduce those stubborn People to a proper Obedience of the Law'. The report added that 'a Judge's Warrant is come down for taking into Custody upwards of 40 of those Persons, for divers Offences',[54] but there is no record that any colliers were actually prosecuted.

One of the puzzling features of these riots concerns the possible involvement of gentlemen in stirring them up – or at least in failing to act in support of the law – and the extent to which local tensions between Whigs and Tories may have been implicated in at least some of the disturbances. There are several pieces of evidence which draw attention to the divisions within the local governing elites. The eight gentlemen who sent a letter to the Duke of Newcastle on 30 September 1727, seeking his assistance in subduing the colliers, complained of the lack of support from some of their neighbours.[55] John Oldmixon, writing a few years after these events, attributed the failure of the turnpike endeavours not only to the 'Mutiny of the Kingswood Colliers', but also to the fact that there had been disputes between the trustees appointed from Bristol and those from Gloucestershire and Somerset.[56] In 1731 it was reported in the press that some tradesmen and 'several Gentlemen of Note' were suspected of encouraging and abetting the riotous colliers in the summer of that year; and on 14 July 1731 Codrington was complaining to the secretary of state, on behalf of himself and Blaithwaite, both of whom had been objects of the colliers' displeasure, that some of the county justices 'did not come to our assistance when the Colliers were soe outragious'. 'I am afraid my Lord', he continued, 'that those wretches would never have been so impudent if they had not beene prompted by men of some fortune & figure.'[57] A letter of 1734 from Henry Creswicke, a land-owner in Hanham (a hamlet of Bitton), to John Scrope, the secretary of the Treasury and Whig member for Bristol who was defeated in the election of 1734, indicates the manner in which the colliers' 'insolence' could be laid at the door of some gentleman. Creswicke was very aggrieved, claiming that Sir Abraham Elton, MP for Bristol between 1727 and 1742 and a major force in city politics, had circu-lated a story that he, Creswicke, had encouraged the colliers' risings and given them money. He also alleged that Elton had tried to find a witness to swear an affidavit against him. Creswicke, pleading his innocence, claimed that the truth was that 'I myself rode to the head of above 200 of them [the colliers] and read his majesty's proclama-tion to them and dispersed them myself, which my antaggonest would not have done except he had a Company of Soldiers at his heels.' He concluded by expressing friendship for Scrope and 'those Gentlemen that are his majesty's sincere friends'.[58] Creswicke's pro-fessions of innocence are probably to be believed, for as a turnpike trustee, apparent Whig, and one of the eight signatories of the letter of 30 September 1727 to Newcastle, he does not fit the role of an agitator. The incident, at any rate, illustrates the sorts of tensions in genteel society which could become associated with the colliers' inter-ventions in public affairs.

What are we to make of the suggestion that party contentions may have influenced the behaviour of the colliers and the character of the riots? Although the evidence currently available does not allow us to pursue this question very far, we can point to a few facts which may be relevant to a more complete assessment. There is no doubt that party conflicts were well developed in Bristol and its Gloucestershire hinterland. In Bristol itself there was a fairly even balance in party strength, though the Whigs controlled the city corporation – and it was the corporation which had sponsored the turnpike Act of 1727. It was claimed by one person in 1734 that in other parts of Gloucester-shire, Whig-supported turnpikes were more susceptible to popular attack than those promoted by Tories (he reported that in the Gloucester area 'the Cry of these Rioters has all along been Bathurst and Chester, and no Turnpikes', Bathurst and Chester being the two Tory candidates in the general election).[59] It is certainly possible – perhaps even probable – that the Kingswood colliers favoured the

Tory interest in the Bristol region. It was alleged by a partisan pamphleteer that a body of Kingswood colliers ('these High Church Colliers', he called them, who 'hardly ever heard of Religion, till Cheverel was the Word') had been employed by the Tory interest in opposition to the Hanoverian succession during a major political riot in Bristol in 1714; and on a later occasion, in 1735, it was claimed by a government paper that a disorderly Tory mob in Bristol had been reinforced 'by a great Number of Colliers (supposed to be hir'd for that Purpose)'.[60] A Jacobite informant clearly thought that the colliers were well disposed towards the Tories.[61] Several of the most important landed families and proprietors of the coal mines in the Kingswood region were opponents of Walpole's government, including the Berkeleys, the Chesters, and the Newtons, though it should be added that they were all also turnpike trustees. There is as well a little evidence that some Tories may have viewed the question of road improvements in a manner which was more likely to elicit popular approval, for in 1732 and 1733 the party introduced bills in Parliament which were intended to shift the 'responsibility for road maintenance from the poorer to the more affluent inhabitants of each parish' (the bills were defeated).[62] But though the colliers may have had their reasons for preferring Tories over Whigs, or at least for being disaffected from their Whig rulers, there is no direct evidence that any Tory gentry actively urged them on in their attacks on tollgates. Indeed, there would surely have been substantial risks in so doing, even if some Tories may have disapproved of certain turnpike arrangements. Eighteenth-century observers of popular risings were too inclined to see outside agitators where there were none, and to exaggerate the importance of the supposed 'encouragers and abettors' of crowd action; and they were usually disposed to play down – in fact, they often failed to perceive – the substantive reality of popular interests and grievances. As we have seen, and will see further, the actions of the colliers can, for the most part (though with one significant exception), be adequately explained in terms of their own norms and perceptions and the changing events which impinged upon their lives.

The turnpike issue virtually disappeared from the Bristol scene for a decade. It was revived again in 1749 when the trustees petitioned Parliament for a new Act, partly on the grounds that the previous Acts, which had been granted for only twenty-one years, were soon to expire. Many of the roads leading out of Bristol were said to be still in a poor state; the earlier Acts had, for the most part, not been implemented, the toll-gates, according to one witness, 'having been pulled down long ago' (though it is clear from other evidence that a few gates were still standing). Thomas Chester and Norborne Berkeley, the two Tory members for Gloucestershire (and also substantial coal proprietors), were appointed to the five-man committee which was charged with preparing and bringing in an appropriate bill.[63] The Act which emerged in the end (22 Geo. II c. 28) continued the exemption for the carriage of coal; it added five new roads to the twelve original ones, three of them in Somerset and only one near Kingswood; and it appointed a huge total of 615 named individuals as trustees, these persons to be in addition to the surviving trustees from the previous Acts. After suitable preparations the taking of tolls on the roads to be turnpiked began on 19 July, and most of the new gates which were initially constructed appear to have been on the Somerset side of Bristol.

This emphasis on the Somerset turnpikes helps to explain the character of the series of riots which occurred during the following two weeks, for the initiative in these protests was taken, not by the colliers, but by the country people around Bristol, mostly farmers and labourers from Somerset who attended the city's markets and found themselves, for the first time, 'being obliged to pay their Passage'. The risings against the new tolls began in earnest on 24 July and continued for much of the following fortnight. Most of these disturbances occurred in Somerset, on the roads leading from Bedminster to Long Ashton and Dundry, and those running through Whitchurch and Brislington, though there were also at least three attacks on toll-gates on the Gloucestershire side of Bristol. Numerous gates and toll-houses were blown up, cut down, or set on fire, sometimes at night and by men in disguise; there were cries of 'Down with the Turnpikes! Down with the Turnpikes!', the people claiming that 'they would have a free Passage'. Several of the leaders of the riots were on horseback, suggesting (as does other evidence) that some of the protestors were farmers of at least moderate substance. Hardly a day passed without some sort of disturbance; gates which had been re-erected were soon destroyed again, and normal trade in Bristol ground to a halt. The whole area was in a great uproar. Feelings were running so high that it was thought necessary to give special protection to one of the assize judges on his journey from Wells to Bristol.[64] Bristol itself was said to be 'under the most terrible Apprehensions', the city gates were shut at 10 p.m., and the constables were ordered to be ready for any emergency.[65]

But the authorities asserted themselves to resist these risings with considerable firmness and determination. As one report put it, given the failures which they had suffered over the earlier turnpike Acts,

the Commissioners are absolutely determin'd to put all the Laws strictly into Execution: And if the Turnpike Gates are ever so often cut down and destroy'd, they will as often be erected, and the Tolls levy'd in Consequence of the Power given them, let the Opposition be ever so great.

The commissioners worked assiduously in defence of their turnpikes and employed a variety of strategies to enforce the law. On the day after the toll-gates at Bedminster were first cut down,

the Commissioners took it by Turns, about a Dozen in a Body, to stand at the Gates . . . to give an Awe to the People, and oblige them to pay the Toll. Notwithstanding which, the same Morning, several Persons attempted to force their Passage with some Cattle and Colts for the Fair, and insulted the Gentlemen; and one of them, who held the But-End of his Whip over one of the Commissioner's Head, in a menacing Manner, will, we hear, have an Information lodg'd against him in the Crown-Office.

Two days later a body of commissioners, armed with muskets and pistols, ventured several miles into Somerset in search of some of the rioters, though they returned with only one prisoner to their credit. Some 'stout Men' were employed to protect the more vulnerable toll-collectors, and when further threats against the turnpikes were heard, gangs of seamen were hired to reinforce the authority of the commissioners and the constables. On 1 August, during a confrontation near Knowle between the rioters and these *ad hoc* police forces, around twenty-five persons were taken into custody; it was said that the seamen, 'who upon such Occasions shew but little Favour, wounded some of them in a desperate Manner with their Cutlasses'. There were subsequent threats to release the prisoners from their confinement in Bristol, and fears that the city might be invaded, so special measures were taken to secure it from attack and mount a strong guard at the gaol. On 5 August two troops of dragoons arrived from Stroud after 'a forc'd March from that Place, by express Command of the Secretary of War, in order to protect the City against any riotous Attacks that might be made'. More than thirty rioters had been committed to gaol, several of whom were seriously wounded, and by the end of the following week six troops of dragoons were quartered in Bristol. Faced with this vigorous demonstration of force and determination to enforce the law, the turnpike rebels dispersed and refrained from further direct action.

The Kingswood colliers were completely uninvolved in the first ten days of these disturbances. It was not until Wednesday, 2 August that they chose to participate in a rising which had been initiated by others: a correspondent from Bristol reported that day that 'We next expect the Gloucestershire Colliers, who have been preparing Fire-Arms and other Weapons ever since Two o'Clock this Morning, and who give out that they will rescue the . . . Prisoners now in Newgate' who had been captured in Somerset the previous day.[66] The rationale of the colliers' involvement in these riots is by no means clear. In fact, there is little reason to think that their interests were being newly threatened in any important way, and it is hard to see that they had any clearly defined or deeply felt grievances. It was suggested by a local newspaper report that some of the colliers had been incited to rise 'by two Somersetshire Farmers, who gave some Money among them'.[67] One must not accept such allegations uncritically, of course, but it is possible that the Somerset dissidents, having already been worsted by the turnpike posses that had been reinforced with gangs of sailors, decided to hire their own strong-arm men for attacks on other turnpikes and turned to the Kingswood colliers as the most likely source of such assistance. Everyone certainly would have remembered the colliers' steadfastness in previous years on the subject of turnpikes.

The proposition that the colliers had no clearly focused grievances at this time is supported by the evidence concerning the manner in which their rising was mobilized and the disunity which marked its development.[68] It was reported by one observer that on the 2nd, when the rising began, some of the colliers went 'from Pit to Pit, [and] compelled the Underground Men, either by Threats or Strategem, to ascend and join them'. Another account of these events similarly stressed the role of these tactics of coercion:

they went to the Cupulo's and obliged all the Workmen they could lay their Hands on to join them; they did the like from Coal-Work to Coal-Work, and from House to House round the Country for some Miles. Those who were at work under Ground, and refus'd joining them were compell'd to it, by being threatened to have their Ropes cut, and the Pitts fill'd over their Heads.

There seems, certainly, to have been a decided lack of unity and agreed objectives in this rising, in contrast to most of the other disturbances in which the colliers were involved. After 'uniting' together, they 'went in a large Body to Toghill, and there cut down the

Turnpike leading from thence to Bath, erected by Virtue of other Acts of Parliament, which had stood there untouched for many years'. Then a party of the Kingswood men marched to Brislington, hoping to arrange to join forces with the Somerset colliers. It was said that they 'dispersed in the Evening in a seeming Discontent and Resolution not to assemble again', and the next day some of them were reported to be bringing coals into Bristol as usual. However, numerous Kingswood colliers were still gathering together on 3 and 4 August, and some were imposing levies on travellers. On the morning of the 5th a party of colliers destroyed the turnpike-house at Yate, north-east of Bristol, 'long since erected there, by Virtue of the Sodbury Act'; there was at least one other skirmish involving the colliers the same day, and a few of them may have been taken prisoners. There is little doubt that through all this the colliers were divided among themselves. It was reported, for instance, that

At Kingswood several principal Gentlemen concerned in the Coal-Works, and who are Commissioners [of the turnpikes], expostulated with those People the real imminent Danger they would run themselves into, if they persisted in their Design of opposing the Laws, etc. Some would not give Ear to Reason; but others more prudent, and sensible that as the Colliers are exempted from paying Toll, and had free Liberty to go to and fro with Coals and Provisions, thought it but reasonable to give Way to the Caution given them, and so divided from their Brethren.

Given this disunity and the warnings which were being delivered (there was much public talk of how the destruction of turnpikes was now a capital crime), and with the arrival of troops on the 5th, the rebellious colliers were deterred from engaging in further unlawful activities.

The apparent collapse of the Kingswood rising, and the reluctance of the colliers to persevere in the war against turnpikes, helped to sour their relations with the colliers on the Somerset side. According to one account,

A Body of 3 or 400 Colliers, who came from Clutton, Paulton, and other Coal-works, in order to join their Brethren in Kingswood, return'd back on Saturday [the 5th] over the River to Keinsham, greatly enrag'd against those in Kingswood, for disappointing them, after so many Threatnings, that caus'd them to leave their Works; and were very near on the Point of dispatching one of the Kingswood Leaders, and pulling his and some other of the principal Colliers Houses down.[69]

Here was a golden opportunity for the magistrates to deflate the reputation of the Kingswood colliers, weaken their leverage in the Bristol region, and enhance the stature of established authority among other groups of labouring people. They wasted no time in seizing on these congenial developments and exploitingt heir possibilities, for a few days later

Three of his Majesty's Justices of the Peace for the County of Somerset . . . made a Visit to the Colliers of Paulton, Timsbury, Clutton, and other Coalworks, and severely reproached them for their late maroding March to Kingswood, with full Purpose to join their Brethren there, and then all in a Body to proceed to Bristol, and demand the Turnpike Prisoners from the several Jails; and laid before them the great Danger they had run themselves into, and the bad Consequences that were likely to ensue thereupon, to the Ruin of themselves and Families. They plead in Excuse, that they were forced to it, by Letters sent them from the Colliers in Kingswood, who therein, on Refusal of joining them, threaten'd to come in a Body, cutt off their Ears, and fill up their Coal Pits, let who will be in 'em. The Gentlemen then turn'd upon 'em a smart Retort for their Cowardice, and wonder'd that such a large Number of lusty stout Men should be intimidated by the trivial Threatenings of the Kingswood People, and thereupon so suddenly to quit their Works, when at the same time they were superior in Strength, and capable to have withstood such a Summons, and even to have handsomely drubbed them, and sent them back, had they attempted to have put their Menaces into Execution; and as this was the Case, one of the Justices in particular advised them all, 'to pull off their Breeches, and give them to their Wives, who perhaps might make a better Use of them!' But before they parted, the Gentlemen caution'd them, that if ever such an Instance should happen again, that they would behave like Men, and by all Means give them immediate Notice of it, when a Supply of Arms should be ready to be given them, and they would head them in Person. The Colliers expressed their Concern for what was past, and gave their Promise never more to be concerned in such an Affair; and at the same time bitterly cursed the promoters of their last Expedition, vowing Revenge the first Opportunity that should occasionally happen.[70]

The standing of the Kingswood colliers did not emerge untarnished from the events of the summer of 1749.

The political background to the authorities' efforts was not as harmonious as it might have appeared. In fact, there were important disagreements among the various men of influence, most notably dissension between the turnpike commissioners and the city magistrates. The mayor of Bristol complained to the secretary of state of 'the indiscreet warmth & precipitate measures of the acting Trustees in carrying the Act for erecting the Turnpikes into Execution', and he criticized them for certain unilateral actions they took without the approval of the city authorities. In addition to this 'forwardness' and 'severity' on the part of the commissioners, he also drew attention to 'the Inactiveness of the Neighbouring Justices of the peace and Gentlemen of the Two Counties', who seem to have been unwilling to commit prisoners to gaols in their own jurisdictions.[71] Meanwhile, the turnpike trustees were letting it be known that the Bristol authorities had been lax in their handling of the disturbances, and were so arguing in their representations to the Duke of Newcastle. In reply to the trustees' claims, Mr Justice Foster, who had visited the city just after the riots, approved of the way in which the magistrates had attempted to preserve the peace 'without Bloodshed', and he argued that 'if they could have prevail'd on the Commissioners to have acted with the same tempers, the Blood that has been shed, which has provok'd the County in general to a great degree, might have been prevented'.[72] The Lord Chancellor, Lord Hardwicke, to whom details of the dispute were referred (he was also High Steward of Bristol), wrote to Newcastle on 18 September 1749 that 'it is not material at present to enter into the Dispute between Them', and having thus put aside matters of substance, he proceeded to resolve the issue in a suitably partisan manner:

I take the original difference to have proceeded from hence, that, in the nomination of Commissioners in the last act of Parliament, the Tories prevail'd to get a Majority, and the Magistrates of Bristol are generally Whigs. This indeed ought not to influence the merits of the Case in any degree, but I dare say Your Grace will think that a Sett of Magistrates so well affected to His Majesty's Person & Government, who act so worthily in administring the affairs of that great & populous City, & I verily believe intended to do their Duty on this occasion, deserve all that Regard & Countenance, which Justice & Reason will admit.[73]

As Hardwicke well knew and had often revealed in the past, the processes of the law could not be allowed to turn a blind eye to the realities of political expediency.

Despite the continuing opposition to turnpikes among many of the country people in Somerset – the mayor received a couple of incendiary letters, rumours were heard of plans for further attacks on toll-gates, and there were threats to cut off food supplies to Bristol – security and order were effectively re-established. Troops continued to patrol the city, toll-gates were re-erected, and the machinery of prosecution was resolutely activated.[74] Everyone of influence was determined to make the best possible use of the criminal law 'in a Case of such open and publick insult upon government and the Laws,' as the attorney general put it; the local gentlemen, it was said, were 'desirous of a speedy and Solemn Trial, in order to strike a Terror in the most effectual manner'.[75] There was the customary hope that, as a result of well-orchestrated criminal prosecutions, it would be demonstrated to the people, 'by fatal Experiment, that the King's Laws will have their Course, and must be obeyed'.[76] In the end a large number of men were prosecuted for their part in the turnpike disorders (most or all of them were from Somerset): three were tried at the Taunton assizes in April 1750, two of whom were executed; and at Salisbury in the same month, where eighteen other prisoners had been removed under a strong guard for a special trial at the Crown's expense (the authorities hoped to find a less hostile body of jurymen in another county), not a single conviction was secured, thanks, it seems, to a sympathetic jury. (Five prisoners had already died in goal of the smallpox.) But whatever magisterial disgruntlement these acquittals may have caused, there is no doubt that the long-term objectives of the authorities were realized, for thereafter toll-gates remained securely in place. As for the Kingswood colliers, although evidence against them had been collected by the turnpike commissioners, it had proved extremely difficult to bring them to trial. On 12 September an armed party of bailiffs went into Kingswood in order to take one of the colliers' leaders, for whom a reward of £100 had been offered.

They beset his House, and broke open his Door; but he retiring to an upper Room, barricaded the Stairs with a Bed and Chest, and with large Stones and a Pitchfork kept all the Assailants off, several of whom he wounded. . . . Since which a great many Colliers have furnish'd themselves with Pitchforks, and other Weapons, in order to defend themselves against such another Incident.

By the following week the colliers were patrolling Kingswood every night with firearms, 'several Parties of them keeping Watch by Turns, to prevent any of their Brethren being seiz'd unawares, on Account of destroying the Turnpikes'.[77] No further efforts were made to intervene in their territory.

While the risings during the generation that especially concerns us involved turnpike tolls more often than any other issue, on several occasions the colliers had other grievances which also brought them into conflict with the defenders of the law. An analysis of these different disturbances sheds further light on the character of their relations with the established authorities, and the ways in which they regarded and responded to the actions of those entrusted with enforcing the law.

The sole occasion of a major industrial dispute in Kingswood occurred during the autumn of 1738. A price war had broken out among the proprietors of the coal mines, and to reduce their costs as much as possible some of the employers were trying to lower the colliers' wages from 1s. 4d. to 1s. per day. Many of the colliers, faced with a 25 per cent wage cut, were determined to resist this reduction and defend their traditional standards. They combined together and forced others to join them in a general stoppage of work. They prevented the carriage of coals to Bristol and took over some of the roads, and 'as they are poor and not able to subsist without working, to supply their Necessities' they began to organize forced collections of money and food – a kind of strike fund drawing on the 'contributions' of non-colliers. The rising began on Monday, 9 October, and the newspaper accounts tell of a general rampage through the neighbourhood which lasted for four days: of attacks on public and private houses in search of food and drink; of a gentleman trying to buy them off with pails of beer; of a procession of colliers through Bristol 'hallowing and shouting'; of attacks on some of the coal pits and coal-carriers; of robberies on the highways; and of active attempts to find, and presumably punish, one of the colliery bailiffs. They also 'visited several Gentlemen who have large Concerns in the Coal-Works, and by threatening to fill up their Pits, have extorted from them divers Sums of Money'. 'They have play'd such mad Pranks', complained one writer, 'that one would think they had forgot there were still any laws in Being for the Government of a People, and to secure the Peace and Property of the Subject'. The whole area was said to be 'in the utmost Consternation', and the Bristol magistrates became particularly anxious after the incident in which a body of colliers marched noisily through the city, armed with axes and clubs, a demonstration of force much like the one which had been witnessed in the early summer of 1727; the colliers were also threatening to dump into the water any coal they found on the city's quays. After this disturbance in their city, the Bristol authorities were quick to communicate with the secretary of state, fortify the city guard, and arrange for emergency coal supplies from the Forest of Dean. By the end of the week the disorders were over, coal was again being brought into the city, and evidence was being collected against some of the rioters in an effort 'to have Examples made of some in order to deter Such Villainory proceeding for the future'. (It should be noted that the grievances of the Kingswood colliers were probably not shared by other labouring people in the area. It was said that some of 'the civilized Colliers' in Brislington, who may not have been threatened with wage reductions, were compelled by force to join the Kingswood rising; and there were attacks by the colliers on several of the coal-drivers, who may have been similarly unaffected by the dispute, as they were carrying their burdens to Bristol.)[78]

It is not clear whether the colliers had any success in this rising: success in forcing the local industries (especially the glass-houses) to pay the usual prices for coal, and in getting the coal adventurers to abandon their price competition, and thereby attaining their objective of ensuring the maintenance of the customary wage-rates for mining. Our only slim piece of relevant evidence, suggesting that they had not succeeded, is a report of 25 November on their threats to destroy the river locks between Bristol and Bath (in order to prevent the trans-port of coal), where it is said that they vowed 'that they had as good be hang'd as they and their Families to starve'.[79] In the material available the colliers' grievances are completely submerged by the widespread concern for public order. The dispute, moreover, com-pletely slips from view until 2 November, when the colliers, as one observer put it, were 'pleased to show a little more of their ungovern-able Authority'. This rising was in response to two recent initiatives by the authorities: the magistrates were meeting at an inn just east of the city to inquire into the damages caused during the recent disorders and to collect evidence against the rioters, and the colliers were hoping to prevent witnesses from appearing before them; and a pitman sus-pected of being involved in the riots had been 'apprehended by Strategem' the previous night and committed to prison, and his fellow colliers were intending to release him. It was reported that the colliers had 'cast a great many Bullets at Grimsbury, and fir'd divers Times to bring their Arms in Tune, as they said, against they went to War'. Since it was feared that the colliers might march on Bristol, troops were ordered to stand guard at the eastern approaches to the city, and on 3 November,

the better to oppose the Colliers from fulfilling their Threatnings, a large Detachment of Soldiers march'd into Kingswood, in Search of those against whom abundance of Informations are made, with Orders absolutely to fire on the Colliers, if they made any Opposition: but instead of that, they took to their Heels, and fled out of the Wood; and the Soldiers, in searching their Houses, seized what Fire-Arms they could find, and made one Samuel Wilimot, a noted Ringleader, Prisoner, who they brought to accompany the other Collier in Bridewell.

After this military intervention, the colliers refrained from taking any further direct action.[80] Despite determined efforts on the part of the authorities – warrants were issued for the arrest of thirty-six colliers – great difficulty was experienced in apprehending any other of the October rioters; the two colliers who had been taken were admitted to bail at the Gloucester assizes in April 1739, and there is no evidence that they were ever prosecuted.[81]

The remaining Kingswood disturbances of importance were all occasioned by the high price of grain. Little is known about the earliest of these risings, in May 1709, a year of inclement weather and large exports of grain to the continental army, when about 400 colliers marched on Bristol, demanding cheap bread; in response to this pressure, the city magistrates assured the crowd that wheat would be sold at 6 s. 8 d. per bushel, around two shillings lower than the prevailing market price. Some of the wheat was bought up by the corporation and sold at a loss.[82] The second and better-documented price disturbance involving the colliers occurred in September 1740, and it nicely illustrates the sorts of pressures and responses which characterized their relations with established authority. The previous winter had been unusually severe (it was one of the coldest in the century), and in many parts of England there had already been serious grain shortages, drastic price rises, profiteering and food riots; at least fourteen counties had experienced disorders prior to the Kingswood incident.[83] The colliers, like many other labouring people, were completely dependent on public markets and bakers for their supplies of grain and bread, and they had a strong interest in the effective regulation by the justices of the prices of these basic necessities. If the authorities failed to ensure reasonable prices, the people were prepared to remind them of their duties at law and, if necessary, to take direct action themselves in order to secure a 'just price'.

The Kingswood rising of 1740 began on 18 and 19 September with threats against several local mills, and there was talk of the colliers visiting Bristol on the 20th 'to lower the Price of Corn to six shillings a Bushell' (wheat at this time was selling for 8 s. 6 d. per bushel). As it happened, troops were already quartered in the city, and their colonel shrewdly employed his soldiers to good dramatic effect: he reported that he 'drew out the Regiment in the great Square, and delivered out Powder & Ball to them in publick; which had its desired & Expected

Effect; for they did not come that day'. The colliers met to reconsider their tactics, and two days later they 'gather'd again to a great Body, obliging one another to desist from Working, severely threatening those that did not join them, complaining loudly at the high Price of Corn; that there was good Living enough in the Land, and whilst it was to be had they would have a Part'. Because of the presence of troops, the colliers thought it prudent to send only a portion of their members into the city, and these 'without their usual Armour of Clubs and Staffs, as their Representatives and Complainants to the Mayor (the rest waiting near the town for an answer)'. In the afternoon they marched to the Council House, along with some weavers, colliers' wives 'and Abundance of other Women' in order to negotiate with the authorities; a delegation was admitted to parley with the mayor, and an elderly man represented their grievances, saying:

'That they came with no Intent to hurt any Man, but for the Good of their Country; that for his Part he had good Bread, good Cheese, and good fat Beef enough; but that there were Hundreds of poor Families starving round him; and therefore demanded Redress to their Grievances, by having Corn allowed them at 6s. per Bushel.' The Mayor was pleas'd to return them this Answer: *Gentlemen, I'll take Care that you shall Have Justice done you.*

The colliers, 'complimenting the Court with Huzzas', then left the city, thinking that their demands would be met, but this expectation was not to be fulfilled: the mayor, writing the next day to the Duke of Newcastle, admitted that the price of wheat was 'excessive', but argued that in the present circumstances nothing further could be done about the matter, 'the Assize of Bread being already settled as low as possible'. The colonel of the troops reported that the colliers 'had mistaken the setting of the assize of bread, for lowering the price of Corn, [and] have threatened to come into this place a second time in a different manner'. Grain prices remained high, but further and more vigorous direct action was deterred by the round-the-clock watch maintained by the troops in the city 'in order to keep the Colliers in Awe'. The mayor still feared that the peace of the city was in 'imminent danger of being broken'; threats were heard about plundering the granaries, but nothing further transpired. Some gentlemen tried to persuade the colliers that such disturbances tended to discourage merchants and farmers from bringing their provisions to the city's markets. Fresh imports of wheat were expected, and these may have materialized, for by the middle of December the price of wheat was down to 6 s. 6 d. per bushel.[84]

Charles Wesley, who happened to be in the Kingswood area at this time, offered a rather different perspective on the rising. On 22 September he met around a thousand colliers on their way to Bristol and tried to dissuade them from continuing their march, especially those whom he referred to as 'our colliers'. 'Wherever I turned', he claimed, 'Satan lost ground; so that he was obliged to make one general assault, and, by the few violent colliers, forced on the quiet ones into the town.' He said that he

found afterwards that all our colliers to a man had been forced into it. Having learned of Christ not to resist evil, they went a mile with those that compelled them, rather than free themselves by violence. . . . near twenty of Mr. Willis's men they got by threatening to fill up their pits, and bury them alive, if they did not come up and bear them company.

(There is evidence of similar forms of pressure being exerted in both 1738 and 1749, though only on the latter occasion were they apparently unaccompanied by any general sense of grievance.) The Rev. Charles Wesley also remarked on the peaceful and orderly character of the colliers' conduct in Bristol, though his explanation of this restraint was decidedly spiritual. 'All who saw were amazed', he said, 'for the leopards were laid down. Nothing could have more shown the change wrought in them [by faith] than this rising.' He, like his brother and George Whitefield, was convinced that the missionary work in Kingswood, which had been started in early 1739, was helping to transform the 'primitive' culture of the colliers and cultivate among them new and more civilized modes of conduct. On 23 September he lectured the colliers on 'the things they would have done in the last rising, had not grace restrained them'.[85]

The final rising of the colliers during this generation – and for them perhaps the most traumatic – occurred in the spring of 1753. Although 1753, unlike 1740, was not a year of generally high grain prices in England, the Bristol–Somerset area seems to have experienced especial difficulties, and there were vigorous expressions of popular discontent in several parts of the region. On 11 May, for instance,

about 700 Coal-Miners assembled in a riotous Manner in the Town of Shepton-Mallet, in Somersetshire, on Account of the great Quantity of Corn exported abroad. They went to all the Inns where the Corn was lodged, carried it into the Market, and obliged the Owners to sell it at such Prices as they thought proper.[86]

The colliers of Kingswood were similarly aggrieved by the fact that

(in their opinion) the local markets were not being adequately supplied, and on the morning of Monday, 21 May they began to gather
in Kingswood, protesting about the high price of grain – caused, they
thought, by its export from the region – and threatening to march on
Bristol: they said that 'they were going to Bristol to get their Bread
Larger'. When the city authorities heard of this gathering, the mayor
dispatched a scout to Kingswood 'to observe their motions'. The
colliers' collective action began in a manner much like that of 1740.
In the afternoon, along with some 'Country People', they marched
unarmed into Bristol, 'headed by a Captain and Colours', a typical
sort of demonstration of popular unity. They proceeded to the Council House, where the corporation was already meeting, and four of
their leaders presented a petition to the mayor 'representing the
Straits they were in by the Dearness of Bread, etc. and praying for
Redress of their Grievances. They were mildly received, and promised Relief as soon as possible, to the Satisfaction of the major
Part of them'. Some of the protesters, however, remained uncon-
vinced that appropriate action would be taken, and this dissatisfaction may have been reinforced by an apparently rather premature
reading of the Riot Act to the crowd assembled outside the Council
House. Rather than retire from the city, the people decided to act in
their own interest. They departed for the quay, boarded a ship which
was loaded with seventy tons of wheat bound for Dublin, and began
to remove the grain from the hold. But they were soon interrupted in
the course of this work by a body of constables who arrived to protect the vessel. Numerous skirmishes broke out, the constables quickly
gained the advantage over the unarmed protesters, and the crowd
dispersed through the streets. Shortly thereafter the people regrouped
and rallied their forces and rescued some prisoners whom the constables had taken; stones were thrown at the windows of the Council
House and most of them were broken, 'by which some therein were
much hurt'; the colliers then left the city, declaring that 'they would
arm themselves and repeat their Visit'. It was said that the magistrates, 'having examined such as were taken, after proper Reproofs,
discharged them on Promise of good Behaviour for the future',
though it is clear from later evidence that at least one rioter was
detained in custody.[87]

Thus far, it seems, the disorders had not been particularly extraordinary, though one would not want to minimize the impact of these
crowd actions on the city's sense of security. The substantial citizens
had certainly been much frightened and the magistrates were very

anxious about the possibility of future invasions, especially considering the threats which they were hearing from the colliers. This, after all, was the first time that the colliers had actually employed any physical force within the city itself; on previous occasions they had confined their actions in Bristol to processions, demonstrations and the ritualized conventions for negotiating the redress of their grievances. Moreover, there were no troops in Bristol at this time; the nearest forces were quartered in Gloucester, almost forty miles away. The city authorities acted quickly to prepare for future confrontations: the mayor wrote to the secretary of state requesting troops, the militia was raised, many citizens were enlisted as special constables and guards were posted throughout the city. On Tuesday and Wednesday stories were heard of further gatherings in Kingswood, but no attempts were made to enter the city gates. On Thursday a large crowd of 'Colliers, Country People, Weavers, etc.' approached the eastern entrance to the city in a menacing manner, but the guard prevented them from advancing any further. On Friday morning, the 25th, some fifty soldiers arrived from Gloucester, but shortly thereafter a large body of people, estimated to number between 1000 and 2000, succeeded in entering the city, some of whom were bent on releasing a prisoner taken earlier in the week. At this point the level of violence rapidly escalated. The crowd was able to break into the gaol and rescue the prisoner, but only after a bloody struggle during which one of the rioters lost his life. In the various battles which followed the rioters were frequently fired on, not only by the guard but also by some gentlemen and merchants who had armed themselves in preparation for the return of the protesters. This was the most intense day of direct conflict in the recorded history of the colliers' collective actions. In the course of the day's encounters four of the crowd were killed and about thirty men, some of them dangerously wounded, were committed to prison. In retaliation for their losses the colliers captured several of the armed gentlemen, and though some were retaken at Lawford's Gate as the crowd retreated, at least two citizens were carried off to Kingswood (where, as the stories had it, they were confined in a coal pit), an indication, thought the mayor, of 'the spirit of resentment which rages among them'.

A serious incident had clearly developed. Much blood had been spilt, violent conflicts had for the first time occurred within Bristol's own borders, and the authorities' anxiety was heightened by the fact that many of the labouring poor of the city were apparently in sympathy with the grievances of the Gloucestershire populace.[88] Many colliers (as many as fifty) lay wounded in Kingswood; provisions and medical assistance were sent to the forest in the hope of inducing the colliers to release the one prisoner they continued to hold; and more troops were dispatched to secure the city.[89] The whole area remained in a very disturbed state for at least two weeks, and the colliers were reported to be intent on revenge. They were making assiduous efforts to capture one John Brickdale, a woollen draper whom they held responsible for the killing of one of their fellows and who had been obliged to flee the neighbourhood.[90] They also tried to use the processes of the law in an effort to avenge themselves against Brickdale, apparently with the assistance of a sympathetic coroner. They exerted pressure on the conduct of the coroner's inquest on the dead collier, which twice returned verdicts of murder against several gentlemen (the attorney general said of the first inquisition that it 'appears to have been taken under the Influence of force'), and the attorney general was obliged to intervene – on more than one occasion – to quash these proceedings. He recommended that the matter be disposed of for good in the court of King's Bench, for otherwise, he opined, 'the Riotous Colliers may find Means to procure new Inquests as fast as the Old ones shall be quashed'. In November Brickdale was still afraid for his own safety, for he had heard that the rioters were intending to indict him for murder at the next Gloucester assizes.[91] By this time, however, the colliers were mostly on the defensive, for the processes of the criminal law had already been mobilized against them. In July substantial rewards were offered by the Crown for the arrest of five men considered to be ringleaders in the riots, four of them colliers (though not one of them, it seems, was ever apprehended). In early September a special commission at the Crown's expense was held to try those rioters who were still in custody. Although many of the prisoners were acquitted because of the failure of witnesses to appear against them, eight colliers were successfully prosecuted and sentenced to two years in prison. Bills of high treason were found against two of the unapprehended colliers. The disturbances had cost the city corporation, for various services, almost £600.[92]

This whole affair must have been a great blow to the colliers. Their losses had been considerable and they had accomplished very little. The authorities, as on previous occasions, were determined to teach the colliers a lesson, and this time they may have had some success. Never before had the colliers paid such severe penalties for their direct actions, either in losses during the course of the disturbances (which were largely 'unplanned' by the authorities) or through the calculated retribution of the criminal law. Death, injuries, imprisonment, bills of high treason: all these descended upon them. Only in 1733 had any of them previously been punished, and then the losses they suffered had been much less extensive. In January 1754 the eight imprisoned colliers were reduced to sending an obsequious petition to the Duke of Newcastle, begging for clemency and pleading the distress of themselves and their families (they alleged that the weavers had forced them to participate in the riot against their will). The attorney general was unsympathetic, for, as he said, the intention of the convictions was to 'make the deeper Impression on the minds of the Colliers, and operate in terrorem, so as to deter them the more from Joining in the like Attempts for the future'. The colliers were still in confinement in March, and 'having nothing but Gaol Allowance to subsist on', they were begging for assistance and humbly thanking those who had already given them a little relief. (On 17 July 1753 John Wesley had reported that 'At their earnest desire, I preached to the poor colliers confined in Newgate on account of the late riot. They would not hear the gospel while they were at liberty. God grant they may profit by it now!')[93] So vivid were people's memories of the events of 1753 that the details of the riots were readily called to mind many years thereafter.[94] Indeed, it is noteworthy that very much later, in the spring of 1795, when the colliers were once again protesting about the high price of food, one of the newspapers pointedly drew attention to the defeat they had suffered in 1753:

It is to be hoped these deluded people will consider the situation they brought themselves into about forty years ago, when several of them lost their lives, and their families were reduced to wretchedness and ruin. For it is certain no good end can be obtained by rioting.[95]

During the second half of the eighteenth century the Kingswood colliers appear to have become considerably more quiescent. In fact, there is no evidence that they were involved in any further disturbances until the 1790s. In 1756–7 and 1766–7, when high food prices sparked off popular protests and price riots in many parts of England, the colliers did not engage in any risings.[96] Perhaps they remembered only too well the disagreeable events of 1753. But the authorities and people of wealth may have remembered them, too, for it would seem that the food subsidies and relief measures which were organized during these years of dearth were remarkably ambitious and well planned.[97] Perhaps such ameliorative measures were an expression of prudence and foresight after the regrettable upheavals of 1753. There were renewed disturbances at the end of the century – industrial protests in 1790 and 1792, and a food riot and tithe dispute in 1795 – though none of these incidents appears to have been as serious as many of the disorders earlier in the century.[98] By this time, certainly, the colliers of Kingswood no longer deserved any special notoriety. Indeed, by the nineteenth century they had come to be regarded in an entirely different (in fact, virtually benign) light. A former vicar of Bitton recalled in the later nineteenth century that 'Whatever the colliers may have been in former times, it is a pleasure to me to say, that during my long residence amongst them, from 1817 to 1850, they were, with very few exceptions, the cleanest and most industrious parishioners.' Another observer in 1834 referred to them as 'an industrious, contented and inoffensive race. . . . though uncivilized and ignorant, they appear to be neither immoral nor disorderly'.[99] Their tradition of rebelliousness was now a thing of the past. When Bristol's most spectacular riots ever occurred in the autumn of 1831, hardly any colliers were implicated, and while the city underwent several days of dramatic convulsions, Kingswood itself remained completely undisturbed.[100]

What can we conclude from all this about the conduct of the established authorities and the constraints which they experienced? It is clear that the Gloucestershire magistrates were in a weak position to deal with the colliers. There were few gentlemen in the Kingswood area and the local justices were confronted with a large and rapidly expanding population of relatively independent, and 'undisciplined', industrial workers. Patriarchal authority was weakly implanted in the neighbourhood of Kingswood, many of the miners worked their pits (just as the coal-drivers conducted their trade) in an independent or semi-independent manner, and the landlords and coal proprietors had as yet little control over their everyday behaviour. Moreover, the central government was not normally disposed to place troops in the Kingswood region at times when disorders occurred (it was, perhaps, not unaware of the thinness of the local support for Whig rule), and without military assistance men such as Codrington and Blaithwaite were unable to discipline the colliers with any effectiveness. In contrast, the authorities in Bristol, which enjoyed the status of a county borough, were much more energetically supported by their fellow Whigs in Westminster, though it is clear that during the initial stages of any Kingswood disturbance the interventions of the colliers in Bristol's public life caused great consternation, especially at times when no troops were quartered in the city. Kingswood was near Bristol but beyond its jurisdictional control; it was alien territory, a potential threat to the city's tranquillity. As the mayor, writing in May 1753, said of the colliers, 'the place they come from is very populous, & has in it a great Number of Under Ground Workmen, who are but little known and on that account very desperate fellows'.[101] For the most part the corporation was content to keep the colliers at bay, to exclude them from the city itself; they seldom attempted to extend their authority into the colliers' own territory. Similarly, the colliers were usually cautious about exercising their muscle within the city: except for 1753, they always confined their actions in Bristol to processions, demonstrations, and negotiations for the redress of their grievances. They certainly were not inclined to invade the city on whim. When the authorities became anxious about public order, as they normally did at the first appearance of the colliers, they made haste to mobilize the resources immediately at their disposal (constables, citizen pickets, and the like) and to solicit troops from the secretary of state. The presence of troops was essential to ensure peace for the city, though the soldiers might be very careful about the way in which they exercised their power. In September 1740, for instance, the colonel of the troops who was called upon to secure the city against a possible food riot justified his cautious action by noting that 'Captain Porteous's unhappy Fate was too fresh in my memory not to make me act with the utmost Caution & Security.'[102] (Captain John Porteous had, of course, suffered grievously for his role in trying to control an Edinburgh crowd at a public hanging on 14 April 1736.) Moreover, the soldiers stationed in Bristol usually refrained from intervening in the colliers' own district. The relationship between Bristol and Kingswood was, it seems, an uneasy stand-off: a somewhat delicate relationship in which neither side normally violated the other's territory.

The Kingswood colliers, like most labouring people, had a clear set of ideas concerning how authority should be properly exercised: they held specific expectations as to the duties and responsibilities of those entrusted with enforcing the law, and these expectations sometimes differed from those of the authorities themselves. Moreover, they felt relatively few inhibitions about taking direct action in defence of their conceptions of what was legitimate and lawful behaviour. Their public encounters with the law occurred, of course, mostly at times of 'crisis': when traditional standards of subsistence were threatened, and when popular liberties were being challenged by new, officially sanctioned exactions and impositions. They took the position that the authorities should be held *accountable* for certain actions (or inaction) – those which they perceived as illegitimate or contrary to law – and they were frequently determined to exert pressure on the authorities in order to induce some alterations in their conduct. Their various protests and risings may be seen, I think, as regulatory mechanisms intended to change public policies and to articulate values which were not satisfactorily represented through the conventional political process. They employed supplications, threats, demonstrations of power and collective attacks on objectionable targets in an attempt to attain their ends. Sometimes they won concessions, on other occasions the authorities stood firm. If the colliers' exertions were resisted with armed force, they might be compelled to beat at least a partial retreat, but the authorities could seldom rest assured that further challenges would not emerge. Moreover, it always proved to be extremely difficult to employ the criminal law against them. Satisfactory evidence was sometimes hard to obtain, arrest warrants could seldom be executed and witnesses and jurymen might be encouraged to think better of the colliers' supposed 'offences' after suitable forms of intimidation. On numerous occasions the colliers exhibited a capacity to resist or manipulate the processes of the law, or even to usurp the functions of the duly constituted authorities. Considering the large number of indictable offences they committed, very few colliers were ever apprehended and brought to trial. The authorities might hope to be able to *contain* the colliers, but for many years they could not realistically expect to accomplish much more.

The history of the Kingswood colliers after the mid eighteenth century, and their changing relations with the established authorities, cannot at this time be examined in detail. We know, of course, that Kingswood played a major role in the early history of Methodism, though it is difficult to assess with any precision the actual impact of Methodism on the colliers. John Wesley himself was fairly confident in pointing to the social transformations which he thought had taken place: in 1768 he observed that 'no Indians are more savage than were the colliers of Kingswood; many of whom are now an humane, hospitable people full of love to God and man; quiet, diligent in business; in every state content; every way adoring the Gospel of God their Saviour'.[103] Although it is likely that the Methodist leaders often exaggerated the success of their early ministry, there is no doubt that in the long run Methodism became well established in the Kingswood area and gained a substantial body of adherents, thereby helping to transform the values and behaviour of many colliers. We can suggest, very tentatively, that Methodism may have introduced into Kingswood a new form of authority, a set of religious imperatives which attracted at least some of the colliers to a new outlook on life and a new set of aspirations. Methodism tended to have its greatest impact in areas where patriarchal structures of authority were weakest, and from this point of view Kingswood was clearly a 'dark corner of the land': there was something of a psychological vacuum to be filled, and Methodism offered spiritual renewal as an alternative orientation to the worldly independence of the colliers. The early preachers brought to Kingswood, not only a compelling personal dynamism, but also a message of concern and compassion and personal salvation to people who had stood alone – and some of them may have realized that they could not stand alone much longer. Outsiders were certainly inclined to credit Methodism with much of the change which was thought to have occurred in Kingswood. Methodism was thought by one writer in the early nineteenth century to have been responsible for 'the amelioration of the savage manners of the colliers', and a local observer in 1794 drew attention to similar changes: 'The colliers of the forest', he said,

were 40 or 50 years ago, so barbarous and savage, that they were a terror to the City of Bristol, which they several times invaded; it was dangerous to go among them, and their dialect was the roughest and rudest in the Nation; but by the labours of Mess. Whitefield and Wesley, by the erection of a parish Church and some meeting-houses, and the establishment of several sunday and daily schools, they are much civilized and improved in principles, morals and pronunciation.[104]

It is possible, then, that a new sort of discipline was emerging in Kingswood. A parish church (St George's) was constructed in Kingswood in the 1750s, largely to provide accessible accommodation for the previously neglected people of the forest, and thus for the first time established religion became a visible presence in the area. In 1756 a friendly society was formed among the colliers, a society whose articles emphasized the maintenance of good order and proper conduct and of loyalty to the established government.[105] Kingswood, like many other forest areas, was no longer relatively insulated from outside interventions: the spreading suburbs of Bristol were threatening to absorb it; and with the decline of social and cultural isolation it became more subject to forces of authority and disciplines which were mostly not of the colliers' own making. And as many colliers accepted or submitted to these various disciplines, the social basis for collective action and plebeian independence probably contracted. In the long run Kingswood was tamed, and its eighteenth-century turbulence was succeeded by quiescence during the nineteenth century. The limits of authority had expanded to incorporate Kingswood within its territory of social discipline.

4 The Wilkites and the law, 1763-74: a study of radical notions of governance

John Brewer, Yale University

Advertisement Extraordinary.

Whereas a gang of notorious robbers have for some years past infested the neighbourhood of St. James and the Treasury, and have in a daring manner, and in open defiance of the laws of the land, plundered the public of several millions sterling, to the great loss of his majesty's liege subjects; and have lately absconded loaded with their plunder. These are therefore to require all good and well disposed people, born on this side of the Tweed, to apprehend such traitors and robbers, and bring them to justice, and in so doing, shall on conviction and execution, receive the reward due to the distinguished Patriots of Old England and be recorded in history for future generations.

Middlesex Journal, 7 November 1769

I look upon the administration of justice as the principal and essential part of all government. The people know and judge it by little else. The effects of this are felt every day by the meanest, in the business and affairs of common life.

LORD HARDWICKE, *Parliamentary History*[1]

Most historians, when they discuss the career of John Wilkes and the varied fortunes of his supporters, think immediately of political reform. The Wilkites, it is usually argued, created in embryonic form a movement that was destined to reach maturity with the Great Reform Act of 1832. As the progenitors of parliamentary democracy and responsible government, they were early but powerful advocates of a free press and of an uncorrupt, open legislature, two necessary conditions of representative rule.[2] It is not my intention in this essay to quarrel with this particular interpretation, but to imbue what may be taken more or less as received wisdom with somewhat different meaning by examining the relationship between much-studied reformist politics and the rather less frequently scrutinized reformist notions of law. The union between radical conceptions of politics and of law was essentially a conjugal bond: a marriage between two separate entities which was seen to affect the nature of each. To ignore the bond between the two when considering either of them is, therefore, to provide an incomplete account of both, and it is this partiality in the existing historiography which this discussion sets out to remedy.

But any account of Wilkite radicalism, no matter what approach it adopts, cannot afford to neglect the chief political incidents in Wilkes's chequered career, particularly the major crises of 1763–5 (the so-called 'general warrants' affair) and of 1768–74, which hinged on the controversies caused by Wilkes's election as M P for the county of Middlesex. The general warrants affair began in April 1763 when Wilkes and a number of printers and their servants were arrested on a general warrant as the suspected printers and publishers of a putative libel on the government, the *North Briton* no. 45. Wilkes, imprisoned in the Tower, secured his release by suing for a writ of habeas corpus in the court of Common Pleas (in itself an unusual procedure, as such writs usually went to the King's Bench), and promptly commenced his attack, which eventually proved successful, on the supposed legality of general warrants that failed to name the accused but merely specified the crime, and that entitled the executioner of the warrant to seize indiscriminately the papers and personal effects of any suspect. Despite this success Wilkes was unable to avoid expulsion from the House of Commons; shortly thereafter he was badly wounded in a duel with a government supporter and, with legal proceedings against him pending, he considered discretion the better part of valour, and fled to the continent. There he remained in exile (spending much of his time in the arms of his mistress, Mlle Corrandini) until 1768, when his return to Britain and candidature in the general election of that year sparked off a new series of incidents. Successfully elected as M P for the county of Middlesex, Wilkes surrendered himself to the authorities and was sentenced to twenty-two months in the King's Bench prison for his authorship of the *North Briton* and of the notorious (though rather tedious) obscene parody on Pope entitled *An Essay on Woman*.

Wilkes's election, at a time of considerable economic hardship, had prompted riots and demonstrations in Westminster, the City of London and, over the Thames, in Southwark. These came to a head on 10 May 1768, when a number of the crowd that had gathered in St George's Fields by the King's Bench prison to cheer the imprisoned Wilkes were shot and killed by troops. Shortly afterwards Wilkes published correspondence from the secretary of state, Lord Wey-mouth, together with a covering note implying that the deaths were part of a government plot. For his pains he was ejected once more from his parliamentary seat. But the electors of Middlesex refused to give up their hero, and as often as the government expelled Wilkes the voters returned him again, until the government was forced into the invidious position of having to declare the candidate with a minority of votes to be duly elected.

By mid 1769 these incidents had blown up into a crisis of major proportions. Disorder, especially in London, was widespread, and the political nation divided. In December 1768, after a riotous by-election at which two of his supporters were killed, John Glynn, Wilkes's legal counsel, was returned for the second seat at Middlesex. The violence of the followers of Glynn's opponent, a government supporter, and the support given by the administration to Colonel Luttrell, a notorious and ill-regarded rake who replaced Wilkes as one of the Middlesex MPs, pushed many moderate men into the radical camp. Parliamentary opposition and public opinion gravi-tated towards the Wilkite cause. The radicals established their own, independent, extra-parliamentary society, the Society of the Sup-porters of the Bill of Rights (hereafter SSBR) to co-ordinate their support, and a major petitioning campaign was launched with the aid of the chief opposition groups in the legislature. But the impact of the Wilkites was most strongly felt in the metropolis. They successfully infiltrated the government of the City of London, and in 1771 used their power in the nation's greatest corporation to defy the House of Commons by preventing the arrest of printers of parliamentary debates. Although a schism occurred among the radicals in 1771, and though they obtained only twelve seats at the general election of 1774 they continued to dominate London politics and became a permanent if not terribly prominent feature in the political landscape.

Throughout these activities the leading Wilkites evinced a strong commitment to reform. They fought valiantly, and with considerable success, for the liberty of the press, and from June 1769 tried to bind parliamentary candidates and their followers to a scheme that would have produced more frequent parliamentary elections, the removal of government placemen from the Commons, and a 'more fair and equal representation'.[3] In sum, the Wilkites began by objecting to particular acts and attitudes of the government but progressed to making demands for structural reform which would have rendered the

legislature free from ministerial control and accountable for its
actions to the people it was supposed to represent. Such is the conventional wisdom of historians, though they debate the precise nature
of the radicals' demands, the legitimacy of their grievances, and the
extent of their support.

But what of Wilkite attitudes towards the law; where do they fit in
with Wilkite politics? To tackle these questions – some of which have
been touched upon in writings on the freedom of the press[4] – I have
divided the discussion into three parts. The first examines legal issues
and their relationship to politics in general in order to reveal the
obvious political dimensions of much legal theory and practice, and
to demonstrate how much political ideology was concerned with
questions of law. Secondly, I look at how the Wilkites used the law
itself as a political weapon, exploiting the highly ritualized theatre of
the courts and the labyrinthine complexity of the criminal law to
propagandize their cause, defend themselves and wreak vengeance on
their enemies. And finally, I consider the question of whether the
Wilkites were simply exploiting the existing legal system for narrowly
political ends, or actually raising questions about the nature of law
and justice in the society as a whole. I argue that the Wilkite view of
the law was not exclusively instrumental – as it was for some prosperous London thieves who used every loophole in the law[5] – but that
radical litigation and legal claims were also statements about and
attempts to achieve a particular sort of polity.

The Wilkites were well placed to employ the law as a political
weapon, because so many members of the S S B R, a society chiefly
composed of professional men, merchants and tradesmen, were
attorneys or advocates who could use their skills for the radical cause.
John Glynn, Wilkes's counsel, John Reynolds, Wilkes's attorney,
William Ellis, George Bellas of Portsmouth, Robert Morris, the
secretary of the society, Arthur Lee, the Virginian, Watkin Lewes
from Wales, Charles Martin, Sayer and Dayrell were all members of
the S S B R and of the legal fraternity.[6] About one in ten members of
the society was a lawyer, by far the largest occupational group, and
they played a disproportionately important role in the activities
of the S S B R because their legal expertise made them the obvious
men to compose, draft and engross instructions, petitions and
remonstrances.

These lawyers spearheaded Wilkite activity in the courts; it was
they who exploited the loopholes in the law, generated drama in the
courtroom, and proclaimed their legal and political tenets from the

public platform of the assize and the central courts of King's Bench and Common Pleas. It is tempting to try to distinguish the instrumental use of the law, the enunciation of legal principle, and the development of political argument as separate categories of Wilkite activity, yet, as much as one tries to distinguish them, they collapse in on one another. For example, the indictment of a magistrate for murder because of his presence as an active JP at St George's Fields on the day of the massacre was a typical piece of Wilkite theatre, designed to dramatize the horrors of that day and to air radical grievances. The justice, one Gillam, was an unwilling but peculiarly effective actor in this performance: ashen-faced and dressed in black, he was petrified that the London jury would find him guilty and, before he was acquitted, he fainted twice during the proceedings.[7] All this was grist to the Wilkites' mill, but it was also an instance of the radicals' determination that all those who exercised judicial authority should be accountable for their actions; this view, in turn, was part of an understanding of politics that emphasized the centrality of accountability and consent. For the Wilkite radicals politics and law were not easily distinguished; indeed, it was a distinction that they felt no need to make: questions about law necessarily had a political dimension, and politics was never far from the proceedings of the courts.

The radicals, of course, were not unique in their conflation of politics and the law. Almost all eighteenth-century Englishmen would have agreed that liberty – an Englishman's liberty – was the highest political value, and that this much-vaunted artefact of the British constitution was sustained and protected by English law. How law was made (by Crown, Lords and Commons), how it was administered (by a burgeoning bureaucracy including customs and excise officers as well as bailiffs and parish officials), and its modes of judicial execution (by JPs, judges and juries) were all, therefore, highly material considerations to the preservation of an Englishman's liberty and, most importantly, of his rights. Good governance constituted a proper administration and execution of justice. Thus a protagonist in the Newcastle election of 1774 defined a good Whig as one who

looks upon all governors and legislators but as trustees to the public, but as stewards to the public purse, and makers of laws for its own good, and impartial executors of them, when made, for its safety; that if they use the trust more for their own private advantage than for the good of the whole, if they embezzle the money he pays in taxes, if they made laws more favourable to themselves than to him; if they execute the laws more favourably to one than to another, or stretch them to an oppressive purposes to serve their own ends – they should be displaced, from the prince to the parish officer; and others chosen in their stead.[8]

Though this description would undoubtedly have provoked contradiction from other self-confessed Whigs, it underlines the all-embracing character of the eighteenth-century term 'magistrate', which was applied with equal alacrity to the king and the local justice of the peace. The powers and duties of the one were directly analogous to those of the other. Similarly, different bodies concerned with the law were directly compared: the House of Commons was the grand jury or the grand inquest of the nation, and it seemed perfectly natural for a provincial newspaper to draw a parallel between a judge and a packed jury and a minister with a packed Parliament.[9] The questions of the fair administration of local justice and of good governance at Westminster (both in Parliament and in the major law courts) were seen as common problems which should be tackled in the same way, even if they did not admit of a single, simple solution.[10]

Such a perception of politics and the law was reinforced by most Englishmen's experience of governance. Many corporate bodies combined what we today would distinguish as political and judicial functions. The House of Commons, for example, enjoyed a judicial as well as legislative capacity (though most members were hard put to define the scope of the former); aldermen both ruled and dispensed justice in their boroughs; and grand juries, as well as determining whether indictments were 'true bills', were seen as the proper body to initiate the petitioning process that brought political grievances to the attention of those at Westminster. Most Englishmen experienced government and understood politics through their dealings with the law. What I am arguing, therefore, is that political ideology and the law as ideology were intertwined, and that legal bodies and processes (many of which had an overt political function anyway) were frequently the foci of political expression and political conflict.

The Crown, the king's government, judges and lawyers, as well as the radicals, were fully aware of this. The quarter sessions and the assize held in July and August 1768 at Guildford in Surrey serve as an excellent example of the courts as a forum for political contention. At the quarter sessions Sir Fletcher Norton, a resolute government supporter known to the radicals as 'Bull-face Double-fee', sentenced a Wilkite rioter, John Perceval, a pewterer, to two years in gaol for chalking the number forty-five on a magistrate; he took the opportunity, when condemning the prisoner to what nearly all considered a savage sentence, to expatiate for an hour and a half on the importance of loyalty, obedience and good order and on the egregious sins of riot and radical politics.[11]

In August, the Guildford assize witnessed an even more overt political clash. Both Wilkites and the supporters of government saw the occasion as a major confrontation, when both rioters and the troops who had shot radical demonstrators were to come to trial. Both sides were out in force, determined to show how much enthusiastic support they could each command. Local inns were packed: the price of an 'indifferent bed' rose to a guinea a night.[12] The father and friends of William Allen, whose death in the St George's Fields Massacre had elevated him to the status of a martyr, were treated by the populace, and when Wilkes himself arrived to give testimony at the trials, he was 'received with ringing of bells and general acclamations of the populace'.[13] The government countered by giving Wilkes miserable, flea-ridden lodgings, while the judges – Mansfield (the radicals' great enemy) and Smythe – 'were complimented by the Corporation in their formalities, who thought that at this critical period the Ministers of Justice could not be distinguished by too many marks of veneration'.[14] (Similar sentiments animated the High Sheriff of Hertfordshire at that county's assize in 1768: the judges were met at the border of the county by double the usual number of javelin men; the sheriff came further from the town than ever before to meet Mansfield and Smythe, and he wined and dined them sumptuously because 'in these licentious times, when so many people had attempted to trample on the laws, he could not treat his Majesty's chief magistrats of justice with too much respect.')[15] When authority was threatened, whether by smugglers, grain rioters or dissident politicians, it felt it necessary to increase the majesty of the law.[16] At Guildford, as at most of the venues on the home circuit in 1768, and throughout the country in 1769, the judges began their charge to the grand jury with an encomium of government and a warning of 'the dangerous tendency of riots'.[17] Such fastidiously composed and portentously delivered exhortations were, as Douglas Hay has pointed out, a customary means of enjoining a subject's loyalty and obedience;[18] they were specifically designed to curb discontent among the grand jurors – a cross-section of the county elite – and to pre-empt any attempt on their part to organize a petition of grievances to Parliament. For the assize was one of the few regular opportunities for the 'county', i.e. its gentry and bigwigs, to come together and assess the local political climate. At the assize dinner – where the toasts proposed were seen as a crucial indicator of political senti-ment[19] – at the assize ball and after the assize sermon, county political opinion was canvassed and local intrigue begun. In sum, when the judges arrived on circuit in a county town, it was never purely a judi-cial affair: whether or not politics actually entered into the litigation – as it did in Guildford – the assize had its political dimension, for it was one of the ways in which government conveyed its views, through the mouths of the judges, to the locality; and, conversely, it was an established means of expressing local political views which were meant to be heard by those at Westminster. This travelling train of justice, with judges, clerks and barristers, linked the centre with the localities, enabling not only loyal servants of the Crown, but also radical dissidents, to publicize their views in the provinces. Thus Robert Morris, the secretary of the SSBR, used his presence as an assize lawyer on the Welsh circuit in the spring of 1770 to organize a local celebration of Wilkes's release from gaol.[20]

All parties – government, radicals and spectators – therefore, were fully aware of the politics of the law. They recognized the potency of its symbols and rituals, knew how significant a platform its institutions provided and what a powerful legitimizing force its endorsement could be. But if there was such unanimity on the power and use of the law, can we in fact successfully distinguish radical, Wilkite attitudes towards the courts, litigation and justice?

Certainly it is possible to isolate particular sources of Wilkite views on the law. Above all there are the cases – over the freedom of the press and as a consequence of riot – brought by Wilkites to the courts, and pleaded, with extraordinary skill and tenacity by John Wilkes's right-hand man, advocate and fellow MP for Middlesex, John Glynn. His speeches in the courts of King's Bench and Common Pleas and at the local assizes encapsulated radical feelings about the law. These views were developed in the instructions, petitions and remonstrances drafted by Wilkites in the City of London, Westminster, Middlesex and Southwark. Drawn up by such radicals as the Rev. John Horne, George Bellas, John Reynolds and James Townsend (all of whom were SSBR members), they included in their catalogue of crimes and grievances bitter complaints about the nature of English justice. Equally illuminating are the many self-proclaimed radical journals which frequently discussed what they regarded as the anomalies and vagaries of the law. The *Middlesex Journal*, William Bingley's *North Briton* and *Freeholders' Magazine*, William Moore's *North Briton Extraordinary*, *Whisperer* and *Parliamentary Spy*, and John Almon's

Political Register, together with a raft of radical pamphlets, all published articles, anecdotes and polemics expressing their criticisms and plans for reform. Yet the radicals were not always critics of authority *per se* for, on occasion, and especially in London and Middlesex, they actually *were* those in authority. In their capacity as local JPs, radicals such as Wilkes, Sawbridge, Townsend, Bull and Crosby all sought to effect certain reforms and to act as exemplary justices, fulfilling what they considered to be the correct role of the magistrate. They attempted legal reform through example.

The Wilkite view of the law that emerges from their advocates, articles and actions was – to put it in the very broadest terms – one dominated by four main themes. First and foremost the radicals demanded accountability: they wanted to ensure that those who made, administered and executed the law were answerable, through that self-same law, to the public for their actions. Secondly, the radicals sought to eliminate what they regarded as partial justice, whether in the form of protection from the law for those in high places, unequal access to the law, abuse of the law for personal gain by petty officialdom, or socially discriminatory or anomalous legislation such as the laws covering game and indebtedness. Thirdly, they were adamant about an Englishman's right to what we would call due process within the law, by which they meant trial before both a grand jury and a petty jury according to laws which were publicly known and strictly construed. Finally, in the face of the widespread disorders of 1768–9, which raised in the acutest form the whole question of how magisterial authority ought to be exercised, the Wilkites, in formulating notions of a good magistracy, emphasized the vital importance of governing by means of public consent rather than overt force, and stressed the use of the civil power on behalf of the public rather than the deployment of military power on behalf of the Crown.

These deeply felt and loudly voiced opinions were, of course, neither unique nor novel; indeed, they could be described as part and parcel of one conventional idealization of the English law and its processes. A similar impulse and comparable attitudes seem to have animated the reformism of the 1730s with its hostility to the courts' use of Latin, its concern with the state of prisons, the use of processes circumventing trial by jury, and with the fate of those incarcerated for debt. In the wake of a 'crime wave' after the War of Austrian Succession, a Commons committee had been established in 1751 to seek means of enforcing and reforming the law. Though the committee made little headway, it deployed for the first time many of the arguments that were to become reformers' commonplaces in the second half of the eighteenth century.

Indeed, by the 1760s when the Wilkite movement began, there was far from universal satisfaction with the state of the criminal law. The nature and status of capital punishment for crimes against property was being called into question, even by the likes of Blackstone, and a great many common lawyers were both anxious and annoyed by the burgeoning of statute law effected by what the lawyers saw as an over-enthusiastic and legally incompetent body of country gentlemen. The publication of Beccaria in English, William Eden's *Principles of the Penal Law*, and Sir William Meredith's parliamentary committee into the state of the criminal laws 'as relates to capital offences', together with the disparaging remarks of lawyers about a blundering legislature, all attest to dissatisfaction with the *status quo*, even though these misgivings are more plausibly explained by legal professional pride and the emergence of a new sociology rather than by commitment to radical politics.[21]

We can, of course, exaggerate the extent of this equivocation – it certainly did not lead men to challenge the rights of property – but we should not ignore it. It is possible, by arguing in a thoroughly reductionist manner, to assume a consensus about the law in this period, but, in doing so, one loses all sense of the acrimonious differences that existed among lawyers, politicians and patricians generally, and of the highly ambiguous attitudes that were held towards what Sir William Meredith described as a code that breathed 'the spirit of Draco'.[22]

Wilkite attitudes towards the law, therefore, were neither new nor peculiar to them. The same can be said of the specific grievances taken up by the radicals or raised by their followers. Imprisonment for debt, the game laws, impressment, the role of bailiffs, the overweening power of judges and the legal powers of customs and excise officers were all complaints of long standing. But what distinguished the Wilkites was their ruthless determination that the old shibboleth, that all Englishmen enjoyed certain rights and liberties under the law and that all Englishmen had an equal right to recourse to the law, should be more than a hoary cliché. It was the Wilkites' readiness to act upon their view of the law that made them radical and threatening, and which prompted the fairly frequent suggestion that they were 'confounding the principles of equality with those of liberty'.[23]

The Wilkites, in other words, made explicit the political and legal or judicial connections between long-standing popular grievances and broad questions of governance that affected Parliament as much as the local JP, constable or bailiff. This tactic tended to link expression of popular grievances with a particular (Wilkite) political view, and drew those who felt especially aggrieved into the radical fold, where the political apprehension of their plight was intensified and some-times transformed into a general critique of government.

This goes some way to explaining how the Wilkites were able to win a popular constituency. The bulk of Wilkite support was in Lon-don and the provincial towns. True, there were many gentry who supported the Wilkite petitioning campaign but, on the whole, their adherence to the Wilkite cause was narrow, being chiefly confined to the issue of the rights of electors; very few of them were prepared to endorse the SSBR's proposals for parliamentary reform.[24] The hard core of Wilkite support – the people who raised money for him, formed Wilkite clubs in such towns as Newcastle, Bristol, Norwich, Worcester and Durham, and demonstrated in his favour – were of humbler origin. The typical Wilkite was a man of business or a trades-man: a victualler, an innkeeper or tavern-keeper, a printer, a pew-terer, an apothecary, a poulterer, a small master in the textile trade, a hairdresser or just a plain shopkeeper; sometimes, in the countryside, he was a tenant farmer.[25] These men of small property were those most injured by the practice of imprisonment for small debts, and most likely to have regular and unpleasant dealings with customs and excise officers whom they regarded as arbitrary officials interfering with legitimate business. And they shared with the poor – indeed, with all members of society apart from the rich – an implacable hatred of the punitive and socially discriminatory game laws, the vicious press gang, and the greedy, venal bailiff.

It is often said that the Wilkites managed to win the support of the middling sort, and we know that the labouring poor were willing to riot in their favour, but little explanation is offered of this allegiance beyond a presumed attachment to the formal propositions of liber-tarian politics. Rather more plausibly, it can be shown that Wilkite criticism of some of the more mundane aspects of governance and authority helped win them such support. The *Middlesex Journal*, like other radical papers, encouraged its readers to bring their grievances to the attention of the public through the good offices of the paper; we can hear the authentic voice of the humbler Wilkite from its pages, complaining bitterly of small but deeply felt injustices and seeking redress in the best Wilkite manner by the public exposure and humiliation of those who perpetrated abuses.[26]

The process of knitting together popular grievances and the radical cause was a gradual one whose complexities can only be revealed by a detailed examination of the central themes of Wilkite reformism and by placing Wilkite activities in the contest of a series of crises and incidents. The Wilkites were not always agreed on what complaints required swift redress (Wilkes himself, for instance, seems to have dragged his feet over imprisonment for debt), and the radicals never had a concerted plan for reform. Rather, they responded in both a flexible and sometimes highly opportunistic way to grievances as and when they occurred. Thus, although there is no doubt that the Wilkites did at least agree on general principles about the law, it would be misleading to see their actions as either a consistent or self-less attempt to act out a very detailed or coherent view of what English law and justice ought to be.

Indeed, like many another group that used the courts, the radicals were perfectly capable of deliberately and theatrically manipulating the law for their own (usually political) ends. Take, for example, the case of Alderman James *Townsend* v. *Hunt*. This case was an elbo-rately contrived attempt to use the law courts to show that Wilkes, though rejected by the House of Commons, was in law the true mem-ber for the county of Middlesex. From about March 1769 there had been rumours that the freeholders of Middlesex, deprived of their true representative, namely John Wilkes, would, on the basis of the American adage, 'no taxation without representation', refuse to pay their taxes. Meetings were held, money raised to fight a test case over a tax strike, and a strategy prepared.[27] One newspaper reported:

Their plan is this: On the collector's application for the tax, they are deter-mined to refuse payment: He, of course, will make a distrainer, agreeable to the law; and this they propose quietly to submit to. They then intend bringing an action of Damages against the Collector, Constable etc, which must then be tried by a jury, and as it will be a special jury of Middlesex freeholders, it will rest with them to judge whether the county is properly represented or not; and, of course, whether the inhabitants of the county are liable to the King's tax or not; and according to that judgement, to determine the merits of this important contest.[28]

And this is exactly what occurred: in June 1772 Townsend took collector Hunt to court, claiming damages. Lord Mansfield, the pre-siding judge, succeeded, however, in getting the case quashed, though not before one of the jurors, a Mr Long, had bitterly complained about the Lord Chief Justice's instructions.[29] *Townsend* v. *Hunt*, in other words, was one example of the deliberate and knowing manipulation of the judicial process, using its mechanisms to engineer a confrontation between the radicals and the government. The Wilkites were using their knowledge of the law to put pressure on Parliament, seeking to oppose the legitimacy of a vote of the House of Commons by the sanction of the courts.

Townsend v. *Hunt* achieved only limited success for the radicals, but in the previous year the Wilkites had won a remarkable victory over the House of Commons by the unscrupulous exploitation of loopholes in the law. The so-called 'printers' cases' of 1771 centred on the right of newspapers to publish parliamentary debates. Though this was technically a breach of parliamentary privilege, the radicals, with their commitment to an accountable legislature, were naturally eager that proceedings should be open and publicly known. Wilkes, together with the secretary of the radical SSBR, Robert Morris, therefore concocted a plan to protect the printers of debates from the wrath of the Commons. Three newspapermen, Wheble of the radical *Middlesex Journal*, Roger Thompson of the *Gazetteer* and John Miller of the *London Evening Post*, were persuaded (quite easily: they were old cronies of Wilkes) to defy the Commons and to refuse to appear before the House for the offence of printing its debates. Wheble, through his lawyer (none other than Robert Morris) even issued a statement arguing that his summons was illegal as the Commons was not a properly constituted court of law. On 14 March 1771 the radicals' plan went into action. Wheble (whose arrest carried a £50 reward offered by royal proclamation) allowed himself to be apprehended by his servant, Edward Carpenter. He was brought before Wilkes – in his capacity as a City alderman and magistrate – and released on the grounds that he was a London freeman, that Carpenter was not a City peace officer, and that the cause of arrest was neither a felony nor a breach of the peace. Wheble promptly countersuited Carpenter and charged him with assault. On the same day a more serious incident occurred when William Whittam, a messenger of the House of Commons, tried to apprehend Miller. The printer had a city constable at hand and had Whittam arrested for assault and false arrest. Only after the messenger had given bail before the Lord Mayor and aldermen Oliver and Wilkes was he released. It became clear, in other words, that the Commons had no power to execute its orders within the precincts of the City of London.[30]

Opposing the corporate privilege of the House of Commons by the jurisdictional autonomy of the City of London in order to protect the printers was a brilliant move, executed with characteristic audacity by Wilkes and his compatriots. Their legal stratagems were an almost unqualified success. Though the Commons clapped Mayor Crosby and Alderman Oliver in the Tower, where Glynn was unable to obtain habeas corpus for them, and though the case against messenger Whittam was quashed by the attorney general, Carpenter was found guilty of assault and sentenced, and the House was unable to punish the printers of its debates.[31] Moreover, by imprisoning two of the City's most senior officials, the Commons helped push the London citizenry (aldermen, common councilmen and freemen) even more firmly into the arms of the radicals, and prompted massive demonstrations in support of the printers. In effect, and if only tacitly, the Commons was forced to relinquish its claim to control the publication of its proceedings. After 1771 the House could only close its galleries to the public; it could not prevent any 'stranger' once present, from making its deliberations known to the world at large.[32] Radical support had been increased, the Commons humiliated, and a major political victory won, because of Wilkite manipulation of the law.

It is possible to treat nearly all the cases in which the Wilkites were involved simply as instances of radical use of the law as a tool or instrument, a means of making political points and of discomforting political enemies. (Few radicals, however, were as explicitly instrumental in their manipulation of the law as John Horne who, in 1774, deliberately libelled the Speaker of the House of Commons in order to be called before the house, so that he could air the grievances of his friend, William Tooke, when arraigned before the legislature.)[33] But in using the judicial process the Wilkites also made explicit their ideas about how that process should operate and what its animating principles ought to be. So that, if we are to appreciate fully the contribution that the radicals made, we have to examine other examples of Wilkite use of the law in the context of those principles which they thought essential to the just and fair operation of the British judicial system, namely notions of accountability, equality, the rights of jurors and of a good magistracy based on consent.

The right of the magistrate arises only from the right of private men to defend themselves, to repel injuries, and to punish those who commit them: that right being conveyed by the society to their public representative, he can execute the same no further than the benefit and security of that society requires he should. When he exceeds his commission, his acts are as extrajudicial as those of any private officer usurping an unlawful authority, that

is, they are void; and every man is answerable for the wrong which he does.
A power to do good can never become a warrant for doing evil.

The Whisperer, no. 30 (8 September 1770)

If there was one single general principle that bound nearly all radicals, it was that the magistrate – whether he be a justice of the peace, MP, the king or a lowly parish officer – was a servant of the public, appointed to execute their will and to look after their general good, and that, in consequence, he was accountable to the people in law for his actions. If he acted illegally, or in a manner that denied the purposes for which he was appointed, then he forfeited the privileges of his office and could be cashiered.[34] (Some radicals argued that illegitimate acts by those in authority – unjustifiable arrest, for instance – produced a state of nature in which the victim had the right of self-defence, and therefore was not liable for any injury, assault or murder that he might perpetrate against the offending officer.)[35] William Moore summarized the radical position in the *North Briton Extraordinary* no. 23:

the greatest happiness any nation can enjoy, is being governed by laws made by the consent of the people, either collectively or representatively, and of having a right to call the principal magistrates intrusted with the execution of those laws to an account for maladministration.

Accountability in law was, of course, a time-honoured notion which had frequently been invoked by the victims of authority. The very detailed accounts of the correct forms and the entitling circumstances for the arrest of offenders in such legal manuals as parish officers' guides attest to the care that officials had to take to stick to the letter of the law if they were to avoid facing prosecution by the putative lawbreaker.[36] But the chief question for the radicals was not one of the wisdom or legitimacy of accountability – they could all agree with Wilkes's counsel, John Glynn, that all men were beneath the law and liable to its strictures[37] – but of how to ensure that those in authority were answerable for their actions. In practice there were two tactics open to the radicals: either they could take officials to court, or they could engage in the 'policing' of authority, relying on the public exposure of abuses – usually through the radical press – to shame those in authority into reformation.

The former stratagem was frequently employed by the Wilkites both in cases arising from the arrest of printers of radical journals, and in the litigation that emerged from Wilkite riots and demonstrations. Thus in 1762 and 1763, when the purported authors, publishers and printers of the *Monitor* and of the *North Briton* no. 45 were arrested on a general warrant issued by the secretary of state, Wilkes and his printer allies retaliated (largely at Wilkes's own instigation) by countersuiting officialdom: those who had not in fact produced the journals in question, but who had been apprehended in the usual general 'round up' of printers, sued for false imprisonment and trespass, while others more directly involved – including Wilkes – attacked the legality of general warrants, because they failed to specify by name the persons who allegedly committed the crime, and allowed for a general seizure of their papers and effects. The success of this counter-attack was truly remarkable. Once the court accepted that the secretaries of state and their messengers (who had actually executed the general warrants) were not justices of the peace and constables and were therefore not protected in law, the radicals were able to wreak their revenge. By June 1764, only a little more than a year after Wilkes's arrest as the author of the *North Briton* no. 45, fourteen printers had won successful verdicts for damages against the messengers of the secretaries of state. The secretary himself, Lord Halifax, despite his repeated attempts to stave off proceedings, was successfully prosecuted by Arthur Beardmore and by Wilkes, who received damages of £1500 and £4000 respectively.[38] Moreover, by going to court, the radicals succeeded in ending the use of general warrants against printers. The Lord Chief Justice in Common Pleas, Camden, a known sympathizer of the radicals and the political ally of William Pitt, condemned general warrants as 'subversive of all the comforts of society' in a masterly judgment in *Entick* v. *Carrington*, and his extensive and well-reasoned opinion was endorsed by the *obiter dicta* of Lord Mansfield.[39] The government had its talons clipped, public officials were humiliated, and the cases themselves resoundingly affirmed the radical dictum that no man, no matter how elevated his office, was above the law. See, said the Wilkites, what can be done to the overweening magistrate and the arbitrary minister: they can be brought to answer for their crimes at the bar of British justice.

The radicals sought to sustain this principle in a series of cases which they brought after the so-called St George's Fields Massacre of 10 May 1768. On that day, the date of the opening of the new parliamentary session, huge crowds gathered in St George's Fields, Southwark, to cheer Wilkes. The magistrates feared that the crowds watching him at his window in the King's Bench prison would try to effect a rescue, and they therefore requested military aid. In the ensuing affray two incidents occurred which led to the deaths of demonstrators and innocent bystanders. First, shortly after he had read the Riot Act, Gillam, one of the Surrey magistrates, was struck by a brickbat. Captain Murray and three guards were ordered to chase and apprehend the assailant, but they bungled the job, contriving to shoot dead a young cowman, William Allen, who was almost certainly innocent of any involvement in the demonstration. Later the same afternoon Gillam was again struck by missiles hurled by the demonstrators and, on this occasion, he ordered the troops to fire on the crowd. It was at this juncture that several people were shot and killed, including a weaver, William Redburn, who was wounded in the thigh and died two days later in the London Hospital. Whether or not Redburn was an active participant in the riot, there is no doubt that in this second incident a number of citizens going about their lawful business (in fact returning home from work) were mown down by the military.[40]

The response of the leading Wilkites to these events was swift and incisive. On the very day of the massacre, the Rev. John Horne and other radicals sought to obtain warrants for the murderers of Allen. John Reynolds, Wilkes's attorney, was active in collecting information, and the day after the massacre a coroner's jury found one of the soldiers, D. Maclane, to be guilty of the cowman's murder. On 14 May an inquest was held on the death of Redburn, and it brought in a verdict of murder by person or persons unknown. Reynolds, assuming a role that he was often to play in litigation instigated by the Wilkites, urged Redburn's widow to take action against Gillam, while Serjeant Glynn helped William Ellis, another radical lawyer, to draft an indictment for murder against the magistrates who had been active at St George's Fields. Although both Gillam and the soldiers involved were acquitted – the evidence on who shot Allen was contradictory and confused, while Redburn had been killed more than an hour after the reading of the proclamation, a fact that legally absolved the JPs – the legal actions implemented and encouraged by the Wilkites helped perpetuate the memory of the massacre (which was also the subject of an annual admonitory sermon by the radical Dr Free) as an especially heinous example of the brutal use of the military to suppress the legitimate, if boisterous activities of true-born Englishmen.[41]

The prosecution of those in authority, and even the knowledge that there was a group of determined radicals prepared to act against magistrates if they showed the least semblance of exceeding the letter of the law, undoubtedly acted as a deterrent to the presumptuous exercise of power. Indeed, the activities of the Wilkites may, in part, explain the tardiness and prevarication of the magistracy during the Gordon riots of 1780. Yet almost as effective a constraint on authority was the deliberate exposure in the radical press of even minor abuses of power. Actions against constables for wrongful arrest or assault were often reported; London's thieftakers – including the notorious William Payne who operated in at least eight city wards[42] – were singled out for special scrutiny; bailiffs were criticized; trading justices were regularly exposed.[43] A characteristic item was the complaint in the *Middlesex Journal* of 24 August 1769 that:

There is at this time, a most infamous place close to the [Westminster] Abbey, called the *Little Ambory*; it is become a terror to the whole neighbourhood: it is filled with *thieves*, *whores* and *murderers*.

One of his Majesty's *trading justices of the peace* has planted himself in the midst of them, and they certainly are rather worse than better. The more quarrelling and drinking, the better his trade. A shilling for a warrant to take them up, and another immediately to discharge them, bring in a great deal of money. The worse, therefore, and more wicked the place is, the greater profit to his worship's shop.

Occasionally the paper would even mention miscreants by name. Thus John Keeling, a Middlesex trading justice, was attacked for 'usurping' the water from the parish pump of St John's Clerkenwell, and the local churchwardens encouraged to take action against him.[44]

This policing of magistrates and of officialdom is, of course, indicative of how the Wilkites thought that authority ought to be exercised in the society at large, and how office-holders had an obligation to act for the general good. As men who had been consigned certain powers by the public, authorities of all sorts were beholden to those who had created their offices and sanctioned their appointments. Wilkites argued that, even if, as a result of (reprehensible) historical developments which they broadly characterized as oligarchy and corruption, it was no longer true that officials were actually elected, the public still had both a civic obligation and the right to scrutinize the activities of the magistrate, for it was in their interest – both collective and individual – that he exercised power.[45] (Not all of them, however, went on to draw the conclusion of Bingley's *North Briton*, that all magistrates, without exception, should be publicly elected rather than appointed by the Crown.)[46] In other words, the radicals maintained, much in the manner of grain and turnpike rioters, that the citizenry were entitled, in their own different ways, to remind authority what its duties were and to take action if it reneged on its obligations. Hence the grain rioters' direct action against those who failed to enforce the assize of bread, the turnpike rioters' attacks on justices who, by joining the turnpike trustees, overrode their obligation to the entire community in order to further special interests, and the Wilkite attempts to regulate authority of all kinds, from bum-bailiffs to the secretary of state. Of course, there is a difference between obtaining accountability through the courts, and securing it by direct action or by shaming authority. But all three methods embodied a clear conception of justice, all entailed a remarkable knowledge of the law on the part of those seeking accountability, and, most significantly, all were explicit affirmations of the right of subjects and citizens to determine what was in the public interest or for the public good.

Sure Justice now is at an end
For how can pow'r go further
Since Englishmen are kept in Gaol
And Scotchmen bail'd for murder.[47]

The Wilkites, therefore, saw the law as a public instrument which should work for the benefit of all members of society. In asserting this, they simultaneously committed themselves to the notion of all subjects' equality before the law. 'The laws', wrote one pamphleteer, 'are only the sums of the smallest Portions of the private liberty of each individual.'[48] Great care, argued another, must be taken 'in the foundation of the law so as to render it of equal benefit to the meanest and the highest subject'.[49] The radicals, of course, did not argue that equality before the law obtained in Britain. They were too well aware of the way in which officials and the socially well-connected enjoyed tangible benefits and far greater advantages than the poor under existing legal practices; they also knew full well that access to the legal system, though ostensibly every Englishman's right, was limited by the imposition of fees and by the level of legal costs. And last, but by no means least, the radicals recognized that the law itself contained socially discriminatory legislation that directly defied the principle of equality. As one of them wrote:

A melancoly reflection! Yet too true, that however more useful members of the state, the *Poor*, are found to be than the *Rich* (a point universally allowed) yet their liberties and personal security should rest on slighter and more precarious grounds; which is directly repugnant to the principles of a constitution like ours, where the rays of freedom beam alike on every individual in the state; and diffuse their influence so powerfully throughout the whole, that the monarch and the mechanic have only one common source to resort to, in ascertaining their freedom.[50]

Noble sentiments, indeed, even if, in the context of the existing legal code, they seemed no more than pious aspirations. Yet the Wilkites were prepared to work towards the goal of a more equitable system, largely because they believed that their own experiences had taught them how unfair the law could be. Surprising as it may seem, in view of the legal victories that the radicals gained over the government and their political opponents, it was a common Wilkite complaint that the law was used to aid and abet their enemies and to hinder the radical cause. Much of this was simply special pleading. Almost the same complaints were levelled by the friends of administration against the radicals: Wilkites, it was claimed, used the law partially and maliciously to obstruct the just endeavours of the king's ministers and to exact vengeance upon their political enemies.[51]

Yet, unabashed by these counter-accusations, the Wilkites methodically assembled evidence for the partiality of the law. Why, asked the radical newspapers and the petition of William Allen's father, were those accused of Allen's murder at St George's Fields allowed bail, so that one of their number (and probably the man who did shoot the cowman) could flee from justice?[52] Why, when Justice Gillam was charged with the murder of Redburn and was prosecuted by the Crown, was he allowed both the attorney general and the solicitor general as his defending counsel?[53] Was it, perhaps, that the government operated a double standard of justice? The radicals pointed to other anomalies. They complained of the selective prosecution of printers because of their support for the Wilkite cause, and of the refusal of the king's ministers to publish a threatening letter against a printseller in the *London Gazette* (it was usual to print the epistolatory threat and offer a reward for the apprehension of its author) because the prints in his shop were hostile to government.[54] Why, they asked, were felons – 'murderers and rapists' – allowed bail, in violation of customary procedure, when it had been denied Wilkes who had committed a much less heinous offence?[55]

These acts of discrimination against the radicals were boldly contrasted with the special treatment of those who were sympathetic to government. It was an outrageous abuse, the Wilkites fulminated, for public funds to be used to pay the fines and legal costs of the secretary of state and his messengers after they had lost the general warrants cases. Taxpayers' money was being appropriated to pay for the crimes of royal servants.[56]

Equally exasperating for the radicals were the events surrounding the Middlesex by-election of December 1768. Serjeant Glynn stood as the radical candidate and was opposed by a court supporter, Sir William Beauchamp Proctor. The contest itself was a riotous affair, especially on the first day, when a hired mob, wearing favours marked 'Proctor and Liberty' in their hats, stormed the hustings and succeeded in suspending the poll.[57] Two of Wilkes's supporters – George Clarke, a young lawyer, and George Hopkins, a headborough – were killed in the affray. The Wilkites, with their customary expedition, and largely through the efforts of Charles Martin, Robert Jones, a Welsh member of the SSBR, and the indefatigable John Horne, managed to apprehend two of the hired men – Lawrence Balfe and Edward McQuirk or Quirk, also known as the Infant, presumably because of his enormous size.[58] Both were charged with murder, found guilty at the Old Bailey and sentenced to death. But they gained repeated stays of execution, and the government obtained medical opinions – given by surgeons who in fact never saw Clarke's body – contradicting Dr Foot's evidence that Clarke had died as a result of a blow to the head. These doubts led the king to grant McQuirk an unconditional pardon.[59] During the trial it had been revealed that the two Irishmen had been hired by a man called Tatum or Tatam, an agent, so it was claimed, of that old enemy of the radicals, Lord Halifax.[60] It looked very much as if ministerial influence was being used to shelter hired thugs, and that the royal prerogative of pardon was being deliberately abused.

This discrimination against the Wilkites and in favour of their arch-enemies prompted the radicals to involve themselves more generally in the question of inequality and the law. They began by taking up complaints of those whose grievances were comparable to their own. In 1770, for instance, they took up the cause of a London widow whose husband had been murdered in an affray on Westminster Bridge. The crime itself was straightforward enough. Widow Bigby's spouse had been a nightwatchman on the bridge, until he had been brutally beaten to death at his post by two Irish brothers called Kennedy who were returning home one night after an extremely drunken and acrimonious evening at the local tavern.[61] Both were tried for murder and found guilty, but were pardoned largely through the intervention of aristocratic friends of their sister, Polly, a highly successful *fille de joie* who was kept by 'two gentlemen of quality'[62] and who is preserved for posterity on one of Reynolds's canvases. Polly, who consorted with a rakish set, belonged to the socially parasitic *demi-monde* that catered to the baser tastes of the courtly aristocracy. This connection enabled her to act in her brothers' favour. The case, as the Wilkites quickly perceived, was an especially apposite example of the abuse of influence and power, an instance of what Junius called 'the mercy of a chaste and pious prince extended cheerfully to a wilful murderer, because that murderer is the brother of a common prostitute'.[63] There could be no clearer instance of the potential for abuse inherent in the discretionary power of pardon conferred on the Crown, nor of the unjust way in which the privileged enjoyed advantages that were not open to much more worthy but less well-connected citizens. Why, it was asked, should unfortunate Spitalfields weavers, driven to desperate acts by penury and indigence, be executed for loom-cutting, when such vicious brutes as Matthew Kennedy, having smashed open the skull of a humble watchman with a poker, escaped with a commuted sentence?[64] Such questions led the radicals to respond wholeheartedly when Mrs Bigby's attorney asked the Rev. Horne for their help. They raised a substantial subscription to fund her case and John Glynn began an 'appeal of murder' against the pardoned brothers.[65] An 'appeal' was an alternative means of bringing cases to court to the use of an indictment or information. Action by appeal was a complex, expensive and difficult proceeding. The prosecutor or appellant had to sue in person, and might be punished if the appeal failed or be liable to damages; even if he won the case he had to pay costs. Not surprisingly, by the eighteenth century the practice was virtually obsolete. But the Wilkites used the process of appeal for one very good reason. As Blackstone put it:[66]

If the appellee be found guilty, he shall suffer the same judgement as if he had been convicted by indictment: but with this remarkable difference; that on indictment, which is at the suit of the King, the King may pardon and remit the execution; on an appeal, which is the suit of a private subject, to make an atonement for a private wrong, the King can no more pardon it, than he can remit the damages recovered in an action of battery.

In other words, a successful appeal would have made it impossible for the Kennedys to shelter behind their sister and her friends. Unfortunately for the radicals the case foundered, in part because of the legal complexities of bringing an appeal ('this uncommon species of proceeding', as the law reporter described it),[67] but chiefly because Mrs Bigby was unwilling to pursue her cause to the bitter end. There were dark rumours that she had been bought off, but it is also possible that the radical subscription ran out of cash.[68]

The Wilkites' concern with equality before the law was not always so narrow or specific. Radical journals systematically exposed what they considered to be legal anomalies and publicly 'fingered' anyone who tried to use the law to prey on the poor, the ignorant and the gullible. Spunging houses, with their exorbitant charges for everything from a bed to a glass of water, arrest for personal gain or profit and the exploitation of clients by conniving attorneys were all condemned by papers like the *Middlesex Journal*.[69] In November 1769, for instance, the *Journal* drew its readers' attention to a poor woman who had bought some furniture on twelve months' credit, but who had been served with a writ for payment after six months and had been encumbered with the additional burden of legal fees. An attorney and furniture upholsterer had connived in this action. 'Glorious protection for the laws of England!' thundered the paper. 'The attorney lives very near the upholsterer, and we recommend them to the public notice.'[70] Such newspapers and journals kept an eagle-eye open for all such abuses.

Of equal concern to the Wilkites was the question of access to the judicial process. Clearly, if the law was not open to all, it could hardly be regarded as egalitarian, nor could it be portrayed as the guardian of all men's rights. The imposition of legal fees for access to the court both as a litigant and a spectator was, of course, the most flagrant instance of the restricted availability of justice as well as a grievance of long standing. The imposition of perks and perquisites for the various officials of the court could place men in the most invidious of situations.[71] Isaac Fell, the printer of the *Middlesex Journal*, while in the King's Bench prison for debt, found himself unable to attend the court of King's Bench to defend himself against a charge of libel because he could not pay the court fees. Since he could not afford to appear in person, the court declined to pass sentence on him, and so he languished in gaol. 'Good God!' protested the *North Briton*,

What a crime is poverty? How inexorable are the forms of human justice! A man cannot be legally sentenced to prison in England, without bribing the officers of justice to get sentence passed on him! And yet he should be confined there, sine die, for want of money to purchase a legal period to his misfortunes.[72]

Situations such as this led Wilkes and Bull, when they were elected sheriffs of the City of London, to insist that no fees were to be charged for access to the Old Bailey, and that a public notice to that effect should be prominently displayed outside the court. (As a result of this the court was absolutely packed on the first occasion that Wilkes and Bull sat on the bench, and there were complaints about the indecorous, not to say riotous, spirit that prevailed.)[73] There were attempts to extend this practice to other courts. Robert Morris, the secretary of the SSBR, began an action for extortion against the court keepers of the court of Common Pleas, because they had refused him admission unless he paid them a fee. He won his case, successfully asserting 'the constitutional principle that the courts of law should be free and open'.[74] The radical objection to fees was not simply confined to the way in which they restricted the access of both spectators and litigants to the courts and were socially discriminatory. The sums of money extorted by the courts, bum-bailiffs and prison wardens introduced a personal motive – profit – among officials and officers, whose first concern should have been the public good, and rendered far more probable all sorts of abuses to which the poor and legally inexperienced were most vulnerable.[75]

This same group, whose protection, most radicals argued, was one of the chief purposes of the law, also suffered because of socially discriminatory legislation. Though it is hard to demonstrate that the Wilkites were directly concerned with such matters as reform of the Game Acts and the alteration of Hardwicke's Marriage Act so as to facilitate cheap weddings, the persistence of rumours linking the radicals with these causes is certainly evidence of popular knowledge of their attitude towards the law.[76] Information on Wilkite involvement in the questions of impressment and imprisonment for debt is, however, altogether more concrete.

Impressment was a long-standing cause of complaint, and the press gang had often been resisted with great violence by the populace at large. Members of the press gang had been killed by citizens resisting seizure (their right of self-defence had been established in *Rex* v. *Broadfool* in 1743); press rooms, where the successfully impressed were held, were broken open; tenders used by the gang were attacked.[77] Few practices were as inimical to the populace at large as impressment and few regarded as a more conspicuous infringement on an Englishman's liberty. There were many specific objections to the practice of seizing able-bodied men for service at sea.[78] Press warrants, as the radicals were quick to point out, were *general* warrants, such as those which had been declared illegal when used against radical printers. They deprived an individual of his liberty without allowing him a proper trial or due legal process; they involved the military in civil affairs, were an example of government by coercion rather than by consent, and were socially disruptive, interfering with trade and encouraging violence. Above all, they penalized the humbler members of society, the poor and the middling sort, who were far more likely than any gentleman to find themselves unceremoniously dragged into His Majesty's senior service.[79] The social bitterness felt on this issue is well illustrated by a contributor to a newspaper who complained that the press gang had seized his 'devil', i.e. messenger, and suggested that they would be better occupied impressing the idle and disorderly, namely country squires who destroyed game and young bloods who fought with watchmen.[80]

The question of press warrants came to the fore during the war scare of the autumn of 1770 when, as a result of a quarrel over the Falkland Islands, it seemed as if Britain and Spain would shortly join hostilities. The press gangs were out in force,[81] but Wilkes and his fellow radicals acted swiftly to curb their activities. Wilkes himself first raised the issue of impressment in October 1770, claiming that freemen of the city could not be impressed and casting doubt on the overall validity of press warrants. Shortly thereafter city magistrates took action against press gang lieutenants who acted without an accompanying city constable, and in November Wilkes, Sawbridge and Oliver, and eventually a somewhat reluctant Lord Mayor, refused to execute the warrants and instructed constables to that effect. At the same time, the Common Council, in a move paralleled in Bristol and Newcastle, agreed to augment the bounty for naval volunteers: it was thereby hoped that incentives to obtain a willing naval force would successfully replace the coercive violence of the press gang.

The radicals differed over the precise legal status of impressment. Junius, as well as the counsel that the City Aldermen consulted, thought the practice justified on the grounds of state necessity, provided that the military press gang was accompanied by a civil officer. London freemen, it was agreed, enjoyed immunity from impressment. Some radicals, however – and Wilkes seems to have been one of their number – appear to have regarded the practice as an intrinsic violation of subjects' rights and therefore without any legal justification. But, regardless of their differences, the radicals used their power as city officials and the jurisdictional autonomy of the City of London to protect the City's freemen. The tactics, in other words, were exactly those used in 1771 in the 'printers' cases'. Quite possibly the success of the radicals' stratagems over impressment helped inspire their plans of the following year.[82]

The problem of imprisonment for debt was altogether more intractable. This grievance, discussed much more fully in Chapter 6, was again one of long standing. As in the case of impressment, a veritable barrage of arguments was used against the practice, but one of the chief objections was the distinction drawn between the bankrupt and the small debtor. 'By the laws of England', the *Middlesex Journal* declared in its usual stentorian tones, 'if a man owes ten pounds he is left to die in gaol, if he owes 10,000 £. he becomes a bankrupt, obtains his certificate, and begins the world again: what has the small debtor done that his punishment should be greater than that of the large one?'[83] Wilkes himself, a man with notoriously large debts, does not seem to have been over-concerned with the issue until attacked by James Stephen, the chief protagonist for small debtors, who accused him of reneging on his reforming principles, and who even tried to bring a case against him for falsely imprisoning a debtor named Grimshaw. Wilkes conceded that the laws needed reform (he probably had to, in order to preserve his radical credentials), and made a speech to the London livery expressing the hope that a new code of practice would be introduced by the legislature. As most of the radicals agreed, the quarrel between Wilkes and Stephen distracted from the fundamental question of imprisonment for debt, which was undoubtedly in need of reform, but which probably required a major change in existing law.[84]

The great province of a jury in criminal matters is to make true deliverance of the subject from false accusations, and especially from oppressive prosecutions of the crown.

ROBERT MORRIS, *A Letter to Sir Richard Aston* . . .[85]

For my part, my Passions are very warm for the Memory of King Alfred, who hang'd 44 Judges in one year, as Murthers of the Law.

North Briton Extraordinary, no. 83

Ensuring that the law operated fairly and did not discriminate against particular groups or individuals was never seen by the radicals as an aspiration that could simply be achieved by eradicating legislative anomalies and by ensuring that all had equal access to the law. For the Wilkites, together with many other Englishmen, were sure that a fair legal system could only work if it had clearly defined and publicly known procedural rules which were strictly adhered to, and which guaranteed the rights of the subject. Due process, in other words, was every Englishman's birthright, and by due process all commentators meant trial by both grand and petty juries. As the pamphleteer, the 'Father of Candor,' put it:

By the old constitution, and afterwards by Magna Charta, no man could be put upon his trial for any offence, until a grand Jury had found a bill of indictment, or of their knowledge, made a presentment thereof; and then the person so charged, was to be tried upon that indictment or presentment by a petit Jury of his Peers.[86]

This was the much-vaunted and universally praised system which was felt to be a powerful bulwark of liberty. 'While the trial by juries subsists in its proper vigour', ran one characteristic paean, 'and criminal judicature thereby remains with the body of the nation, no avenue will be open to oppression.'[87] The great virtue of a jury was that it was a *representative* institution, and not merely a cog in the judicial machine.[88] Trial by jury was supposedly trial by one's peers, before a tribunal that was, in the words of the *North Briton*, 'a small part of the people'.[89] Juries represented the public at large and acted, as it were, as the attorney of the people. (The radicals always insisted on the jury's right to question and cross-examine the accused.)[90] An independent jury, therefore, was as much a manifestation of true 'public opinion' as an uncorrupt House of Commons; indeed, the two were frequently compared as the chief means of preserving subjects' liberties.[91] Thus radical tactics in the case of *Townsend* v. *Hunt*, when the jury was asked to determine if Wilkes was the truly elected MP for Middlesex, were an explicit attempt to treat jurors as representatives of the people.[92] If a corrupt House of Commons refused to seat Wilkes, perhaps an independent jury would act as a responsible public body.

These views on the jury were, of course, a constitutional cliché. Many claimed that the jury was as old as the civil polity itself and that it had the imprimatur of the twenty-ninth chapter of Magna Charta.[93] When Serjeant Glynn, in his first charge to a jury in his capacity as Recorder of the City of London, echoed the words of Lord Willes and waxed lyrical on the specially privileged position that Englishmen enjoyed by virtue of the jury system, he was merely giving his own (admittedly very forceful) expression of an old saw.[94] But both Willes and Glynn were led to reiterate what were regarded as well-established truths because the conflict between the government and the radicals had raised in an acute form two major questions: what were the respective roles of judge and jury in criminal proceedings, especially libel trials; and what was the legal status of certain procedures – notably *ex officio* informations and writs of attachment – which side-stepped the jury process?

It was clear from the very beginning that the radicals intended to put enormous pressure on the jurors involved in cases between the Wilkites and the government. Most of the trials, as we have already seen, were overtly political, and radical counsel, especially Serjeant Glynn, made a naked political appeal to jurors, simultaneously trying to flatter them and to fill them with a sense of their own importance. This was a deliberate and self-conscious move. Glynn, in preparing for the case of *Wilkes* v. *Wood*, wrote,

An opportunity may be taken . . . to possess the jury with a just idea of their own Dignity and Importance that Liberty in her last gasp must look up to them only as her truly constitutional and firm protectors; that if the day should come (which heaven avert) when Parliaments should vote *ex post facto* indemnities of the violators of their most ancient privileges yet that an English jury will always be uninfluenced intrepid and uncorrupt assertors of the rights and privileges of their country-men.[95]

By emphasizing that the cases in which the radicals were involved were not matters of personal recrimination or vengeance, but *class* actions which affected the rights and liberties of all subjects, Wilkes's counsel placed the jury in the highly responsible and special position of arbiter of Englishmen's freedoms. 'The security of the subject', it was argued, 'requires a spirited and exemplary decision which may convince ministers that the Liberty of an Englishman is not to be sported away with impunity – The manner of conducting the Defence makes this cause a matter of general concern.'[96] Wilkes himself usually sought to reinforce this view of the trials by speeches that he made in court – most notably in Common Pleas in 1763 and in the King's Bench in 1768 – reiterating the general nature of his crusade against tyranny and in the cause of liberty.[97] Both Lord Mansfield and the attorney general, De Grey, complained about the way in which the radicals portrayed Wilkes's private cause as one of national concern.[98]

Glynn and Wilkes's attorney, Phillips, tried every tactic they could think of which could 'alarm and awaken the attention and jealousy of an independent and sensible jury'.[99] Their efforts at flattery and their attempts to impress upon the jury the portentousness of the occasion were accompanied by other, none too subtle tactics to increase pressure on the jurors. In *Rex* v. *Wilkes* the jurors were supplied with pamphlets advocating freedom of the press, and with an account of the trial of Zenger.[100] In the general warrants cases, and in the trials of the printers of Junius's *Letter to the King* – an overt epistolatory attack on George III – the individual names of the jurors, accompanied by comments about their connections and employment, were published in the chief newspapers.[101] And when the main publishers of Junius's letter were acquitted because of the juries' conduct, their names were put up in gold lettering in the London Guildhall to remind their fellow freemen of the way in which these citizens had preserved the nation's liberties.[102] This public exposure of the jurors, the radicals argued, helped ensure that the special juries requested by the Wilkites' opponents (and made up of senior freeholders) would not be corrupted, but would act as a proper representative of the public interest.

In seeking to win the favour of the jurors and in asserting their central place in determining cases of constitutional importance, the Wilkites not only pursued a highly effective stratagem to give them victory in the courts, but also challenged existing legal practice in the law of libel. It was the law, as construed by nearly all members of the bench, that in libel cases the jury had to confine itself to the facts of the case, and that it was the court that determined the law.[103] In other words, when Wilkes was accused of publishing a seditious libel, it was the court – the judges – who decided whether or not what had been published was a libel; the jurors' sole task was to decide if the evidence proved that John Wilkes was the publisher. Serjeant Glynn first challenged this in *Rex* v. *Williams* in 1764, when he was defending the printer for publishing a collected edition of Wilkes's *North Briton*, which included the notorious no. 45. After delivering the usual encomiums on liberty and trial by jury, he asserted that 'in the matter of libel, they [the jurors] were the proper judges of the law as well as the fact; that they had a full right to determine, whether the defendant had published the *North Briton* with the intent as laid in the Attorney General's information'.[104] But he was promptly contradicted by Lord Mansfield, the presiding judge, and Williams was found guilty.[105]

Once they had raised the question of the relative powers of judge and jury, the radicals were determined that it should not sink into obscurity. The issue became the subject of an extensive pamphlet debate in which the Wilkites argued that there could scarcely be a more appropriate body than a jury to determine what constituted a libel, because libel was a matter of public opinion.[106] The crucial test for the radicals' case came in 1770 when the government brought to trial several of the printers of Junius's *Letter to the King*. After the initial conviction of John Almon, Glynn deliberately appealed to the jury, asserting the right that Englishmen had to express their grievances publicly, and the role that the jury could perform in deciding on the nature of the libel. The jury in this trial of Woodfall brought in the verdict of 'guilty of printing and publishing only'; the second, despite strict instructions from Lord Mansfield, returning 'not guilty', and so did the third.[107] Newspapers all over the country announced the verdicts with the simple words, NOT GUILTY, set out in large capital letters.[108] By the time of the trial of George Robinson of the *Independent Chronicle*, the radicals' victory was complete and the jurors totally won over. One of their number leapt to his feet as the judge was delivering his charge, exclaiming, 'You need not say more, for I am determined to acquit him'.[109] Success in these cases did not, of course, actually alter the law of libel, which was not emended until Fox's Libel Act of 1792, but apart from providing the Wilkites with the pleasure of repulsing the Crown's attack on the newspapermen, the litigation served as a forceful and well-publicized reminder of the radicals' commitment to due process.

Seeking to limit the power of the judges in general, and of Lord Mansfield in particular, complemented the radical attempt to enhance the power of juries. The Wilkites were extremely suspicious of the judges' claim to be independent of the Crown and of administration. They were certainly sceptical of the effect of the much-vaunted decision at the beginning of George III's reign which, it was claimed, ensured judicial independence by giving the judges tenure for life. They pointed to the salary paid to the Speaker, who was a judge, and to the sums obtained by three others who were Commissioners of the Great Seal.[110] Besides, judges, unlike juries, were neither representatives of the people, nor answerable to them, except through the cumbersome process of impeachment. Judges, it was argued, should therefore confine their activities in court to seeing the jury regularly returned and duly sworn, permitting the accused his lawful challenges, ensuring that only lawful evidence was admitted, examining witnesses, summarizing the evidence and taking the verdict of the jury. They should never browbeat, coerce or bully jurors, or attempt through their decisions to establish new legal principles.[111] These general observations stemmed from a number of particular grievances of the Wilkites. They objected to the way in which Mansfield had altered the information against Wilkes (he was acting as a prosecutor, not a judge, they argued), and resented his instructions to the jury (which they claimed were false law) in the printers' trials.[112] In sum, they opposed judicial discretion for they maintained that all problematic matters were the proper concern of the jury.

This explains the Wilkites' involvement in the case of *Smith* v. *Taylor*. Smith was a Surrey tavern proprietor who was stabbed to death by a Scottish soldier, Taylor, after the latter had been forcibly ejected from Smith's hostelry. The jury wanted to find Taylor guilty of murder, but was bullied into returning a special verdict which was determined by the judges as manslaughter. The trial had quite strong political overtones: the tavern brawl had originated because of Smith's servants' insults to 'Lord Bute's countrymen', and Smith himself had complained to the soldiers that, 'Because you have red coats on, you think you have a right to come into any man's house and do what you will.'[113] The Wilkites persuaded Mrs Smith, the victim's widow, to bring an 'appeal of murder' against Taylor, thereby effecting a retrial in an attempt to avoid judicial discretion. As in the case of *Bigby* v. *Kennedy*, however, the appeal proved unsuccessful.[114]

Though they criticized all the judges, the radicals' special target was Lord Mansfield. Bingley's *North Briton* was especially harsh on the Scottish Lord Chief Justice:

the judge has little more to do than to superintend the trial, and to preserve inviolate the *forms* of justice. Would to God that this was always the case! ... But can this compliment be paid to a judge, who confounds, controuls and browbeats a jury? Who changes, garbles and packs a jury? Who in all his speeches, is perpetually talking of supporting the measures of the government, that is the prerogative of the crown, but never once of supporting the privileges of the people; as if the sole duty of a judge were to assist the *great* in opposing the *little*, and not to protect the *little* against the oppressions of the *great*? Who, not only in his private but in his judicial capacity, affects to despise the sentiments of the public, whom he politely calls the giddy mob, the giddy multitude? And whom it must be ingenuously confessed, he very cavalierly treats as such.[115]

Underpinning these criticisms was a basic difference between Mansfield and the radicals about the exercise of justice. The Wilkites' view of the law was in the best strict common law tradition. Forms had to be adhered to punctiliously and exactly: a misspelling or the tiniest legal nicety rendered a trial null and void. Radicals were strongly committed to strict construction of a publicly known law because they believed that this was the surest guarantee of a subject's rights, and because it reduced to a minimum the opportunity for discretion which was, as far as they were concerned, the opportunity for abuse.[116] Mansfield's own view could scarcely have differed more. He had gained a brilliant reputation as a judge who had brought equity and reason to bear on the law, and had thereby successfully adapted it to the needs of the mercantile and business community. Mansfield had brought into the Court of King's Bench a substantial body of commercial litigation, made judgments that had rationalized the law governing contract, insurance and bills of exchange, and had streamlined procedures. These reforms had been welcomed by many merchants, but had provoked hostile comment from common lawyers who thought that Mansfield's equitable and reasonable construction of the common law smacked too much of his Scottish civil law background. In the words of Lord Revesdale,

Lord Mansfield had on his mind prejudices derived from his familiarity with the Scotch law, where law and equity are administered in the same courts, and where the distinction between them which subsists with us is not known; and there are many things in his decisions which show that his mind had received a tinge on that subject not quite consistent with the constitution of England and Ireland in the administration of justice.[117]

The *North Briton*'s attacks on the chief justice therefore struck a welcome chord with some common lawyers. They knew exactly what the paper meant when it said of Mansfield,

I have seen, upon occasions too many to be repeated, your declination from the tightness of rules, your uneasiness under the limits of jurisdiction, your contempt of precedents, and your eagerness to free yourself from every controul, which the law has laid upon you.[118]

The traditional practice of strict construction was justified on the grounds that it was better that ten guilty men be acquitted than one innocent man be found guilty. A rigorous adherence to the common law was an important means of preserving a subject's rights. Mansfield's unwillingness to suffer fools gladly, whether on the bench or in the jury, and his reputation as a civilian or prerogative lawyer, meant that his enemies, both in the legal profession and among the radicals, could stigmatize him for rejecting this tradition; it also meant that they could compare him in the same breath with those notorious bullies, judges Jeffries and Scroggs.[119]

The radicals' attack on discretionary power, as exercised by the likes of Lord Mansfield, was not confined to their attack on the judges. They were also far from happy with the power – the prerogative – of mercy or pardon enjoyed by the king. It introduced an element of uncertainty into proceedings that hampered the deterrent effect of capital punishment (most radicals agreed with Beccaria that punishments should be both graded and constant), and it meant that the Crown reserved for itself a means of altering the determinations of the courts. This, of course, partly explains why the radicals used the procedure of 'appeal of murder': it precluded the use of the prerogative of mercy. Equally it explains the extreme reluctance of Sawbridge and Townsend, when sheriffs of London, to execute two weavers, Doyle and Valline, after they had been capitally convicted of cutting looms. The court had ordered that the condemned men be executed at 'the usual place', i.e. Tyburn, but the Crown wanted them hung *in terrorem* near Bethnal Green church as a warning to other loom-cutters involved in industrial action against their employers. Sawbridge and Townsend claimed that 'the King cannot by his prerogative vary the execution, so as to aggravate the punishment beyond the intention of the law'. Once such a principle was admitted – as it would be, they argued, if Doyle and Valline were killed in their home territory – the monarch would be able, at least hypothetically, to alter punishments at will; there could even be private or secret executions, and there would be no *public* guarantee that the right criminal – particularly if he was affluent – would be the man actually on the scaffold.[120]

It is important to emphasize just how hostile the Wilkites were to nearly all those discretionary aspects of the law which Douglas Hay has shown to be an essential part of the customary functioning of the Hanoverian criminal code.[121] Though the Wilkites never suggested that there should be a public prosecutor, and though they certainly thought that the citizenry should take the law into their own hands and implement prosecutions, they were also adamant that such action should not be malicious or a matter of personal vengeance or recrimination, but for the public good. They therefore policed prosecutors in the same way that they policed those in authority, exposing their malicious actions in the radical press.[122] As we shall see, they also objected to the discretionary powers granted to the JP when he heard offences which came under summary jurisdiction, and they wanted to keep the discretion of judges to a minimum; according to the Wilkites the only body in the court that could be permitted any leeway was the jury. It also seems that in the Kennedy brothers case the Wilkites challenged the practice of allowing evidence other than the actual proceedings of the trial to be considered in granting a royal pardon.[123] They sought, in other words, to end the system by which 'mercy was part of the currency of patronage'.[124] A number of Wilkites, like T. B. Bayley, the Manchester magistrate, opposed all forms of mercy and discretion; in good Beccarian fashion, they wanted a law of nicely weighed and carefully graded fixed pains and penalties.[125]

So far we have looked at radicals' attitudes towards such powers – judicial and royal – as might constrain or limit the scope of juries within the legal process. But the Wilkites were equally hostile to the use of procedures that actually circumvented or avoided the use of juries altogether. First and foremost amongst these was the practice of the attorney general of issuing *ex officio* informations against libellers. The procedure was a simple one in which, if the attorney considered a particular piece of writing to be a libel, an information would be issued against the publisher of the offending item (to all intents and purposes the printer and any seller were considered to be publishers), and they would be required to appear to defend themselves. The case would then be tried by a petty jury. The objection to this procedure was that it avoided presentment before a grand jury, and placed enormous powers in the hands of the attorney general. William Bingley described the situation in the *North Briton* no. 175:

Informations for printing and publishing libels, if the prosecution is instituted at the suit of the Crown are filed in the Crown Office, by and in the name of the Attorney General, *ex officio*; in which case, as the paper in question hath not been declared libellous by any judicial authority, the Jury seem to have both the law and the fact submitted to their consideration, by the very mode of proceeding, otherwise the Attorney General, where he files an information *ex officio*, unites the several distinct and incompatible characters of Accuser, Judge and Jury, in one and the same person.[126]

Such prosecutions for libel were entirely at the personal discretion of the attorney general. Moreover, as pamphleteers pointed out, he did not have to pay for the action, and if the court failed to find his information to be true, the accused could not recover costs. Informations, therefore, could be used to harass critics of the government, putting printers to considerable inconvenience and expense. This method of proceeding, like the use of writs of attachment, was condemned as a legal vestige of the prerogative court of Star Chamber, a device that had survived after that tyrannous court had been abolished, and which, in conformity with the tradition from which it stemmed, continued to be used to invade Englishmen's rights. One refinement of the procedure seems to have been an eighteenth-century innovation, namely that 'Attorney Generals, upon the caption of a man supposed a libeller, could insist upon his giving securities for his good behaviour, before he should be admitted to bail and delivered from confinement.' In other words, very substantial securities could be called for *before any trial* and simply because of the accusation of the attorney general; the unfortunate printer would therefore either have to assume a potentially crippling financial burden or languish in gaol.[127]

If the use of *ex officio* informations circumvented the grand jury, writs of attachment could be used to forgo any jury trial at all. Originally the use of such writs had been established to enable the court to control its own officers, to publish contempts in the presence of the justices or in the face of the court, and to enforce obedience to the king's writ. But in the eighteenth century a new usage developed which was first employed in 1720 and which enabled the court to punish a stranger, i.e. one who was not present in, or an official of, the court, for a libel on the court.[128] This procedure was used by the court of King's Bench against John Almon in *Rex* v. *Almon* of 1765 for his publication of a pamphlet accusing Mansfield of wilfully altering court records (namely, the information against Wilkes), and of seeking to defeat the intentions of the Habeas Corpus Act. Subsequently, the process was employed against William Bingley, for his *North Briton* nos. 50 and 51 attacking Mansfield's overall judicial career. The objections to such a process were threefold: the accused was hauled before the court and could be summarily punished by the judges; he could be bound over to answer interrogatories – the means of determining if a contempt of court had been committed – thereby committing himself to answer questions which might entail self-incrimination; and, most notoriously, the judge – in these particular cases Mansfield – could exercise 'the province of party, judge, evidence and jury'.[129] In sum, the cards were stacked in favour of authority: the process of writs of attachment conferred enormous advantages on the judge, granting him virtual immunity from criticism as a public official, and the opportunity to harass his enemies and political opponents.

The case against Almon was dropped on a technicality (the rule of the court read *Rex* v. *Wilkes* and not *Rex* v. *Almon*),[130] but the case against Bingley proceeded. He, in the best Wilkite manner, defied the court, refused to answer interrogatories, and began his own campaign against attachments. He published an extensive justification of his conduct in the *North Briton*, printed a sworn affadavit refusing to answer interrogatories even if he were tortured, vindicated his right to a jury trial and bitterly poured forth his grievances against Mansfield. Even if he had been indicted for treason, he pointed out,

> I should be intitled to have *a copy of the charge alledged against me*, and to have council [sic] assigned me by this honourable court. . . . So that *every means* of *defence* could then be allowed me; and on judgement, I might move an arrest, or bring in a writ of *error*. – Now, every means of ensnaring me, without a possibility of defending myself, may be made use of – Interrogatories settled at leisure, and with deliberation, by able council, with questions of every kind, in the most artful manner; and thus prepared, tendered to me to answer on *oath*, at *my peril*; without any copy, without even a previous sight; unassisted by council, or any other person whatsoever.[131]

Such cruel procedures, together with the general debate about the role of juries, prompted many of the radicals to insist that instructions and petitions should include the reaffirmation of the principle of jury trial, and should call on Parliament to investigate and to curb any court that violated the right of due process. Protests about the attack on the rights of electors, the peculation of public funds and the government's attitude towards the American colonists were accompanied by equally vociferous complaints about judicial abuses. The City of London's instructions of February 1769 to its M Ps opened with the recommendation:

> that you exert your utmost endeavours, that the proceedings in the case of libels, and all other criminal matters, may be confined to the rules of law, and not rendered dangerous to the subject by forced constructions, new modes of enquiry, unconstitutional tribunals, or new and unusual punishments, tending to take away or diminish the benefit of trial by juries.[132]

Although, as the City's instructions indicate, the issue of jury trials was principally confined to the law of libel, its discussion was so widespread that it could not help but be applied more generally. Summary jurisdiction through informations before petty sessions of justices for offences against both the excise and game laws were criticized as denials of due process.[133] In this way the radicals' objections to the law of libel and its proceedings were linked with long-standing and widely felt grievances. The issue that had begun as a question that primarily affected grub-street gazetteers and metropolitan printers was, in the best Wilkite fashion, elevated into a matter that affected all freeborn Englishmen.

The policing of authority, the attempt to obtain an equitable judicial system and the strong emphasis placed on due process were all seen as a means of securing 'good governance'. What the radicals understood by this term is best revealed in the debate over the exercise of authority by the magistracy during the fraught and violent period between 1768 and 1774. Radical riots and demonstrations, together with strikes and collective bargaining by riot which occurred during these years of economic hardship, combined to create a crisis of authority.[134] How was the magistrate to preserve the peace and to maintain good order in the face of such violence and contentious dispute? What had to be done to recreate the confidence in authority that both the government and the radicals saw as a *desideratum* of successful rule?

This was no academic question. London in 1768–9 was the scene of repeated rioting and demonstrations; magistrates and constables struggled to control the crowds, and troops were called in. The events of April and May 1768 indicate the gravity of the situation. On 20 April, as a result of an on-going dispute between London coal-heavers and their employers, there was an all-night gun battle between a band of coalheavers and an 'undertaker' or agent of the employers. A week later the London crowd seized Wilkes while he was in custody and *en route* for the King's Bench prison; they whisked him off to a Spitalfields tavern where he was cheered and saluted by a large crowd. On 5 May London sailors went on strike, calling huge rallies to march on Parliament with petitions for higher wages. In the following week there were strikes and demonstrations by watermen, glass-grinders, hatters, coopers and journeymen tailors. From 27 April until the fateful 10 May there were almost continuous demonstrations in St George's Fields, outside the King's Bench prison where Wilkes was confined. On 10 May, apart from the St George's Fields Massacre, there were riots outside the London Mansion House and the House of Lords; a sawmill was destroyed by 500 sawyers, and the dwellings of two Surrey magistrates who had been present at St George's Fields were attacked. Before the month was out sailors and coalheavers were involved in bloody affrays over the unloading of fuel from ships in the port of London.[135]

The radicals had their own distinctive analysis of these highly alarming events. They argued that the appointment of reliable, socially respectable and independent JPs in the metropolis had been deliberately neglected by the administration, to provide an excuse for the introduction of military power. The instructions of the free-holders of Middlesex in January 1769 called on their members to implement an inquiry into the county commission of the peace,

a branch of the police, that has been shamefully neglected, in order to furnish a reason, or rather a pretext, for the introduction of another kind of authority, namely, for that of the military power, which, on account of the real or supposed weakness of the *posse comitatus*, has been already employed to the danger, and even to the destruction, of the lives of many of his majesty's liege subjects. But while the commission is filled with men of such worthless and insignificant characters as many of those are who now compose it . . . can we possibly wonder, that the commission itself is fallen into contempt?[136]

The radicals therefore explicitly linked the political designs of the government – which they took to be a conspiracy to subvert subjects' liberties by such means as the introduction of military power – to the inability of the bench to control or command the confidence of the citizenry. Trading justices, venal and despised, responsible for creating crime rather than curbing it, were the natural concomitant of a corrupt administration: hence the radicals' demand, formalized by a parliamentary motion made by James Townsend, that there be a new commission of the peace.[137] This, of course, was a political ploy, designed to capture the commission for the radicals and to sweep out their enemies on the bench (who, regardless of their competence, were always referred to as 'trading justices').

But the demand for a reformed magistracy stemmed from a notion of how magistrates ought properly to act and, when the radicals themselves held office, they attempted in a self-consciously didactic way to show how the virtuous JP should conduct himself. Thus they invariably refused military aid in executing their duty, even when it involved them in personal danger.[138] True justice and the exercise of authority was not based on naked coercion, the power of the bullet and the bayonet, but upon the consent of the people to acts per-formed by those whom they respected. In October 1769, during the violent dispute between the Spitalfields journeymen weavers and their masters, sheriffs Townsend and Sawbridge set out to prove exactly this point:

It is said they are determined to enquire into the complaints of the poor journeymen as well as their rich masters; and by doing impartial justice to both, to prove to the publick the possibility of keeping the peace without the assistance of the military, or to lose their own lives in the attempt, to preserve the constitution and civil power of this kingdom.[139]

A similar motive prompted the same sheriffs to refuse military aid at the Spitalfields execution of the weavers Doyle and Valline, although there was a serious possibility that the condemned men might have been rescued from the scaffold. The peril of the magistrates was nought compared with the danger to the public from military rule.[140]

Good governance was not merely confined to excluding the military, but also included punctilious attention to a magistrate's duties, particularly as they affected the rights and liberties of the subject. Wilkes and Bull, when they became sheriffs of the City, ensured, as we have seen, that no charges were made for access to the Old Bailey, and also suspended the practice of bringing prisoners into court bound in fetters or irons. They refused to execute press warrants. Sheriff's officers who exceeded their powers or tried to extort money were disciplined, and the sheriffs themselves regularly visited Newgate and the city compters to examine conditions and to hear personally the grievances of prisoners. When Wilkes and Bull reviewed their first six months in office they could proudly boast that complaints against bailiffs had been redressed, and that the City had been thankfully free of legal abuses. By acting assiduously and by envisaging their duty as the exercise of authority for and on behalf of the people rather than over and against them, the two radical sheriffs had sought to exemplify the conduct they had tried to obtain in others by policing their actions.[141]

As the people have a share in legislation, to prevent improper laws being passed; so likewise have they a share in the administration of justice, that these laws may not become engines of oppression.

A Letter to the Jurors of Great Britain (1771)

Is it proper that the administration of justice should be influenced in any respect by the temper of the times?
Whether any state, power, or court of justice have, constitutionally, a right to exercise a discretionary power?

Motions for debate at the Queens Arms, Newgate Street, 26 May and 17 June 1769

What are we to make of the Wilkites' attitude towards the law? It is easy to belittle the importance of their views or to explain them away. The Wilkites certainly did not command the support of most members of the parliamentary classes and their actions had little tangible or lasting effect on those spheres of the criminal law that affected the bulk of the populace. They were not responsible for any new legislation nor did they succeed in moderating a penal code which most of them came to see as excessively harsh and gratuitously brutal,[142] though they did alter the common law in the general warrants cases. Judged by results, the Wilkites do not score very highly.

In addition, they never questioned the rights of property except in their attempts to redefine posts of responsibility as public trusts rather than private sinecures. Both grand and petty juries, with their property qualifications, were essential parts of the Wilkite legal fabric. The Rev. John Horne, for all his declarations in favour of subjects' rights, was perfectly willing to act as the key prosecution witness against the thief of a Wilkite's handkerchief, and to see him transported.[143]

Equally the Wilkites viewed the industrial disturbances and the distress of 1768–72 in a remarkably narrow way. True, they disliked the new capital statute against loom-cutting and they attempted to mediate in industrial disputes, but their outlook was primarily that of the employer or master, and their chief concern was to use the issue of unrest to win control of the magistracy. Though they were prepared to take some remedial measures, such as acting against forestallers, they would not go so far as to enact paternalist legislation governing wages.

One could even argue that there was precious little about the Wilkite view of the law that was radical at all. Most men would have agreed that officials should be accountable, though they might have differed on the forms that accountability should take; equality before the law was a cliché mouthed by many patricians, no matter how conservative their politics; and no magistrate in the kingdom would have denied the importance of due process, while many would have approved the Wilkite conception of good governance. What the Wilkites appear to have done, therefore, is to have distilled the essence of the law and to have blamed their opponents for failing to maintain its purity. They were critics operating within the framework of the law, using the well-tried and singularly successful tactic of castigating the government for denying the ideals it professed to uphold. Put like this, the Wilkite view seems much more akin to that of the parliamentary classes than as a viable alternative to it.

Lack of results, the failure to challenge property, the seemingly platitudinous view that the Wilkites took towards the law: all these apparently belittle the Wilkite achievement. Or do they? The absence of long-term success for the Wilkites, the failure to make the sort of gains so beloved by Whig historians who seek the present in the past, should not be allowed to obscure the extraordinary impact that the radicals had, even if the effects of their actions were short-lived. The feeling they induced among the nation's leaders – politicians and judges – was one of continuous irritation, periodic anger and occasional panic. For several years the government was on the defensive and the execution of justice, as conventionally conceived, became a fraught and arduous task. The Old Bailey and the court of King's Bench became, together with the House of Commons, the chief arena of a political battle that was viewed with undivided attention by a large part of the political nation. The challenge to authority in the courts was especially provoking to those who administered justice. Imagine oneself as Lord Mansfield: to have men come into your court of law, make overt political speeches, impugn your integrity and challenge the legitimacy of the court's procedures and jurisdiction. There were times when it appeared as if the legal fabric was coming apart at the seams. The extant law and its officers were ceasing to command the respect that they needed if they were to work successfully: the potent myth of their neutrality, equity and fairness was explicitly and savagely attacked. It is very hard to calibrate this process of demystification: intensity of feeling and depth of commitment, as well as changes of outlook and mind, do not lend themselves to aggregation. But there is no doubt that the Wilkite challenge to judicial authority helped them win the zealous and active support of the middling sort and the artisans of London and many provincial towns. Moreover, Wilkite political aspirations had a contagious effect, leading more and humbler men to challenge the courts in the way that Stephen did over imprisonment for debt. The impact of this attack on 'the powers that be' is well illustrated by an incident in the court of King's Bench on 9 November 1770. The description is a long one, but it is worth quoting in full:

A prisoner in the King's Bench came into the court of King's Bench on Friday, and begged his Lordship to read the copy of his commitment, explain it to him, and point out what Authority the court had to deprive him of his liberty: his copy of causes being read, it appeared to be an attachment against the body, for the nonperformance of an arbitration bond, which the court calls a supposed contempt of court. The prisoner observed, if he had been guilty of any contempt, he looked on himself bound by the Laws of this free country, to pay implicit obedience; but if a thing imaginary, he hoped it was not sufficient to deprive a Briton of his Liberty – Mr. Lucas, *ex officio*, spoke in opposition to the prisoner, on which the court said, You have been ordered to pay a sum of money, and you must do it. The prisoner observed, that was impossible, he was not able: begged his Lordship to consider the case, and point out a remedy. 'Your Lordship has given the plaintiff two remedies, as I stand discharged from his suit, for want of an execution, and you now desire me on an attachment, which is tantamount to an execution, and besides, my Lord, that is a breach of a civil contract, not mentioned in the committment, and your Lordship has no business with it – for by the 11th article of Magna Charta, you are expressly forbid the holding of Common Pleas, and without a manifest breach of the 29th Article you cannot remand me'. His Lordship said, 'Take him away'. The prisoner replied, 'It is contrary to Law, and I will not go'. His Lordship again said, 'Officer, why don't you do your duty'. The prisoner again said, 'My Lord, it is my duty to resist'. Upon which Mr. Holloway seized the prisoner, and dragged him out of court. The prisoner said, 'If you rob me of my Liberty, you have no occasion to keep my Hat,' upon which he was suffered to return, got his hat, and made Lord Mansfield a very complaisant bow, smiled in his face, and told him he was acting contrary to law. . . . Lord Mansfield seemed very angry on the occasion.[144]

This particular challenge to authority, it could be said, was even less successful than that of the Wilkites, but it was also symptomatic of a changing attitude and sensibility: one that challenged existing legal practice and which saw that challenge as a political act. The forging of this particular link was the Wilkite achievement.

The Wilkites, it must be conceded, did little to challenge property rights. But this does not mean that their conception of law or of the social relations affected by law was just a patrician shibboleth. Indeed, it is very hard to see how the Wilkites' vision of the law can be accommodated to either a patrician or a plebeian model. They opposed the entire patrician edifice: they abhorred the use of capital punishment as *in terrorem* – on the grounds that it had no value as a deterrent, was contrary to natural justice and deprived society of useful citizens;[145] and they were wholeheartedly against legal discretion, since it smacked of royal prerogative, was an intrinsic part of the corrupt clientage system and because it made impossible the fair application of a regular, finely weighted system of pains and punishments. Nor were the Wilkites especially plebeian. It is true that they supported a number of popular grievances such as hostility to impressment, and that they opposed, by and large, intrusions by the state upon traditional liberties – hence their antagonism towards customs and excise officials. They also attacked forestalling, short-weight bakers, price-fixing butchers and commodity speculation in general.[146] Yet this concern to alleviate the lot of the poor and to expose abuses did not necessarily entail subscription to the paternalism of the 'moral economy'. Wilkite charity, on the whole, was strictly regulated and selective, not indiscriminate largesse, and a number of leading Wilkites – most notoriously William Temple of Trowbridge –were powerful advocates of an unfettered market economy.

These ambiguous attitudes were further confused by two some-what contradictory impulses in Wilkite thought. One, associated with Wilkes himself, can only be described as libertarian: a minimal state and popular rights come hell or high water. This is the sentiment reflected by the convicts and pirates who wore Wilkite cockades on their way to transportation or the gallows.[147] The other view, one which commanded a great deal of support amongst Wilkes's trades-men followers, was altogether more regulatory. Despite talk of sub-jects' rights and liberties, the protagonists of a more ordered polity were eager advocates of rigorous street policing. They wanted to see vagrants and streetsellers prevented from impeding the smooth work-ings of city trade and local business. The radical attack, led by James Townsend when sheriff and later as mayor on hawkers, vagrants and pedlars, together with the fruitsellers (many of whom were prosti-tutes) who lingered near the Royal Exchange and St Paul's, epito-mized this willingness to use the law as a regulatory device in favour of men of moderate property.[148] Shopkeepers were not willing to be undersold by hawkers or to see their customers solicited by *filles de joie*. Hence the launching of such schemes as the plan implemented by the trusty burghers of St Martin's Ludgate in December 1769, when they appointed a salaried official – they refused the help of a well-known thieftaker – to clear Ludgate Hill of the prostitutes who were repeatedly distracting tradesmen's customers.[149] Such schemes of street policing, together with plans for street lighting and night patrols to cut down local crime, indicate a greater sensitivity to the fate of movable property than to the misfortunes of the labouring poor. Wilke's own much-publicized libertarian tendencies, and the tender consciences among some of their number, enable the Wilkites to be viewed as friends of the poor, but most of them distinguished themselves from plebeian and patrician alike. If we are to give their attitudes a class connotation, then it should be bourgeois: theirs was the mentality of the shopkeeper and the trader.

5 'Our traitorous money makers': the Yorkshire coiners and the law, 1760-83

John Styles, University of Bath

In a kingdom like Great Britain, the most commercial, and for its extent the richest perhaps that ever existed in the world, every branch of circulating medium, of whatever it may consist, should be founded on solid, wise and honest principles.

CHARLES JENKINSON, LORD LIVERPOOL (1805)[1]

Why does Britannia mourn and cry,
That every man has got his die?
And are so bold as to purloin,
And cheat old England of her coin:
As there is nothing further in't,
Than to maintain the *Yorkshire Mint*.

'The Yorkshire Mint, a New Song' (1773)[2]

Eighteenth-century commentators, both native and foreign, agreed that England enjoyed a prosperity unparalleled among the nations of Europe. Most echoed Daniel Defoe and ascribed the country's burgeoning wealth to the expansion of English commerce.[3] Yet, during much of the century, the primary medium of commercial exchange, the coinage, was defective, both as to quality and availability. The inadequacies of the coinage were rooted in government's failure to come to terms with the major discrepancies between England and other countries in the values of coins made from precious metals.

In the seventeenth century the English Mint coined in both silver and gold, but silver had traditionally been the English standard. Its status was confirmed by the silver recoinage of 1696–8. That recoinage was undertaken, after acrimonious debate, according to principles enunciated most notably by John Locke. These principles were to be a major influence on government coinage policy throughout the eighteenth century. Locke argued that silver was by its very nature the universal measure of value: gold was 'not the money of the world and measure of commerce, nor fit to be so'.[4] Ironic then that in the twenty years after the recoinage, the newly minted silver coin all but fled the country. Gold became, by default, the national standard. Immediately after the recoinage the face value of silver in circulation was estimated at £6.75 million, compared with a gold circulation of £9.25 million. By 1776 a gold circulation of £26 million almost eclipsed a silver circulation of, at best, £2 million.[5]

The flight of silver was the result of international disparities in the relative values of gold and silver. The mints of most countries in Europe, outside the Iberian peninsula, offered more gold for a given quantity of silver than the English Mint. Though the Mint price of gold was lowered in England in 1699 and 1717, the Mint price of silver bore a ratio to it of over 15 to 1 for the rest of the eighteenth century. In some European countries the ratio approached 14 to 1, in India 12 to 1 and in Japan 9 or 10 to 1.[6] As long as the face value of a quantity of English silver coin was less than the value it commanded on the international market as bullion, it was inevitable that new silver coin would rapidly be consigned to the melting pot and exported, despite the legal prohibition on both activities. The East India Company shipped out enough silver bullion for a silver coinage of £5.73 million between 1700 and 1717.[7] After 1717 silver bullion continued to command a price well in excess of that offered by the Mint, often by the order of 10 per cent.[8]

Only a residue of old, worn and underweight silver coin remained in circulation. Through the eighteenth century, this was supplemented by foreign silver, which passed at an exaggerated value, and counterfeits. By the second half of the century, most silver shillings and sixpences were mere blanks.[9] The Mint's output of silver coin in the eighteenth century was derisory (see the graph below), but then the silver recoinage of 1696–8 had been exceptional. In the eighteenth century the Mint reverted to its traditionally passive role as receiver of whatever silver bullion happened to be supplied for recoinage at the Mint price. It was hardly surprising that little silver came to the Mint when silver bullion consistently enjoyed an advance over the Mint price.

Hence in the eighteenth century, despite Locke's strictures, gold became the primary circulating medium, effectively the British standard. The Mint price of gold was firmly fixed after 1717, and gold coin became legal tender for all transactions.[10] However, the preponderance of gold coin in the eighteenth-century national circulation was no guarantee of its quality. There had been no recoinage of gold in the 1690s. When hammer-struck gold coin minted before 1663 was withdrawn from circulation in 1733, guineas and half guineas that were already seventy years old remained current. The gold coinage therefore became progressively worn and underweight.

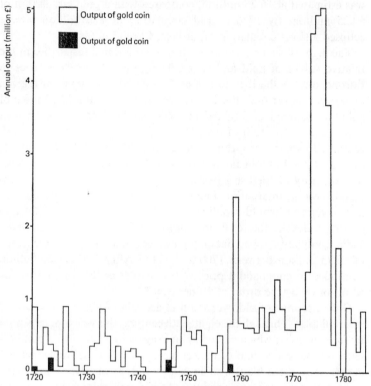

NOTES: One pound weight of gold was worth approximately fifteen times the value of one pound of silver. Annual production totals of gold and silver coin amounting to under £20,000 are not shown.

SOURCE: 'An account of the weight and value of all the gold and silver coined, 1660–1850', PRO MINT 9/61.

Mint output of gold and silver coin, 1720–84

Many late seventeenth-century guineas had entered circulation with a deficiency of 3 per cent or more in weight, as a result of the Mint's lack of precision in manufacture at that period.[11] Various estimates suggest that in the course of 100 years of normal wear, a guinea would lose 4 per cent of its gold content.[12] By the 1760s, therefore, the oldest guineas might circulate with a deficiency in their gold content of one shilling and sixpence in value. Yet they remained legal tender at face value.

Under these circumstances, much of the new, full-weight gold coin issued from the Mint was melted for export. By the mid eighteenth century, the bullion price of gold had advanced considerably above the Mint price (although not to the same degree as the bullion price of silver). Over the sixteen years, 1757 to 1773, the average price of gold bullion was 1 s. 4½ d. (1.74 per cent) above the Mint price of £3 17s. 10½ d. per ounce Troy. In some years it advanced to £4 1 s. per ounce Troy.[13] Matthew Boulton wrote in 1772 that the gold coin in circulation 'is much diminished and will be diminished as long as the refiner or manufacturer can buy more than a thousand pounds worth of gold coin with a £1000 bank-note, which is the present case'.[14]

The condition of both the gold and the silver circulations aroused considerable public complaint in the eighteenth century. Many commentators laid the blame for the problems of the coinage on the undoubted greed and inefficiency of the sinecurists who held office at the Mint.[15] There is no doubt that in the mid eighteenth century the Mint's attitudes and costly work practices discouraged positive action to correct the fundamental problems which beset the currency.[16] However, a much more powerful restraint on corrective action was eighteenth-century governments' fear of the economic disruption and attendant political embarrassment that threatened to accompany any major alteration in currency values.[17] Government reluctance to initiate fundamental changes was reinforced by the continued attachment, against all the evidence, of commentators, the Mint and successive administrations to Locke's principles of the silver standard and the immutability of the established Mint price for silver.[18]

Government was no more anxious to sustain the quality of coin already in circulation at the existing Mint prices than to initiate major reform in monetary values. The official responsibilities of the Mint extended only to the production of new coin and the prosecution of illegal abuses, such as counterfeiting and clipping. It had no responsibility to maintain or correct the ravages of normal wear on coin already in circulation. There was no system of regular, general recoinages to uphold the quality of the currency.[19] Recoinages in England were extraordinary government decisions, reluctantly taken. Eighteenth-century administrations were discouraged from embarking on such exercises by the disastrous experience of 1696–8. That recoinage had been forced on government by catastrophic public abuse of the silver currency. It entailed commercial dislocation, huge expense, fraud, popular hostility and political acrimony, yet it entirely failed to provide a secure silver coinage.[20]

In the middle years of the eighteenth century the Mint did continue to manufacture some gold coin [see table on page 174], but this output did not necessarily influence the volume or quality of guineas in circulation. The work was undertaken mainly for the Bank of England, which was willing to supply bullion for coining at the Mint price (and therefore often at a loss) in order to sustain the convertability of its note issue.[21] Adam Smith pointed out that these 'operations of the Mint were . . . somewhat like the web of Penelope; the work that was done in the day was undone in the night. The Mint was employed, not so much in making daily additions to the coin, as in replacing the very best part of it which was daily melted down'.[22] The result was an acute shortage of English gold coin, which was only partially mitigated by a massive influx of Portuguese gold in the years 1700–60. Imported as coin in settlement of England's massive surplus on trade with Portugal, a proportion of this Portuguese gold avoided the melting pot because it passed current as coin at a value greater than its intrinsic gold content.[23] In 1742 Portuguese moidores were described as 'in great measure the current coin of the Kingdom'.[24] Tiny Portuguese gold coins circulated widely, because, in the absence of silver coin, the cash shortage was particularly severe among small denominations. An unwilling Mint was pressed by the Bank of England to issue one quarter or one-third guinea pieces.[25]

If the condition of the gold coin was thus defective, and that of the silver abysmal, the copper coinage had effectively ceased to merit the name. A 1787 Mint inspection of a random sample of coppers in circulation revealed that 8 per cent bore some resemblance to Mint coin, 43 per cent were blatantly inferior, 12 per cent were blanks and the rest (37 per cent) were 'trash which would disgrace common sense to suppose it accepted for coins'.[26] The Mint did undertake some copper coinage in the eighteenth century, but this was not strictly its responsibility under the Mint indenture. Nor was copper coin legal tender for many transactions. However, the huge demand for substitutes for small-denomination silver provided a ready market for counterfeit copper, which flooded the country and was estimated at anything from two-thirds to one and a half times the legal issue.[27]

Counterfeiting copper was widespread. In 1751 it was said 'of counterfeit halfpence [that] there are now almost infinite sorts. Every town and village has its mint where many of our master manufac-

Two concepts of order

Above A group of 'good fellows at the alehouse, from the title-page of Thomas Randall's ballad, 'The High and Mightie Commendation of the Vertue of a Pot of Good Ale', published in London, 1642

Left Presentment of the jury for the hundreds of Hinckford and Witham, Essex, October 1644, signed by the jurors

The Wilkites and the law, 1763–74

Above 'Midas; or the Surry Justice', from the *Oxford Magazine* (1768), shows Justice Gilliam, the magistrate who ordered troops to fire on the demonstrators at St George's Fields, May 1768

Right 'Mr Alderman W———s in his Magisterial Character' illustrates the exercise of radical justice. From the *Oxford Magazine*, 1770

'Our traitorous money makers'

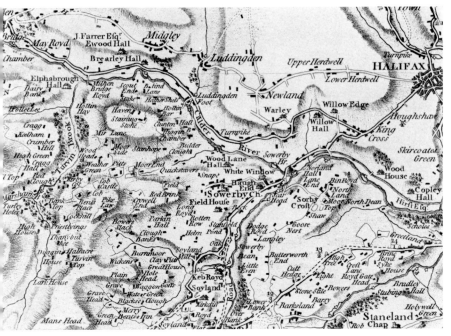

The area between the Turvin valley and the town of Halifax, from Thomas Jeffrey's map of Yorkshire, sheet 12, published in 1775 (scale 1 in. = 1 mile). The district was surveyed by Jeffrey's assistant between 1767 and 1769. The area on the extreme right is shown in greater detail on pages 202–3

A pair of dies for striking counterfeit moidores, with a collar for holding them in place during use. They were discovered during the 1830s, concealed in the wall of a house near Hebden Bridge

The King's Bench prison in the later eighteenth century

An 1808 engraving of the front parade of the King's Bench prison. The prison at this time had essentially the form that it assumed after the rebuilding of 1780–1. Note, on the right, the awnings over the shops on the ground floor and, on the left, racket players and the prison pumps

King's Bench prisoners tossing a bailiff in a blanket, from an 1825 engraving. Note, on the right, the two men standing at the prison entrance; one, possibly a turnkey, holds a mug of beer

turers get them coined as cheap as they can for their use to pay their workmen with'.[28] Profits were immense, estimated by the Mint at 50 per cent on the best quality counterfeits in 1755 and 300 per cent by a Lancashire magistrate in 1783.[29] An Act of 1771 made counterfeiting copper a felony.[30] Before that date the offence was a misdemeanour, subject to two years' imprisonment after 1742.[31] This status restricted the ability of magistrates to have premises searched for evidence or to commit offenders. Many of the so-called counterfeits bore so little resemblance to genuine copper coin that their manufacture was not construed as an offence. The production and distribution of these counterfeit coppers enjoyed widespread public sanction. Manufacturers and tradesmen were often customers for counterfeits in bulk, to alleviate the acute shortage of small coin. These were the very men who in cases of theft were most anxious to use the criminal law to protect property. Workmen, although entitled by law to be paid in silver or gold for sums of 6 d. or more, accepted counterfeit copper from employers when the alternative was delayed wages. The counterfeit coin they received, often in five or ten shilling parcels, was recirculated through small retailers, with whom it found a ready acceptance for similar reasons.[32]

The gold and silver circulations were not subject to the extraordinary degree of penetration by counterfeits that characterized the copper currency. Yet their poor condition, limited availability and the diversity of their national origin did facilitate both counterfeiting and other forms of abuse. Indeed, foreigners found the plethora of false coin of all kinds worthy of special remark.[33]

Illegal abuse of the gold and silver coin was in important respects a more serious undertaking than the production of false coppers. The manufacture of silver and gold counterfeits tended to require greater skill. Of course, there were many methods of producing all kinds of counterfeits, as there were many degrees of worn coin. Copper could be bought commercially in the form of rolled sheets or as cut button blanks. The latter might pass as coin, without reworking, but the most lucrative copper counterfeits were those which bore appropriate impressions on both faces. A coining die for that purpose was the work of a skilled engraver or die sinker. The impression was struck on to the blanks by means of a hammer or a press.

As usually practised, counterfeiting gold and silver required the additional skill of mixing base metals to imitate coin, as well as the appropriate equipment, in particular melting pots or crucibles. The latter were difficult to conceal or explain away as an aspect of the button trade. A simpler technique for counterfeiting silver and gold coin, though one more easily detected by scratching or rubbing, was to plate lower denomination coin, or base metal imitations, with a chemical wash. Even here special skill was required if the counterfeiter was to manufacture, rather than purchase, his wash.

Counterfeiting the gold and silver coinage, diminishing it,[34] or possessing appropriate coining tools were all capital offences.[35] The potential consequences of detection and prosecution were therefore considerably more serious than those associated with offences against the copper currency. Unlike bad coppers, counterfeit gold and silver coins were rarely accepted knowingly by the general public. The holder of an intrinsically worthless counterfeit guinea or thirty-six-shilling Portuguese piece suffered a considerable loss if it would not pass. Worthless gold and silver counterfeits made from base metals never enjoyed ready public acceptability. Those who counterfeited the precious metal coinages could not, therefore, rely on the indulgence of the public as a means of reducing the considerable risks of detection and prosecution.

Although the manufacture and circulation of gold and silver counterfeits involved greater risk than the production of false coppers, many coining enterprises in this field were heavily capitalized, geographically extensive and sophisticated in organization. To ensure greater security in manufacture, such illegal enterprises depended on secrecy. A favourite device was to use a variety of premises for coining, all specially located and adapted to facilitate warning of discovery, concealment of equipment and escape.

Putting off the products of these secret workshops, although a non-capital offence, was the most exposed component of the typical counterfeiting operation. Prosecutions for uttering gold or silver counterfeits (a misdemeanour) were much more frequent than those for coining. Here risks could be reduced by attention to the quality of the product and by providing for its distribution through a small number of expert and trusted dealers. Peripatetic retailers and middlemen, such as badgers and hucksters, whose legitimate business involved transactions based on cash, enjoyed particularly good opportunities for putting off counterfeits, without excessive suspicion or risk.

Thomas Lightowller was the doyen of eighteenth-century English coiners, a counterfeiting entrepreneur who enjoyed a notoriety in his own trade that matched the renown accorded to an Arkwright or a Wedgwood in theirs. His activities were well documented and will serve to illustrate some features of a large coining operation in the 1740s and 1750s.[36] Lightowller was an exceptionally skilled metal-worker, 'a mechanical genius',[37] and was later in life to be employed as a mechanic in Austria by Maria Theresa.[38] Born at Walton le Dale in Lancashire, he coined in South Wales, the West Midlands, Lancashire, Yorkshire and the Isle of Man during the middle decades of the eighteenth century.[39] In 1756 – Lightowller was charged with high treason at Lancaster, where he was acquitted against the evidence, and at Coventry, where he was discharged without prosecution.[40] Evidence taken at the time revealed that Lightowller had introduced associates in Lancashire, Yorkshire, Coventry and the Black Country to the mysteries of coining and had managed their operations. Alderman Hewitt of Coventry recalled that 'between twenty and thirty . . . were concerned in the Mint at Coventry, as appears by letters, all of whom had learnt to do business in the absence of Thomas Lightowller; who besides this company . . . was at the head of others in different parts of the kingdom'.[41]

Lightowller's trade involved the production of counterfeits of gold and silver coin from mixed or base metals. A Londoner ordered Pinchbeck guineas and white metal crowns from him by post in 1755.[42] Files and crucibles containing mixed metal were found concealed in the garret of a house at Coventry belonging to one of his associates.[43] Occupational information is available for five of his West Midlands customers for false coin (mainly counterfeit shillings). Two were pedlars and three bakers.[44] A London cheesemonger ordered 'goods' from him in 1752 at fifteen for a shilling.[45] Food dealing and peddling were both trades that depended heavily on cash transactions. Lightowller's business was geographically extensive and his associates many, but he did not rely on popular endorsement for of the eighteenth century.[39] In 1756 – Lightowller was charged with the reduction of risks. His activities were characteristically secretive. He moved frequently between his far-flung groups of associates, his coining shops were carefully concealed and the distributors of his product appear, on the available evidence, to have been drawn from a few, appropriate trades.

By mid century the contdiion of the gold coin in circulation was so poor that another illegal abuse of the gold coinage was provoking complaint.[46] In 1752 Peter Vallavine, a Kent clergyman, submitted a paper to the Mint entitled *To prevent the diminishing of the current coins*.[47] He pointed out that 'custom gives countenance and security to the breach of the law . . . and there is neither danger nor discredit in passing away guineas which are known to have been filed'.[48] The cutting or filing of a small quantity of gold off the edge of a guinea was not likely to excite attention if most guineas were already battered. The activities of Joseph Wood and his associates, exposed in 1757, provide a well documented example of the kind of large-scale filing operation that came to flourish during the late 1740s and 1750s.[49] Wood obtained immense amounts of gold coin near full weight from the Bank of England, which had a reputation for holding good and often newly minted coin. From each of these guineas he filed gold worth, on average, 9 d. or 12 d.[50] The milling was restored to the guineas thus diminished and they were then used to procure provincial bills of exchange, for which they were readily accepted. The bills of exchange were discounted at London banks and payment received in Bank of England notes, which were then exchanged at the Bank for more full-weight guineas. Wood created some suspicion because he was 'so very shabby a man',[51] but in two years he circulated over £40,000 for a profit of over £2000 in gold filings.[52] Filing was conducted with extreme secrecy by Wood and his associates in a number of premises kept for the purpose, including a summer house in the gardens at Islington, where Wood also kept a mistress. Risk arose from the incongruity of 'so very shabby a man' circulating such immense amounts of cash. This probably led to his capital conviction at the Old Bailey in 1757. His reliance on the wider community was minimal. The extreme secrecy of his filing operations ensured the success of his enterprise as long as banks and dealers accepted his diminished coin without excessive suspicion. As Vallavine had remarked five years earlier, there was no necessary public discredit or danger in passing such coin.

The attitude of the public in the mid eighteenth century towards the various forms of illegal abuse of the coinage requires careful examination, because massive public support was to be a novel and distinctive feature of the clipping and coining operations in Yorkshire in the 1760s. Public toleration for the circulation of filed guineas, like that for counterfeit coppers, stemmed from the shortcomings of government coinage policy. Government condoned the circulation of guineas that were underweight as a consequence of almost a century of normal wear. Yet the circulation of guineas underweight, to the same degree, as a result of illegal filing was officially condemned. The public remained impervious to this legal distinction, which was of little practical consequence. There was general unconcern as to how coins came to be deficient, when most were already underweight and were passed despite their deficiency.

Government's almost complete failure to provide legal copper coins encouraged ready public acceptance of counterfeit coppers, often with a low copper content. However, as has been pointed out, this kind of endorsement did not extend to counterfeits of the precious metal coins. Although the gold and, especially, the silver circulations were allowed to decline in quality and availability in the eighteenth century, their condition never approached that of the copper coinage. The public remained generally hostile to receiving worthless counterfeits as substitutes for high denomination, Mint-struck coins, which, though worn, retained a substantial bullion value. Men like Thomas Lightowller, who dealt in base metal counterfeits of these coins, imposed on a public that was unwilling to be defrauded. Yet despite public reluctance to receive such counterfeits, there are some indications that those who manufactured them were occasionally extended the kind of public sympathy enjoyed by the dealers in false coppers.

In the middle years of the eighteenth century there were several spectacular instances of juries acquitting against the evidence in capital coining cases. Thomas Lightowller himself was acquitted at Lancaster summer assizes in 1756 against the evidence, while Richard Wrag secured an acquttal on a capiital indictment at York Lent assizes in 1761, 'contrary to the opinion of the judge, who told the jury he hoped they would not hereafter complain if they received bad money'.[53]

Juries were composed of freeholders, middling men of some property such as farmers, small manufacturers and tradesmen. Such men handled large amounts of gold and silver coin in the course of their commercial transactions and were familiar with both the inadequacies of legitimate coin and the prevalence of counterfeits. Acquittals against the evidence may therefore have reflected a deep-seated hostility on the part of this section of the population towards the Mint monopoly, which, through its failure to provide an adequate circulation for commercial purposes, facilitated the manufacture and circulation of bad coin.

However, this evidence is ambiguous and must be treated with caution. Such individual acquittals may have resulted merely from the peculiar circumstances of each case. The chances of being capitally convicted on a capital coinage indictment were much higher than on an indictment for capital theft.[54] However, before a prosecution was allowed to proceed, the evidence against a capital coinage defendant, unlike that against a defendant accused of capital theft, was specially vetted by the Crown law officers for its reliability. Those capital coining prosecutions which were allowed to come to trial were selected because they were likely to succeed. The conviction rate, therefore, might be interpreted as disproportionately low.

Unfortunately it is impossible to confirm such an interpretation of the conviction rate, because capital coinage cases were characterized by other peculiar obstacles to securing convictions. These derived principally from the nature of the offences and the evidential standards of the courts.

Superficially the laws against abuses of the gold and silver coinage were expressly constructed to encourage successful prosecution. In practice the conventions of the courts and the prevailing method of prosecution inhibited it. Coining or clipping the current English gold and silver coin, and possessing or making tools for that purpose were high treason.[55] A reward of £40 was available to those who apprehended and prosecuted clipping or coining offenders to conviction, and offenders who gave information leading to the conviction of two others were offered a free pardon.[56] Informing was also encouraged against those selling or possessing clippings (a noncapital offence) by the grant of half the £500 fine to the informer on conviction.[57]

These incentives did not extend to equivalent offences against Portuguese coin, which was not current in the technical sense. To counterfeit or clip it was not high treason, but misprision of treason, punishable by life imprisonment, forfeiture of goods and loss of profits of land during life.[58] Treasonable offenders against the coin were exempt from certain safeguards available to defendants in other treasons. Defendants in coinage treasons did not enjoy the privilege of a copy of the indictment before trial, nor of lists of jurors and witnesses. Nor did a successful prosecution technically require more than one witness.

These encouragements to prosecution were compromised in the courts. Judges were solicitous to the accused. By the eighteenth century, judges in most criminal cases refused to accept the evidence of accomplices, without strong corroborating testimony.[59] This practice prevailed, despite Parliament's anxiety, expressed repeatedly in legislation, to promote convictions on the evidence of accomplices by offering them pardons and rewards. It bore heavily on capital coining prosecutions. Because the act of counterfeiting was itself private and could be easily concealed, such prosecutions relied disproportionately on the evidence of accomplices. Extraordinary lengths were taken to secure this evidence. The uncle of a suspected coiner who attempted to help his nephew escape from prison in 1756 was prosecuted only so that the nephew, tho' acquitted might be induced to make 'the best discovery he was able'.[60]

Yet the nephew had been acquitted on a capital coining charge, 'the judge being of the opinion that circumstantial evidence was not strong enough to support the evidence of an accomplice'.[61] In practice, the standards of evidence required by judges were much more stringent than the letter of the law demanded, and could be exacting. At the trial of Joseph Stell, executed at York in 1768, even the discovery at his home of mills suitable for coining was not enough to convict him, in spite of his having no occasion for them in his business. This evidence, it was pointed out to the mayor of Newcastle upon Tyne, 'would not do, nor, do I believe, would he have suffered, but coin was found upon him'.[62] These rigorous evidential standards, which were a brake on the successful prosecution of suspected counterfeiters, rendered convictions for clipping and filing virtually impossible, because they could be undertaken without either special equipment or accomplices.

Ironically, another hindrance to the successful application of the criminal law against coinage offenders was the very availability of official finance for prosecutions. Offences against the gold and silver coin were distinctive, in that finance and direction were provided for prosecutions by the Mint. Most other eighteenth-century criminal prosecutions were privately conducted and financed, although a patchwork of statutory rewards, county reimbursement and parish or association funds was available to some prosecutors under certain circumstances.

In charge of coinage prosecutions, after 1715, was the Mint Solicitor.[63] His duties were described, in 1798, as general attention to all circumstances leading to the discovery of offenders against the Mint laws, attending magistrates in London on such subjects and 'corresponding with magistrates in the country . . . and giving them directions for their conduct'. In addition he was expected to assist in taking copies of evidence, to arrange that evidence so that the propriety of prosecution could be determined by the Crown law officers, to manage cases through the courts, and to pay those who undertook prosecutions.[64] The Solicitor had a salary of £60 per annum, and received other fees proportional to the work and expenditure undertaken. The holder of the office was usually a practising London solicitor, who combined the Mint post, which generated work intermittently, with his own regular business.

Like other eighteenth-century officials, and especially Mint officials, the Mint Solicitor was often accused of abusing his office. Those abuses and derelictions of duty which took place were not merely the consequence of a predisposition on the part of successive Solicitors to exploit the financial rewards of their position while ignoring its responsibilities. In the middle decades of the eighteenth century, the Mint Solicitor's activities were hampered by financial constraints, imposed by Parliament and the Exchequer, and by the supervision to which his activities were subjected by senior government law officers.

From 1709 to 1742 the money available for Mint prosecutions was limited to £400 per annum, irrespective of the amount of business brought to the Solicitor's attention.[65] An Act of 1742 raised this figure to £600.[66] The Solicitor's accounts for his expenditure were settled only after the end of the accounting year. If the expenses exceeded the limit there was no statutory provision for any payment at all. Fountaine Cooke, Mint Solicitor between 1748 and 1755, was forced into bankruptcy and emigration because the Treasury refused to pay any of the money owing to him for prosecutions in years when his expenditure had exceeded the £600. In 1764 he claimed he was still owed £1220. His accounts were not finally settled until 1771.[67] His successor, William Chamberlayne, exceeded the £600 ceiling in his first full year of office, 1756, but thereafter kept his expenditure well within bounds. Between 1757 and 1769 it never exceeded the £600 limit, averaging £298 per annum.[68] Yet Chamberlayne suffered financial embarrassment too. Although a proportion of his expenditure was imprested to him before the passing of his annual accounts, the settlement of the balance was very slow. Thus in 1765 Chamberlayne was still owed £195 on his accounts for the previous three years, and, in 1770, £550 on the previous five years' accounts.[69]

Under these circumstances Chamberlayne positively discouraged business. The Marquis of Rockingham complained in the late 1760s that 'the Solicitor of the Mint, on some informations being communicated to him, declared that his salary did not allow him to carry on prosecutions'.[70] The Solicitor gained a widespread reputation for parsimony and negligence. Alderman Hewitt of Coventry, when investigating Thomas Lightowller and his associates in 1756, was warned by Mr Wyrley, a Warwickshire justice, not to 'be too forward in expences lest he should meet with the disappointment he had done, with respect to the due attendance upon my proceeding, as well as the repayment of my expences'. Hewitt later remarked, 'the business ended as Mr. Wyrley prognosticated'. Never paid by Chamberlayne for his expenses, he considered the Mint Solicitor had bungled the trials by failing to retain counsel and by unjustifiably allowing some of the accused to be discharged without trial.[71] The affair emphasizes the conflicting pressures that could make the Mint Solicitor's position an invidious one. According to the Solicitor's accounts, these prosecutions were dropped on the instructions of the attorney general, to whom the Solicitor had to submit all cases for approval before Mint finance and assistance could be provided.[72] Nevertheless, the opprobrium generated in the localities by such occurrences fell upon the Solicitor and was a considerable discouragement to the activity of local magistrates.

The Mint Solicitor himself had cause to suspect the competence and enthusiasm of local magistrates. Models of magisterial incompetence in coinage cases are not difficult to come by. In a Durham case in 1776 'the Justice who committed [the offenders], having omitted to bind the evidence to appear against them, they kept out of the way and the prisoners were necessarily discharged . . . for want of prosecution'.[73] A North Riding justice was berated on the occasion of an escape in 1773 'for not finding securer place of confinement for a traitor than *an alehouse*'.[74]

Most justices were more reliable than these, but their experience and characteristic methods of handling the bulk of their criminal business were not well suited to the distinctive demands of investigation and prosecution in a coinage case. They were accustomed, in most criminal cases, merely to process complaints and evidence brought before them by aggrieved parties. It was only occasionally that a magistrate directed the detailed investigation of an offence. Yet coinage cases often required the management of extensive detective work and sustained liaison with prosecutor and Mint Solicitor alike.

The standards of evidence that justices were accustomed to meet in their regular criminal business were determined by their personal experience, by discussion with colleagues or lawyers and by reference to law books, in particular the justices' manuals, such as Burn or Dalton.[75] Such standards could prove counterproductive in coinage cases. The evidential requirements of the courts were far more stringent than the letter of the law indicated. Moreover, the physical evidence of coining, that was so often crucial in court, was notoriously difficult for the layman to understand. Only a handful of provincial justices had any direct experience of capital coinage cases because in most localities prosecutions were never common. The unfamiliarity of magistrates with such cases was often the immediate reason for calling in the Mint Solicitor.

The variety of legal and institutional constraints on the prosecution of capital coinage suspects, combined with the ability of offenders to conceal their activities, made it difficult to prosecute successfully in the mid eighteenth century. This is not to suggest that coiners were left to ply their trade unhindered. Between 1732 and 1769, there are only four years for which the Solicitors' accounts survive, when no capital prosecution is recorded. Moreover, the convicted offender had good reason to fear a capital sentence, for the proportion of capital coinage convicts who actually suffered at the gallows was much higher than the equivalent proportion of those convicted of other capital offences against property.[76] However, after 1757, when William Chamberlayne instituted his restrictive policy on prosecution expenses, the number of cases that came to court was strictly limited. The combination of Chamberlayne's efforts to discourage business with the many other disincentives to prosecution ensured that those who abused the gold and silver coinage in the 1760s enjoyed considerable immunity from the rigours of the law.

At no point in the eighteenth century was the condition of the gold coin in circulation as poor as in the 1760s and early 1770s. Throughout these years gold bullion prices were constantly well in excess of the Mint price for gold. Cash continued in short supply. Joseph Wood's extraordinary profits between 1755 and 1757 had been facilitated by the willingness of London bankers to accept guineas deficient by 10d. or 14d. in order to dispose of country bills of doubtful origin.[77] The far more extensive clipping and coining operations carried on in the West Riding of Yorkshire and adjacent areas of Lancashire in the 1760s were also dependent on an exceptional demand for cash, but in other respects they were very different from the undertakings of Thomas Lightowller or Joseph Wood.[78] In Yorkshire clipping and coining were combined, the clippings being remanufactured, often with no adulteration, into counterfeit moidores and other gold coins. Mint-struck gold coins were diminished by clipping 'to an amazing degree',[79] and guineas generally recirculated that were 5s. 3d. or 5s. 4d. deficient, over five times the deficiency that had ensured such huge profits for Joseph Wood. In the coining heartland, broadly the area between Halifax and Rochdale, the illegal trade was sustained by massive and active popular support. Such support allowed the trade to proceed in a remarkably overt manner. Accessibility and popular support combined to underpin the lavish prosperity of the business. Indeed, so much did it prosper that by 1773 a Norwich M P could complain to his Yorkshire nephew of a plague of diminished guineas in Norfolk, the worst of which, 'the bad guineas wanting 2/6d and 3/-, are called Yorkshire guineas'.[80] Good money followed bad and Yorkshire set the pace for the debasement of the national circulation.

Various commentators noted that clipping and coining were new to the Halifax area in the 1760s, and strictly limited to it. The Mint Solicitor recorded that it was only 'in the summer of 1765 that I then began to hear vast complaints out of Yorkshire'.[81] The first comment in the local press did not appear until 1768, and in 1769 coining was still described as a 'manufacture lately established in this country'.[82] In 1755 and 1756 Thomas Lightowller's associates had been active in the Craven area of Yorkshire, thirty miles north-west of Halifax, and in Leeds, but their operations did not involve clipping.[83] There were no prosecutions for capital coinage offences in the Halifax area in the thirty years before 1765.[84] However, by

the years 1767, '68, and '69 the gold coin circulated in and about Halifax was greatly diminished, and numbers of counterfeit moidores and other pieces were constantly passed in payment, . . . [which] were circulated throughout the neighbourhood, but were not payable elsewhere.[85]

An irate correspondent to the Leeds newspapers reported in 1769 that 'this re-manufactured gold coin will pass in payment nowhere but in this manufacturing country'.[86]

The success of this highly localized and distinctive coining enterprise was based on the peculiar opportunities for clipping and coining which the regional economy generated during the 1760s. The purely local predisposition to accept exceptionally diminished and counterfeit coin was itself the result of an acute local shortage of specie in that decade. The Mint Solicitor later pointed out that in the area about Halifax 'the want of cash for circulation gave a currency to everything that bore the face of a guinea'.[87] 'I found the great demand for cash to be such that the [difficulty] of getting induced everybody to overlook the smallness. I found everybody afraid to make an objection to the cash for fear of not being supplied with it.'[88]

Shortage of cash of all kinds was, of course, a national complaint throughout the eighteenth century. But the particular degree of shortage in the West Riding in the 1760s can be explained, at least in part, by the vicissitudes suffered by the region's staple industry in those years.

The town of Halifax was one of the chief market centres for the West Riding woollen and worsted industry. This manufacture dominated a belt of country running west from Leeds and Wakefield, up the valleys of the river Aire and Calder and their tributaries, and across the intervening hills. The trade continued uninterrupted through the Pennine moorlands into the Colne, Rossendale and Rochdale districts of Lancashire. Defoe, writing in the 1720s, described this textile country as 'one of the most populous parts of Britain, London and the adjacent parts excepted'.[89] This description held true forty years later. Between the principal market-towns, settlement was scattered thickly across all except the highest hills (see the plate of Jeffrey's 1775 map of Yorkshire). Many families were able to combine handloom weaving or other domestic textile employment with agricultural pursuits, but by the second half of the eighteenth century agricultural by-employment was declining, especially in the worsted branch. The prosperity of the population of the area depended overwhelmingly on its staple industry.

Within the broad swathe of this textile region, the industry was geographically specialized. The area between Halifax, Huddersfield and Rochdale had traditionally been the stronghold of the narrow cloth manufacture. Kersey, a coarse cloth used for army uniforms and clothing the poor, was the principal variety of narrow cloth produced. But from the early eighteenth century the district between and to the north of Halifax and Rochdale became dominated increasingly by the manufacture of worsteds.[90] By 1770, the West Riding worsted industry, concentrated in this district, vied with that of Norwich, the traditional seat of the industry.[91]

Woollen and worsted production in the West Riding relied disproportionately on export markets.[92] This was to bring considerable difficulties during the 1760s. North America was the principal market for Yorkshire worsted exports and, during the Seven Years War, trade had flourished.[93] A cloth manufacturer wrote to the *York Courant* in December 1765 to point out that 'while the war lasted we had a brisk trade, goods sold well, and were generally wanted (for very obvious reasons)'. However, by 1765, Yorkshire manufactories were 'in a languishing condition, more especially that part of them in the worsted way'.[94] This recession he explained as the product of readjustment to peacetime conditions. Peace brought to an end the artificially inflated prices that had obtained under conditions of wartime demand.

Yorkshire's worsted industry was not the only section of the British

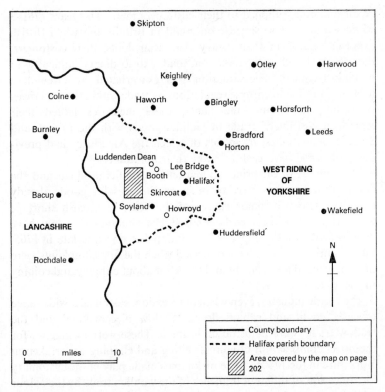

The Lancashire–West Riding border

economy to suffer recession in the mid 1760s. The national economy entered a depressed phase with the major slump of 1761–3, which was relieved only by the short-lived post-war boom in 1764.[95] However, the West Riding worsted trade suffered especially badly, as a result of its dependence on the North American market. American purchasing power underwent a severe cut with the reduction of military expenditures in the colonies at the end of the war. American consumption of British goods was also hard hit by the British slump and the stagnation that followed. Even those colonies which were not major direct exporters to the mother country were profoundly affected, as a consequence of their trade with the colonies which did rely on British markets.

The slump was particularly severe for British exporters to North America because, during the rapid expansion of their trade to the colonies in the preceding decade, they had extended unprecedented credit on goods supplied to their customers there. The years 1761–3 witnessed an intense squeeze on credit in Britain, but when British exporters called in their heavy American debts, their customers, themselves faced with recession, had extraordinary difficulty in making payment. The situation was exacerbated by Grenville's measures in 1763 to enforce regulations on trade within the Americas. According to Halifax merchants, these measures halted their American customers' trade in Halifax goods with the French and Spanish West Indies, by means of which the Americans had previously obtained hard cash to make their remittances.[96]

The collapse of the principal market for Halifax products and the failure by customers there to make remittances for goods already supplied were two major causes of the acute local cash shortage which developed in the early 1760s.[97] The situation can only have deteriorated with the impact of the Stamp Act boycotts late in 1765. Significantly, this was the very period when the first complaints were made to central government and the Mint about clipping and coining in the area.

The textile industry, even when in recession, sustained a wide range of cash, credit and capital flows. 'Yellow piecemaking' and the 'yellow trade' were parasitic upon them. These were nicknames for the novel combination of counterfeiting and clipping undertaken in Yorkshire in the 1760s.[98] The nicknames made play of the customary identification of different branches of the woollen trade by the colour of the cloth produced, as in 'white kerseymaking'. They emphasize the extent to which coining was regarded by the local population as a legitimate business equivalent to the local wool textile trade. In fact the yellow trade was a sophisticated illegal business, which in some aspects of its organization mirrored the local staple industry.

To describe the yellow trade as an illegal business is not to apply a gratuitous label. There are important distinctions to be made between different types of eighteenth-century criminal organization. Criminal activities from horse-stealing to poaching were frequently undertaken (though by no means invariably) by groups of offenders, who used a set of well-established procedures to exploit opportunities inherent in the legitimate order. The yellow trade differed from most of those in the sophistication of its organization, and, more importantly, in the emphatically commercial character of its relationship with the population at large.

That relationship is best illustrated if the yellow trade is contrasted with Thomas Lightowller's activities in the 1750s. At that period

Lightowller manufactured counterfeits of silver and gold coins from base metals. They were intrinsically almost worthless and were not knowingly accepted by the public. The poor condition of legitimate coin facilitated the deceitful circulation of such counterfeits. Lightowller used this opportunity to perpetrate a barefaced cheat upon the public.

By contrast, the entrepreneurs of the yellow trade offered the public in the Halifax locality a product and a novel source of income which, together, were widely marketable. The yellow piece-makers manufactured counterfeits not from worthless base metals, but from gold. These counterfeits had an intrinsic bullion value not far short of that which characterized legitimate gold coins in circulation in the 1760s. Acute local cash shortage ensured that they were generally, if sometimes reluctantly, accepted in circulation. Indeed, in the locality, they enjoyed a similar currency to the underweight legitimate coinage, which they closely matched in gold content. Like the latter, they were paid and received at face value, or, in bulk, at a slight discount.

The ready circulation of these counterfeits was further encouraged by their association with the clipping branch of the yellow trade. Heavily clipped gold coins circulated remarkably freely in the locality as a consequence of the peculiar severity of cash shortage there. This presented local people with a widely accessible method of supplementing their incomes at a time of economic hardship. To realize a cash profit from this source they were dependent on the yellow piece-makers, who used clippings as raw material for their counterfeits. The yellow piece-makers purchased clippings direct from the public and offered a premium to anyone who could lend them legitimate gold coin of sufficient quality to clip. Recompense was naturally made in clipped or counterfeit coin, thereby enhancing the acceptability of that coin in local circulation.

The yellow trade, therefore, resembled smuggling, the greatest eighteenth-century illegal business, in that it took commercial advantage of opportunities generated by the workings of government monopoly. It differed from the trade in contraband because it was strongly localized and flourished only briefly. Yet these limitations permit a detailed and comprehensive account of its organization as an illegal business. Such an account is essential in order to understand the popular support enjoyed by the yellow trade and the obstacles which the trade presented to the application of the criminal law against its practitioners.

The organization of the yellow trade as an illegal business is here assessed from three distinct perspectives. First, as a structure of activities, in which individuals participated in different ways: for example, in the supply of raw materials, in their manufacture and in the distribution of the product. Second, as an association of individuals, with reference, for instance, to their social background, internal differentiation and cohesiveness. Third, as a specifically illegal enterprise which faced peculiar problems of risk reduction. Although distinct, these three perspectives should not be regarded as independent of each other, for no one aspect of the organization of the enterprise can be understood except in relation to the others.[99]

The outstanding feature of the organization of the yellow trade as a structure of activities was the symbiosis between coining and clipping. Coining, or yellow piece-making, required specialized skills and facilities if output was to be maximized. It was therefore dominated by a few leading entrepreneurs. The manufacturing activity of this few depended on a multitude of individuals throughout the locality who never coined but supplied clippings or coin to clip. It was an advantage unique to the Yorkshire coiner that this multitude was simultaneously both customer for his manufactures and supplier of his raw material. It has already been pointed out that those who supplied clippings, or coin to clip, were themselves dependent upon the coiner to realize a cash profit. This relationship between coining and clipping was the key to the massive penetration of local circuits of cash and paper currency, which the yellow trade had achieved by the late 1760s.

Clipping involved cutting a thin sliver of gold from the edge of a guinea, restoring the milling with a file and then returning the diminished coin into circulation. Jonas Tillotson, a shalloonmaker, described the procedure. The landlord of the Wheatsheaf in Halifax, John Bates, had clipped a guinea to convince Tillotson 'how beneficial a branch [of trade] it was'. The coin was

clipp'd with a common pair of large scissors and was afterwards filed even at the edges, and then milled by being turned upon the edge upon a cross cut file and by striking upon the upper part of the guinea, or otherwise weighing upon it with a nicked piece of wood as it was turned round upon the file.

Bates cut gold worth two shillings or half a crown from the guinea.[100] Guineas were clipped to a deficiency of 5s. 3d. or 5s. 4d., but it was difficult to get guineas that were not already underweight by two shillings.[101] Between 15s. 6d. and 16s. was the lowest acceptable weight for recirculation. John Sutcliffe clipped some guineas to such an extent that they were worth, in gold content, under 15s. 6d., 'so little that [they] would not be paid'; he had to beat them out with an axe head 'and afterwards crooken them so that they looked large enough and was easily paid'.[102]

Clipping was an easily accessible activity, though a skill of a sort. A virtuoso like James Green had a 'very strong' pair of scissors specially obtained from Sheffield.[103] On the other hand the diffident Joseph Murgatroyd was anxious that a more expert man should 'take notice whether or no I do them as well as other persons'.[104] Yet it was easily learnt, and as the Mint Solicitor pointed out, 'every wool-comber in the country was possessed of everything necessary . . . his implements of trade did all the business'.[105] Under other circumstances disposing of the gold so obtained would have involved a considerable risk, but the clipping woolcomber 'easily avoided that risk by carry-ing the produce of four guineas to a Mint hard by, of which there were two or three, where for a shilling he could have it coined into half a guinea'.[106]

Because clipping was so easily learnt and relatively free of risk, 'the middling sort, finding that a light guinea was as good to them as a heavy one, could not resist the temptation, but diminished every one they got before they parted with it'.[107] However, the opportunity to come by gold coin that could be clipped was available to men of widely differing degrees of wealth. Poor weavers and woolcombers were often paid intermittently, or in groups, with large denomination gold coins, which they had every opportunity to clip. Moreover, a weaver or woolcomber could partake of the benefits of the yellow trade on a considerable scale by soliciting heavy gold coin for clip-ping. It was 'a constant, regular trade to give twenty shillings for the use of twenty guineas for a couple of hours. Two shillings for two guineas for half an hour'.[108] Over two shillings' worth of gold were usually clipped from each guinea, ensuring a considerable profit to the clipper, at a time when a weaver might earn only seven shillings a week, if regularly employed.[109]

Enormous income from clipping was available to those who handled large quantities of cash in the course of legitimate business. In the Halifax area such men were mainly wool textile manufacturers and merchants. Some clipped their own coin. Samuel Magson, a Skircoat merchant, was taught to clip by a leading coiner, and thenceforth sold him the clippings.[110] However, for many it was both convenient and reduced risk to contract this work out, like various processes in the textile industry. John Thomas, a manufacturer of Burnt Stubb in

Erringden township, regularly employed a man to take gold for clipping to John Wilcock, a nearby farmer and weaver.[111]

Merchants and manufacturers could use commercial credit facilities to procure coin for clipping. In 1768 Samuel Magson supplied a
fellow merchant with approximately £150 in gold coin for clipping,
obtained at York on bills of exchange. Magson also borrowed £50 to
£60 to clip himself from Brian Dempsey, a Halifax merchant, which
Magson repaid via his drawing rights on London. In 1765 Dempsey
had made available £300 in cash to a Halifax watchmaker for the
same purpose, which was to be repaid in bills or cash. Magson paid
Dempsey a premium of 6d. per guinea (2.38 per cent), a small sum
by prevailing standards. When later questioned, Dempsey was at
pains to stress that, although he well suspected the gold would be
clipped, the affair had the character of a normal business transaction,
'cash bearing a premium for bills at the time'.[112] A Lancashire magistrate pointed out that many of those involved were 'considerable
people, . . . both in property and iniquity'.[113]

The coiner provided the specialized services on which ultimately
depended the conversion of clippings into a cash profit. He was the
lynchpin of the illegal business system. Counterfeiting from base
metals was conspicuous by its rarity in the Halifax–Rochdale area in
the 1760s.[114] Counterfeits were usually produced from clippings
without adulteration, although small amounts of silver and copper,
cut from coins, were sometimes mixed with the gold. The counterfeits were deficient as to weight by comparison with the face value of
the coins they imitated. Counterfeit moidores, with a face value of
27s., usually contained gold worth only 22s.[115] However, this deficiency was not much greater than that of some of the underweight
Mint coin, which circulated freely in the locality at face value.
Moidores were the coin most frequently counterfeited, but other
Portuguese denominations and guineas, half guineas and quarter
guineas were imitated too. The only other counterfeiting process
widely resorted to was to heat up guineas, half and quarter guineas
and overstamp them with the die of a moidore, half or quarter
moidore, thereby increasing their face value by 30 per cent.[116]

Overstamping guinea denominations could, with appropriate
equipment, be undertaken in any house with a fire. One peripatetic
coiner carried moidore dies, a pocket anvil and a pocket hammer for
this purpose.[117] Small-scale production of crude counterfeits from
clippings was hardly more demanding. It involved a three-stage process. First, the clippings were melted down into small gold buttons,

of a size appropriate to the coin to be imitated. Second, these buttons were hammered into flat plates, while still warm. Third, the warm plates were inserted between a pair of coining dies and the impression struck by a hammer blow on the upper die (see the plate of a pair of dies). However, the manufacture of good quality counterfeits on a large scale could be accomplished most efficiently at a permanent establishment, which could provide a fixed block for striking the dies and rollers to prepare blanks for stamping, along with other specialized equipment, such as crucibles, files and emery dust. An establishment of this character called for a permanent site and considerable capital investment, both to provide equipment and to minimize the increased risk which permanency entailed.

It was reported in 1769 that 'there were not above four shops where they coined'.[118] One such establishment was the house belonging to William Varley, isolated in an area of dense but scattered settlement on South Owram Bank, overlooking the town of Halifax. It was colloquially known as the 'Halifax Mint'. It contained 'a stone near the fire under which there were several crucibles'. There was also a hammer fixed into the side of the house, which was designed to strike a die positioned in a wood and iron block. The block itself fitted into a special socket in an upturned flagstone. The equipment was so designed that when everything had been replaced 'nobody could see that any such business had been carried on there'. Indeed security was so important that 'if they were at work, there would be an old woman standing at the door watching'.[119] The Mint Solicitor visited an establishment of this kind and found 'the situation such that it was impossible for anybody to come near the house, but they must be seen at a distance of half a mile. They must be seen time enough to get everything out of the house'.[120]

Though they dominated production, these mint masters never had a monopoly on coining. There were always many more men in possession of coining tools than operated permanent and well-established mints. Coining dies were both manufactured and marketed in the Halifax–Rochdale district. The area was an established centre for the manufacture of clocks and watches, a trade which generated skills appropriate to die-making.[121] Thomas Sunderland, who 'made for many of the coiners', was a clock engraver and painter of considerable ability.[122] He manufactured dies for sale, offering a commission of one-third of the selling price to those who would market his products.[123] He charged £2 for a pair of moidore dies.[124] Others with less appropriate skills learnt to make dies too, including Robert Iredale, a friend of Sunderland's and a woolcomber, and Joseph Shaw, a weaver.[125] Sunderland cut durable dies from iron or steel, but many were crudely made from spelter (zinc) and had a very short working life.[126] Dies were much sought after and were rented out, sometimes in conjunction with other facilities at an illegal coining shop.[127]

The risks that most eighteenth-century counterfeiters were obliged to undergo in order to pass off their product were considerably reduced in the yellow trade with its dependence upon clipping. The man who used the services of a coiner to make up his clippings into counterfeits had to pay them off himself. He also had to recirculate the coin he had clipped. Those who obtained a novel form of interest by hiring out their cash for clipping were repaid in clipped or counterfeit coin.[128] For a busy manufacturer who had large quantities of coin clipped, it was both convenient and it reduced risk to employ someone to dispose of the diminished coin. John Thomas, the manufacturer from Burnt Stubb who used a man to deliver his coin for clipping, employed the same man to put it off.[129] Of course, by acquiring appropriate change, passing off could itself become a source of more coin to clip.[130]

The mutual dependence of clipping and coining in the yellow trade dictated that the relationship of the Yorkshire coiner with his public was very different from Thomas Lightowller's. Lightowller shared his profits only with his immediate accomplices and a select group of putters-off. In the Yorkshire operation the financial benefits of coining were extensively diffused. Yet the opportunities which the yellow trade offered for profit to a vast multitude in the locality, should not obscure the special status held by the few great entrepreneurs of the trade. The novel source of income enjoyed by that multitude was especially dependent on the skills and facilities that the leading mint masters commanded. With the assistance of small coteries of trusted associates, they used this command to exploit every avenue for profit which the business offered.

The mint masters provided a commission coining service for those who clipped independently, and instruction in how to clip for the uninitiated. At the same time, they themselves aggressively solicited coin to clip. This dual approach secured maximum penetration of the gold circulation in the immediate locality and beyond. Maximum penetration was essential, because, on average, clippings from twelve guineas were required to produce a single counterfeit moidore. Therefore the mint masters' profits, as indeed the prosperity of the yellow trade as a whole, depended on a continuous supply of heavy coin to clip. This was assured by encouraging the individual enterprise of a large proportion of the local population and combining it with the leading coiners' own endeavours, in particular their appropriation of the commercial paper circulation in the area. Large Yorkshire and Lancashire manufacturers already made a practice of scouring the country for cash to pay their work-force.[131] It has been noted that the yellow trade offered them an opportunity to use coin they could procure to obtain what amounted to a novel form of interest. Nineteenth-century local historians asserted that the leading coiners effectively operated as a banking company for manufacturers.[132] Certainly they systematically appropriated the manufacturers' bills of exchange in order to obtain heavy gold from outside the coining heartland. A letter from Halifax published in the Leeds newspapers in July 1769 describes the practice with a bitter humour:

These very ingenious gentlemen ingross the bills drawn upon London, through the persuasive influence of a large discount upon their newly-reformed coin, with its auxiliary numbers begot upon it and, by an extensive correspondence, are in a fair way of drawing half the gold in the two Kingdoms into this happy country, with giving still larger premiums with the bills for gold coin (brought out of distant parts) that has not partook of their improvements.[133]

The rewards available to those at the apex of the hierarchy of production in the yellow trade must have been considerable. The local author of a reply to the letter quoted above asserted that he 'could produce several instances of persons who, a few years since, had scarce the necessaries of life, and can now, by their skill and industry in the gold trade, live at the rate of above a hundred a year'.[134]

The structures of association which sustained these large profits are not easily penetrated by the historian. Information about the yellow trade derives principally from sources associated with the concerted effort to suppress it in 1769 and 1770. This material is a reliable guide to the various activities which comprised the illegal business at that period. It is a less trustworthy source for the background and relationships of those individuals who participated in the trade.

The most detailed accounts of individual involvement are found in nearly a hundred depositions taken before local magistrates between 1765 and 1773.[135] The shortcomings of these accounts are not simply the product of deponents' characteristic tendency to confirm a magistrate's expectations in their testimony. The authorities' search for evidence was biased towards the leading coining shop proprietors and their close associates. While these groups appear repeatedly in depositions, those who supplied clippings or coin to clip are probably underrepresented. Hence these sources almost certainly mask the numbers of merchants and other men of great wealth involved in the trade. Their characteristic role was said to be the supply of coin for clipping, which was an infrequent ground for accusation, criminal intent being so hard to prove. Those depositions taken in the autumn and winter of 1769–70 (the majority) form such a tangled web of accusation and counter-accusation that the credibility of evidence against any particular individual is often in doubt. As the surviving depositions are only a proportion of the original series, the difficulty is compounded.[136] In assessing the occupational profile of those incriminated between 1765 and 1773, these shortcomings must be taken into account.

Occupational information survives for eighty individuals from the Halifax–Rochdale area, who were accused in depositions, in the courts or in the press of capital offences against the coin, between 1764 and 1773 (see the table facing). Although individual accusations may have been false, it is probable that the vast majority of those accused had been involved in the yellow trade in some capacity. However, the utility of the available descriptions of occupation is compromised by the wide variations of status and income within particular trades. The most important victim of such ambiguity is the key distinction between employer and employee in the textile industry.

The staple worsted and kersey industries of the Halifax–Rochdale area were characterized by marked, though not extreme, differentiation between master and men. A few manufacturers commanded enormous enterprises and great wealth. Sam Hill of Soyland enjoyed an average turnover of £30,000 per annum between 1744 and 1750.[137] More typical of the scale of industrial organization was the business of Robert Heaton, of Ponden Hall near Haworth. In the later 1760s Heaton's annual output of worsted cloths amounted to between 500 and 600 pieces, worth from £800 to £1000.[138]

A *minimum* estimate of the work-force required to sustain this output would include three woolcombers and nine weavers, all men, and thirty-five spinners, mainly women and children.[139] Yet Heaton styled himself merely a 'woolcomber', a description, which, if it appeared in a deposition, would offer no possibility of distinguishing him from his employees. Heaton's case would suggest that *woolcomber* was a self-description as acceptable to the small manufacturer as the unambiguous 'stuffmaker' or 'piecemaker'. If an estimate of the proportion of small manufacturers among the accused is based

Occupations of those accused of clipping, coining or possession of coining tools in the Halifax–Rochdale area, 1764 to July 1773, for whom occupational information is available[140]

Textile occupations

Clothier	4
Master cloth dresser	1
Piecemaker (stuffmaker/shalloonmaker/kerseymaker/manufacturer)	14
Dealer in yarn or wool	2
Woolcomber	7
Weaver	24
	—
Total	52

Other occupations, including cases of dual occupation in textile and non-textile activities

Farmer	1
Farmer/weaver	3
Husbandman/weaver	1
Miller	1
Innkeeper	10
Butcher	3
Clockmaker	2
Painter/engraver	2
Tanner	1
Carpenter	1
Healdstriker/staymaker	1
Badger/weaver	1
Labourer/charcoal burner	1
	—
Total	28

on these unambiguous descriptions of occupation alone, it must be recognized as potentially deficient.

The most striking feature of the occupational profile of the accused when set against the local occupational structure (see appendix, pages 308–9), is the extremely high proportion of those *explicitly* described as small manufacturers among those accused men who resided outside the town of Halifax itself. On the other hand the proportion of those described as weaver is relatively low. Also striking is the high proportion, among those accused men resident in the town of Halifax, of retailers, craftsmen and middlemen. They comprised 26 per cent of all the accused and nearly half of their number were innkeepers. Bearing in mind that the proportion of small manufacturers may well be an underestimate (for the reasons set out above), the prominence of men of small capital is very marked.[141] The yellow trade was never the preserve of the very poor, although opportunities for their participation were legion. It revolved around money and, in particular, transfers of cash. Comment in the Leeds newspapers confirms that innkeepers were prominently involved.[142] With their traditional control of local systems of credit, innkeepers were well placed to manipulate small cash transactions for the purposes of the yellow trade.

Detailed information about the lives and characters of the accused is sparse. The few individuals whose lives are particularly well documented were not necessarily representative of the accused as a whole. However, several significant features do emerge.

A number of the accused were men with respectable reputations. Those who supplied coin to clip and clippings included established local merchants and tradesmen, and even an overseer of the poor. William Roberts, a Bacup innkeeper committed for clipping, was described as having previously been 'a man of good instance'.[143] James Oldfield, hanged for coining in 1770, was a manufacturer and founder member of the Independent church at Booth in Midgeley township.[144] All this appears to confirm a report in the *Manchester Mercury* in May 1770 that the characters of many of those involved in coining in the Halifax locality had previously been 'fair and unquestionable'.[145]

The yellow trade also enjoyed the participation of minor local office holders under the law. A deputy constable of Halifax town was among offenders who absconded in 1769, and two Halifax bailiffs were accused of clipping.[146] Bum-bailiffs and hired constables were hardly figures of respect in eighteenth-century England, but their incorporation among the fraternity of the yellow trade posed important obstacles to the use of the law against its practitioners.

The careers of some of the accused directly reflect the vicissitudes suffered by the local textile industry during the later 1760s.[147] One accused merchant and one accused master woolcomber were bankrupts, while two of the accused worsted piecemakers had been imprisoned for debt.[148] If their involvement in the yellow trade was a response to their commercial difficulties, as one of the bankrupts claimed, this may be a significant indication of the predicament and motivation of other businessmen involved in the trade.[149] However, it is equally possible that they overextended their credit in order to secure coin for clipping.

Eighteenth-century commentators were apt to use the term 'gang', the customary designation for any collectivity of criminals, to describe the character of the association between the yellow traders. The local newspapers chose to group all the practitioners of such a strongly localized form of illegal activity in a single gang.[150] No doubt, under duress, the yellow traders could act in concert. In 1769, when it was considered necessary to murder an interfering supervisor of excise at Halifax, the killers were paid by subscription among coiners throughout the area, including Halifax, Leeds, Bradford, Otley, Bingley, Keighley, Colne and Burnley.[151] However, for the purposes of their regular business, the leading practitioners of the yellow trade were grouped into a number of loose coteries, each of which was associated with a particular shop and its proprietor.

These groups of associates around each coining shop were geographically differentiated and heirarchical in internal structure. Their characteristics are well illustrated by the group associated with David Hartley. Hartley lived and coined at Bell House, high on the moor edge overlooking the Turvin valley, some six miles west of the town of Halifax. The son of a local family, he was the district's outstanding coining entrepreneur. The Mint Solicitor was told by an informant that Hartley 'was one of the first persons that brought this unhappy thing into this country, which it is said he learnt at Birmingham, where I believe it is carried on to perfection'.[152]

The coterie surrounding David Hartley had an identity distinct from other groups. To those yellow traders living near Halifax town, he and his associates were sometimes described as the 'Turviners', after their native valley, but they were better known as the 'upper hand people' and their locality as the 'upper hand country'.[153] Of 156 individuals in the Halifax–Rochdale area who were accused between 1765 and 1773 of illegal involvement in the yellow trade and were identified by township of residence, sixty-six lived in one of the three townships adjoining the Turvin valley. Precise residence is known for thirty-four of that sixty-six (see the map on pages 202–3). The distribution of the thirty-four suggests that many of the 'upper hand people' were close neighbours, particularly those who occupied farmsteads on the moor edge to the west of the valley. Links between neighbours, friends and acquaintances were reinforced by the bonds of kinship and employment which permeated such a community. Thomas Spencer was brother-in-law to Thomas Clayton, a leading coiner.

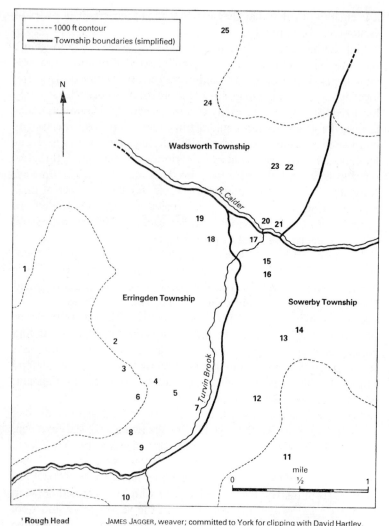

¹ **Rough Head**	JAMES JAGGER, weaver; committed to York for clipping with David Hartley, October 1769
² **Bell House**	DAVID HARTLEY, 'King David', weaver; hanged for coining, April 1769
³ **Keelham**	JOHN WILCOCK, farmer and weaver; accused of clipping; absconded winter 1769/70
⁴ **Crumber Hill**	DANIEL GREENWOOD, weaver; committed to York for clipping, January 1770
⁵ **Sandy Pickle**	BETTY CROSSLEY, spinner; wife of William Crossley; accused of paying to have clipped coins put off
⁶ **High Green**	THOMAS DEWHIRST, listed as a suspected coining offender
⁷ **Paper Mill**	JAMES WHITELEY, accused of putting off bad guineas and listed as a suspected coining offender
⁸ **Hill Top**	DAVID GREENWOOD, white kerseymaker; accused of coining; hedge solicitor to King David
⁹ **Old Cragg**	JOHN DEWHIRST, stuffweaver; accused of clipping

[10] **Turley**	JOHN HEAP, listed as a suspected coining offender WILLIAM HELLIWELL, accused of going to Preston to obtain heavy guineas for clipping
[11] **Collinbob**	JAMES BROOK, listed as a suspected coining offender
[12] **Wood**	ABRAHAM KERSHAW, worsted dealer; acquitted of uttering counterfeit guineas at Leeds borough quarter sessions, April 1769 JAMES KERSHAW, listed as a suspected coining offender
[13] **Bent**	JOHN LISTER, listed as a suspected coining offender
[14] **Stannery End**	THOMAS CLAYTON, 'Royal Clayton', worsted stuffmaker; accused of clipping; absconded September 1769 MATTHEW NORMANTON, worsted stuffweaver; accused of clipping; one of the murderers of William Deighton, Halifax supervisor of excise
[15] **New House**	THOMAS SPENCER, brother-in-law of King David, weaver; organizer of Deighton's murder
[16] **Hall Gate**	JAMES BROADBENT, charcoal burner and weaver; informer against 'upper hand country' coining offenders
[17] **Elphaborough Hall**	ISAAC HARTLEY, 'Duke of York' and brother of King David, yeoman; absconded in winter 1769/70; organizer of Deighton's murder
[18] **Buckley Gate**	JOSEPH BROADBENT, 'Belch', weaver; informer against coining offenders
[19] **Burnt Stubb**	JOHN THOMAS, piecemaker; accused of sending coin to John Wilcock (see 4 above) for clipping
[20] **The 'Dusty Miller'** Mytholmroyd Bridge	THOMAS BROADBENT, uncle by marriage of Matthew Normanton (see 15 above), innkeeper; committed to York in January 1770 for the rescue from custody of a coining suspect
[21] **Mytholmroyd Bridge**	JOHN SUTCLIFFE; accused of clipping
[22] **Wadsworth Banks**	THOMAS GREENWOOD; 'Great Tom o' the Bank', piece maker; committed to York for clipping, December 1769 ROBERT THOMAS, labourer; brother-in-law of Thomas Clayton (see 14 above), one of Deighton's murderers
[23] **Wadsworthrow**	JOHN PICKLES, farmer and double-piece weaver; accused of clipping; committed to York, September 1769
[24] **Armory Well**	JOHN SLADDIN, weaver; travelled through the coining districts to collect money to pay for Deighton's murder, autumn 1769
[25] **Popples**	DANIEL GREENWOOD, weaver; committed to York, December 1769; died in York Castle while awaiting trial

NOTE: The area covered by this map is indicated on the map on page 189. It also appears on the extreme right of that portion of Thomas Jeffrey's map of Yorkshire shown in the section of plates. The plate illustrates the pattern of late eighteenth-century settlement in the locality, of which the residences listed above formed a part.

The 'upper hand country'. Known places of residence for those accused and their associates[154]

Matthew Normanton worked for Clayton as a weaver. Execution literature and depositions provide outline life-histories for Thomas, Normanton and Spencer.[155] They emerge as men rooted in the Turvin locality. Apart from Spencer, who left to serve in the infantry during the Seven Years War, they passed their whole lives in the area.

David Hartley was renowned throughout the coining districts as 'King David'. This dignity was considered 'an honorary reward for saving his country from the formidable enemy – Poverty'.[156] In depositions, the justices' clerks were repeatedly obliged to append 'David Hartley' to the royal title used by their informants, in a hopeless battle to contain popular respect for this monarch. 'King David's' brothers were the 'Duke of York' and the 'Duke of Edinburgh', and Thomas Clayton, a close associate, was popularly 'Royal' Clayton.[157] The proliferation of royal nicknames suggests a hierarchy of authority among the 'upper hand people'.

King David was not the only coining monarch. He was only one of 'two Gentlemen, of moderate fortunes . . . dignified with the title of Kings'.[158] The identity of the other crowned head is unknown. However, other coining shop masters reigned over local coteries similar to Hartley's. The evidence available for these groups illustrates some aspects of their internal working relationships, which are not available for the Turviners. Only a few intimates were permitted, or competent, to use all the facilities of a coining shop. Only six men appear accused in the depositions of actually having coined at William Varley's 'Halifax Mint', and eight at Isaac Dewhirst's.[159] A larger number of associates, who probably never coined, came to the mints in order to have coin clipped, or clippings made up into counterfeits. Ten men were accused of having visited Isaac Dewhirst's to have commission work of this kind undertaken. How firm their allegiance was to a particular coining shop is unclear, although the necessity of mutual confidence between proprietor and client probably called for an established and consistent relationship.

The coteries around each mint, though distinct, were never exclusive, at any level. John Bates, a Halifax innkeeper, used facilities at William Varley's, Isaac Dewhirst's, John Cockroft's and his own home both to clip and coin.[160] Joshua Brigg, a woolcomber from Halifax town, sent clippings to the 'upper hand country', to be made into counterfeits by King David, but he also did business with intimates of coining shops nearer Halifax.[161] As early as 1765, King David had deliberately established contacts in the vicinity of Halifax town with wealthy men, such as Joshua Stancliffe, a watchmaker, and

Samuel Magson, the Skircoat merchant, who could supply coin and bills.[162] His early command of such relationships was probably the key to his pre-eminence. This interlocking set of associations spread through Halifax parish and beyond. The Mint Solicitor was informed of 'a set of people that came from Howorth [sic] to the Spread Eagle in Halifax . . . [who] will lead you into the parishes of Howorth, Bradford, Leeds, and Wakefield, and [Thomas] Sunderland, if he will inform, will bring you into Hodersfield [sic] and other parts of the country'.[163] The attention which the legal records, in particular, focus on Halifax parish, and certain groups of coiners within it, may therefore be unrepresentative, although Halifax and Rochdale were without doubt 'the great marts of this new commerce'.[164]

As an illegal business the yellow trade faced risks not associated with legitimate commercial activity. Yet certain branches of the trade were carried on remarkably overtly, in particular clipping and dealing in heavy coin and bills. Indeed, easy public access at this level was vital for the trade's continuing prosperity. It was reported in 1768 of the many tradesmen, manufacturers and merchants who took diminished gold for bills, that 'they do this in the face of the sun, with their eyes open; and what is worse, they suffer both the deceit and the deceiver to pass with impunity'.[165] A man uninitiated in the mysteries of clipping 'might light of chaps in many places by all reports';[166] all that was required was a visit to an inn frequented by reputed clippers. The only precaution adopted was to wait for the particular room in the inn to be vacated by strangers before exchanging coins. The clipping was often done outside the inn as the customer waited.[167]

An attempt to prosecute a Turvin man for clipping in 1765 was dropped by the Mint Solicitor on the advice of the attorney general.[168] The reasons for discontinuing it are not recorded, but thereafter those involved in the yellow trade remained immune from prosecution on their own territory until 1769. This immunity reflects, in part, the fact that it proved very difficult to secure evidence of sufficient quality to convict those who clipped, because clipping was easily undertaken without special equipment.[169] Those who coined on a peripatetic, fireside basis were also relatively invulnerable, because they could work alone and their only specialized equipment was an easily concealed pair of dies. The greater risk run by the proprietor of a permanent (and therefore vulnerable) coining shop was reduced by means of the traditional criminal devices of concealment and vigilance.[170] However, the yellow traders' immunity from prosecution and the

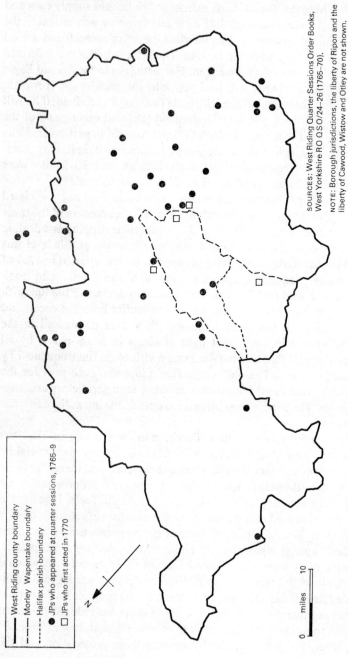

SOURCES: West Riding Quarter Sessions Order Books, West Yorkshire RO QSO/24-26 (1765–70).

NOTE: Borough jurisdictions, the liberty of Ripon and the liberty of Cawood, Wistow and Otley are not shown.

West Riding county boundary
Morley Wapentake boundary
Halifax parish boundary
● JPs who appeared at quarter sessions, 1765–9
□ JPs who first acted in 1770

N

0   miles   10

Justices of the peace acting in the West Riding, 1765–70

extraordinarily overt manner in which the trade was conducted can only be fully understood if account is also taken of the shortcomings which characterized the enforcement of the coin laws in the locality and the massive popular support which the trade enjoyed there.

The rise of the yellow trade in the Halifax locality was facilitated by the isolation of the locality from those sources of formal and informal authority which sustained eighteenth-century law enforcement. Like neighbouring rural–industrial parishes in both Yorkshire and Lancashire, the parish of Halifax was extensive and populous. Institutionally it was divided into a patchwork of twenty-three townships covering 118 square miles. In 1764 the total population of the parish was computed at 8244 families, which were estimated to represent at least 40,000 people. 1272 of those families lived in the town of Halifax.[171] The parish was an early centre for Methodism and a stronghold of the small freeholder.[172] Apart from the Hortons of Howroyd, it had few resident gentry. Large landowners like Sir George Savile and Lord Viscount Irwin were non-resident. The wealthiest inhabitants were the great manufacturers and merchants. However, their relationship with the small masters and outworkers did not involve that close control and subordination which characterized the dependence of tenants and labourers on the landowner in some rural parishes.

The absence, since the 1740s, of an acting justice of the peace in such a populous parish was a source of local complaint in the mid 1760s, for reasons unconnected with coining.[173] At this period there were two justices resident between the towns of Halifax and Bradford, but they were the only justices in the whole Wapentake of Morley, the most heavily populated in the West Riding (see the map opposite). The majority of the Riding's acting justices resided in the agricultural areas to the east and north-east of that Wapentake. The few Halifax men in the Commission of the Peace were discouraged from taking out their dedimuses by the heavy potential work-load.[174]

The acting justices of the peace did not ignore the yellow trade in the mid 1760s, but their efforts to contain it were weak. The Mint Solicitor reported that in the summer of 1765 he received complaints and letters from the Halifax area on the subject, but

my only answer was I was sorry for it, but if there could be no evidence provided, it was impossible to prosecute. I recommended it to the justices, whenever informations were laid before them, necessary to grant a search warrant, to collect their tools, or something of that sort, for with such circumstantial evidence it could answer no purpose.[175]

The justices' seeming inability to secure firm evidence may have resulted from their ignorance of the evidential requirements of the courts. However, it probably also reflected their reluctance, remarked on in theft as well as coinage cases, to issue any search warrants, even those giving only the most restricted of powers.[176] A possible explanation for this reluctance was offered in a letter to the *Leeds Intelligencer* in 1769. Its author remarked that no 'justice durst issue out warrants to search for *coining* tools, or clippings of gold', as a result of the ruling against general warrants secured by John Wilkes in the Common Pleas in 1763.[177]

Although the Mint Solicitor's criticism of the local bench finds confirmation elsewhere, it was in part an attempt to conceal his own negligence. The mid 1760s was the very period when he was most actively discouraging business, in order to avoid the financial embarrassment suffered by his predecessors. In 1769 the Marquis of Rockingham complained to the secretary of state that complaints and informations sent to the Mint Solicitor had been ignored, and this is confirmed by other evidence.[178] The Solicitor had made finance available for the abortive 1765 prosecution, but the initiative behind the prosecution was not his and he did not appear in person to supervise it. The discouraging image presented by the Solicitor to local magistrates was relieved only by the success of a Mint-financed prosecution for coining against a Keighley man taken up at Sheffield in 1768.

The yellow traders' active subversion of legal authority reinforced the deleterious effects on law enforcement of the local magistrates' inadequacies and the Mint Solicitor's neglect. A correspondent in the Leeds newspapers claimed that the trade had 'nothing to fear from the bugbear of those obsolete laws which inflict pains and penalties upon ingenuity of this interesting kind, as those whose particular business it is have good reason, no doubt, for neglecting and discountenancing informations'.[179] It has already been pointed out that minor local law officers participated in the trade. There is no evidence (other than the innuendo in the quotation above) of involvement by local magistrates in the trade, or of their having been bribed to provide immunity to coinage offenders. However, officers of the law, at all levels, were certainly intimidated. 'They set constables at defiance and threatened magistrates with destruction if they offered any disturbance to them.' Informers could be discouraged by 'bribing some and intimidating others'.[180]

Yet it is unlikely that intimidation and bribery to prevent informing were required very frequently prior to the start of the organized campaign against the trade in 1769. The yellow trade's strongest defence against the terrors of the criminal law was the participation and support of the local populace. A correspondent in the Leeds newspapers commented that 'the old proverb, everybody's business is nobody's, is a sufficient protection from prosecution'.[181] Clipping and coining were redefined in the locality as legitimate business activities, and enthusiastically defended.

The strength of popular support was well illustrated in 1774, when the body of a coiner, executed for killing and robbing the Halifax Supervisor of Excise, was hung in chains on Beacon Hill, overlooking Halifax town.

It was rumoured in Halifax that he would be brought there late on Sunday evening, on which account an innumerable multitude assembled, in order, as supposed, to have prevented his being put up, but about midnight, their patience being exhausted, they almost all went home.[182]

The body had to be placed on a special iron-clad gibbet at four the next morning. The same procedure was required in 1775 to hang up alongside the body of an accomplice.

Those who supported the trade did not just act in its defence; they also argued its merits. James Oldfield, the manufacturer executed for coining in 1770, had been a founder member of the Independent church at Booth in Halifax parish. On the occasion of his execution, the minister at Booth preached a sermon entitled *God's indignation against sin*.[183] He emphasized the particular seriousness of sin by those who professed to be good Christians, and singled out for condemnation 'those enemies of the Lord' who, with reference to the execution, 'have taken occasion at these things to blaspheme'.[184] He continued:

It is amazing to think, that so many are endeavouring to extenuate this crime, and speak as if it was of a trifling nature, and commit it in so daring a manner, when it is so far contrary to laws of the realm, an act of so high reaason and rebellion against our most gracious Sovereign, so prejudicial to trade, and injurious to our fellow subjects.[185]

The eighteenth-century criminal law purported to classify man's actions as good or evil. Yet the didactic morality of the legislators was not necessarily shared by those subject to their laws. Many practices which were defined in law as criminal were considered legitimate by various, broad sectors of the public. Smuggling, poaching and wrecking were all forms of illegal appropriation which were redefined as legitimate, both by men of middling rank and by the poor. That redefinition has not been analysed by historians merely in terms of the economic benefits bestowed by such activities. It has been pointed out that these practices were all unequivocally defined as traditional rights or customs, and that a clear distinction was made between the goods involved and other property. Communal solidarity and support were not easily mobilized against the definitions of the criminal law. The legitimating notions which informed such solidarity had to draw on deep communal allegiances. They also had to differentiate between the type of illegal appropriation at issue and casual theft, for loss by theft was a common complaint at every social level.[186]

The yellow trade enjoyed the general support of work-people, piecemakers, tradesmen and many merchants in the Halifax–Rochdale area. Yet there is no evidence here of any notion that the trade was a traditional right or custom. This is hardly surprising, given it was so new to the locality. Nevertheless, it is possible to detect in the support for the trade a set of legitimating ideas. The trade was clearly distinguished from other forms of coining and illegal appropriation and was defended as a harmless source of advantage to the public, in an area suffering from industrial recession.

The legitimacy accorded by so many in the locality to the yellow trade may, for some, have merely reflected their ignorance of the law. A handbill issued by the Mint Solicitor in 1769 generously suggested that 'there is great reason to believe that numbers of persons have been drawn into the commission of the said offence [clipping], not knowing at the time that by the laws of this realm the same is declared to be high treason'.[187] Certainly the laws against some of the offences which comprised the yellow trade had received very little publicity through the medium of the courts. During the 1750s and 1760s there were only a handful of Mint prosecutions anywhere in the country for clipping gold coin and relatively few for manufacturing counterfeit moidores.[188] Moreover, in law, there was ambivalence enough in the status of the gold coin to sustain genuine confusion, or at least provide a peg on which to hang a local redefinition of the yellow trade as less treasonable than other coinage offences. Clipping and coining English gold coin were, of course, treason, but in some respects the gold circulation enjoyed lesser protection from the law than the silver. The authority which the law vested in government agencies and any member of the public to cut and withdraw from circulation clipped silver coin, tendered in payment, did not extend to gold.[189] There was therefore no official facility to prevent the circulation of clipped gold. Most counterfeits in the Halifax area were false moidores. To counterfeit or clip moidores was not high treason but the non-capital offence, misprision of treason. Also non-capital was the possession, buying or sale of clippings from English gold coin.

However, among the yellow traders an explicit denial of the legitimacy of the law was more characteristic than thoroughgoing ignorance. According to a Lancashire magistrate, many practitioners of the yellow trade were impudent enough to call it 'their lawful business'.[190] Yet practitioners and supporters alike clearly condemned and eschewed other forms of coining. John Bates, a Halifax innkeeper, had been easily persuaded that 'there was no harm' in the trade. Yet he insisted that:

I never had any concern with plated or gilded money, neither did I ever know of any person excepting John Utley of Luddenden Dean that came and told me he could wash and plate money and he told me if I could put off for him every twenty-seven that I paid he wd. give me 7 shillings. I told him I would not have anything to do with any such thing for I made it a matter of conscience more than the other, because I was sure it would hurt but King and Country, so I never had anything to do with him.[191]

Bates's prejudice against base-metal counterfeiters was shared by many others in the locality. A correspondent in the *Leeds Intelligencer* caricatured their attitudes towards base-metal counterfeiting in such a way as to emphasize the prevailing image of the yellow traders as honest dealers:

As for the little, rascally pettyfoggers, who vend for gold what is only *base metal, washed* or *plated*, they deserve hanging, and no tradesman of honour will have any concern with them; and if they are not stopped, they will actually bring an evil report upon the country, and ruin the honest dealer.[192]

Because they considered the yellow trade as an honourable one, unlike the fraud of counterfeiting in base metals, its supporters were able to argue that it deserved immunity from the Mint laws. Their case is caricatured by the *Leeds Intelligencer*'s correspondent:

I understand there are some obsolete laws against *coining*; so there are against profaning the Sabbath, and against masters paying their workmen with anything but cash: And yet the Sabbath is profaned and the poor workman is obliged to take meal, and other eatables, at an exorbitant price, in lieu of his wages. Is it ignorance, or what shall I call it, that made [a Halifax correspondent] to open his mouth and draw his pen against a trade that is so beneficial to individuals and to the community, and to his own town and parish in particular?[193]

Caricatures offered in sarcastic letters to the press and excuses proffered to examining magistrates by arrested offenders have to be treated with due caution. Yet it is possible to discern here the outline of the legitimating notions which informed popular support. The justifications offered for redefining the yellow trade as legitimate may have involved no appeal to custom, but they did present its case in terms of the public interest. The trade was not harmful to the public interest – to 'King and Country' – because its counterfeits were made of gold, like legitimate coins. Prosecution under laws designed to prevent public injury by the fraud of base-metal counterfeits was therefore unjustified. Did not those in authority turn a blind eye to the transgression of other obsolete or inappropriate legislation? Far from being harmful, the trade generated widely diffused economic benefits in a locality suffering massive impoverishment.

It was spurious for apologists for the trade to imply that the Mint laws were designed merely to discourage counterfeiting in base metals. They were intended to defend the ancient royal monopoly over the production and standard of the gold and silver coinage as a whole. Yet eighteenth-century Englishmen were no respecters of government monopolies for their own sake. In the mid eighteenth century the Mint's monopoly was not exercised to provide a gold currency adequate for the requirements of the public. Government was more concerned to avoid the expense and political embarrassment of recoinage. It therefore allowed the circulation of gold coin that was grossly underweight, irrespective of whether it had been diminished by normal wear or illegal abuse. The yellow traders could plausibly argue that their local manipulation of the coin could not be very harmful to the public interest, when government already condoned general deficiency in the gold circulation. Like the export of new gold coin as bullion or coin, which was so widely sanctioned by the wealthy,[194] the yellow trade permitted those who owned coin to benefit from the otherwise unhappy consequences of government coinage policy. From this point of view the crime, if any, of the practitioners of the trade was to flout an unsatisfactory Mint monopoly, not to harm the public. They merely turned the advantage which government obtained, by avoiding a recoinage, to the private profit of the public who suffered by governmental negligence.

However, the benefits which government acquired by neglect of the gold circulation, and the yellow traders by their depredations on it, were obtained at a high price. By the early 1770s an accelerating decline in the standard of the gold coinage as a whole threatened national commercial dislocation. The effects of the yellow trade were particularly serious. Increasingly it attracted coin from far beyond the Halifax–Rochdale area, in order to diminish it to a degree unknown elsewhere. Yet the widespread local belief in the trade's public benefits persisted because, in the main, the local population experienced only its benevolent aspects. It was the local cash shortage, not the activities of the yellow traders, which initially obliged local people to take exceptionally diminished gold coin. Though the burgeoning illegal business must have perpetuated the shortage of heavy coin in the area, it provided ample additional supplies of light gold, in the form of counterfeits and clipped coin. Purchases by the poor and the legitimate business transactions of men of small capital, so prominent in the yellow trade, were overwhelmingly local. As long as exceptionally underweight gold was readily accepted in the locality, the illegal business did not appear to compromise their livelihood directly. Of course, the purely local circulation of highly diminished coin gradually undermined national confidence in the commercial credit of the region as a whole. However, the only individuals to suffer directly were those few great manufacturers and merchants who were obliged to sustain credit and make considerable payments outside the area. Many such men remained well disposed towards the yellow trade because, despite its unhappy effects on their legitimate businesses, it offered them an alternative source of profit through the manipulation of their commercial paper to secure heavy coin.

The popular image of the yellow trade as harmless was reinforced by its commercial character. Within the locality it presented itself as a web of innumerable business transactions between individuals, rather than a monstrous conspiracy against the integrity of the coinage. For local people the trade amounted to dealing to mutual advantage in property which they considered theirs, to dispose of as they pleased. These transactions were indistinguishable, in many cases, from the legitimate and profitable trade in cash, which had arisen as a direct result of the shortage of specie.

Although the evidence is sparse, it is probable that these transactions were untainted with criminal associations. Prior to the collapse of the yellow trade in 1773 there is no indication that any of its practitioners was involved in theft or other criminal activities. The many unflattering descriptions available of those concerned with the trade, include, at this stage, no references to careers in any other type of illegal appropriation. This did not mean that the yellow trade was necessarily closed to other types of offenders. Indeed, its many, disparate transactions could themselves be used as a cover for fraud. Two brothers from Colne, both tinkers, who were hanged at York for a highway robbery near Halifax in 1767, plausibly claimed that the prosecution against them was a malicious one, spitefully undertaken as a result of a fraud they had perpetrated under cover of a coining transaction.[195] However, the prominence among the yellow traders of respectable men of small and middling wealth indicates that normally the trade was conducted according to the usual standards of business probity. Such men, and especially textile manufacturers, were the members of the local community most vulnerable to theft and the most active in undertaking prosecutions against it. Their enthusiastic participation in the illegal business suggests that it was considered distinct from most other offences against property.

The innocuous aspect which the yellow trade presented in the locality sustained the popular notion that it caused no public injury. The conviction that, on the contrary, it was advantageous to the public stemmed directly from the economic benefits it diffused so widely, at every social level, during a period of acute recession in the area's staple industry. It was as financial beneficiaries that the local population extended legitimacy to the illegal business itself and to the reign of the yellow trade's royal entrepreneurs. In the Halifax–Rochdale locality the trade was 'everybody's business'. The relationship between mass popular participation and the prosperity of the trade was a reciprocal one. The trade offered to all a novel opportunity for profit, but was itself dependent on widespread participation for both a continuous supply of raw material and a ready market. This reciprocal relationship was to pose insuperable obstacles to the concerted attempt mounted in 1769 to crush the trade by means of the systematic application of the criminal law.

By 1769 the practitioners of the yellow trade were 'so firmly estab-lised in the neighbourhood of Halifax as (almost) to bid defiance to the civil power'.[196] It was commented, in that year, that 'the merchants of Halifax, and the worsted piece makers in the country, understand too well the utility of a trade that brings in ten per cent, either to give it up or to discourage it'.[197] Yet 1769 was the first year to see sustained public complaint in the local press about the ever-

increasing number of clipped and counterfeit gold pieces in circulation, both within the coining heartland and beyond.

The ravages of the yellow trade on the legitimate activities of some
of those who had to sustain credit outside the West Riding were
sufficiently severe, by 1769, to prompt a concerted attack upon the
trade. This systematic attempt to use the criminal law to crush the
yellow trade was mounted by two interests with no jurisdiction over
the coinage: the excise service and large-scale worsted manufacturers.
William Deighton, supervisor of the Halifax excise district from 1759
to 1769, undertook a personal crusade against the trade, which eventually cost him his life. As supervisor, he had no direct responsibility
for the state of the coinage. His duties involved overseeing the work
of subordinate excise officers in his district, as well as assisting the
collector of excise at Leeds, his immediate superior, in taking payment
of the tax at Halifax.[198] However, there is no doubt that Deighton
and the collector were greatly inconvenienced in their returns to
London by the exceptionally diminished coin they were obliged to
accept, for want of any other, in the Halifax area. This was the
principal reason for Deighton's exertions against the yellow trade.[199]

The earliest evidence of Deighton's taking the initiative against the
trade dates from 1765, when he was prominent in the unsuccessful
prosecution of a Turvin man.[200] The failure of that prosecution may
have been a temporary discouragement from further activity. There
is no evidence that he renewed his efforts to secure convictions until
1769. However, in that year, according to Isaac Hartley, brother of
King David and himself 'Duke of York', 'Deighton did his best to
run at the lives of us upper hand people.'[201]

The large-scale worsted manufacturers did not act against the trade
until 1769. By the middle of that year, it had become 'a difficult
matter to get any gold coin in the [West] Riding but which is greatly
short of weight'. The manufacturers complained that the proportion
of diminished coin in the local gold circulation was so large and the
difficulty of making payments with it 'in distant parts' so great, 'that
not only the trade and credit of the said Riding in general, but also
the interest of individual persons who may happen to have large
sums of such diminished coin in their custody are in danger of suffering thereby'.[202] In response they joined with some local gentlemen to
undertake prosecutions of offenders. Of course, many of the great
manufacturers and merchants in the immediate vicinity of Halifax
were either active participants in the yellow trade, or unwilling to defy
local opinion by opposing it, thereby risking public abuse and private

vengeance. Significantly the manufacturers' campaign was organized from Bradford rather than Halifax.

Co-operation among large manufacturers and West Riding gentlemen to further their interests in the wool textile industry, which sustained their rents or profits, was not new. The worsted manufacturers were already organized in a voluntary association to secure convictions for false reeling and other frauds by outworkers. Since 1764 a permanent committee had managed a subscription for this purpose.[203] Manufacturers and gentry had long been accustomed to associate in a variety of campaigns on behalf of the local staple industry, like that against the false winding of fleeces in 1752, as well as general projects to encourage regional economic prosperity, such as the Leeds and Liverpool canal in the late 1760s.[204] John Stanhope of Horsforth, the senior barrister on the northern circuit, and Samuel Lister of Horton, a particularly active magistrate, were two local gentlemen involved in the manufacturers' campaign against the yellow trade who were also leading figures, along with some of the manufacturers themselves, in the canal project.[205]

Major obstacles to the successful application of the criminal law against the yellow traders were the strength of popular support for the illegal business and its practitioners' ability to intimidate and suborn. To overcome them, Deighton and the manufacturers conducted their investigations by means of secrecy, deception and bribes.

The manufacturers, after a false start, secured evidence against offenders by using their private industrial police as *agents provocateurs*. Since 1764, the committee of worsted manufacturers had employed several inspectors to detect and prosecute outworkers who embezzled work materials.[206] Two of these inspectors were directed 'to get acquainted with some of the persons reputed to be principal [coinage] offenders, and, if possible, make a discovery'. However, mere surveillance proved unrewarding and, in July 1769, John Stanhope and Samuel Lister were authorized by the manufacturers to employ the two inspectors in any way they 'thought necessary and expedient to detect the persons guilty'. Stanhope and Lister had decided to have the inspectors secure irrefutable evidence by trading with known offenders. This obliged the inspectors to break the law themselves, by offering for clipping coins that had previously been marked and weighed. They were promised immunity from criminal proceedings and 'reasonable satisfaction for their trouble'.[207]

The need for secrecy was such, in an area steeped in sympathy for the yellow trade, that the employment of the inspectors as *agents provocateurs* was concealed from most of the manufacturers and gentlemen involved in the campaign. The secret was divulged only to one leading member of the manufacturers' committee, and to a trusted Bradford attorney. To further ensure concealment, the latter took down the inspectors' depositions, in preference to Justice Lister's regular clerk.[208]

Deighton's efforts too were conducted with considerable secrecy.[209] Between April and October 1769, he covertly purchased information from two men resident in the upper hand country who were intimate with leading offenders there.[210] 'For the better concealing what intelligence he got, [he] carried the witnesses to be examined before a Justice of the Peace in the County of Lancaster'.[211]

In the autumn of 1769, the employment of secrecy, deception and bribes reaped a rich harvest of offenders committed to prison and absconding. Between 30 August and 9 September four men were committed to York Castle on the evidence secured by Deighton's hired informers and the worsted inspectors, to face trial at the subsequent assizes.[212] Many others, against whom information had been laid, were obliged to evade capture by fleeing the district, or by going to ground in the locality.[213] Once information had been sworn, warrants issued and committals undertaken, the deterrent potential of the ferocious coin laws began to be realized. The threat of prosecution, combined with the reward and statutory pardon available to accomplices who informed, became an effective weapon for breaching the coiners' accustomed silence. Joseph Shaw, one of those apprehended in early September 1769 on the evidence of the two inspectors, was not committed to York but taken into temporary custody at Bradford. There, on 10 and 14 September, he informed against twelve other offenders.[214] Over the next two months his evidence probably secured at least two more committals.[215]

The success of the simultaneous initiatives by Deighton and the manufacturers against the yellow trade was celebrated by the local printing presses. The *Leeds Mercury* reported that in the second week of September 1769 'a great many persons, chiefly landlords, absconded from Halifax. . . . Upwards of 100 persons, we hear, in Halifax, etc., are informed against'.[216] A flysheet published at Halifax expressed the pleasure of those local notables who now felt secure enough to discountenance the illegal business publicly: 'we now have the pleasing satisfaction of seeing the bands of these formidable set of villains broken: terror and dismay have taken holden of them, and they no longer care to face the injured public'.[217]

The achievement of Deighton and the manufacturers in securing the committal and discomfiture of leading practitioners of the yellow trade was reinforced by a public meeting held at Bradford on 12 October 1769, at which they and local justices were present. Newspaper advertisements requested the attendance of

all gentlemen merchants, traders and others in the [West] Riding, who choose to discourage such practices . . . in order to consider the most effectual means to bring to justice all such offenders, and to endeavour to prevent the like practices for the future.[218]

An Association for Prosecuting Diminishers of the Coin was established.[219]

This meeting also marked the culmination of Deighton's personal crusade to break the upper hand people. Deighton brought James Broadbent, of Hall Gate in the Turvin valley, to the Bradford inn where the meeting took place. Broadbent was to lay an information against King David before one of the magistrates present. He had been in Deighton's employment as an informer for some time, but had long been reluctant to inform against the coining monarch. He later claimed that Deighton persuaded him on this occasion only by means of an offer of £100, while he was 'in liquor'.[220] Nevertheless, the information served to secure a warrant. King David was taken up and committed to York Castle, charged with clipping. His apprehension was interpreted as the single most important blow against the yellow trade up to that time.[221]

However, the yellow traders' discomfiture, though considerable, was not as complete as the celebrations in the local press might suggest. By the end of October 1769 only seven offenders had actually been committed to prison to face trial.[222] The practitioners of the trade showed themselves able to apply in their own defence a range of techniques which mirrored those which had been used by Deighton and the manufacturers to subvert their accustomed security. Popular solidarity was bolstered by bribery, intimidation and the deceitful use of the law.

Despite the special care taken by Deighton and the manufacturers to conceal the provision of informations and the identity of informers, the yellow traders were quickly able to penetrate these secrets. As soon as warrants were issued out on the evidence of the two worsted inspectors, 'an information was made against . . . James Crabtree [one of the inspectors], in order . . . to take away his evidence against the persons by him informed of'.[223] Hence the yellow traders demonstrated that they were as conscious as the authorities, if not more so, of the stringent evidential standards demanded by the courts in coinage cases, and that they were well able to use this knowledge to subvert the course of justice.[224]

The coiners' ability to mobilize in their defence resources of men, money and legal expertise is best illustrated by their attempts to save their monarch, King David. Their response to his committal moved progressively through the exploitation of legal process to outright assassination. Hartley's associates discovered that James Broadbent had been the source of the incriminating evidence only after the committal. Immediately 'Hartley's brothers and friends got about him and he then, through their persuasions, declared that what he had sworn against Hartley . . . was totally false and that he had been induced by promises from [Deighton] to lodge the information.'[225] Initially Hartley's associates set out to use Broadbent's new story to reverse the legal process.[226] The informer was taken to York Castle by Hartley's brother Isaac and made to plead forgiveness for his *lèse-majesté* before the coining monarch. He recounted his revised story to the governor of York Castle, who did not release Hartley, and then to a York attorney, who took down a statement. The attorney was consulted by Hartley's brother about obtaining bail, but this was not normally available in capital coining cases. The next ploy of Hartley's friends was to have Broadbent recant before the committing magistrate, in order thereby to obtain the reversal of the committal. Broadbent was accompanied before the justice by David Greenwood, a kerseymaker and neighbour of King David (see the map on page 202), who acted as hedge solicitor to Hartley in the affair.[227] A prominent local attorney, James Carr of Birstall, was hired to go with them. However, this array of legal talent was of no avail. The magistrate prevaricated, refusing on two occasions to hear Broadbent without Deighton present. The supervisor of excise naturally refused to co-operate, for as long as Broadbent's information stood to secure the committal, other, more reliable witnesses might be acquired to obtain a conviction.

Deighton's steadfastness led directly to his death. 'Hartley's friends, when they saw they could not get him set at liberty, they therefore resolved upon the murder.'[228] Isaac Hartley was the prime mover and secured finance and guns. He promised 'that if the job could be done . . . he would insure one hundred pounds reward'.[229] Like their tormentors, the yellow traders were able to use subscription to provide finance. Several of the upper hand people contributed sums of £10 or £20, and Isaac Hartley sent an associate on a tour of the coining districts beyond Halifax parish, to collect further sums.[230]

Thomas Spencer, King David's brother-in-law, and Royal Clayton, who had gone to ground locally after Deighton secured a warrant against him, persuaded two weavers from the upper hand country, Matthew Normanton and Robert Thomas (see the map on page 202), to carry out the murder.[231] After two abortive attempts, Deighton was shot about one o'clock on the morning of 10 November 1769, in the road near his home on the outskirts of Halifax town. After killing him, Normanton and Thomas emptied his pockets of ten guineas and returned to Normanton's cottage at Stannery End, where Normanton's wife declared that they were 'brave lads, and that trade would now go briskly on'.[232]

In reply to the threatened judicial killing of their monarch at the gallows, the coiners had arranged their own deterrent execution. However, the exciseman's murder did not, as its perpetrators had hoped, re-establish the unrestricted prosperity of the yellow trade. On the contrary, the price of suppressing Deighton's evidence was an intensification of the campaign against the trade and its practitioners.

The most important consequence of the murder was to transform the way in which the illegal business was perceived by the authorities, both in the locality and in London. No longer was it regarded just as a serious threat to local economic interests, but also as an outright public challenge to the power and status of civil authority. Prior to the killing, the principal concern of those involved in the campaign against the yellow trade had been to halt its ravages upon their particular economic interests. They believed that this objective could be achieved by a concerted effort to overcome the shortcomings of the officers of the law and the blandishments and popular solidarities which had previously defended the yellow traders. By bringing offenders to justice, the deterrent potential of the coin laws would be reactivated. Deighton's murder was a most emphatic public challenge to this policy. It served notice of the coiners' intention ruthlessly to contest *any* attempt to apply the civil power against what they considered their legitimate business. In the prevailing context of public support for the trade, an impenetrable and defiant murder threatened further to intimidate local magistrates and publicly to undermine the credibility of civil authority.

The initial reaction of many of the substantial inhabitants in the area was panic. Some of those who had participated in the campaign against the yellow trade were so much alarmed that they talked of being obliged to leave the vicinity.[233] In the aftermath of the murder, therefore, local notables at Halifax had two immediate objectives: first, to prevent further assassinations, by apprehending the murderers; second, to obtain assistance from national government to crush the threat posed by the trade, which they now considered themselves incapable of confronting unaided. It proved extremely difficult to secure evidence against the killers, as they had got clear away on a dark night and were shielded by public sympathy.[234] Suspicion immediately fell upon James Broadbent, as a consequence of his bizarre role in the apprehension of King David and its aftermath, but he denied any knowledge of the murder. Application was made to the secretary of state for the affair to be laid before the king, in order to obtain a royal proclamation of a pardon and £100 reward to any accomplice who would make a discovery. The proclamation was granted and a subscription begun to finance the reward, which soon amounted to double the sum offered. The pardon and reward were advertised about Halifax by handbills.[235] On being informed of the terms of the proclamation, Broadbent characteristically agreed to provide an information, claiming he had been present at the murder. He incriminated the two murderers, as well as another man who was innocent.[236] All four were committed to York Castle.

Outside assistance was also solicited in the form of troops. One of the local magistrates wrote to the war office to seek 'military assistance to preserve the peace and to be assisting in apprehending and conveying . . . offenders to prison' for 'there is great reason to apprehend the fate of the said Deighton will deter the constables and other persons who ought otherwise have been instrumental in apprehending the rest of this dreadful gang'.[237]

However, the murder did not stifle the continuing efforts of the Bradford-based large manufacturers to suppress the yellow trade by bringing the law to bear against its practitioners. On the contrary, they redoubled their exertions. Leading Bradford manufacturers summoned local notables from Halifax and Leeds to a meeting of the Association for the Prosecution of Diminishers at Bradford on 22 November. Its purpose was to consider new measures for bringing to justice both the murderers and coinage offenders. A new committee was established to manage the association's affairs, composed of 'a select number of gentlemen' from each of the three towns. It was agreed to open subscription lists in each town, to offer £10 rewards for information leading to the conviction of coinage offenders and to publish descriptions of absconded suspects in the Leeds and York newspapers. The descriptions were also distributed about the West

Riding in the form of flysheets, parcels of which were dispatched as far afield as Skipton, Otley and Wakefield.[238]

Central government also reacted vigorously once confronted with a defiant murder which challenged the exercise of civil authority. Not only was a royal proclamation granted against the murderers and the call for troops acceded to, but, in addition, the secretary of state approached the Marquis of Rockingham, lord lieutenant and *Custos Rotulorum* of the West Riding, asking him to take 'such steps as you shall think most likely to put a stop to a practice so very dangerous to a trading town' and to 'restore security to that part of the country'.[239]

The request had the character of a royal command, for the king had taken a personal interest in a matter that affected his royal prerogative over the coinage. Rockingham had heard little of the affair previously, although he had been resident for most of the summer and autumn of 1769 at Wentworth, his Yorkshire seat, only twenty-five miles south-east of Halifax.[240] Henceforth he was to act energetically to manage affairs at Halifax, serving both as representative of central government in the locality and as intermediary between the locality and London.

However, Rockingham's energetic conduct of affairs at Halifax was not prompted merely by his obligations as lord lieutenant and *Custos Rotulorum*.[241] He also had a personal political interest in being seen to campaign vigorously against the yellow trade. Rockingham was a dominating political figure in Yorkshire, as well as a major national political personality. The assiduity he was to display in helping the beleaguered gentlemen at Halifax in 1769 contrasted with the lassitude he sometimes evinced with regard to national political affairs.[242] Indeed, his dedication to Halifax in 1769 was at the expense of those national responsibilities, at a time of growing national political tension.[243] By putting himself at the service of Halifax men who were some of his most active political sympathizers in the county,[244] he could secure considerable local political benefits. The episode illustrates the prime importance that Rockingham attached to cultivating his local political base. His domination of Yorkshire politics had been carefully nurtured by attention to the politically significant interests in the county, especially the wool textile industry. Rockingham's activity against the yellow trade was to reap lavish praise from that quarter.[245]

Neither Rockingham's instructions nor his reading of events at Halifax prompted him to reassess the feasibility of the objective set by Deighton and the great manufacturers. Like them, he assumed that the yellow trade could be rooted out, by bringing the ferocious coin laws to bear effectively against offenders. Indeed, the activities of Deighton and the manufacturers appeared to demonstrate that, despite a climate of intimidation, bribery and popular solidarity, the concerted efforts of those well disposed to the law could secure evidence, committals and, therefore, convictions. However, Deighton's murder had served notice of the yellow traders' ruthless tenacity in the face of such a challenge and of the vulnerability of the local authorities. Rockingham considered that the active and successful prosecution of legal proceedings against the yellow traders was therefore all the more necessary, in order to sustain the credibility and confidence of civil authority. But he also recognized that the civil power would require considerable encouragement and reinforcement if the terrors of the criminal law were to have their desired deterrent effect.

Nevertheless, Rockingham resisted the deployment of troops at Halifax. He recognized that, because soldiers could provide little security against private assassination, their use would be inappropriate to the kind of policing problems posed by the yellow trade. Drawing on his experience in suppressing the grain and militia riots of 1756 and 1757 at Sheffield, he believed that the local authorities could and should enforce the law against an illegal activity of this character, without military assistance. He was particularly concerned about the implications of the manner in which the trade was suppressed for the future credibility of the law and the civil authorities. He pointed out that

the confidence which arises from troops must always bring along with it the certainty of an alarm reviving whenever those troops are again removed. On the other hand, the confidence arising from the exertion and support of the civil power in any neighbourhood is permanent.[246]

In the long term, obedience to the law, indeed order itself, depended on popular belief in the ability and willingness of the civil authorities to put the laws into execution (and to forgive, threaten, or protect). The use of troops, even when both appropriate and efficacious, tended to detract from that belief. It was only if the local civil authorities were seen to be capable of dealing with the yellow trade by the use of their own legal powers that their credibility could be restored and the humiliation inflicted upon the civil power by a defiant murder reversed.

To stimulate the exertion of the civil power, Rockingham mounted a calculated and ostentatious display of solidarity for the beleaguered civil authorities at Halifax. This highly theatrical exercise in exhortation and example was contrived to revitalize the activity of local notables and to overawe the populace with the weight of social authority gathered in support of the law. Thereby, Rockingham intended to terrorize the yellow traders and to restore the confidence of that majority of local people, whom he assumed to be well disposed towards the law. In this way he hoped they would be persuaded to defy intimidation and to assist the authorities.

The principal part in this theatrical display was played by Rockingham himself, who made a brief but impressive visit to Halifax at the end of November 1769. He was anxious to see for himself the state of affairs at Halifax, but he also considered that

the very appearance of my coming at this juncture . . . might have the effect of frightening and alarming many of the lower persons concerned in clipping and coining, and . . . some of them might, by the additional alarm, be more ready to come in and make discoveries.[247]

Appropriately, his arrival in the town was impressed upon the public by a longer peal of bells than any of those rung for the victories of the Seven Years War.[248]

Rockingham's visit to Halifax was all the more impressive because he summoned a large number of West Riding gentlemen, particularly those in the Commission of the Peace, to join him in the town for a meeting on 28 November. Forty-three West Riding gentry, merchants and attorneys attended. Resolutions were passed commending the prior exertions of local notables.[249] Rockingham was determined publicly to demonstrate 'that the activity which has been shown by many of the gentlemen and townsmen in Halifax deserves great approbation'. He considered that 'perhaps the seeing their activity particularly countenanced may have some effect as an encouragement to others'.[250] Hence he wrote to London extolling local zeal and passed on to Halifax the personal commendation of that zeal by the king.[251]

However, he was not concerned merely to spur local notables to even greater exertions, but also to ensure that, subsequently, their efforts should not flag through lack of support. To this end, the 28 November meeting pledged the Halifax notables the assistance, in future, of all West Riding magistrates and of polite county society in general. Rockingham also agreed that Sir George Savile, his personal friend, Halifax landowner and Member of Parliament for Yorkshire, should visit the town late in December to sustain the enthusiasm of the civil authorities there.[252]

The related objectives of Rockingham's exercise in exhortation were the reversal of the humiliation suffered by the authorities and the promotion of an effective application of the criminal law against the yellow traders. However, he was not prepared to sacrifice his overriding concern with thoroughly rooting out the trade merely to provide an enhanced theatrical effect in the short term. Hence his opposition to the suggestion, put forward at the Halifax meeting, that, because 'a speedy execution would make great impression', those suspects already in custody should be tried at once before a special commission. He considered that delay until the Lent assizes in March 1770 would be advisable, so that more evidence could be collected and 'the fullest possible discovery . . . made of *all* who [had] followed the practice [of clipping and coining]'.[253]

Rockingham recognized that to achieve 'the fullest possible discovery', the revitalized efforts of the civil authorities would require further *practical* reinforcement. This he provided in two ways. First, he set out to persuade local gentlemen already in the Commission of the Peace to act as magistrates, even 'if they would only engage to act for six months'.[254] Within eight months four new justices had begun to act (see the map on page 206).[255] Second, he applied to London for the attendance of Mint officers at Halifax, to advise on the collection of technical evidence, and for government personnel and funds, to undertake prosecutions.[256]

This application received the personal endorsement of the king and was unhesitatingly acceded to by the Treasury. William Chamberlayne, the Mint Solicitor, was ordered to Yorkshire, with an assistant and a promise of unlimited funds.[257] Despite a pessimistic assessment of the feasibility of prosecutions, Chamberlayne did 'make shift to collect evidence'.[258] During his eleven-day visit to the Halifax area, in mid December 1769, he and his assistant conducted searches of at least six premises and held co-ordinating meetings with local notables and justices at Halifax, Bradford and Rochdale. To stimulate public awareness of the gravity of the offences and of the availability of rewards for information, he placed advertisements in the local newspapers and circulated handbills.[259] Chamberlayne's presence at Halifax was clearly crucial in stimulating the efforts of the local authorities to secure informations and committals. No committals were made to York from the area on capital coinage charges during the five weeks between Deighton's murder and Chamberlayne's arrival. Nineteen were made during, or soon after, his visit.[260]

By the end of March 1770, when the Yorkshire Lent assizes took place, at least twenty-seven men had been committed to York, charged with capital coinage offences. Four others were imprisoned there, charged with Deighton's murder. Coinage offenders from the Halifax area comprised more than half the total complement of prisoners awaiting trial.[261] At the assizes, four men were tried and three convicted: David Hartley, James Oldfield and William Varley (the proprietor of the 'Halifax Mint'). Oldfield and King David were executed at Tyburn, near York, at the end of April. Varley received a free pardon. The rest of those committed or bound over for coinage offences were discharged. Of the four men charged with William Deighton's murder, James Broadbent was to serve as king's evidence and the other three were not indicted until the Yorkshire Lammas assizes in August. There all three were acquitted. Of four men committed to Lancaster to face trial at the assizes there during 1770, two were acquitted and two discharged without prosecution.[262]

Yet even such a royal example at the gallows as the execution of King David failed to deter the practitioners of the yellow trade from their calling. Admittedly committals and abscondings in 1769 and 1770 temporarily disturbed the operations of the trade and the authorities' activity stimulated some internal dissension among its practitioners.[263] However, once the assizes were over, it prospered anew. In January 1771 the *Leeds Intelligencer* reported that 'our correspondent from [the Halifax] neighbourhood informs us that those iniquitous villains, the clippers and diminishers of the current coin of this Kingdom, still continue that vile and destructive practice'.[264] Complaints from Yorkshire to the Treasury and to members of the government in London indicated that the campaign of 1769 and 1770 had changed essentially nothing. The yellow traders remained defiant and the plight of the authorities in the locality had once again become a sorry one. By 1773 local gentlemen were reduced to pleading, in terms very similar to those of November 1769, for government assistance, in particular the provision of troops and more stringent legislation.

We are horribly distressed in the woollen manufacturing country by clippers and coiners. The magistrates are actually afraid to act and do their duty, especially those who live about Halifax. The poor, ignorant manufacturers take this stuff and we can scarce get one guinea, not reduced very much. A regiment of foot seems to me to be absolutely necessary to assist the civil power at Halifax in searching the houses and apprehending suspected persons. Whether any additional law is necessary for this purpose should be considered. . . . What must be done? These rogues are desperate fellows and as ready to commit murder, as to do anything else.[265]

In the aftermath of the 1770 trials the carefully orchestrated campaign to use the criminal law to root out the yellow trade had been abandoned. These renewed requests for government assistance from local magistrates failed to secure its resumption. Rockingham appears to have taken no active interest in affairs at Halifax after 1770. Between 1771 and 1773, local notables, with some Mint finance and advice, did undertake proceedings against seven capital offenders from the Halifax–Rochdale area. However, these were essentially sporadic efforts, not a concerted sweep of the district like that during the winter of 1769–70. They provided no convictions.[266]

Rockingham's management of affairs at Halifax in the autumn of 1769 had been shaped by the assumption (which had been shared by Deighton and the manufacturers before him) that the means most likely to put a stop to the practice of the yellow trade was a determined execution of the existing coin laws. Yet, the energetic campaign to execute those laws was abandoned, despite the fact that the trade continued to flourish. To explain this dramatic reversal, it is first necessary to examine those obstacles which obstructed the campaign during the winter of 1769–70; in particular, the considerable difficulty which the authorities experienced in obtaining evidence of sufficient quality to ensure convictions.

The problems of evidence confronting the authorities in their attempts to convict known offenders are amply illustrated by the state of the case against Deighton's murderers, in 1770. The authorities were well aware of the murderers' identities and of the manner in which the crime had been perpetrated. Yet they could not obtain convictions because the sole *positive* proof was provided by the untrustworthy James Broadbent. The other evidence available was sufficient only to put the prisoners 'on their defence'.[267] In the coinage cases, too, general information was not difficult to secure, but evidence of sufficient quality to convict was usually unforthcoming. This was evident to the Mint Solicitor even before he left London for Yorkshire in December 1769. He reported that 'it so often happened that in almost all the cases there being nothing but the evidence of the accomplices, one against another, that the then Attorney and Solicitor General said they thought the best thing to happen to me was to have them all run away before I got down'.[268]

These problems were, in part, the consequence of those obstacles to procuring evidence inherent in the character of clipping and coining from clippings as illegal activities. The coining shop proprietors were vulnerable to a thorough search of their premises, but those who coined on a peripatetic basis were much less so. Clipping could be perpetrated in secret, without special equipment. But the authorities' difficulty in obtaining effective evidence also reflects the incompetence of the local magistrates and the continuing resistance of the yellow traders and their supporters.

Through the autumn and winter of 1769, several local magistrates displayed considerable zeal and energy in collecting evidence. Yet the evidence which they procured was often useless, as a consequence of their seeming ignorance of the stringent evidential requirements of the courts in capital coinage cases. This came to light when the Mint Solicitor arrived in Halifax in December 1769. He reported that the justices had 'depended too much upon the positive evidence of accomplices, without looking out for circumstantial evidence to corroborate them, without which it is impossible to expect convictions'. A false notion prevailed that one witness was sufficient to secure a conviction. Chamberlayne still had to impress upon the magistrates the need to grant search warrants at the same time that warrants were granted for apprehending offenders. Soon after his arrival in Yorkshire, he reported to the Treasury, 'I shall apply myself while I stay here to the obtaining of [circumstantial] evidence, but with no prospect of obtaining much of that sort, now so general an alarm has been given.'[269]

Rockingham's contrived display of patrician solidarity at Halifax and his efforts to sustain the activity of the magistrates had been intended to counteract local support for the yellow trade and the determination of many of its practitioners to defend it. The activity of the authorities did generate alarm among the yellow traders and major breaches in the solidarities which had previously protected them. However, these successes were limited. In early 1770, a Lancashire justice could still complain that the attempt to collect evidence was being sabotaged by the blandishments of the yellow traders and their supporters. Many had 'eluded an *effectual* discovery of their connections and guilt (tho' not very strong suspicion of both) by bribing some and intimidating others of their accomplices. . . .Very few . . . dare come to lodge information against the *most* capital offenders, for fear of sharing poor Deighton's fate'.[270]

Unfortunately it is impossible to gauge the precise impact of such blandishments, even on cases which did enter the judicial machinery. In most cases of acquittal, or failure to proceed with prosecution, there remains no direct evidence as to the reasons behind the decision of the jury, or of the prosecutor. It was recorded, however, that the two men tried on capital coinage charges at Lancaster Lent assizes in 1770 were acquitted as a result of 'the principal evidence to prove the filing having been apparently suborned to omit part of what he swore before the justice'.[271] There is no doubt that much intimidation did take place. The extraordinary strength and persistence of general popular sympathy for the trade has already been remarked upon.[272]

During the winter of 1769–70, as these obstacles to the acquisition of effective evidence became apparent, they provided considerable discouragement to the authorities' efforts to root out the yellow trade by means of a concerted application of the criminal law.[273] Yet it is unlikely that such evidential problems were *in themselves* decisive in persuading the authorities to abandon their campaign against the trade. In spite of such difficulties, three prominent offenders were convicted at the York Lent assizes in 1770, and two executed.[274] Moreover, there is no reason to believe that there could not have been some additional convictions, either in 1770 or later. The three convicted men were found guilty on the evidence of accomplices and the worsted inspectors, notwithstanding the Mint Solicitor's pessimism, in December 1769, about the possibility of obtaining guilty verdicts using this kind of witness.[275] Evidence of the same kind was available against many of those who were committed in 1770, but never tried. More could have been collected, had the concerted campaign of the autumn and winter of 1769–70 been sustained.

Why then was the campaign abandoned, if convictions were, against all the odds, available, and when the two executions of April 1770 had manifestly failed to stay the progress of the trade? The leaders of the campaign have left no comprehensive account of its abandonment. However, it is possible, on the basis of the evidence available, to indicate the other considerations which shaped their decision. At the heart of that decision lay the authorities' loss of confidence in the ability of additional convictions and executions to deter the practitioners of the trade from their calling. The whole campaign had been conceived on the assumption that the yellow trade was susceptible to control by an application of the terrors of the ferocious coin laws. As the campaign unfolded, that assumption was called into question. It became increasingly clear that it had been based upon a mistaken assessment of the character of the trade.

In the autumn of 1769 the authorities had assumed that the number of participants in the yellow trade was limited, that their relationship with the mass of the population in the locality was a hostile, exploitative one, and that support for the trade was not widespread, even at the bottom of the social scale. Sir George Savile commented, early in December 1769, that

it is as near impossible as anything can be, that the persons interested in coining can bear such a proportion to those injured by it as to want actual strength to resist or quell them. The general spirit, even of the lowest orders, must at worst be, in such a case, rather on the right side.[276]

These assumptions did not represent an accurate assessment of the social relationships and public attitudes associated with the yellow trade. They bore a much closer resemblance to the relationships and attitudes associated with a large-scale operation for counterfeiting the gold coin in mixed or base metals, like that run by Thomas Lightowller during the 1750s.[277] This suggests that, in the beginning, the authorities assumed that the yellow trade was similar in organization to the general run of eighteenth-century coining. This would hardly have been surprising, given that the trade was new and unfamiliar, and the authorities were ignorant of the technicalities of coining and of the coinage laws.

Had the yellow trade been similar in organization to base- and mixed-metal counterfeiting, there would have been good reason to expect a concerted application of the law, along the lines envisaged by Rockingham, to break the Yorkshire coiners. The determined use of the coin laws had succeeded, in 1756 and 1757, in destroying a mixed- and base-metal counterfeiting operation as extensive and sophisticated as Lightowller's. Although Lightowller was acquitted, four of his associates were convicted and hanged. Of course, it must have been obvious in the autumn of 1769 that the degree both of intimidation and popular solidarity in the Halifax area was far greater than that associated with the general run of mid-eighteenth-century mixed- or base-metal counterfeiting. Yet Rockingham's ostentatious theatrics and his efforts to revitalize the activity of local gentlemen were specifically designed to counteract this.

During the early months of 1770, the extent to which the authorities had misunderstood the character of the yellow trade gradually became evident. In May 1770, the *Manchester Mercury* reported that:

So great a number of persons, besides those formerly found out, are discovered to have been concerned in coining his Majesty's current money, in
and about [the county of] York, and the characters of so many of them have
always been so fair and unquestionable that the gentlemen of the law are
quite puzzled how to act in such embarrased circumstances.[278]

There has survived no explicit account of the precise rationale for
this embarrassment at the discovery of the unexpected social realities
of the yellow trade. However, there is little doubt that the 'gentlemen
of the law' were nonplussed primarily because their discovery indicated insuperable obstacles to a successful deterrent application of
the criminal law. The extent of participation in the trade was indicative of its distinctive character as an illegal business. The yellow trade
was very different from the general run of mid-eighteenth-century
counterfeiting, in that coining was combined with clipping. Participation at almost every social level in the locality was massive,
because clipping was so accessible, so lucrative and because it carried
with it such a small risk of detection. Once the degree of temptation
presented by the trade was revealed to be so enormous as to persuade
huge numbers of formerly 'respectable' men to succumb, the authorities' initial confidence that a sustained application of the terror of the
law could deter offenders was quickly dissipated. The Mint Solicitor,
the most influential 'gentleman of the law' in the affair, was in no
doubt that because clipping was 'so easily executed, with but a small
degree of care [and] without a possibility of detection', the coin laws
could never prevent it.[279]

Doubtless the determined use of pardons, rewards and informers
could have secured some additional executions, in spite of the
obstacles which the trade presented to the collection of effective
evidence.[280] However, additional executions can hardly have
appeared of great value to the authorities, when they considered the
temptations of clipping to be so great that 'the execution of the law,
if it had an execution once a week, would by no means remedy the
evil'.[281] Under such circumstances, additional executions would have
served merely to emphasize the authorities' revengeful impotence and
to subvert that belief in the majesty and strength of the law, which so
much effort was customarily devoted to promoting.[282]

However, the campaign to apply the criminal law against the yellow
traders had not been undertaken merely to prevent the flouting of the
coin laws. Rockingham had also been anxious to reverse the humiliation which the authorities had suffered through the defiant murder
of William Deighton, and to restore the credibility of the civil power.

The abandonment of such a highly public campaign, on the grounds that the criminal law was ineffectual in the face of the unforeseen implications of the organization of the yellow trade, threatened to expose authority and the law to additional contempt. It was a particular concern of those who administered the criminal law in the eighteenth century to avoid such exposure, as Douglas Hay has pointed out.[283] The pattern of discharges, prosecutions and pardons in 1770 suggests that the authorities set out to manage the abandonment of their campaign in such a way as to conceal the actual weakness of their position.

In March 1770 at least twenty-seven offenders from the Halifax area were imprisoned in York Castle to await trial on capital coinage charges. Yet it was decided to try only four at the subsequent assizes and discharge the rest. After three of the four had been convicted, 'the King's Council, fearful of an acquittal, chose rather as an act of lenity of the Crown to produce no evidence than hazard the ill consequences of an acquittal on an attempt to convict'.[284] Three convictions having been achieved, it was evidently considered preferable to feign mercy than to expose any weakness. In coinage cases elsewhere, however, the authorities were by no means so coy about acquittals. At the trials of members of Lightowller's gang on capital coining charges at Lancaster in 1756, the effort to secure convictions was continued, even after two men had been found guilty. Five others were acquitted.[285]

The pattern of prosecution in the Lightowller affair strongly suggests an attempt to maximize the number of convictions and deterrent executions, even at the risk of embarrassing acquittals. The equivalent pattern in Yorkshire is much more suggestive of a desire to minimize humiliation, in the context of the abandonment of any thoroughgoing effort to use convictions and executions as a deterrent tool. The Yorkshire pattern can best be interpreted as an attempt to achieve a respectable minimum of convictions (relative to the huge number of offenders charged) at the lowest possible cost in humiliating acquittals.

Clearly, the authorities considered that it was of primary importance, if they were to retain any credibility, that King David, the most notorious offender in custody, should be convicted. Unlike the other defendants, he was arraigned on four separate indictments.[286] It was only after he had been convicted that further prosecutions were abandoned.[287] Moreover, it appears that, out of the three convicted men, Rockingham was anxious to execute only the coining monarch himself (although, in the event, two of the three were executed).[288] It is unlikely that, alone, even such a royal example at the gallows could have been considered a genuinely deterrent permutation of the bloody arithmetic of pardon and execution, when the yellow trade had been so extensive and had involved such a direct challenge to the exercise of authority. All four members of Lightowller's gang convicted in 1756 had been executed. Rockingham's willingness to execute only King David indicates that the authorities' primary concern was for a suitable public affirmation of the illusion of power, in order to mask their retreat from a profoundly embarrassing exercise in law enforcement, which threatened to expose their weakness.

It had been to protect King David that William Deighton had been assassinated. In order to counteract this most blatant act of defiance against authority, it was clearly essential in 1770 for the authorities to convict and punish the murderers, who had been in custody since November 1769. At the Yorkshire Lent assizes in 1770 their trial was postponed until the Lammas assizes in August, in order to collect additional evidence.[289] The decision in August to have the murderers tried must have been taken in some desperation, for the authorities were well aware that their case was still a very weak one.[290] However, the potential humiliation of allowing men whose guilt was common knowledge to go free was as great as that of a failure on an attempt to prosecute. In the event, the three accused were acquitted. Yet it is significant that, unlike the discharged coinage offenders, the two acquitted men who had actually perpetrated the assassination were pursued with determination and ferocity for the next five years.[291] The double humiliation which they had inflicted on the authorities, by the murder and the acquittal, could not be permitted to go unpunished. Indeed, it called for a particularly savage exercise in exemplary counter-terror. When finally convicted and hanged in 1774 and 1775 (for robbing Deighton's body after the killing), it was ensured that the two murderers were made an especially 'notorious example to the public'.[292] After public execution at Tyburn near York, their bodies were hung in chains on Beacon Hill, overlooking the town of Halifax. Hanging in chains was a gory refinement of the ritual of execution, which was only applied when circumstances were considered to require exceptional deterrent severity. At Halifax it was given an additional symbolic twist by contriving the irons so that the right hand of at least one of the corpses pointed 'at the very place where the robbery was committed'.[293]

If the authorities' realization that clipping presented an insuperable temptation was at the heart of their decision to abandon the campaign against the yellow trade, the government's refusal to take any effective steps to reform the coinage can only have further contributed to their disillusionment. Clipping was rendered so extraordinarily accessible, profitable and free from risk in the Halifax–Rochdale area by a combination of the appalling general condition of the coinage and the acute local cash shortage, which facilitated the ready acceptance there of exceptionally diminished coin. Although an eighteenth-century government could hardly have remedied the local coin shortage by legislation or decree, it was within the power of government to restore the quality of the coin by such means. As legislation in 1773 was to demonstrate, measures to restore the quality of the coinage could eliminate the yellow trade virtually instantaneously. However, as the Mint Solicitor pointed out, diminished 'money is permitted to circulate, in vain are all prosecutions of diminishers'.[294]

In December 1769 a number of woollen merchants and manufacturers in the Halifax area made a voluntary agreement to refuse diminished and clipped coin. However, they were well aware that, faced with the local cash shortage, their agreement would be of little use without government support.[295] A large proportion of the local cash circulation passed through the hands of the local receivers and collectors of taxes. The merchants and manufacturers depended on them for cash to pay their workmen and suppliers. In conditions of cash shortage, they dared not refuse what the collectors and receivers offered, for fear of being denied any cash in future. Hence the requests from the Halifax–Rochdale area in 1769 and 1770 for a Treasury order to the receiver and collectors 'not to receive any money diminished so much as to be impassable in any other country and to cut it when offered them'.[296] Three Lancashire magistrates chided the Treasury board with the comment that 'if such an order had been given some years ago, very little bad money would have been made and very little good diminished'.[297]

The Lords of the Treasury were prepared to recommend the collectors of the land tax and the excise 'to co-operate with the gentlemen of the country in any proper measure for preventing the circulation of the debased coin', but they considered that they had no legal authority to give orders to refuse or cut diminished gold coin.[298] Mere recommendation was unavailing because the collectors, if they were to make their returns to London, were as much obliged to take what they could get as the local manufacturers. Voluntary agreement entirely failed to prevent the circulation of diminished and counterfeit coin.

There is no doubt that at law the Treasury had no power to order the tax collectors to refuse and cut diminished coin. The Act of 1698, which required such treatment for diminished silver, did not extend to the gold circulation.[299] However, government was unwilling in 1769–70 to take steps to alter the law, despite pressure from the Halifax locality and the Mint Solicitor. To have required the collectors to refuse and cut diminished gold coin, at a time when the general condition of the gold circulation was atrocious, would inevitably have led to a national gold recoinage. The prospect of a recoinage was unwelcome to any mid eighteenth-century government. Not only would it prove expensive, technically difficult to execute and disruptive of commercial life, but it threatened to reawaken embarrassing debates concerning the fundamental principles of the coinage and the responsibility for its regulation.[300]

However, within three years the accelerating decline of the quality of the gold coin in circulation forced the government's hand. The quality of the gold coin was rapidly deteriorating throughout Great Britain, but 'Yorkshire guineas' set the standard for diminishing elsewhere. It was renewed complaints from the West Riding in 1772 that eventually persuaded the Treasury to reconsider its refusal to regulate the coin.[301] The Mint Solicitor's opinion was consulted. He reaffirmed his belief that only by ordering the collectors of taxes to cut diminished coin could diminishing be prevented. Such a policy was tentatively decided upon. However, legislative action was delayed until mid 1773, as a result of the complexity and sensitivity of the issue.

The Treasury did not choose to proceed upon matters of such nicety without taking every advice they could, both from those who were best judges of the political consequences and those who were best judges of the points of law. Upon that ground the propositions were referred to the law officers of the Crown. It [sic] was for some time under their consideration and seldom had they had a matter which required a more ample consideration.[302]

The leading government figures in the affair – the prime minister, Lord North, and Charles Jenkinson, a man with considerable experience in the Treasury – were haunted by the precedent of the disastrous silver recoinage of 1696–8.[303] It had involved enormous frauds at public expense and consequently massive taxation. In order to avoid politically embarrassing additional taxes, it was decided, in contrast to 1696–8, initially to offer no compensation to the holders of unlawfully diminished guineas. Gold coins were to be withdrawn from circulation at their bullion rather than their face value. The scheme obliged those who had for years innocently accepted diminished coin at face value to bear directly the cost of restoring the quality of the coinage.[304] Implicitly, government had chosen to repudiate responsibility for having permitted diminishing to flourish. Although the scheme was the only practical method of preventing fraud and hence massive additional government expenditure, its inequity generated bitter public complaint and political dissension.[305]

However, the government proved able to weather the political storm, in part because opponents of the measure were presented with a *fait accompli*. A bill was surreptitiously slipped through Parliament, with a minimum of debate, in June and July 1773, unusually close to the end of the session.[306] It required Exchequer tellers, and permitted others, to cut any gold coin that appeared to be counterfeit, or to have been diminished other than by reasonable wear. The collectors of revenue were, in practice, ordered to cut coins according to a table of weights, which varied with the age of the coin. The oldest guineas were allowed to pass if deficient by no more than one shilling's worth of gold. This standard was chosen, not on the basis of estimated wear over a given time span, but rather to avoid throwing too much coin out of circulation at once, especially in Yorkshire.[307] Approximately £3.8 million were withdrawn under the July 1773 Act, at a loss to the holders of the coin estimated at £300,000.[308]

The table of weights adopted in 1773 still offered the diminisher the opportunity to clip heavy coin down to the arbitrary weight thresholds adopted for guineas of different ages. In order to prevent further diminishing, it was essential to bring the gold circulation as a whole as close to the Mint standard as was considered technically and commercially feasible. Further measures in 1774 and 1776 progressively removed from circulation all coins deficient by more than 2d. in value.[309] The total charge on the Exchequer for the whole recoinage was in excess of £750,000.[310] Over a period of four years, gold coin valued at over £16.5 million was withdrawn from circulation and recoined.[311]

At this price was bought the eradication of the yellow trade. When the 1773 Act came into operation, clipping in Yorkshire ceased within days.[312] It became customary to weigh all gold coin. Guineas worth less than twenty shillings by weight were liable to be cut by the collectors and therefore ceased to enjoy currency in general transactions. In Yorkshire, by 1773, few guineas were worth even twenty shillings by weight. One consequence of this was temporarily to exacerbate the already severe local coin shortage. Local commercial life was disrupted as a result, and considerable complaint generated.[313] However, the extremely poor quality of most coins in Yorkshire, relative to the threshold weights established in 1773, also rendered the potential there for continued clipping especially restricted. Some 'old offenders' did manage to acquire heavy guineas and diminish them to the threshold weights,[314] but any unlawfully diminished coin, of whatever weight, was likely to be cut. The 1776 regulation brought the threshold weight for guineas in circulation so close to the standard Mint weight that diminishing was hardly worthwhile, unless an impossibly large circulation could be sustained.

The recoinage removed the preconditions which made the practice of the yellow trade possible. Confronted with a newly minted gold currency, the popular solidarities that had defended the trade so tenaciously against the application of the coin laws were of no avail. Yet a multitude in the Halifax area had partaken of the lavish financial benefits of the trade. How they reacted to its demise is poorly documented. The trade's extinction can only have added to the widespread economic distress which characterized the Halifax locality in 1773. The recoinage coincided with and exacerbated a major national economic depression. This hit the West Riding worsted industry especially hard. Most of the period between the Seven Years War and the War of American Independence was difficult for that industry, but the years 1773 and 1774 were particularly bad. In both years, employment and piece rates were at an exceptionally low level.[315]

The available evidence, which is of variable quality, suggests that at least some former participants in the yellow trade responded to these circumstances by taking up other forms of illegal appropriation. However, these were forms of illegal behaviour which had previously been clearly differentiated from the trade. It was widely believed in the Halifax area, during the immediate aftermath of the 1773 Coin Act, that 'the rascals who are now prevented from diminishing the gold coin' would turn to theft.[316] There appears no significant increase in the number of indictments for theft emanating from Halifax parish between the year ending July 1773 and the year ending July 1774.

However, the local newspapers carried an unprecedented number of reports of thefts, break-ins and burglaries at or near Halifax during the latter period. Local gentlemen were already so alarmed in August 1773 that they decided to shoulder the expense of a watch to patrol the streets of the town during the ensuing winter. One local merchant with tenters in a rural area of the parish suffered so many thefts during the winter of 1773-4 that he eventually set man-traps in his tenter fields. In November 1774, a Halifax correspondent in the *Leeds Intelligencer*, reviewing 'the frequent and almost daily robberies committed in this parish' pinpointed as one of the principal causes the fact 'that all the persons who of late years were employed in the iniquitous practice of coining, and who had contracted a habit of idleness and extravagance, are let loose upon the country, whilst their trade is quite ruined'.[317]

If the opinions expressed in these newspaper reports can be accepted as reliable, it would appear that at least some of those who had benefited from the yellow trade may have turned to theft after its demise. Much more direct evidence from the legal records indicates that several leading yellow traders took up other varieties of illegal appropriation, in particular forgery of the paper currency, production of bad coppers and counterfeiting the precious metal coinages, in mixed or base metals. In character, these activities bore a closer relationship to the yellow trade than did theft, but like theft, they had not been associated with the trade during the years of its prosperity. Clipped gold as a raw material for counterfeits had disappeared with the extinction of clipping, but the skills of those whom the yellow trade had taught to coin in gold could be transferred to counterfeiting in mixed and base metals. The unprecedented cash famine in the West Riding between 1773 and 1776 facilitated the circulation of such counterfeits and forged notes. Yorkshire newspapers during those years were full of warnings about counterfeits in circulation, especially plated ones.[318] Eight men were indicted at York assizes for coinage offences committed in the Halifax area between 1774 and 1782.[319] Three were charged with possessing coining tools and the rest with counterfeiting the silver or copper coinages. Four of the eight had been among those incriminated in 1769. One of this four and another man incriminated in 1769 were tried in 1776 for forging paper currency. In one case, the offence involved the small denomination guinea banknotes which were issued in Yorkshire to mitigate the cash shortage.[320]

In assessing responses to the demise of the yellow trade, the most intractable problem concerns the attitude of the local public to these illegal activities, and to the participation in them of leading former yellow traders. It is improbable that the men of small capital, formerly so prominent in the trade, were in general sympathetic to any former associates who turned to indiscriminate theft. Especially if they were small manufacturers with tenters, they were particularly vulnerable to such depredations. Neither base- and mixed-metal counterfeiting, nor the forgery of commercial paper involved that intimate and reciprocal relationship with an extensive public that had characterized coining in the yellow trade (although the production of false coppers was more ambiguous in this respect). The relative ease with which base- and mixed-metal counterfeiters from Halifax parish were convicted on capital charges at York between 1774 and 1782 might indicate a significant popular unwillingness to extend the solidarities associated with the yellow trade to those who took up these pursuits.[321] On the other hand, the high conviction rate may have owed more to the extensive range of materials and equipment required for counterfeiting of this type. This tended to minimize the problem of collecting material evidence, which had proved so intractable when the authorities attempted to prosecute the activities comprising the yellow trade.[322]

Other evidence indicates that popular support and indeed respect for leading former yellow traders did not disappear with the material basis for mass participation in the trade. The huge crowds that attended at Beacon Hill in 1774 and 1775 to prevent the hangings in chains of the bodies of Deighton's murderers demonstrate continuing popular solidarity with the yellow traders and hostility to the authorities. The significance in this respect of the events leading to the public execution in 1783 on Beacon Hill of Thomas Spencer is less certain. Spencer, King David's brother in law and a prime mover behind the exciseman's murder in 1769, was the last of the leading yellow traders who can be identified as having suffered at the gallows. Yet he hanged, not for a coinage offence, but for a theft. The crime was perpetrated in the course of a grain riot and *taxation populaire* at Halifax in June 1783. Spencer joined the rioters as they marched through the 'upper hand country' in the direction of Halifax town. He proposed himself as leader and was readily adopted. On arrival at Halifax, he marshalled the rioters and directed their activities.[323] The mob's ready acceptance of Spencer's leadership may have stemmed from the fact that he was an ex-soldier and therefore well qualified to drill a body of rioters. However, it is clear that the extensive diffusion of the benefits of the yellow trade, during the years of its prosperity, had generated enormous local gratitude and respect towards its leading practitioners. The deference accorded to Spencer as riot captain in 1783 may indicate that such sentiments had been so pervasive that they could continue to flourish a decade after the demise of the trade itself.

The current historiography of crime and the law in eighteenth-century England is highly diverse in its methods and objectives. A broad concern among historians of the subject to understand changing patterns of behaviour defined as criminal in terms of prevailing social, political and economic transformations has spawned a wide variety of perspectives. However, two approaches to the central problems of locating changes in criminality within broader socio-economic relationships stand out. First, that approach which has focused on the relationship between secular trends in the incidence of criminality, as measured by aggregate indictment rates, and equivalent trends in various social and economic indicators.[324] Second, that which has stressed the social origins and purposes of the criminal law, with a particular emphasis on the relationship between legislative extensions of the criminal sanction and changing attitudes among the powerful towards property.[325]

Both approaches have major shortcomings. The eighteenth century did witness a redefinition as criminal of many activities that had previously been either outside the purview of the law or merely subject to civil actions. It also saw increasingly harsh penalties applied to pre-existing criminal offences, particularly through the massive extension of capital legislation. There is no question that such transformations are of considerable importance for the study of crime and the law in the eighteenth century, but it is also important to recognize that the status, at law, of the vast majority of those criminal cases which came before the courts of quarter sessions and assize during the century remained relatively stable.[326]

The comparison of secular trends in indictment rates with various indices of social and economic change ostensibly offers an attractive methodology for the analysis of those indictable offences that were not subject to major shifts in their legal status. It addresses the obvious historical questions concerning the nature of and reasons for changes in the incidence of criminality, and draws on a large body of criminological work that has applied similar techniques to modern criminal statistics.[327]

However, the damaging criticism that has been levelled at the use of the modern statistics is even more telling against these analyses of time series derived from eighteenth-century legal records.[328] It is extremely doubtful whether fluctuations in the number of indictments within any jurisdiction during the eighteenth century can be regarded as a measure of changes in some hypothetically quantifiable aggregate of offences that actually occurred. Changes in the number of indictments (and hence prosecutions) over time are at least as likely merely to reflect changes in the sensitivity to offences of victims and the officials who regulated entry into the judicial process, changes in other influences on the propensity of victims to prosecute, or changes in official objectives and policy. Moreover, the shortcomings of this approach are not restricted to the problem of the quantitative relationship between fluctuations in the numbers of indictments and the hypothetical 'dark figure'. There is also a qualitative problem, posed by the arbitrary legal categories employed in eighteenth-century indictments, which can mask important shifts in the character of offences and offenders. These shortcomings are compounded by others, deriving, for example, from the small annual totals of indictments within most eighteenth-century jurisdictions, which lead to tiny absolute fluctuations in the numbers of indictments acquiring unwarranted proportionate significance, or from the weakness of eighteenth-century aggregate population figures, which inhibit accurate comparisons of indictment *rates* across time.[329]

The history of the Yorkshire yellow trade highlights some of these shortcomings. Coining and clipping the precious metal coinages were offences which had long been capital and did not undergo major changes in their legal status during the eighteenth century. The changing and often conflicting responses of the authorities to the yellow trade cannot be explained by reference to broad shifts in the attitudes of legislators towards property. Indeed, government failed to respond to requests from powerful interests in Yorkshire for harsher legislation.[330] Yet the fluctuations in the numbers of indictments for these crimes are clearly inadequate as a measure of changes in the incidence and character of the offences themselves. Between 1757 and 1769 the single most important influence on the national level of indictments for coinage offences was not the actual incidence of such offences, but the Mint Solicitor's concern to limit his expenditure on prosecutions. Within Yorkshire, the year-by-year fluctuations in the number of capital coinage indictments between 1760 and 1773 bear no consistent relationship to the rising tide of diminished and counterfeit coin, reported in correspondence and the press. Moreover, the cramped definitions employed in these indictments provide no direct indication of the fact that, during this period, counterfeiting in base or mixed metals was eclipsed by coining in clipped gold.

This study of the brief but spectacular flourishing of the yellow trade has therefore adopted a different (although not necessarily wholly incompatible) approach to the problems of understanding the pattern of criminal activity within a broader historical context: an approach that turns on the relationship between changes in the organization of coinage offences and changes in the configuration of control. Indeed, it is a central contention of this study that neither component of that relationship can be understood without reference to the other.

Throughout the study, the term 'organization' has been applied to criminality, not in the restricted sense implied by the phrase 'organized crime', but rather to indicate the manner in which human activity is arranged for the purpose of bringing about any results that happen to be officially classified as criminal.[331] The changing structures of organization, thus defined, that characterized various of the activities proscribed by the eighteenth-century coinage laws have been analysed in terms of the changing opportunities for their practice provided by the legitimate order and the institutions that defended it.

Although this approach can no more offer an accurate and detailed quantitative measure of the changing incidence of these activities than the use of serial indictment statistics, it does provide a much more sophisticated guide to and understanding of the patterns of illegal abuse of the coinage during the eighteenth century. The character and incidence of such abuse, the techniques used to facilitate it and the relationship between those who practised it and the wider public did not remain constant during the course of that century. The most significant of these changes – the massive development, during the middle decades of the century, of diminishing the gold coin – was closely associated with the long-standing deterioration in the condition of the gold circulation as a whole. However, detailed analysis of the yellow trade, as opposed to other diminishing operations, demonstrates that the structures of organization that characterized a particular form of abuse were also conditioned by local social and economic circumstances, as well as by the character and interrelationship of the institutions of control at the local and national levels.

Despite the fact that the coin laws were subject to public, not private prosecution, the way the law was applied against the yellow traders confirms the emphasis placed by Douglas Hay on the highly discretionary character of most eighteenth-century legal process.[332] But neither the manner in which that discretion was exercised nor the interests it was manipulated to serve were monolithic. The powerful and the wealthy in the Halifax locality did contrive to use the law and the courts against the yellow traders as 'a selective instrument of class justice'.[333] However, they had to contend with the yellow traders' own ability to initiate legal proceedings, with the widely divergent ways in which those who staffed the legal system fulfilled the responsibilities of office, and with conflicts of interpretation and interest between themselves and the central government.

The law's discretionary characteristics offered the powerful and the wealthy considerable opportunity to manipulate it for their personal and collective ends. Hence the great West Riding worsted manufacturers, faced with the deleterious effects of the yellow trade on their business transactions outside the region, could invoke the coin laws to defend their interests, and indeed enhance the application of those laws by using their industrial police to collect evidence. For the manufacturers and local gentlemen, the coin laws were a resource to be mobilized in a manner akin to the promotion of a canal or a market hall. However, the subsequent history of the campaign against the yellow trade demonstrates that, though special interests could initiate criminal proceedings for their own purposes, the outcome of those proceedings was severely constrained by the complex and often contradictory influences which shaped the enforcement and administration of the criminal law.

The most spectacular influence inhibiting a successful application of the law was the determined defence of the illegal business by its numerous practitioners and supporters in the Halifax locality. The defenders of the trade undermined the attempt to apply the law not simply by means of their own solidarity and by bribery, intimidation and murder. They also demonstrated an acute knowledge of the law, the capacity to purchase legal expertise and an ability to manipulate legal procedure to their own advantage. Indeed, the events immediately preceding Deighton's murder indicate that such manipulation, rather than the more extreme forms of intimidation, was their preferred first response to the authorities' challenge.

The success or otherwise of criminal proceedings was also shaped by the manner in which the system of criminal justice was administered. Of importance were not merely the formalities and strict procedural rules which placed such limitations on the success of proceedings in the eighteenth-century criminal courts. The multiple and often contradictory sources and levels of authority within the system also operated to inhibit criminal proceedings. The yellow trade, as a result of its distinctive character as an illegal activity, touched on many different interests within the system, or interests influential upon it. It involved a group of offences subject to special prosecution procedures and personnel, it presented a massive public challenge to the wider authority of local officials, and ultimately it called into debate the highly sensitive issue of government coinage policy.

More is at issue here, therefore, than those policy anomalies within the machinery of justice which arose from ignorance, incompetence or the different administrative, financial or personal imperatives associated with particular offices. The outcome of the campaign against the trade also turned on changing interpretations, within the machinery of justice, of the character of the offences concerned and of the capacity of a conventional exercise of the criminal law to prevent them. The initial strategy of the campaign against the trade had been determined by the great manufacturers and local Supervisor of Excise, in an effort to reduce the trade's ravages upon their own financial transactions. As the campaign unfolded, and particularly after Deighton's death, its conduct came increasingly under the control of Rockingham and the Mint Solicitor, men whose allegiance and obligations in the affair were, to a much greater extent, aligned with the broader demands of county and, particularly, national government. As long as they believed that the character of the yellow trade rendered it susceptible to a deterrent application of the coin laws, there was no major conflict of strategy or interest with the original promoters of the campaign. Indeed, as far as Rockingham was concerned, Deighton's murder appeared to reinforce the need for a determined application of the coin laws, in order to counteract the yellow traders' humiliation of authority.

However, from the start, the Mint Solicitor was pessimistic about the possibility of successfully applying the coin laws. Rockingham and others also came to accept that their sanguine expectations of a concerted application of the law were based on a profoundly mistaken interpretation of the character of the trade. Under these circumstances, the overriding concern of those who now directed the campaign against the trade was to avoid the humiliation of an ineffective application of the law and thereby to safeguard the broader social purposes of the criminal law (although in this they were far from successful).[334] The interests of the original promoters of the campaign against the yellow trade were brushed aside. Their calls for the resumption of the legal campaign against the trade and for additional criminal legislation were rebuffed. In addition, their suggestions for administrative regulation of the coinage, designed to protect their interests against the ravages of the trade, were also rejected, because they ran contrary to the immediate political and economic interests of national government. It was only three years later, with considerable reluctance and after a very careful evaluation of the prevailing economic and political climate, that government eventually accepted that overriding economic and commercial considerations made recoinage unavoidable.

Of course, very few of the wide variety of criminal offences that came before the eighteenth-century criminal courts ultimately forced a government to the degree of expense and inconvenience that accompanied a recoinage. In this, as in other respects, the yellow trade was a highly distinctive form of illegal activity. However, in differentiating between the yellow trade and other illegal activities, this study has avoided the unsatisfactory distinction between 'social' and 'normal' crime which has been proposed by some eighteenth-century social historians. Although there is no unanimity among the proponents of this distinction as to what constitutes a 'social' as opposed to an 'ordinary' or 'normal' crime, key distinguishing features appear to be an element of social protest, strong communal support and a conflict of definition between the interpretation placed on the activity in question by those who participated in it and the interpretation imposed by the law.[335]

The principal object of the 'social' crime/'normal' crime distinction is, at its crudest, to isolate a group of eighteenth-century illegal activities as forerunners of popular political movements. These are distinguished, principally on the basis of popular support, from the bulk of criminal offences, which are relegated to the undifferentiated and apparently unproblematic category of nefarious crime. The value of such a teleological and one-dimensional typology is exceptionally dubious, and its applicability has been heavily qualified, on the ground that the evidence does not permit 'any tidy notion of a distinction between these two kinds of crime'. In particular, it has been pointed out, of both types of offender, that 'they inhabit – although perhaps at different edges of it – a common culture, that of the exploited labouring poor'. However, the authors of these qualifications still contend that 'there is a real difference in emphasis at each pole'.[336]

Clearly there were a number of illegal activities that were exceptional in the consistent and unequivocal popular support and participation that they enjoyed. But do even these activities, which appear most unambiguously to qualify for the label 'social' crime, have enough in common to justify that label's retention as a coherent category of analysis, especially when it carries the implication that all such activities were expressions of social protest against the prevailing social order and its values? Attitudes towards the coin in the Halifax area and the social conflicts and alliances which were associated with its abuse suggest considerable doubts.

The yellow trade clearly merits the label 'social' crime, as conventionally applied, in so far as it enjoyed massive support and an enormous degree of participation in the Halifax locality. Yet unlike, for example, poaching or wrecking, there is no evidence here of an attempt to legitimate this breach of the law by reference to a countervailing prescriptive right or customary usage. Nor is there any other evidence of a deep-seated or long-standing hostility in the area to the coin laws, as they applied to the gold coin. Indeed, the yellow traders distinguished their own activities from the deceit of base- or mixed-metal counterfeiting, which was by far the most frequently prosecuted abuse of the gold coinage in the middle decades of the eighteenth century. There is no evidence that the latter was widely supported or practised in the Halifax area in the period prior to the heyday of the trade. Like other eighteenth-century Englishmen, people in the Halifax area appear to have remained hostile to being passed near-worthless imitations of the higher-denomination precious metal coins. Local people at most social levels had some dealings in these coins and were therefore vulnerable to loss by such deceits, in the same way that they were vulnerable to casual theft, and generally disavowed it. Doubtless, base-metal counterfeiters (whose skills were highly appropriate), thieves and cheats all participated in the yellow trade, but most of its practitioners appear to have had no association with such activities. On the demise of the trade, some of its former practitioners did sustain their incomes by turning their new-found skills to other forms of counterfeiting and, perhaps, to theft. Yet, even if popular sympathy persisted towards those individual former members of the yellow trading elite who adopted other illegal activities, there is no evidence that base-metal counterfeiting or casual theft were, in the long term, any more tolerated in the area after the demise of the trade than before and during its existence. Halifax parish certainly did not become a sanctuary for base-metal counterfeiters.

All this is not, however, to suggest that there was ever a deep reverence in the locality for the coinage laws as such. Among those whose transactions were overwhelmingly local, concern for the integrity of the coinage extended only so far as the currently accept-able *local* standard: a standard that was judged in terms of the gold content of the coins that would freely circulate at face value in the locality. They had few scruples about clipping heavy coins that came into their possession, or about having the clippings made up into counterfeits, when, in the 1760s, the local cash shortage, combined with long-standing government neglect of the coinage, rendered the clipped coins and the counterfeits made from gold generally acceptable in the locality. Because the circulation of such coins did not deceitfully impose any direct loss on those whose transactions were local, the activities comprising the yellow trade appeared harmless to the bulk of the local population. They could be legiti-mated as being in no way contrary to the public interest.

One can detect here, as in the hostility of farmers to the game laws, a sense of injustice at the law's denial of the rights of property. The ferocious coin laws defined property that a man held in the form of gold coins as inviolable, thereby denying the owner the right to manipulate it to best advantage under the peculiar local circum-stances of the later 1760s. But this is not to suggest that the yellow trade was grounded in widespread popular opposition to the existence of the Mint monopoly, in the way that smuggling or illegal dealing in excisable goods drew on a profound popular resentment towards the fiscal state establishment. It was the *failure* by the Mint to supply a gold circulation adequate in quality and quantity for national commercial requirements that provided the opportunity to practise the yellow trade. If the Mint had provided an adequate gold coinage in the mid eighteenth century, it is improbable that such an exercise of its monopoly would have been an occasion for general grievance, at any social level. What resentment did exist in the Halifax locality towards the Mint's monopoly focused on its inadequacies.

It also proved possible to justify the yellow trade as being con-sistent with the public interest, because it provided a widely diffused source of income during a period of acute depression in the local staple industry. Indeed, the trade and mass support of it, can, in a sense, be conceived as a popular response or adaptation to the vagaries of eighteenth-century industrial capitalism. If so, then it was not a response that took the form of a conscious challenge to the prevailing economic order, or even a call for official redress of economic grievance. On the contrary, it involved the emphatically commercial exploitation of an opportunity, which, at least in part, was itself a product of the local economic crisis. The relationships of exchange that characterized the exploitation of that opportunity were in important respects similar to those typical of the region's depressed staple industry.

If the trade appeared overwhelmingly beneficent tot hose whose transactions were predominantly local, it also offered extraordinary profits to local businessmen whose transactions extended outside the locality. But it threatened their legitimate businesses and, in the long term, the national credit for all men of substance in the district. The configuration of local support for and opposition to the trade reflects these considerations.

The legitimate transactions of labouring men, tradesmen and the lesser manufacturers were predominantly local. In addition, their economic perspective was short term. Hence they shared in a thoroughgoing solidarity in support of the yellow trade (although it was the men of middling wealth who dominated the trade, by virtue of their much greater access to cash). The great manufacturers and merchants were divided between those who preferred a short-term advantage from participation in the trade and those who looked to the long-term interests of their legitimate business activities. This division may also reflect a geographical split between big businessmen in Halifax parish and those elsewhere in the textile district.

'Popular' support for the yellow trade therefore emerges as the product of a specific set of social alliances, closely related to the different economic implications of the trade for different social groups in the locality. These alliances were not necessarily duplicated in other illegal activities which enjoyed 'popular' support. Although Thomas Spencer led the 1783 grain riot into Halifax market, it is unlikely that those dealers in foodstuffs, who figure prominently with him among those accused of participation in the yellow trade, supported their former associate in this later involvement in a collective illegal activity. Similarly, false reeling and embezzlement of goods in manufacture, although widely practised and regarded as legitimate by putting-out workers in the local textile industries, were generally opposed by large and small manufacturers alike.

The configuration of active local opposition to the trade was shaped by similar consideration to those that moulded support. Unwavering in their hostility were those local big businessmen and gentry whose primary concern was for their long-term economic interests, viewed in a national perspective. However, the opposition of national government to the trade was much more equivocal. Undoubtedly successive mid eighteenth-century governments were not unaware of the dangers for the national economy posed by their continued neglect of the gold coinage. Yet they were prepared to deal with the consequences of their neglect only by recourse to the terrors of the criminal law (and then only under pressure). When the attempt to apply those terrors proved unsatisfactory, they resisted recoinage, fearful of the expense and political embarrassment.

The neglect of the gold coin by successive governments was the focus for the public and parliamentary outcry that accompanied the first steps towards recoinage. It was generally accepted that clipping had flourished only because of the irresistible temptations generated by government neglect. Hence the outrage of many MPs at the ministers' refusal to offer compensation to those whose clipped coin was withdrawn from circulation at its bullion value. This action, they argued, was a rank injustice; an arbitrary repudiation of a moral and financial responsibility towards, in particular, bankers and other wealthy men who had been obliged to hold large quantities of such coin, for want of any other.

This argument rested on an explanation of the extraordinary proliferation of clipping in the middle decades of the eighteenth century which left government answerable for another, weightier injustice. If the responsibility for the spread of clipping actually lay with successive governments, rather than with individual offenders, then the behaviour of those governments, in prosecuting and indeed hanging those who clipped, was grossly unjust. Yet there was only one MP in the 1774 coinage debate who pointed out that for government to 'put people into temptations human nature can't resist [and] then go to prosecute [was] an act of great cruelty'.[337] His colleagues were anxious enough to use the argument that government was responsible for clipping in order to berate the ministry for its denial of compensation. They conveniently ignored the fact that the same argument called into question the assumption that every offender had an absolute responsibility for his transgressions – an assumption that was fundamental to the eighteenth-century criminal law.

6 The King's Bench prison in the later eighteenth century: law, authority and order in a London debtors' prison

Joanna Innes, Girton College, Cambridge

The government of the King's Bench [prison] . . . must be allowed not only mild, but liberal to a degree.

The Debtor and Creditor's Assistant (1793)

It would be highly presuming in your petitioners to attempt to shew that the deprivation of liberty is one of the greatest evils that can befall Man; or that any exaggeration of this evil through the conduct of those to whose custody prisoners for debt are committed is exceedingly reprehensible in itself, and a direct violation of the statutes which the Legislature in their humanity have thought fit to make on behalf of persons in that unfortunate situation.

Petition of prisoners to the court of King's Bench (1782)

Englishmen must and will be free, despite prison, chains and death.

Worcester Journal (1769)

This essay sets out to investigate imprisonment for debt in the eighteenth century by an examination of the King's Bench prison, the largest of the debtors' prisons in England. The discussion is divided into five sections. The first examines the legal process by which debtors might be imprisoned. It seeks to explain both why the debt laws were criticized and why they were defended, as well as demonstrating how the imprisoned debtor's sense of grievance grew out of public ambiguity towards the law and the anomalies of the law itself. The second section describes the prison environment and the nature of officialdom in the prison. Most accounts of eighteenth-century gaols have been written from the point of view of such reformers as John Howard. There has been very little attempt to see the prisoners in their own terms. This essay offers a different approach: the prison environment is not depicted as a world of corruption in earnest need of moral reform; rather, it is portrayed from the point of view of the prisoners (many of whom would have regarded the reformers' proposals as anathema) and as a functioning social environment. This perspective seems especially appropriate as the prisoners had far more influence and impact on the day-to-day running of the prison and the nature of prison life than either those who wielded authority over them or the reformers. The prison officers, as the second section demonstrates, were a weak body whose effective exercise of authority depended upon the support of the prison population. They therefore needed to appear to be acting legitimately in the eyes of the prisoners, and this both served as a constraint upon authority and affected the ways in which it was exercised. The vacuum created by the absence of an effective formal presence in prison life was, as the third section shows, filled by the prisoners themselves. They established their own sophisticated prison economy as well as complex organs of self-government, notably the so-called prison 'college'. Sections two and three portray the imprisoned debtor not as a languishing and impotent figure, but as an individual capable of affecting his own fate and of participating in many ways in what was a viable community.

The fourth section examines the relationship between prisoners' institutions and the formal authorities, and discusses the ways in which the college's notion of harmony either clashed or conformed with the marshal's idea of prison order. It explains how a viable compromise between the college and the prison officers worked, and in what circumstances such a relationship was likely to break down. The final section examines one special instance of this breakdown in 1770–1, with the emergence of a campaign within the prison walls for the abolition of imprisonment for debt on the grounds that such a practice was 'unconstitutional'. This radical campaign is used to illustrate the weakness of authority in the gaol and the use to which the prisoners' institutions could be put, and to make a number of general points about debtors' attitudes towards the law and towards authority in the prison.

The debtor and the law

The eighteenth-century English economy rested upon an extensively ramified network of credit and debt, in which all sorts of men and women, from gentry and great merchants to shopkeepers and wage labourers, were deeply implicated. The reasons for this ubiquitous practice of borrowing and lending were many, notably a shortage of specie, the absence of any great number of formal financial institu-

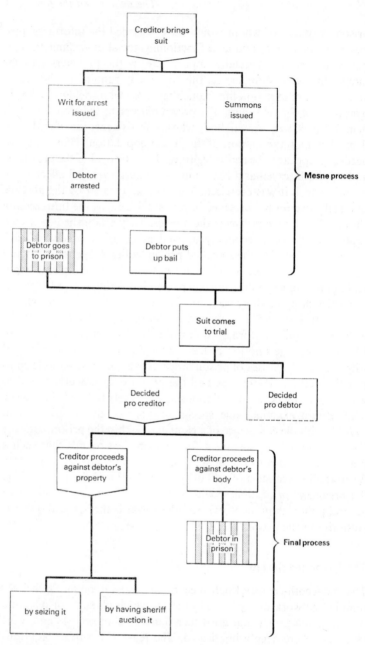

The legal process for the collection of debts: an instrument in the hands of the creditor

tions and the amount of circulating (as opposed to fixed) capital in most commercial enterprises.[1] Legal procedures governing indebtedness were of considerable importance inasmuch as they were supposed to sustain confidence in the system of credit which underlay the English economy.

The foundations of the eighteenth-century legal process governing debt were laid in the later middle ages when the courts first began to offer a general service to creditors of all kinds, to aid them in the collection of debts.[2] The process current in Hanoverian England was a *civil* process, which could be initiated by any creditor owed a debt of forty shillings or more, in any of the more important courts handling civil suits. On commencing the process the creditor acquired a number of powers over his debtor. He could order him to be brought into court to attend the hearing of the suit, either by a simple summons, or by having him arrested and held to bail or, in default of bail, by having him cast into prison (see the diagram on page 252). If, at the trial of the suit (which might occur several months later), the debt was found to be good, the creditor could choose to proceed 'in execution' either against the property of the debtor (by having the sheriff seize and sell the debtor's chattels) or 'against his body', that is, he could have him detained in prison as a pledge for ultimate payment. Thus, two kinds of imprisonment for debt were possible: pre-trial and post-trial, the first called 'imprisonment on mesne process' and the second 'imprisonment on final process'. The debtor imprisoned on final process was, in normal circumstances, dependent upon his creditor for his discharge.[3]

Eighteenth-century critics of this process singled out as its most remarkable and unjustifiable feature its gift of extraordinary discretionary powers to the creditor. Certainly the process is less well described as a system of court-supervised arbitration than as a system of legalized bullying. Throughout, the courts played no more than a passive and procedural role, never attempting to ascertain the debtor's resources nor to impose any kind of settlement. It was normal in civil cases for a suitor to enjoy great latitude in the conduct of his suit but, in the case of suits for debt the debtor's liberty at stake, the creditor's discretion had an exceptionally oppressive aspect.

According to the blackest pictures painted of the practice in debt cases (favoured by eighteenth-century critics and, frequently, by historians), creditors were accustomed to exercise their discretionary powers to the full, seizing upon penniless debtors and casting them into prison to rot. This oppressive proceeding, critics maintained, was encouraged by the inefficiency of the alternative process against a debtor's property: land could not be seized for debt, nor could liquid assets such as bills of exchange; nor could any arrangement be made for tapping future earnings.

Critics of the law saw incarcerated debtors as the victims of a process at once capricious and inefficient. Nevertheless, there was always a substantial body of citizens, usually tradesmen, who defended existing legal arrangements and opposed alterations in the law. They did so, we may suppose, less because they relished the power of incarceration, than because they knew that the law, for all its inadequacies, worked, and sometimes worked well, providing an appropriate mechanism for securing the payment of debts.[4] Most suits reached some kind of resolution so that it was not necessary to gaol the debtor. The long-term imprisonment of debtors was therefore not a necessary consequence of the legal process, but a symptom of its (periodic) failure.

In order to understand the ways in which the debt laws functioned, we have to remember the circumstances of most actions for debt. An action was not usually brought against someone who was penniless or who had a balance of debts over assets; but simply against someone who had contracted a financial obligation which he had failed to discharge. A creditor would commonly try appeals, demands and threats before actually going to law. Only when these failed to move a recalcitrant debtor would a creditor initiate proceedings to gain for himself an enhanced coercive negotiating power.

What a creditor wanted, in these circumstances was, above all, the power to *threaten* imprisonment. A debtor who was brought to court, even if he could put up bail, received a forceful reminder of his perilous situation. Court appearance might well induce a debtor with resources to re-order his priorities and settle outstanding claims. Even a debtor without resources might find himself able, under the shadow of the law, to dredge up sufficient funds from friends and relatives.

In 1791 a House of Commons committee discovered that, from about 12,000 bailable writs issued against debtors in the city of London and the county of Middlesex in the preceding year, only about 1200 commitments to prison had ensued.[5] The greater majority of prosecuted debtors therefore never ended up in gaol. Some, no doubt, evaded arrest, others probably proved so unforthcoming that their creditors, deterred by legal costs, abandoned their suits. But a great many paid up, and they therefore demonstrate the successful application of the debt laws and show the deterrent value of threatened imprisonment.

Of those debtors who were committed to prison in the late eighteenth century, the majority (by the evidence of the same Commons report) were detained on mesne process only, that is, they were imprisoned because they were unable to put up bail.[6] Mesne process imprisonment was not completely indeterminate, and could end when the suit came to trial. Creditors must have hoped that the debtors' desire to get out of prison would drive them to strenuous efforts to pay off the debt. The King's Bench prison books, which record the ground of a prisoner's ultimate discharge, show that creditors' expectations were often fulfilled.[7] Many imprisoned on mesne process settled with their creditors, thus cutting off the suit before it ever came to trial. In many other cases, however, frustrated creditors abandoned their suits when the cold bath of imprisonment failed to have the desired effect. In these circumstances, debtors, after remaining in prison for several months, became 'supersedable' – eligible to apply for a discharge from the court.[8]

Creditors cannot have expected much from the minority of debtors confined on final process. When debtors held out against their creditors long enough to be imprisoned, the chances of their paying were exiguous. Commitment to prison reduced the chance that the debtor would pay still further if only because, when the news spread of a man's going to prison, all his creditors would hasten to slap writs on him. Prisoners for debt thus represented the failure rate of the legal process. As an eighteenth-century proverb had it, 'A prison pays no debts.' And yet creditors argued keenly for the preservation of imprisonment – for the sake of what pickings there might be, and because they wanted their threats to have teeth.

It might appear from this account that the debtor was entirely at the creditor's mercy. But, in fact, debtors were as capable of exploiting aspects of the law as their creditors, and could marshal considerable powers of resistance to their prosecutors. Although the courts made little active attempt to defend their interests, they did hedge the operation of the law with a multitude of restrictions which debtors could exploit to their own advantage.[9] Thus, for example, the bailiffs' powers of arrest were strictly circumscribed. They could not make arrests at night, nor on Sundays, nor could they break into a house in order to make an arrest, and if they did infringe any of these conditions then they were acting without legal authority and could be resisted by force. If a debtor was prepared to regulate his life very carefully, and to be always on his guard, he could avoid arrest more or less indefinitely and, moreover, could probably count on mob support in fighting off bailiffs' incursions. Even when captured, the debtor was under no legal compulsion to surrender what he had, unless the creditor attempted the difficult course of proceeding against his property. If, instead, the creditor chose to proceed against the debtor's body and keep him in prison (strictly an alternative to process against property), the debtor could retain everything he owned and spend it as he pleased.

Because imprisonment actually offered the debtor *protection* for his property, some men chose to have themselves imprisoned by 'friendly actions'.[10] Baffled creditors frequently complained that debtors' prisons were a haven for the spendthrift, and on at least one occasion in the eighteenth century they sought statutory powers to compel their debtors to come out of prison and make some kind of settlement.[11]

Even in prison the debtor did not languish but was able to fall back on a number of expedients to relieve his situation. Certain privileges were available to facilitate debtors' efforts to sort out their affairs.[12] Prison staff often allowed them, formally or informally, to go out of the prison on day trips. But the most important liberty which debtors were allowed was that of living outside prison, usually in the immediate vicinity of the gaol and under the jurisdiction of the prison government. This privilege was not automatically available, and was usually offered only to debtors who could find friends to stand surety for their debts. In the King's Bench the system of allowing debtors to live outside the prison was more extensively developed than anywhere else. Several square miles around the prison, called 'the Rules', was designated as the area in which prisoners might settle. Prisoners living in the Rules could wander freely within the area, but were not supposed to go outside it. As many as one-third of all debtors committed to the King's Bench at one time were settled in the Rules.[13] The privilege of the Rules was especially sought after by tradesmen committed for debt, who hoped, by setting up in business again, to provide themselves with a living income.[14] As prisoners, such tradesmen were not liable for arrest for debt, but presumably they would not have been able to get much credit.

Both in the Rules and the prison itself, debtors called meetings and negotiated with their creditors; they also sought legal advice. They might consult any of a number of debtors' handbooks, published throughout the eighteenth century, which strove both to instruct debtors in the law of debt (particularly those portions which they might invoke in their own defence) and to teach them survival tactics for prison life.[15] In addition, debtors' needs were served by 'gaol lawyers' and by others with legal knowledge (such as former bailiffs, prisoners who were themselves lawyers, or even the prison staff) who provided a minor service industry centred on the London prisons. Such 'gaol lawyers' provided instruction in techniques of manipulating the law to the creditor's loss; they also contributed a sophisticated legitimating rhetoric to debtor activities.[16]

These services helped create a 'debtor ethos' in prisons. Debtor communities developed their own notions of legitimacy which were often at odds with those of creditors. Because it was possible for debtors to do much to advance their own interests within a legal framework, many of them insisted that they had the greatest respect for property and propriety, even as they fought against surrendering to the claims made upon them. Many debtors were prepared to make an even stronger case for their activities. They argued that the state of the law of debt was such that creditors were able to make an arbitrary assault on property and liberty. Their own efforts to resist such monstrous power were, by contrast, a vindication of the spirit of English law.[17]

This 'debtor ethos' derived a certain amount of support from the sympathy that the public at large extended to debtors.[18] For a number of reasons eighteenth-century public opinion never entirely reconciled itself to the fate of the debtor. Ubiquitous credit meant that almost every Englishman was a potential candidate for imprisonment for debt. It was recognized that debtors were not always to blame for their insolvency: some suffered through accidents of fire or theft, trade or health, or even from the vindictive action of an enemy who had chosen to exploit a debt unfairly. And the notion that the blameless were subjected to what appeared to be punishment (though in law it was not) caused some disquiet. In consequence, giving food and clothing to poor debtors was a favourite work of eighteenth-century charity,[19] and some of the charitable even paid off the debts of minor debtors, a project which was institutionalized in the 1770s with the foundation of the Society for the Discharge and Relief of persons imprisoned for small debts, known as the Thatched House Society.[20]

Such interventions were not only privately sponsored. From the late sixteenth century first the Crown, and then Parliament, made efforts to speed the discharge of imprisoned debtors by setting up commissions to investigate individual cases and to force settlements

The legal process for the collection of debts: opportunities for the debtor

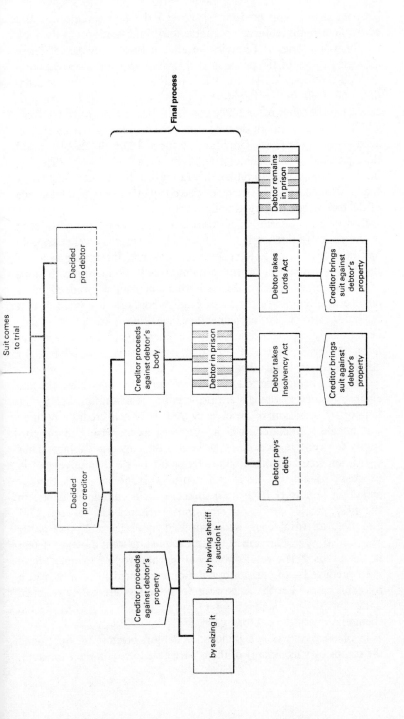

between debtor and creditor.[21] Between the late seventeenth and early nineteenth centuries, parliamentary intervention chiefly took the form of a series of Temporary Relief or Insolvency Acts.[22] These ordered justices of the peace in each county to form a special commission on a named date to invite applications in the form of schedules of assets from all debtors imprisoned (on mesne or final process) at some other named date (previous to the passage of the Act), and to discharge all those who appeared to have given an honest account of themselves. Creditors of the debtors discharged could then proceed against debtors' *property*, as listed in their schedules, but were not allowed to return them to prison for the same debts. By the 1770s such Acts were being passed every other year, and hundreds of debtors were discharged under every Act.[23]

Conceived as charitable gestures these Acts were worthy enough; as the policy of a sovereign legislature, however, they were curiously half-hearted measures. Revealing concern with the inadequacies of the debt law, they yet restricted themselves to tampering with some of its consequences. No doubt Parliament shunned radical interference with the sacred corpus of English law; it is also possible that the half-heartedness of parliamentary intervention was finely judged: because only imprisoned debtors were relieved, and then only irregularly, the basic system of threat and coercion was left intact for creditors to employ as they saw fit.

Far from being a period of great reform in the debt laws, the late eighteenth century saw a stern pro-creditor reaction, marked by the temporary cessation of Insolvency Acts.[24] Much creditor opinion was hostile to the Acts, which were seen as increasing the opportunity for debtors to exploit the law to their own advantage. Thus significant numbers of debtors were said to have themselves put in prison by friendly actions in anticipation of Insolvency Acts, thereby acquiring immunity from imprisonment for accumulated debts. In the 1780s hostile sentiment temporarily triumphed: between 1781 and 1793 all Insolvency Acts proposed in Parliament were either abandoned when Parliament was prorogued or went down to defeat in the Lords.[25] The results were not as catastrophic as might have been predicted – the prison population continued to turn over at a tolerable rate – but the Acts were none the less ultimately resumed under the ardent championship of certain MPs who had associated themselves with the debtors' cause.[26]

Insolvency Acts were significant to debtors because they provided the means by which many of them were able to regain their freedom.

They were also significant in other ways. First, they encouraged debtors to see themselves as suffering under abused power, because they apparently provided evidence that Parliament was not happy with the way creditors were using the legal process. Second, they drew the attention of debtors towards Parliament as a fulcrum of change. From the late seventeenth century, year after year, debtors in all the larger debtors' prisons in England bombarded Parliament with petitions for Insolvency Acts, sometimes making suggestions for the inclusion of specific provisions.[27]

The protests against imprisonment for debt that emerged from the 1770s onwards took up the ideas and rhetoric of nationally resurgent radicalism, but also drew on this long heritage of prisoner activity and resistance to the debt law. The sense of grievance which underpinned debtors' protests was never nurtured in isolation: it thrived on a highly ambivalent public attitude towards the law, and drew sustenance from the ambiguities and complexity of the law itself. These circumstances sustained the imprisoned debtor's belief that he had an enduring legitimate grievance; they also, paradoxically, maintained his morale in circumstances of considerable adversity.

The King's Bench prison: prisoners and authority

All the prisoners in the King's Bench prison were, without exception, prisoners of the court of King's Bench; the vast majority were debtors, prosecuted on the 'plea' (civil) side of the court. The remainder were products of the 'Crown side', or had been committed for contempt of court. These occasionally included felons on appeal from the lower courts, but frequently such difficult prisoners were sent to Newgate; those allowed to remain were minor offenders whose presence made little impact on prison life.[28]

Debtors were committed to the King's Bench prison at the rate of several hundred a year, the annual total rising steeply between 1760 and 1780 and levelling off for two decades thenceforth at a new high level[29] (see the diagram on page 262). The total population of the prison varied widely according to circumstance. Very large numbers were generally confined before an Insolvency Act, while hundreds were released when the Act came into operation. Figures for the total population were reported occasionally; some of these are set forth in the table (page 263). These figures give the total population of prisoners, not that of the prison, which was substantially greater since it included many prisoners' families. In 1791 it was reported

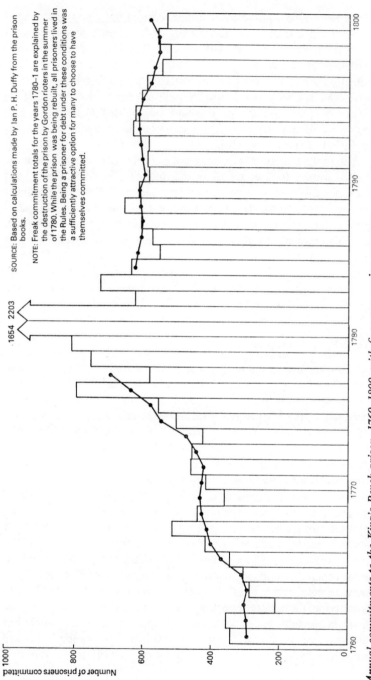

SOURCE: Based on calculations made by Ian P. H. Duffy from the prison books.

NOTE: Freak commitment totals for the years 1780–1 are explained by the destruction of the prison by Gordon rioters in the summer of 1780. While the prison was being rebuilt, all prisoners lived in the Rules. Being a prisoner for debt under these conditions was a sufficiently attractive option for many to choose to have themselves committed.

Annual commitments to the King's Bench prison, 1760–1800, with five-year moving averages

Total population of prisoners, King's Bench prison

Year	Total	Living in prison	Living in Rules
1768	571	330	241
1774	424	324	100
1776 (i)	444	364	80
1782 (i)	457	450	7
1782 (ii)	515	485	30
1783	582	532	50
1787	430	370	60
1788	444	340	104
1781	570	500	70

that of the 570 prisoners, about 340 had wives and children living in the prison.[30]

A sketchy social analysis of the prison population was provided by the prisoners themselves in 1795.[31] Of 800 prisoners they counted

		%
60	military and naval	8
40	mercantile	5
50	manufacturers	7
110	mechanics	14
160	agriculturians	20
150	trade	19
200	labourers	25

The table, which appears to be arranged on the basis of the social hierarchy, suggests the range of the prison population. A category surprisingly not identified, and hard to locate within this table, is that of the professional men – lawyers, clergymen, estate agents, journalists – who seem to have been present in fair numbers.

Almost all the prisoners for debt were men. Married women were not legally responsible for their own debts; the few women debtors were either widows or single, independent women. John Howard, the prison reformer, who recorded the total prisoner population in 1779 and again in 1782, estimated male-to-female ratios of 19:1 and 25:1 respectively.[32] The presence of many prisoners' wives within the prison, of course, ensured that women were not so greatly outnumbered as might appear from these figures.

The prison itself consisted of a number of brick buildings standing in an open yard which was enclosed by a high brick wall.[33] Located on the southern outskirts of London, it stood little more than a mile

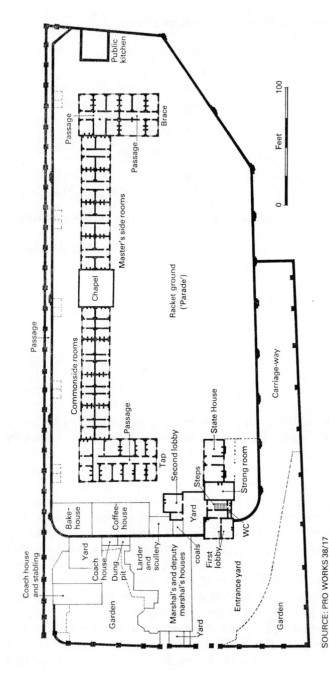

Passage

Coach house and stabling

Garden

Yard

Coach house

Dung pit

Larder and scullery

Marshal's and deputy marshal's houses

Yard

Bake-house

Coffee-house

coals

First lobby

WC

Entrance yard

Garden

Commonside rooms

Chapel

Passage

Tap

Second lobby

Steps

Yard

State House

Strong room

Carriage-way

Master's side rooms

Passage

Brace

Racket ground ('Parade')

Public kitchen

0   100

Feet

SOURCE: PRO WORKS 38/17

A nineteenth-century plan of the King's Bench prison, which shows the basic layout of the prison from the later eighteenth century south of the Thames, by the side of the main road leading south from London Bridge. The Rules of the prison encompassed the whole of St George's Fields, and a small part of Southwark.[34] The site of the prison had been chosen in the 1750s for its healthy qualities, the hope being that prisoners would benefit from the fresh air.[35] By the end of the century, however, roads had begun to branch out through the fields and the metropolis to extend around the prison.

In general plan the King's Bench was a 'free prison', almost without internal barriers. Prisoners were able to move from one part to another as they pleased. The major part of the buildings was taken up with the prisoners' accommodation which was not especially prison-like, except inasmuch as large blocks of rooms were not at this time common in London. Most of the prisoners' rooms were contained in a large dormitory block. A small group of rooms was set aside for Crown prisoners; the rest, reserved for debtors, were various in quality: those under the shadow of the prison wall, the least desirable, were called the 'commonside' rooms (and the prisoners who lived in them, commonside prisoners), the remainder were 'master's side rooms' inhabited by master's side prisoners. A dozen especially luxurious rooms were set apart in a special building called the State House. Rents were charged for all these rooms at moderate rates set by the court of King's Bench: 1s. a week for commonside rooms, 1s. 6d. for master's side rooms, 2s. 6d. for the State House.[36] (A London artisan paid for his rent at this time about 2s. 6d. a week.)[37] Every prisoner had a key to his own room, which he could furnish as he pleased.

In the prison as originally constructed there were twelve rooms for Crown prisoners, twenty-four on the commonside and eighty-four on the master's side, and twelve in the State House: 132 in all, billed as accommodation for 200 prisoners. The new buildings of the 1770s added 108 more rooms; later in the century still more were added. In the 1790s the standard size of the rooms was reported as eleven feet by fifteen feet. The number of rooms in the prison must almost always have been smaller than the number of prisoners. Prisoners frequently shared rooms, therefore, often sleeping two to a bed, also a common practice in London rented rooms at this time. Prisoners were not evenly distributed among rooms, however, and there were usually rooms that contained half a dozen or more people. Overcrowding was, of course, exacerbated by the presence of many prisoners' families. When the prison was very full overcrowding was so acute that many prisoners had to sleep on tables in the prison 'tap', on the pews of the chapel, on staircases, or on benches in the open air.[38]

Other buildings in the prison performed various functions for the support of the community. The kitchen, taphouse (the marshal held a licence to keep a public house), coffeehouse, bakehouse and chapel were arranged around the main street of the prison (sometimes called King street). A large open space, known as the yard or the 'parade', contained the prison pumps, and served as the scene for all kinds of sporting activities, most notably skittles and 'rackets'.

Early in the century the prison yard also contained a set of stocks. It is not clear, however, that any were set up in the new prison. There was, however, a room called the 'strong room' set aside for the confinement of unruly prisoners, especially those who had tried to escape.

The prison was surrounded by a high brick wall, topped by a fringe of spikes, called a *chevaux de frise*. (The rooms on the top floor of the dormitory building were the only ones high enough to give a view over the wall to the 'Surry and Kentish hills' beyond, and were especially coveted for that reason.) The wall was punctuated in two places: once by a massive pair of iron gates, which could be opened to admit building materials (it was through these gates that the Gordon rioters battered their way into the prison in 1780), and once, the more normal entrance, by an arched gateway, in the base of which was the office, called the lobby, of the junior prison officers, the turnkeys.

During the day, when the gate was left open, the turnkeys sat in the lobby, watching the flow of prisoners in and out of the prison – debtors living in the Rules, debtors out on day trips, wives of prisoners, children running messages, friends of prisoners, hawkers, prostitutes and tourists. Only by being acquainted with the faces of all the prisoners were the turnkeys able to prevent escapes; new prisoners were accordingly brought into the lobby to be studied. Even so a prisoner with a little ingenuity could often make his way out unobserved.[39] Attempts to regulate the entrance of commodities were similarly imperfect: spirits, for example, were supposedly banned, but were smuggled in under women's skirts, or in things 'painted like cheeses'.[40] A rule of the prison forbad the importation of arms, but it seems unlikely that any serious attempt was made to enforce this.[41] Some gentlemen still wore swords as a regular part of their dress and did not expect to have to surrender them. There is also evidence of prisoners who had not only swords but duelling pistols as well.[42]

At night, when the turnkeys left the lobby, the gate was closed and left unattended till morning, so that, even if a prisoner fell ill, there was no way of sending for medical assistance.[43]

Beyond the lobby was a small courtyard, at the end of which another arched gateway led out into the street. Within the courtyard were a number of houses intended for senior prison officers. One of these, the house of the 'clerk of the papers', was the prison clerical office, where all new commitments were entered into the prison books, where discharges were reported, and where all prisoners had to go to check that all their debts were settled before they might leave the prison. The clerical office was an important link between the court of the King's Bench and the prison, and all kinds of legal business were transacted there. Other houses were provided for the marshal and deputy marshal. They were described as 'very good houses' but nevertheless the officers repeatedly complained that they were too small for married men with families, and generally avoided keeping residence when they could.[44]

The prison officers constituted one of the two tiers of formal authority that were exercised over King's Bench prisoners.[45] They manned the prison and were answerable to their superiors, the judges of the court of King's Bench, with whom final authority in the prison rested. In modern prisons the prison officers are assigned the task of prison government: as an essential duty they are expected to penetrate prison society with ambitious systems of regulation and control. In the eighteenth century the task of government was not clearly assigned to prison officers, whose role was the more limited one of providing a service to the courts by fetching and carrying prisoners and by keeping them in safe custody. Prison officers, who were generally few in number, were not well equipped to keep up a close surveillance of prison life.

In the King's Bench prison, in accordance with this pattern, the officers constituted a service arm of the court of King's Bench rather than a prison government. Apart from the clerk of the papers and the turnkeys already mentioned, the officers comprised a marshal, who was appointed by the Lord Chief Justice of the court, and who had overall responsibility to the court for the safe keeping of the prisoners; a deputy marshal, who headed the turnkeys, and four 'tipstaffs' who escorted the prisoners back and forth between court and prison. The duties of the marshal and tipstaffs kept them in attendance as much upon the court as upon the prison. Only the deputy marshal and the turnkeys were in close and continuous contact with the prisoners. Numbering only three or four men and faced with a prison population of several hundreds, they concentrated their efforts on maintaining prison security by control of the prison perimeter.

Even considered solely as a bureaucratic and administrative arm of the court, the King's Bench prison regime left much to be desired. The officers habitually discharged their duties in a less than assiduous way. To help them in their work, they all employed assistants, who ranked as their personal servants. Frequently these assistants were left to do the work, while the officers absented themselves. The marshal erred in these respects as much as the junior officers. When he did attempt to exercise his authority to enforce a closer attention to duty, he was frequently not heeded, and sometimes defied.[46]

These flaws and imperfections in the prison regime were deeply rooted. They were in large part the consequence of the prison's financial arrangements. Because there were no public funds made generally available for the support of prisons in the eighteenth century, and because the King's Bench had no local government base to draw upon, it was not possible to provide the prison officers with salaries. They were expected to support themselves by means of fees which they were directed to collect from the prisoners on commitment and discharge, and in return for specific services. The scale of fees was regulated by the court of King's Bench. The incomes that prison officers derived from fees in the later eighteenth century seem to have been comfortable, even substantial, ranging from the turnkey's £50 a year upwards.[47]

The effect of this system was not to motivate the officers to extraordinary assiduity, but rather to endow them with a sense of independence, which encouraged them to discharge their duties by their own lights and to ignore, and even resent, external directives. Deriving their income directly from their work, they expected to have control over the way in which they carried out their duties, and to be immune from criticism so long as the tasks incontestably annexed to their offices were performed. Their attitude was in fact proprietorial: they ran their offices as if they had been private businesses, and the King's Bench judges, though they often lamented the consequences of the officers' attitude, actually buttressed it by recognizing their rights in office as freehold property rights.[48]

Prison security concerned the marshal more than any other of the prison officers. By the terms of an ancient statute designed to curb irresponsibility in gaolers, he was liable to be sued by the creditor of any debtor who escaped.[49] In the later eighteenth century he was paying out a certain amount on this account every year.[50] Naturally he was concerned to keep his liabilities to a minimum, and he attempted to enforce responsibility on his fellow officers by demanding from each a bond in a considerable sum, payable if their carelessness gave rise to any expense.[51] This ought to have ensured effective security, but the officers had, in this sphere as in every other, a keen sense of what they could get away with. They knew that many creditors would not sue; they knew, moreover, that they had a right of recapture. While they could not afford to have large numbers of prisoners escaping, they did not feel compelled to maintain absolute security.[52] The marshal, more mindful of escapes, employed a number of watchmen at his own expense to walk around the prison at night, inside and outside the walls, and prisoners attempting escape were sometimes prevented by the watchmen's vigilance.[53] But even the watchmen were not wholly concerned with security. They were also supposed to watch for fire and to cry the hours, like other eighteenth-century watchmen. And, also like other eighteenth-century watchmen, they seem to have spent much of their time asleep.

The absence of public funding, which made it necessary to reward prison officers by means of fees, also made it necessary to tap private sources to pay for the costs of prison maintenance and for the provision of essential services to the prisoners. A common eighteenth-century solution to this problem was to farm the prison out to the gaoler, who was made personally responsible for prison upkeep and for the provision of services, and who was allowed to recoup his expenses by charging the prisoners for what he made available to them. In the King's Bench prison the marshal performed this role. He received not only a portion of the prisoners' commitment and discharge fees, but also all rents from prison rooms and (of more importance) all profits from the prison tap.[54] His income from these sources amounted to several thousand pounds a year,[55] wealth sufficient to make him quite a substantial figure in the county of Surrey, a commissioner of the land tax, and sometimes a member of grand juries at the assizes.[56] From his income the marshal paid the basic expenses of the prison: taxes and the cost of minor repair works.[57]

Of the other officers, only the turnkeys were much concerned with the life of the prison. They acted as the marshal's agents for most purposes; probably they collected rents for him. They also, characteristically, put some money into prison management on their own account. William Penrice, who was a turnkey in the 1760s, paid for the erection of the *chevaux de frise* on top of the prison wall, after a number of prisoners had escaped. Presumably he wanted to reduce the risk of his being charged for the debts of further escapees. He also paid for a new building to be put up within the prison, apparently as a speculative venture, for he was able to charge exceptionally high prices for his especially luxurious accommodation.[58] It was also a general practice among the turnkeys to furnish and let out at high rents the rooms they were assigned for their own use within the prison. But all these activities were marginal, making no more than a minor contribution to prison life.[59]

Services that the prison officers themselves did not wish to undertake, such as catering, were sometimes farmed by the marshal to a variety of individuals and by a variety of arrangements.[60] The keeper of the tap, for example, who sold beer for the marshal at the ordinary market rate of $3\frac{1}{2}$ d. a pint was allowed to keep a portion of the profits. (By 1815, the tapster's profits were estimated at between £900 and £950 a year.) The coffeehouse keeper, by contrast, kept all his profits, paying only a fixed annual rent. The prison baker also paid an annual rent, and a number of tradesmen – butchers, for example – paid a nominal sum for the right to keep stalls within the prison. Some people, such as the prison cook, were allowed to operate rent-free. Many of the catering franchises and minor employments in the prison were granted to prisoners and ex-prisoners and made up an important part of the prisoners' economy discussed in the next section.

The commercial organization of the prison had both advantages and disadvantages for prisoners. Chief among the disadvantages must be reckoned the general indifference of prison officers for their prisoners' welfare. Only those wants which could be backed up with cash were likely to be regarded. An advantage, on the other hand, was that by means of various small employments, prisoners did have the opportunity of making a living within the prison. And, having cash at their disposal, they were able to procure whatever appealed to their taste with little interference. Moreover, prison officers, who regarded their prisoners in part as their clients, were unlikely to be harsh and rigorous in demeanour. The ambiguous character of the relationship between prisoners and prison officers, and the fate that those of the officers who had most contact with the prisoners – the turnkeys – had often come from the ranks of the prisoners themselves, helped to blur the distinction between prisoners and staff.[61]

Because the cost of running the prison was in fact largely borne by the prisoners themselves, and because the prison officers' income came out of the prisoners' pockets, it was always possible that the prisoners might turn against a system which exploited them in order to finance their own oppression. But the impression is that prisoners in most instances accepted the commercial system as inevitable, and paid for their food and drink and lodging with no more resentment than they would have felt at paying for them in outside life. Even fees seem to have been paid without violent objection. The explanation for this attitude probably lies in the relative financial ease of prison officers in the later part of the eighteenth century.[62] Being comfortable enough, prison officers saw no need to defy the price-setting efforts of the court and screw up prices and fees beyond the limits of tolerance.

The one part of the commercial relationship which did remain highly explosive was that which concerned beer. The marshal held a licence to sell beer within the prison, and the tap had a monopoly of sale. It was possible for prisoners to send out of the prison for beer, but the turnkeys discouraged this practice as a nuisance and a threat to prison security. The prisoners, however, were suspicious of this explanation, believing rather that the marshal was jealous of commercial rivals and intent upon maximizing his own profit. When the beer at the tap was of especially poor quality, the prisoners' resentment with their monopolist gaoler sometimes exploded into violence. In 1771, for example, the prisoners, claiming that the strong beer was unduly weakened, destroyed over fifty barrels of beer at the tap. Troubles over beer played at least a part in several of the more serious disturbances of the period.[63]

Beyond their responsibilities as servants of the court, and as commercial managers of the prison, the prison officers did have some responsibility for, and interest in, the preservation of order within the prison. Although the prison housed a fair-sized community, often of a thousand people or more, it fell outside the normal care of magistrates and constables. The prison officers had a vested interest in ensuring that disorder did not get so far out of hand as to pose a serious threat to their haphazard security arrangements.

For the routine maintenance of order and the enforcement of the law within the prison, the marshal was given the authority of a magistrate.[64] He had the power to commit offenders to the prison strong room, a power which he seems to have exercised most frequently in the case of prisoners who attempted to escape. He could also commit to the local felons' gaol, the New Gaol, Southwark. This power, as one marshal remarked, was of great service in cooling down hot-headed prisoners. There is no evidence that the marshal ever attempted to provide his prisoners with the full range of a magistrate's services. Indeed, when prisoners wished to press prosecutions for assault against each other, or to bring charges for marketing offences, they usually sent for some local Southwark magistrate.[65]

Since the marshal almost never set foot within the prison (he would talk to the prisoners in the lobby, but he feared to demean himself by venturing inside), he could not in any case ever have identified trouble for himself, but was always dependent on turnkeys or prisoners bringing him complaints.[66] The turnkeys were in fact the officers who bore the brunt of the task of preserving order. They played a part within the prison similar to that of the constable on the street. And like most eighteenth-century constables, they were more interested in dispelling or resolving troubles when they appeared than in enforcing any abstract conception of order.

Had the turnkeys been interested in anything more than pacifying the prisoners in the interests of peace and quiet, there was much in the prison that might have attracted their attention. There was much drunkenness and general rowdiness. Gambling, though officially frowned upon, was very popular. Prostitutes frequently came into the prison to ply their trade.[67] Some prisoners, moreover, were actively engaged in traffic in smuggled goods: a raid in 1779 by revenue officers, backed up by grenadiers, resulted in the seizure of contraband goods 'to a considerable amount'.[68]

Because of their lack of numbers the turnkeys could only have suppressed such activities when they had the tacit support of the prison population. Because they lacked both the desire and the capacity to act as a powerful supervisory and coercive force (except *in extremis*), successful prison government depended upon the consent of the prisoners. Naturally this affected the way in which authority was exercised. It was vital that prison officers acted in ways that were regarded as *legitimate* by the prisoners and that they were *seen* so to behave. Consultation, conciliation, mediation: these were the most powerful weapons in the weak armoury of prison government. And all the characteristics of the prison – the attitudes of the officers to their task and their posts, the lack of finance, the system of farming and the employment of prisoners as turnkeys – served to reinforce such a system. The marshal and his officers knew that if harmony, peace and good order were to be preserved in the King's Bench, then they had to develop a good working relationship with the prisoners. They derived their legitimate authority in the prison from their ability to command the support of the prison community, even though they held their offices from the court of King's Bench.

The need to win prisoners' support did not render the officers totally impotent. The prisoners were usually willing to accept the authority of the officers provided that they acted in a fair and equitable manner and maintained a low profile in prison life. However, attempts to regulate or coerce prisoners were usually regarded, in typical eighteenth-century fashion, as the tyrannical abuse of power and were violently opposed.[69] Like other citizens, the prisoners of the King's Bench had a clear idea of the limits beyond which Englishmen should not be pushed around. The authority of the officers was therefore limited, but not entirely invalidated, by the attitudes of the prisoners.

If the marshal lost prisoner support and there was trouble in the prison on a large scale, there were several courses of action which he could take.[70] One, which accorded with the officers' recognition that conciliation and consent were the basis of viable authority, was to attempt to reason with the prisoners to discover the source of their anger and suggest to them some non-violent means of obtaining redress. Magistrates from outside the prison were sometimes imported for this purpose, in the hope that prisoners would see them as impartial arbiters. If this expedient failed, outside help in the form of troops or extra hands might be called in. Such recourse was, however, rare – the marshal had to pay for extra help – and its adoption was always a sign that the harmony and equilibrium between authority and the prisoners had been seriously upset. Troops and extra men often exacerbated the troubles they were brought in to control, because they had no legitimate authority in the eyes of the prisoners. Hostility to the military was, of course, of long standing, and the extra hands were usually bailiffs' men, thieftakers or other prison hangers-on – men who inspired little more than the prisoners' contempt.

In circumstances of conflict both the marshal and the prisoners could appeal to the final source of authority over the prison, the court of King's Bench. The marshal could appeal to the judges' punitive powers over prisoners. The judges claimed jurisdiction over any offence whatsoever which their prisoners might commit. If a prisoner was accused before them, they could order him to be brought into court and, having delivered a solemn peroration, impose a sentence of a few days or weeks in the strong room, or in the New Gaol, Southwark. In the case of more serious offences, which they could try by jury, they might impose sentences of several years in a felons' gaol. In practice the marshal turned to the judges only in exceptional circumstances, when it seemed necessary to make an example of a prisoner.[71]

Prisoners called upon judicial powers more frequently than the marshal, for judicial supervision of the prison meant that they could invoke the judges against the prison officers, and so hope to check officials if they were extortionate or oppressive. Because they recognized the many deficiencies of the prison regime, the judges had offered protection to prisoners over several centuries.[72] Several passages in the eighteenth-century statutes regulating the relationship between courts and prisons, however, required the judges to perform tasks that they had previously undertaken voluntarily. They were ordered to draw up tables of fees to be paid to prison officers, and exhibit the tables in the prison; to look into charity monies due to prisoners, to see that neither trustees nor prison officers were embezzling them, and to have a table of charities likewise exhibited; and, finally, to ensure that prisoners were not prevented by prison officers from sending out of the prison for furniture or bedding, food or drink. These provisions focused on the difficulties and the opportunities for abuse to which commercial and exploitative arrangements of prison government gave rise. The same statutes ordered the judges to draw up general tables of rules for prison government (again refurbishing an old power); these tables were also to be put on public display.[73]

The official concern to make rules *public* was a stratagem for dealing with a situation in which, for the lack of any rigorous system of inspection, the burden of 'pulling up' the prison officers had inevitably come to rest upon the prisoners. The judges had long appointed, as prison Visitor, a 'secondary' or barrister from the Crown Office, who could be reached by the prisoners by letter at any time. He usually responded promptly to complaints, either by visiting the prison himself or reporting the problem to the court. Once a year, usually on Holy Thursday, the Visitor paid a formal visit to the prison, not to make a tour of inspection, but rather to hold an audience. He invited complaints from all the prisoners, forwarded any written petitions to the judges, and, if he saw the need, made a report himself.[74]

Unquestionably this system was perceived by the prisoners as offering a real service. One prisoner told a parliamentary committee in 1791 how he had been able to combat an extortionate prison officer – a tipstaff who demanded from him an inflated fee – merely with the threat of an appeal to the Crown Office.[75] The tipstaff had not merely refunded the money, but promised never to try the same trick on another prisoner. Many instances could be cited of prisoners who wrote letters of complaint, or sent petitions to the judges, and received speedy attention and action – not, of course, invariably in their favour.[76]

At the same time it must be observed that the judges had other purposes in mind in offering these services than merely the protection of the prisoner. Even the system of complaints can be seen as part of the law-and-order machinery of the prison – an important part precisely because the repressive component of the machinery was so weak. Because the prison officers had so little power to put down riots when they did arise, it was vitally important for the judges, if they wished ultimately to reinforce authority within the prison, to prevent riots by responding quickly to every complaint, reconciling conflicting parties and seeing that justice was demonstrably done.

The manner in which the prison Visitor performed his duties bears out the court's emphasis on quelling incipient disorder.[77] On arriving in prison in response to any complaint, he immediately drew the contending parties together, and lectured them on the virtue and necessity of harmony. Disputes were resolved, whenever possible, by mediation and conciliation, rather than by an exertion of power. The Visitor and judges, moreover, were all most anxious to educate prisoners in the use of proper legal channels, and to convince them that it was by proceeding in the proper way that they were most likely to attain their ends.

The success of this system, like the successful exercise of authority within the prison, was entirely dependent on the prisoners' confidence that their interests, opinions and concerns were truly taken into consideration. There were times, of course, when prisoners came to suspect that they were being sold out. At such times they would denounce the judges and prison officers and turn elsewhere and to other means for redress.[78] But for the most part the King's Bench judges seem to have succeeded very well in obtaining the prisoners' confidence.

Though it might be assumed that the incarcerated debtor was rendered powerless to control his own fate in the King's Bench prison, this was manifestly not the case. The mechanisms for redress of prisoners' grievances were highly developed. The weakness of formal authority within the gaol meant that the wishes of the prisoners had almost invariably to be consulted and were often complied with. Moreover, the absence of effective and ongoing intrusion by the prison officers into the environment of the prison created something of a social and political vacuum which the prisoners occupied themselves: they were able to develop not only their own sophisticated local economy but to establish their own forms of local government.

Social and economic relations among prisoners: the prisoners' economy and collective institutions

The fact that imprisonment forced into close proximity people of different classes and social origins, who in society at large might have had little or no contact with one another, was frequently the subject of contemporary comment. 'Debtors' prisons like the grave . . . level all distinctions', wrote the author of a guide to London debtors' prisons in 1793.[79] In fact, the evidence suggests that social distinctions were anything but obliterated. Sustained in part by habit and assumption, the social hierarchy also had, in the prison as outside, a foundation in economic relationships: the prison had its own internal economy, which underpinned a prison class structure.[80]

The form of the prison economy was largely determined by the prison establishment's failure to provide basic services. To some extent, therefore, the economy arose to serve the needs neglected by the authorities. Thus there was no public catering system in the prison. Or rather, although there was a 'public kitchen' and a cook who would prepare prisoners' food for a small fee, prisoners had to provide the food for themselves. To cater for the needs of prisoners, a market was therefore held daily in the main street of the prison, at which fresh fruit, vegetables and meat were sold. Some of the stall-holders were themselves prisoners, who thus met the expense of supporting themselves in prison by pursuing profitable employment within the walls.

Some prisoners found other niches for themselves in the provision of food and catering. Some, holding much coveted ground floor rooms in the main dormitory block, turned their rooms into chandler's shops and sold dry goods. Others ran restaurants in their rooms – every room was provided with a small stove. The prison tap and coffeehouse both offered meals and were staffed at least in part by prisoners.

Other services in demand in the prison were also supplied by prisoners. Doctors and lawyers found plenty of opportunity to pursue their callings.[81] At a humbler level, some prisoners hired themselves out as bootblacks, wet-nurses or valets to other prisoners. Carpenters, plumbers and builders were sometimes employed by the marshal about the prison. Some prisoners made a business of renting furnishings for prison rooms.

Several inmates worked for a greater market than that of the prison. Artisans of many kinds carried on their trades in their rooms. The marshal, discussing prisoners' employments in 1815 noted only one restriction: 'we do not allow joiners to have any large piece of timber'.[82] Those shopkeepers who gained permission to live in the Rules of course could hope to attract general custom. Printers, journalists and poets committed to the prison (sometimes for seditious libel) quite often continued their work within the walls, sometimes selling pamphlets and newspapers from their rooms.[83]

The prison thus contained indigenous shopkeepers, artisans, servants and professional men. It also contained indigenous landlords, for there was a lively market in rented accommodation in the prison.[84] By old custom the right to a room in the prison was determined by seniority. The prisoner thus assigned a room was responsible for paying rent to the marshal. New prisoners were, in theory, parcelled out among the old as 'chums', one to a room until all were double-occupied, then again till all were triple-occupied, and so forth, the most junior prisoner with a room of his own being the most eligible to receive a chum.

In practice, the fact that prisoners had money to spend and that they had spending money in different quantities, combined with the fact that the set rent of 1 s. was far below the market price for a room, gave rise to what might be termed a black market in accommodation. The property rights upon which this market was based were, of course, conventional and had no standing in law, but the prisoners saw room rights as tantamount to a freehold property which could be used to make an income.

This income could be obtained in various ways. A wealthy prisoner, or one who wanted his room for a shop or work-place might prefer to be the sole occupant. In that case he could dispose of any chums assigned to him by paying the chum a small pension of perhaps 5 s. a week. But a prisoner who was not wealthy, or who could not otherwise make use of his space in a profitable way, might choose to set himself up as a landlord. He might take in a paying tenant – perhaps offering his services as a servant, perhaps even vacating his room for his tenant – or alternatively, aiming for the lower end of the market, he might set up a kind of lodging house for dispossessed chums or other stray prisoners. Such lodging houses might contain half a dozen or even more poor prisoners – each paying 20 s. or even 30 s. a week.

Room renting was obviously a very profitable activity. Prisoners were not the only ones to attempt to get into the market. Turnkeys rented rooms. The keeper of the tap regularly allowed prisoners to sleep on his tables for a small charge. So valuable was the possession of a prison room that some prisoners attempted to continue their claims after leaving prison. It seems likely that a large number of prisoners made some income from the market in accommodation. On the other hand, the cost of lodging must have been a very large item in most prisoners' budgets. And the fact that wealthy prisoners were able to command more than their equitable share of space can only have exacerbated the housing crisis.

Employments within the prison obviously offered a variety of opportunities, but what proportion of prisoners was engaged in some form of profitable activity? The Commons committee of 1791 reported that of 570 prisoners, 470 were completely idle.[85] But this report must almost certainly be qualified. In the first place, it seems probable that prisoners drawing an income from the market in accommodation were not reckoned among the industrious. Second, there is a qualification built into the report: 'There are indeed instances of much industry amongst many of the prisoners; but their industry is generally employed in smuggling, usury, lottery insurances, and all other modes of gambling.' The list of illegal or disapproved activities is not exhausted here. Quite a number of prisoners sold spirits in their room. At one time there were said to be as many as forty 'whistling shops' (places where spirits were sold) in the prison – the name 'whistling shop' referring to the whistle prisoners gave to obtain entry. In the early part of the century there were many reports of coining being carried on in the prison; it is not clear whether that activity survived into this period.[86]

The number of prisoners engaged in some form of profitable activity, then, was almost certainly greater than the meagre total suggested by the 1791 commission, even if not all the activities were considered meritorious. A 1793 guide to London debtors' prisons reported that 'the greatest number' of King's Bench prisoners 'carry on some trade or business, as regularly as if they had been born and bred within the walls'.[87] Since prisoners had to pay their own way, of course, some kind of income was essential.

There was, in fact, another alternative: a certain number of charities had been set up for poor prisoners by pious benefactors; there was, moreover, a constant stream of casual charitable gifts – an alms box by the prison gate appealed to visitors and passers-by.[88] Any prisoner who took an oath before a magistrate that he was worth no more than £5 in the world was entitled to a share of these charities.[89] The pauper prisoners also took it in turns to go about the prison with a begging box. Scorn of charity, however, seems increasingly to have prevented needy prisoners from falling back on such resources, since by 1815 there were only two prisoners 'on the box'; even fifty years earlier there rarely seem to have been more than about thirty.[90]

Gainfully employed or not, all prisoners were in some manner implicated in the prison economy. A web of economic relationships bound together the prison community, which thus came closely to resemble society beyond the walls. Even the problems of debt and credit that bedevilled the country at large were echoed within the prison. Many prisoners were chronically in debt to the shopkeepers within the prison.[91] One of the officers in 1815 described how prisoners would vary their eating habits, moving between public kitchen, coffeeshop and tap: 'when they are in debt at one place they go to another; and when they are able to pay off the debt, they come back again'.[92] So the very process which brought so many debtors there was repeated even inside the prison.

The network of economic relationship within the prison sustained a system of social relationships closely resembling that which prevailed beyond the walls. Prison society was quite as hierarchical as free society: it included labourers and mechanics, a middle class of shopkeepers and 'freeholders', a pseudo-gentry class of lawyers, doctors, clergymen, authors and army officers, and an elite of wealthy prisoners, landowners or merchants. These different classes of prisoners were distinguished in several ways. They had different living conditions, purchasing power and social habits. The gentleman's world centred on the prison coffeehouse, that of the lower classes on the tap.[93]

But if prison society was hierarchically structured, it was also knit together with bonds of community and mutual aid. Prisoners banded together to form drinking clubs such as those common in taverns outside the prison. There is a record, from the early 1750s, of a masonic lodge within the prison, later removed to the Rules.[94] Prisoners combined their funds and set up subscriptions for charitable purposes or to finance improvements to the prison. Sometime before 1776, for example, lights were erected in the main street and yard of the prison by subscription of the prisoners.[95]

The inmates also pooled their resources to celebrate public festivities. National events such as royal birthdays or occurrences of special importance to the prisoners, such as the passage of an Insolvency Act, were sure to be enthusiastically celebrated.[96] Such displays of mutual good feeling were sometimes sponsored by the wealthier prisoners who, for all their sense of superiority and distinctiveness, still recognized their obligations as patrons and leaders of the prison community.[97]

But the most important manifestations of the prisoners' sense of community were the corporate bodies established among the prison population.

Prison communities in debtors' prisons had developed certain organs of self-government as early as the sixteenth century.[98] In organizing themselves as self-governing communities, debtors evidently borrowed administrative and disciplinary structures and a technical vocabulary from such social organizations as municipal corporations, guilds and convivial societies. Prisoners seem to have regarded themselves as a kind of corporation or fellowship, appointing officers from their own number, perhaps by rotation, to discharge certain duties of common concern.

The King's Bench prison community spawned not one but two such corporations. The smaller, the corporation of commonside prisoners, concerned itself especially with the supervision of prison charities. The larger, the corporation of master's side prisoners, concerned itself with numerous other aspects of prisoners' welfare.

The commonside corporation consisted of the twenty or so prisoners 'on the box', that is, in receipt of charity.[99] Two or three of these were appointed as 'assistants'; their chief duty was to supervise the charities. This comprised the organization of prison begging, collaboration with a 'steward' who was the receiver of prison charitable endowments and the distribution of charitable proceeds. The court of King's Bench encouraged the prisoners to supervise prison charities, according formal recognition to the assistants in its 1729 code of rules.[100] The steward, appointed by the court, was always nominated by the prisoners, whose recommendation the court accepted, subject to the approval of the marshal. In the later eighteenth century the prisoners usually nominated the clerk of the papers as their steward.[101]

The 1729 rules also ordered that the prisoners should be provided with a common room for 'devotion or conversation, and a fire to be kept therein as the season requires'.[102] This room, in which the 1729 rules were exhibited, was the venue of meetings held to settle affairs of common concern. Its title, 'the court room', designated it as the proper meeting place for the officers of the prisoners' corporation –

just as, say, the Bank of England had a court room where its governors assembled.

The assistants not only regulated charities but exercised certain powers of government over their fellow prisoners, though these lacked any formal approval by the court of King's Bench. One of their number was designated 'mayor' and the other(s) were known as clerk or deputy. They arbitrated quarrels, checked brawling and penalized debauchery or immorality. The most powerful sanction at their disposal was that of excluding offenders from the charities, though this punishment was invariably revoked on appeal to the judges.

Prisoners serving as assistants were sometimes accused by their fellows of behaving in an overbearing and oppressive manner, and even of enriching themselves by appropriating an excessive portion of the charities. It does seem, however, that they were usually zealous in two areas of general interest: in attempting to maximize charitable funds, and in attempting to restrict numbers in receipt of charities.

Unlike the commonside corporation, the master's side corporation, much the larger of the two bodies, enjoyed no kind of recognition from the court of King's Bench. This did not prevent the prisoners from feeling, however, that their organization had a high degree of legitimacy. The master's side corporation was called by its members the 'King's Bench college', and each member a 'collegian'. The college originated no later than the late seventeenth century.[103] In the first half of the eighteenth century custom was adduced as an argument for the legitimacy of the college on several occasions when its authority was challenged. On one occasion an ancient prisoner was called in from the Rules to testify that the college had existed as long as his memory served him.[104] In the second half of the century, however, justifications were more often functional and utilitarian. The college was praised for its contribution to the welfare of the prisoners and for its services in preserving peace and harmony within the prison.[105]

A very abstract essay in justification, aimed primarily at members of the college, appeared in the preamble to a rule book of the college, printed in 1782:

Whereas it is requisite for all communities to have rules for the promotion of good order and harmony amongst themselves; so it is necessary that such regulations should be established by the general consent, as shall be needful from time to time, with a view to alleviate the miseries and to obtain every convenience for the unfortunate members of the college.[106]

The college, in other words, was a representative institution which, like other forms of authority in the prison, depended upon the consent of the prisoners. The corporation and its officers performed several functions. They facilitated 'good order and harmony' among the prison population by providing a formal mechanism for the resolution of the numerous minor disputes that occur within any community. They legislated and enforced petty regulations that ordered and eased day-to-day prison life. And they acted as the collective voice and the corporate representative of the prisoners when dealing with those outside the college community.

The college consisted of the several hundred prisoners lodging in the master's side rooms of the prison – the great majority of debtors – and the small minority of criminal prisoners who were barred from the benefit of the charities by a rule of the court. The officers of the college, who were elected by the prisoners in general assembly (in case of a disputed election, by ballot), are nowhere authoritatively listed, but the most important offices were clearly the president (also described as chairman, steward and lord mayor), clerk or secretary, and treasurer. Other officers occasionally mentioned include sheriff, aldermen and constables: whether these were elected or co-opted is unclear. Juries were convened as the need arose. A number of officers who performed fairly menial duties about the prison seem to have been paid for their work; they were probably appointed or hired rather than elected. They included a clerk of the chapel, scavengers, criers and a cook. This body of officers closely paralleled those found in many small communities throughout the country. Local government clearly provided the model for the prisoners' organization, and college officers mimicked their orthodox counterparts in many details: for example, prison constables, like parish constables, carried white staves as insignia of authority.

The college in the broadest sense – the whole membership several hundred prisoners strong – occasionally met in general assembly. Since the master's side prisoners, unlike the commonside prisoners, had no court room, large meetings had to be held in the open air, in the main yard of the prison. Any prisoner could summon a meeting at any time, on payment of a special fee if for some private purpose, or without charge if for 'the Public Good'. A general meeting had a quorum of thirty. Rules made by a properly constituted meeting were binding. (The printed rule books, drawn up by committees, were presumably approved at general meetings.) Large general meetings were probably infrequent, and most of the routine work of the college was dealt with by the college officers.

Unlike the corporation of the commonside, the college had no outside source of finance. It was therefore the practice to charge new members of the college – incoming prisoners – dues, called variously 'inside fees', 'strummage money' or 'garnish'. The treasurer, who received these dues, disbursed them on such utilities as the commonside prisoners provided for themselves from their charity money: mops, brooms and oil for lamps. He had to keep accounts of all monies received and expended, and to display his books to any prisoner on demand.

The clerk kept the minutes of all general meetings and was responsible for supervising the traffic in rooms. Room vacancies had to be announced at general meetings, so that the next most senior prisoner without a room might know of his right of possession. The clerk was supposed to keep a list of lodgings available, with their prices, for the information of new prisoners. He also had to witness and register all contracts for the exchange or leasing of rooms.

The work of the criers and scavengers within the prison was very like that of their counterparts in municipal government. Criers, armed with bells, made announcements of general meetings. For a fee of 1 d. they would also announce matters of private concern: for example, they would cry out lost property. They also sought out prisoners when requested by visitors to the prison. The scavengers swept the streets of the prison and passageways of the dormitory buildings, cleaned out the water cisterns and 'necessary houses' and lit the lamps. They were responsible for preventing the obstruction of passageways with 'lumber'. These services entitled them to claim 1 d. a week from each prison room. They also made a profit from the sale of urine – which was collected in large tubs in the main street of the prison – to local manufacturers, for use in the processing of leather.

The judicial work of the college was transacted in courts which were probably also general meetings, though they may not have been attended by more than a fraction of the prisoners. Here the president presided, reaching his decisions with the aid of a formally constituted jury, or sometimes by means of a more informal consensus procedure. Problems arising from the administrative work of the college could be brought up in these courts: scavengers, for instance, could call to account any who refused to pay their wages, or could denounce any who had wantonly thrown water or filth from their windows (at a penalty of 1 s. for a first offence, 2 s. 6 d. thereafter). The court claimed jurisdiction over various kinds of problems arising from the prison economy. Shopkeepers using false weights and measures were subject to a fine of 5s. for a first offence, 10s. thereafter 'and no mitigation of fines'. Servants might sue for their wages, or creditors for debts; the college was specifically empowered to make 'legal and binding' settlement in cases of debt. More generally the college claimed jurisdiction over all nuisances and matters of complaint. There is evidence that the courts punished contempts, and there was a specific provision in the rules for the presentment of prisoners who accosted visitors to the prison and demanded pints of beer. There is little good evidence of punishments other than fines inflicted by the court, but it seems that shaming punishments, such as ducking under the prison pumps, were used, that some matters of complaint were settled by a public apology, and that contending parties were encouraged to reconcile their differences.[107] Generally the college courts did much the same work as any court leet or petty borough court, providing the kind of petty regulation and arbitration which was regarded as a vital contribution to social order and harmony in the eighteenth century.[108]

The King's Bench college also resembled other corporations in providing an authoritative voice by which the community it encompassed might address the greater world. By proposing a motion in assembly, a prisoner might promote a petition which would be issued in the name of 'the prisoners of the King's Bench prison'. Applications in the name of the prisoners without the approval of an assembly were not permitted for, as the college rules observed, 'the Dignity and Importance of every Society depends on a strict union among the members'.[109] The requirement that petitions be submitted for general discussion was designed both 'to prevent all absurd and ill complaints' and to ensure 'that the whole strength and influence of the college in support of every reasonable application may be employed'. Several petitions which must have been drawn up by this procedure, signed by several hundred prisoners, survive among the archives of the court of King's Bench.[110]

The evidence concerning college personnel is sketchy but suggestive. Repeatedly the president and those closest to him prefix their names with such titles as 'Captain' or 'Reverend' or claim the suffix 'Esquire'.[111] In other words it seems that the college was headed by the prison elite, the upper-class prisoners who frequented the coffee-house. This is not to say that college government was not rule by consent, or that the leaders did not command wide general support. In 1779 when a small group of prisoners denounced the college as tyrannical, more than 300 signed a petition testifying to their belief that 'any alteration in the internal management of this prison would most materially affect the peace and harmony of the whole'.[112]

Maintenance of peace and harmony was an important function of the college officers. Violence was not uncommon in the prison. Insults and slights between prisoners quickly gave rise to blows. Various forms of cheating or treachery or offences against the customs of the prison (particularly in matters relating to the allocation of rooms) were avenged by small mob actions. The task of the college officers, in these circumstances, was to act as missionaries of order – to intervene, attempt to mediate and reconcile, and to provide minimally violent ways of accomplishing whatever seemed to be a socially desirable end.[113]

Justice as administered by the college, then, was designed to defuse tensions and resolve conflicts. Punishments, when they were enforced, were most likely to be visited upon those perceived as troublemakers, breakers of commonly accepted norms and customs. Justice in all cases had to be seen to be done, so that prisoners would get no support if they wished to exact further vengeance. The kind of order which the college officers sought, commonly described as a state of 'peace and harmony', was very largely defined by the desires and inclinations of the prisoners.

The college was the most important association in the prison. It went beyond all the little clubs and societies that the prisoners founded in providing an image of community. When the prisoners gathered together to send off a petition, they took pride in the spectacle of their united strength. As members of the college they were not just prisoners, they were 'collegians'. They were able to demonstrate within the prison those civic virtues which were so highly esteemed in the eighteenth century, and to feel themselves to be (as, indeed, they were) people to some extent in command of their own lives.

If the college had all these virtues, why was it denounced by some prisoners as tyrannical? On at least two occasions in this period, in 1750 and again in 1779–80, small groups of prisoners waged energetic campaigns against the college and its authority.[114] In each case the motives for the 'revolts' were complex, but certain general grievances stand out. There must have been at all times a certain number of prisoners who felt themselves to be put upon by the college officers, perhaps because they had been penalized for some misdeed, or because they were unable to obtain justice to their own satisfaction. Moreover, a certain number of prisoners probably set their faces against the whole idea of the college, some because they saw it as legitimating popular forms of punishment and questionable moral and legal practices, some because they held the college responsible for such features of prison life as the trade in rooms, or even the lax government of the prison officers. The notion that there was some kind of corrupt bargain between the marshal and the college officers was by no means uncommon. When such prisoners found powerful, articulate leaders, they might coalesce into a discontented faction.

On the whole, however, prisoners seem to have accepted the authority of the college and its officials. They did so because its operation conferred on them important benefits and advantages. The college did much to fill the vacuum left by the indolence of the prison officers. College officials contributed as much as anyone to making the prison a livable environment. Moreover, when the mass of prisoners were moved by great passions against the prison regime or against the law of debt, the college provided them with a forum and with certain traditions of collective action which helped to shape their behaviour.

Harmony and conflict: the prison officers, the court and the college

We have seen that the King's Bench prison was governed by three separate forms of authority: the prison officers, the court of King's Bench and the prisoners' college. All three needed, to a remarkable degree, to secure the support of the prisoners, in order to wield authority effectively. Each served different though related functions: the prison officers guarded prison security, the college organized much of the day-to-day life of the prison, and the judges acted as (admittedly infrequently invoked) arbiters of prison government. All of them, in their different ways, were committed to the maintenance of order and harmony within the prison walls. This was true even of the college, for although it represented prisoners with an undoubted sense of grievance, its members were well aware of the advantages of maintaining a working relationship with prison staff. The three sources of authority in the prison did not, of course, altogether and invariably agree on how order and harmony were to be maintained, and this was a persistent source of friction in the gaol.

However, the attitude of the marshal and his officers to the prisoners' college was one of easy tolerance, even encouragement, for reasons which are quite easy to discern. Since the marshal and his officers wished there to be order in the prison, and since they neither wished nor were able to obtain it by direct intervention, the college officers usually appeared to them as useful allies. Even if the prison officers did not approve of all college activities, they were ill-advised to interfere as long as the college had the support of the majority of the prisoners.[115]

The King's Bench judges' attitude towards the college was, however, much more disapproving and, on occasion, downright hostile. One step further removed from the actual problems of prison government, the judges – possibly because of reformist pressures – attempted in the second half of the eighteenth century to push the prison officers into playing a more conscientious and assertive role in the organization of prison life. With the aim of preventing the college from undertaking tasks that they felt to be the proper duty of the prison officers, the judges adopted a twofold strategy: on the one hand they tried to suppress the college and to restrict its activities by including in their prison rules (notably those of 1759) provisions explicitly confining powers to the marshal and his officers that were customarily exercised by the college;[116] on the other hand, in a more positive vein, they sought to cajole the officers into greater activity.[117] Both tactics foundered, however, because they depended for their execution on the zeal of the prison officers, who repeatedly demonstrated their capacity to ignore orders from above. The prison officers disregarded the judges because they knew that inaction was in their best interests. The judges rarely punished them for their recalcitrance, while renewed interference in prison life would almost certainly have upset the delicate series of calculations, concessions and compromises upon which the officers' rule of the prison was based. There was little point in seeking to enforce rules whose enactment would only have provoked unrest and a general deterioration of the relations between the prison officers and the prisoners. Thus in 1781 the judges' rule that henceforth wives and children were not to be allowed to stay in the prison overnight, and that the turnkeys had to ring a bell at closing time every evening as a signal for visitors to leave, was of little avail. Prisoners with families disliked the rule and prison officers saw no good reason to antagonize them. The officers therefore contented themselves with ringing the bell as ordered, leaving to visitors and families the responsibility of ejecting themselves. Thirty years later, when the old rule was brought to the judges' attention, it was remarked that the prison was as full of women and children as ever.[118]

No rule that assigned a more active role to prison officers in the second half of the century was unambiguously enforced. As long as there was tacit agreement among the prisoners and officers about the extent of the officers' powers and the nature of order and harmony in the prison, there was little that the judges could do to affect life inside.

Nevertheless there does seem to have been a minor revolution in the prison government in the early 1780s.[119] Possibly the marshal was responding to pressure from the judges, or perhaps he felt that the reopening of the King's Bench prison (which had been closed to repair the damage wrought by the Gordon rioters) provided him with the opportunity to start prison government on a fresh footing. For whatever reason, the marshal began to claim the right to appoint the criers and scavengers who had previously been appointed by the college. Apparently a minor change – for the marshal did not break with the college custom of appointing prisoners to these posts – this development was nevertheless seen as significant and stirred up considerable ill feeling among the prisoners. For the marshal gained for himself a piece of patronage previously in the hands of the prisoners (both criers and scavengers made a fair income from their work) and simultaneously established his power a little more firmly in the heart of the prison by adding to the number of officers whose responsibility was primarily to himself.

This attempt to alter the balance within the prison provoked an outbreak of violence, for the college did not at once surrender its right to make the same appointments. Marshal's scavengers and criers, and college scavengers and criers, roamed the prison, falling upon each other when they met. The marshal was moved to complain to the court of King's Bench against the college officers, securing, as might be expected, permission to lock them in the prison strong room for a few weeks. The court judges seem to have hoped that the college might be altogether suppressed as a result of their disciplinary action. If so, they were only to experience one more in a long run of disappointments.

The clash of 1782, however, did have some long-term consequences. The marshal does not seem to have surrendered his claim to appoint criers and scavengers henceforth, and the beginnings of a slight shift in the balance of power within the prison might be dated from this year. By the end of the century prison officers were evidently taking a greater share in the internal management of the prison than they had fifty years before: some effort was being made, for example, to implement the judges' directive of 1759 requiring the marshal to be responsible for the allocation of rooms.[120]

And yet the implications of this shift in power were not very profound. The college, albeit shorn of one piece of its powers, continued to flourish well into the nineteenth century.[121] And if the criers and scavengers were now marshal's men, they did not discharge their duties in any innovative way. Even their appointment may well have involved an accommodation between the marshal and the prisoners.

Though the college officers naturally resented and opposed the marshal's attempts to erode their powers, they frequently collaborated with the marshal because in most circumstances their idea of a harmonious prison community corresponded with the marshal's aspirations for an orderly prison. Formal and informal authority therefore frequently presented a united front. Prisoners who complained of the college to the marshal usually received short shrift; college officers deprecated disorderly outbursts against the marshal. Marshal and college officers were agreed that there were 'troublemakers' in the prison – the drunk, the quarrelsome and those who resented all forms of authority – whom they both felt it was their task to order and control.

Such an account may seem to imply that the college was little more than an appendage of the prison establishment. This indeed was the view of Dr William Smith, who visited many London prisons in the 1770s. Smith wrote of the King's Bench,

The visitor is kept ignorant of the state of the prison by a certificate fabricated in the lobby vouching for the marshal and turnkeys good conduct in the government of the prison, signed by as many of the prisoners as the keepers can influence, who always retain a party of the prisoners to intimidate the rest, and prevent their making any complaints; and who ever expects a favour at the lobby; or is afraid of being insulted is obliged to sign whether he approves or not.[122]

There is reason to believe, however, that Smith's interpretation was rather crude, for he overlooked two important considerations. First, there was a substantial number of prisoners, not just a small kept party, who wished to cultivate good relations with the prison officers. The college officers, whose authority rested upon the support of the prison body, would not have been able to work with the marshal and his men unless most prisoners had thought this desirable. And the prisoners backed the college officers and the marshal, not because they feared official reprisals, but because they looked on the prison establishment as the ultimate guarantors of order in the gaol. Thus in 1783, when a group of prisoners known as the 'Liberty Boys' chal-

A.U.P—K

lenged the marshal's monopoly by setting up their own tap in prison and defied the turnkeys by importing large beer barrels into the prison, the other prisoners helped suppress the Liberty Boys' activities.[123] Prisoners and prison officers alike agreed that certain elements were disorderly and should be suppressed. Dedication to order and harmony, which the preamble of the college rule book enjoined, could thus be interpreted as militating against protest.

This did not mean, however, that the majority of prisoners never protested, nor that the ideals of order and harmony were invariably seen as incompatible with the challenging of the official prison hierarchy. This was Smith's second misapprehension: he failed to realize that the college sometimes acted, not as an instrument of the prison officers, but as a channel for discontent. In these circumstances, exhortations to unanimity and order were sometimes employed in an attempt to bind prisoners together into a more effective protesting force: harmony came to mean solidarity. And the very college officers and orderly minded prisoners who had so strongly aided the prison officers became their most intractable and determined opponents. In other words, the college's notion of harmony ceased to be compatible with the marshal's idea of good order.

The campaign against imprisonment for debt

Conflicts between the college and the marshal arose for a variety of reasons, but they were usually resolved and some sort of harmony re-established in the prison. In the later eighteenth century, however, a new and altogether more intractable set of circumstances arose: the prisoners within the King's Bench were affected by 'the contagion of liberty' and began in an explicitly radical way to challenge the constitutionality of imprisonment for debt. Not only were new arguments advanced against imprisonment for debt, but new and legally dubious tactics were employed by radicals who believed in *direct* action to secure redress of grievances. This created something of a crisis in prison life, for it produced a widely supported protest movement within the prison which could not easily be pacified or compromised within the usual ways. Prisoners who had previously accepted the authority of the marshal and his minions even if they had not necessarily regarded that authority as legitimate except when it commanded their consent, now withdrew their support in its entirety. Prison officers had to bear the brunt of the prisoners' protests, but they were not in a position to pacify them. The prison officers, after all, did not have the power to grant the prisoners' wishes and release all debtors from gaol.[124]

When they came to challenge the very practice of imprisonment for debt, the prisoners were of course brought up against not only the prison officials but also against higher and more powerful organs of government – the institutions that ultimately sanctioned the policies which prison officers merely put into effect. Over the last few decades of the century, the prisoners' notions about how to challenge authority at these higher levels clearly progressed through several stages of development. Initially, they directed their demands for change chiefly at the courts; when this strategy proved futile they turned their attentions to Parliament, and finally when Parliament proved not merely indifferent but actively hostile – ceasing altogether to pass even temporary Insolvency Acts between 1781 and 1793 – many prisoners came to rest their hopes in the crusade for parliamentary reform. By the 1790s, some prisoners were welcoming the French Revolution as an event of immediate relevance to their own needs.[124]

Lack of space unfortunately makes it impossible to discuss here the conflict over the debt law at this higher level. Some account of the impact of the 'radicalization' of debtors upon the confined world of the prison will, however, illuminate many of the themes earlier explored in this essay. To this end, we may focus upon one relatively brief but well-documented set of events: those which surrounded the first well-orchestrated campaign against imprisonment for debt, which erupted in the prison in 1770.

The arguments which inspired the prisoners in that year were comprehensively set out in a pamphlet written by one of them entitled *Considerations on Imprisonment for Debt*.[125] Characteristically legalistic in its approach, this pamphlet argued that the debt law had the unambiguous sanction of neither common nor statute law, but had simply been thrust upon an unwary people by unscrupulous lawyers. Invoking Magna Charta as the fundamental guarantee of English liberty, the pamphlet urged that existing 'law' should immediately be recognized as invalid.[126]

The author of this pamphlet, a Scots émigré named James Stephen, was evidently a man of forceful personality, whose personal beliefs played an important part in shaping the course of events. A former estate steward, apparently without legal training, Stephen seems to have worked out his theories on the basis of legal studies conducted after his commitment to the King's Bench prison in August 1769.

When he propagated his ideas among his fellow prisoners in 1770 he began a period of prolonged prison agitation.[127] Unlike some later converts to the theory of the unconstitutionality of imprisonment for debt, who thought that suffering under unconstitutional oppression must be patiently borne until the authorities could be induced to bring about change, Stephen was a believer in direct action. It is probably significant that his period of imprisonment coincided with the peak of enthusiasm for the great 'friend of liberty', John Wilkes, who had in fact spent eighteen months in the King's Bench prison before his release in April 1770. Certainly the tactics that Stephen used bore a remarkable resemblance to those employed by Wilkes in the general warrants affair: he had himself brought before the King's Bench by writ of habeas corpus, and challenged the judges to point to the statute that might justify their recommitting him, arguing that since there was no statute he, as well as every other debtor who chose to go through the same process, must be discharged.

Stephen's quest for instant legal redress of grievances was, however, doomed to failure. Irritated but by no means perturbed by his arguments, the judges ordered him to be recommitted to prison. Stephen interpreted his frustration as evidence of deep-seated corruption in the legal profession. He submitted (with appropriate protests) to authority whose legal judgment he doubted, returning to the King's Bench prison as, in his own words, a 'voluntary prisoner', but he also persisted in his stubborn search for some legal avenue of redress. Throughout the summer and autumn of 1770 he explored most of the channels of complaint open to prisoners, applying to the master of the Crown Office, the court of Common Pleas, even to the king. In a pamphlet entitled *Address to the Twelve Judges of England*, reproduced in the Wilkite newspaper, the *Middlesex Journal*, he also laid his case before the public, to whom he appealed for financial support.[128] By November, when Stephen made a new appearance before the court of King's Bench, most of the London and provincial papers were reporting his progress. The support of Wilkes himself had been sought for his final application.[129]

But the last application was no more successful than the first. Lord Chief Justice Mansfield, with the brief comment that 'it was not in his power to comply with his request', ordered the marshal to return him to prison. Stephen's next move may again have been inspired by the recent Wilkite remonstrances. Immediately upon his return to the prison from the court, Stephen, announcing his intention to remonstrate before Parliament, pushed his way past the turnkeys into the street. Almost instantly recaptured, he submitted to a punitive transfer to the New Gaol.

Stephen's doctrines may have been flawed in the eyes of contemporary legal scholars, but what alarmed the prison officers was the fact that he commanded an enthusiastic following within the prison. Stephen, of course, had always discussed his ideas with his friends, several of whom were his warmest supporters: men such as William Thompson, a portrait painter and member of the Royal Academy, John Mein, a Scots bookseller and newspaper editor hounded from the American colonies in 1767 for loyalist sympathies, and W. F. Jackson, a vituperative journalist.[130] But Stephen had also convened special meetings of the college in support of his campaign, had issued his various petitions and letters of complaint in the name of the whole body of prisoners, and had appeared before the courts as a delegate of the college.[131] He had been able, in other words, to exploit the representative institutions of the prisoners to publicize his cause within the prison and to involve the body of prisoners in his campaign.

The extent of his support was shown when he attempted his remonstrance. Large numbers of prisoners rushed the turnkeys with him, and helped him take the main door of the lodge off its hinges, while others tried to break their way out through the windows of the coffee room. (A few took advantage of the confusion to escape.) After Stephen's recapture and removal some forty prisoners 'assembled for several hours outside the lodge in a riotous manner' and at night, announcing their determination to release him, they began to hack their way through the prison wall. The number of prisoners involved in this venture was evidently quite sufficient to overawe the marshal and turnkeys who remained cowering in the lodge, sending word for a party of footguards, whose timely arrival narrowly foiled the prisoners of success.[132]

In a deposition after this incident, two of the turnkeys claimed to believe that 'about one hundred [prisoners] have entered into a combination to break the said prison and say they are in great danger of losing their lives and are apprehensive the prison will be again broke'.[133] A prosecution was initiated against Stephen and several other prisoners on the basis of the turnkeys' account, but was not ultimately pressed. It was intended perhaps as a salutary warning.[134] If so, it failed in its purpose, for when Stephen and his would-be rescuers (who had also been moved to the New Gaol) returned to the King's Bench in January, several months of disruption ensued.

The conflicts that arose on Stephen's return were of two kinds. First, there was the struggle between prisoners intent on breaking out of prison and prison officers dedicated to stopping them. It is important to emphasize that attempts to break out were not really attempts to escape. Such actions by the prisoners were neither furtive nor surreptitious, designed to avoid detection; on the contrary, they were symbolic acts, a form of demonstration, intended to show how prisoners felt about imprisonment for debt. They were a bid for freedom only inasmuch as they were designed to secure a change in the law. The second sort of conflict arose between prisoners made newly sensitive to all infractions of their rights and prison officers more than usually inclined to lay down restrictions. The campaign exacerbated the tensions of everyday prison life which might normally have been resolved, and made the maintenance of order and harmony in the prison much more difficult.

Plans to break out of prison seem to have been encouraged by Stephen himself. Not only did he continue to lecture to assemblies of prisoners on the iniquity of imprisonment for debt, but he also came up with specific plans of action. Thus at one time it seemed to him best that prisoners should march off to Westminster Hall in a body to plead their case; on another occasion he was reported as saying 'that in case they the prisoners were inclinable to break out of the said prison and would give him notice and fix the day and hour of their intention, he would write to all the prisons in England and would engage that all the prisons should be broke on such a day'.[135] When Stephen transferred himself to the Fleet prison in May (where, judging by reports of turmoil, he must also have propagated his doctrines)[136] his dreams seem not to have departed with him: in the same month the newspapers carried a story that a dozen or more prisoners had actually succeeded in breaking out of the King's Bench, but had since voluntarily surrendered themselves to the marshal.[137]

Apart from the gaol-breaks, the prisoners manifested a general militancy that led to outbreaks of violence.[138] A complaint about the quality of beer, for example, was expressed by the large-scale destruction of beer barrels; a new building in the prison yard, said to take up air and space, was levelled to the ground; turnkeys and prisoners employed by the marshal who opposed such mob actions were dragged about the prison garden at the end of ropes, or ducked in tubs of urine. Security precautions which the marshal had undertaken because of the threat of mass escapes also served as provocation for several violent incidents.

Stephen's friends – W. F. Jackson and others – played an ambivalent part in these more generalized disturbances in which the ambiguities and complexities of their conception of order were clearly
revealed. According to the account of the marshal and prison officers,
they were the ringleaders throughout; but according to Jackson and
his allies, all their activities were inspired by a firm commitment to
order. These apparently conflicting accounts both contain an element
of truth; they merely represent different perceptions of the same set
of circumstances. Being sympathetic to the prisoners at large, and
understanding how their sense of grievance was aroused by their daily
experiences, Jackson and his friends not only did not condemn their
tumultuous activities, but at times set themselves at the head of campaigns of destruction, directing the prisoners' endeavours and acting
as their agents in the case of any negotiations with the authorities. To
the marshal there could have been no clearer indication that these
prisoners were troublemakers and that responsibility for all the disturbances in the prison rested on their shoulders. But Jackson and his
allies did not believe that they were actively fomenting trouble. By
their account they were playing the traditional role of prisoners'
leaders – the college authorities: economizing on violence, attempting
to direct the energies of an angry body of men into minimally disruptive channels. The roots of disorder, as far as they were concerned,
lay not in the prison population, but in the prison government. It was
the prison government and, indeed, the law itself which had to be
reordered and reformed if there was to be order among the governed.

So excited were the prisoners by the extraordinary hopes aroused
by radical propaganda, and so unwilling the prisoners' leaders to
suppress disorder that they believed to be a natural response to
repression, that for several months the prison lay almost completely
outside the prison officers' control. The marshal attempted to reassert
his authority, throughout this period, by a series of tentative
approaches, sometimes through the prisoners' leaders – Jackson and
others were unquestionably figures of authority in the prison and
powerful potential allies – sometimes with the help of Surrey magistrates, who went into the prison and tried to reason with the prisoners.
The magistrates' approach was characteristically conciliatory: they
inquired into prisoners' grievances and drew up 'conventions' to
regulate prison government, charging both the prisoners and prison
officers to abide by them. Experience with this tactic, however, was
frustrating. Prisoners quickly relapsed into disorderly ways, accusing
the marshal of having contravened his part of the agreement. One

of the last magistrates to go into the prison – one who was determined to get to the bottom of the troubles – later gave this account
of his mission:

he went into the prison and in the room where great part of the prisoners
were assembled and enquired of them the cause of their complaints and
proceedings when after some trifling suggestions respecting the Marshal
and his officers one of them stood up and sayd that they had not any
material complaint against him nor his officers but that their complaint
was being illegally confined or against Magna Charta and that they were
determined not to suffer confinement in that prison for debt any longer and
on this deponents asking if those were the sentiments of them all they
unanimously answered that they were.[139]

A brief experiment with the stationing of troops in the prison was
scarcely more encouraging: not only were the prisoners hotly opposed
to the introduction of military force, but some of the troops were
more inclined to side with the prisoners than with the marshal.

The troubles were not put down until June. In that month a secondary from the Crown Office went over to the prison to investigate
some complaints regarding pumps and bulldogs. Thomas Bradley

accosted him at the outer door of the prison with a pistol in one hand and
a cutlass in the other and told him they knew the occasion of his coming
But they had appointed a committee to act for them and that they should
Trust their complaints to them and did not want his assistance and one of
the prisoners said . . . we don't want to hear of pumps and dogs and
(shewing a pistol) said these are our bulldogs.[140]

At this point the court of King's Bench intervened. While the prisoners
dispatched their committee to the court with a memorial that explained
that they could scarcely be orderly when so inflamed with a sense of
their wrongs, the judges began collecting depositions for prosecution
of the ringleaders. Eighteen prisoners were indicted at the Surrey
summer assizes for conspiracy and misdemeanour. The prisoners
responded with a prosecution of their own against the marshal,
several soldiers and turnkeys for riot and assault, but the grand jury
did not find for their indictment.[141] Characteristically, the prosecution was, it seems, finally abandoned in favour of a negotiated solution. The prisoners agreed to lay down their arms, and to appeal to
Parliament for redress.[142] Fortunately for the court and for the
marshal, the majority of those who had played a key role in the disturbances were released under an Insolvency Act in the following
year.[143]

In terms of the prisoners' campaign against the debt law – which was to last for several more decades – the significance of the events of 1770–1 lay chiefly in their contribution to the prisoners' political education. Disillusioned by their long battle of any hope that the courts might be induced to reform the law themselves, the prisoners finally came to rest their hopes in Parliament. It was from Parliament that they were subsequently to demand radical redress of their grievances; the corruption of Parliament that they were to blame for the survival of the practice of imprisonment for debt.

An episode which served in its own time to educate the prisoners into a sharper awareness of their political environment in this essay serves the more modest purpose of illustrating points previously made about the balance of power in the prison, and about the nature of the prisoners' attitudes towards law and authority. As the previous discussion should have made clear, in normal circumstances the debtors, though they saw themselves as an aggrieved and wronged group, did not seek to challenge the authority of King's Bench, or of the marshal and his officers. On the contrary, prisoners frequently collaborated with, or at least made use of, the prison authorities. In so doing, however (it has been argued here) they never resigned themselves to a purely passive role. Far from it: prisoners imbued with a strong notion of what powers authority could legitimately exercise over them were able to play a significant part in determining the nature and limits of authority within the prison. They were able to assert themselves successfully in this sphere in part because a prison government weak in manpower and resources was inevitably heavily dependent on prisoner co-operation – and in part because the public attitude towards debtors was sufficiently ambivalent that brutal exercise of force was not the preferred tactic of prison officers and would almost certainly have been politically impractical.

In the events of 1770–1 we see the endemic conflicts of prison life raised to a pitch of unusual intensity. The troubles of this period starkly revealed the weakness of the prison government and the routine dependence of prison officers on prisoner collaboration. They revealed also the potential strength of the prisoners within the prison – maximized, and given shape, by their traditions of collective action.

If the events of 1770–1 lay bare deep-rooted tensions, however, they also suggest what were some of the bases for reconciliation and accommodation. The prisoners, even when they behaved disruptively, were never entirely 'lawless'. Their acts of violence were limited and discriminatory; they had a strong notion of justice; and they had not entirely lost confidence in the ability and willingness of the established authorities to deliver justice to them. Even their breaches of the law were commonly not gestures of blind defiance, but rather attempts to elicit a response from some legal agency or authority.

The prisoners' concern for legitimacy, their acceptance of the necessity of rules and government, their adherence to values of 'order' and 'harmony' clearly provided the essential foundations for the re-establishment of 'normal' rule. In the light of the events of 1770–1, however, it is scarcely that note on which we should conclude. For what the disturbances of these years most dramatically evidence is that adherence to such values did not necessarily entail a passive relationship with authority. And in the particular circumstances of the King's Bench prison, the authorities were certainly very far from having established a monopolistic claim to represent 'the law'. Far from being above conflict, or counterposed to conflict, notions of legality and orderliness, in the King's Bench prison, were themselves inextricably caught up in conflict. That law, justice and order should prevail could, with very little difficulty, become the watchword of revolt.

Appendices

Appendix to Chapter 1

Tables 1 and 2 provide an analysis of all prosecutions initiated in the quarter sessions of Essex and south Lancashire (Salford, Leyland and West Derby hundreds) which were accepted by the courts as 'true bills'. Few of the offences listed are composite. That of 'nuisances' includes various nuisances ranging from keeping a savage dog to spreading malicious gossip. That of 'neglect or abuse of office' deals principally with the offences of petty constables, though a few cases concerned other local officers. Cases of assault, trespass, disseisin, gaming and unlawful sports have been counted as single cases regardless of the number of individuals involved in the particular case.

The three categories into which offences have been divided are, of course, to some degree arbitrary, though I have found them useful and would defend them as having a certain logic. 'Interpersonal disputes' were privately brought cases arising from local quarrels and offences. 'Obligation enforcement' involved the punishment of those who neglected their obligations to the community, while 'regulative prosecutions' involved regulation of the community. Since the placing of particular cases in particular categories involved interpretative decisions, the full tables are reproduced for the convenience of any scholar who might require detailed information. Minor adjustments of the categories would little affect the general patterns of business.

All years sampled include a full four sessions of the court. In the case of Essex the rolls for some years were incomplete and therefore it was necessary to take a year's business which straddled two calendar years, e.g. 1636–7 represents Easter sessions 1636 to Epiphany sessions 1637.

In the case of petty sessions business, I have simply tabulated the cases listed in detailed reports of petty sessions.

Table 1 *Quarter sessions prosecutions, south Lancashire, 1626–66 (hundreds of Salfor*

	1626	1628	1630	1632	1634	1636	1638	1640	164
Interpersonal disputes									
Theft	14	21	20	30	17	27	31	14	1
Assault	50	51	47	36	26	44	43	43	2
Trespass	22	27	35	25	21	26	16	15	
Disseisin	19	11	19	15	14	13	17	20	1
Poaching	3	3	3	0	1	3	5	3	
Obligation enforcement									
Decayed roads and bridges	32	31	20	29	25	24	12	29	4
Default on road work	33	76	79	27	0	0	43	23	6
Neglect or abuse of office	2	10	2	0	2	1	0	1	
Regulative prosecutions									
Unlicensed aleselling	33	8	4	0	0	4	0	0	28
Assize of ale	0	0	0	0	0	0	0	0	
Disorderly alehouses	1	5	1	2	1	1	0	3	1
Drunkenness	2	5	0	1	0	2	0	2	
Tippling	9	0	0	3	0	0	0	0	2
Gaming	2	1	1	5	0	1	0	3	
Unlawful sports	0	0	0	0	1	0	0	0	
Swearing	1	0	0	0	0	3	0	0	
Adultery and fornication	0	0	0	0	0	0	0	0	
Sabbath-breaking	0	0	0	0	0	0	0	0	
Non-attendance at church	37	12	1	0	16	2	62	4	5
Vagrancy	2	1	0	4	7	5	1	4	
Harbouring rogues	0	4	3	1	1	0	0	1	
Taking inmates	11	2	4	5	0	3	5	3	
Cottaging	3	0	5	1	0	0	0	1	
Statute of Artificers	0	4	7	2	19	2	7	2	
Unlicensed baking	2	0	0	0	0	0	0	0	
Unlicensed badging	0	1	0	0	0	0	0	0	
Unlicensed malting	0	1	0	0	0	0	0	0	
Unlicensed droving	0	0	0	0	0	0	0	0	
Other marketing offences	0	0	0	1	0	0	1	3	
Nuisances	7	12	7	3	7	3	10	3	
Miscellaneous	6	5	1	0	0	2	2	2	
Total prosecutions	291	291	259	190	158	166	255	179	58

eyland, West Derby)

1647	1648	1649	1650	1651	1652	1653	1654	1656	1658	1662	1664	1666
11	10	14	28	8	9	6	12	5	5	26	13	24
40	40	22	44	27	38	31	43	32	21	20	25	35
24	19	16	14	19	15	12	18	28	14	17	22	16
19	16	18	17	15	5	13	8	8	7	6	12	6
0	3	1	0	6	3	2	4	2	3	0	1	3
50	32	22	57	77	47	14	14	21	18	31	27	34
25	3	0	121	40	2	18	0	3	7	0	19	0
3	3	4	36	17	10	9	12	5	9	4	8	15
224	148	40	123	250	87	24	11	9	41	0	2	2
95	49	5	18	1	0	0	0	0	0	0	2	1
5	6	0	5	2	4	5	0	6	6	1	1	1
10	0	4	3	8	4	11	1	4	7	1	0	0
6	4	0	1	0	4	23	0	17	8	0	19	3
2	0	0	0	0	0	1	0	1	1	0	1	1
0	0	1	0	0	1	0	1	0	0	0	0	0
0	0	0	1	2	10	8	7	8	5	0	3	0
0	0	0	0	0	7	6	4	2	9	0	0	0
1	0	0	1	0	6	4	0	0	0	0	0	0
20	480	39	10	183	0	0	0	0	0	0	3	1
0	3	0	1	0	1	0	3	2	4	13	1	4
1	2	0	3	0	0	2	0	3	1	0	0	0
4	11	6	41	24	29	17	4	4	7	5	2	1
2	7	0	2	1	1	1	1	1	1	1	1	1
5	1	1	0	2	0	5	1	3	0	15	1	3
0	52	11	1	0	0	0	7	37	3	0	59	0
0	3	0	0	0	0	51	21	4	46	62	43	0
0	6	0	0	0	0	16	0	3	33	0	6	0
0	5	0	0	0	0	0	0	0	28	6	0	0
8	5	1	0	0	3	1	1	0	2	12	11	0
2	6	4	3	3	7	6	3	5	8	20	11	15
0	2	0	3	2	4	4	4	4	4	6	4	5
557	916	209	533	687	297	290	180	217	298	246	297	171

Table 2 *Quarter sessions prosecutions, Essex, 1626–66*

	1626	1628	1629	1630	1631	1632	1634 -5	1636 -7	16
Interpersonal disputes									
Theft	32	14	28	29	46	27	21	35	
Assault	5	10	11	11	11	5	4	10	
Trespass	3	1	2	3	1	1	1	0	
Disseisin	1	0	1	3	1	0	0	1	
Poaching	0	0	0	3	2	3	5	5	
Obligation enforcement									
Decayed roads and bridges	67	97	102	98	107	76	89	77	
Default on road work	56	5	217	112	360	135	128	142	
Neglect or abuse of office	13	16	9	46	31	5	5	13	
Regulative prosecutions									
Unlicensed aleselling	89	60	31	62	80	49	44	43	2
Assize of ale	0	1	58	56	121	7	0	3	
Disorderly alehouses	25	25	83	145	68	38	11	24	
Supplying unlicensed alehouses	1	3	2	4	3	0	0	0	
Unlicensed wine-selling	0	0	0	0	0	0	0	0	
Drunkenness	7	6	7	8	7	5	2	1	
Tippling	4	3	3	13	1	12	0	1	
Gaming	0	2	4	4	1	1	0	1	
Unlawful sports	0	0	0	1	1	0	0	0	
Swearing	5	2	3	9	4	5	0	2	
Adultery and fornication	1	0	0	0	0	0	1	0	
Sabbath-breaking	3	0	3	3	0	1	2	0	
Non-attendance at church	332	110	189	165	136	94	54	102	8
Vagrancy	0	0	0	3	6	2	7	0	
Harbouring rogues	2	1	0	0	1	0	0	2	
Taking inmates	7	6	3	24	15	13	6	11	
Cottaging	18	6	8	12	14	5	6	3	
Statute of Artificers	15	0	0	0	0	5	7	4	
Unlicensed baking	0	0	0	0	0	0	0	0	
Unlicensed badging	0	0	0	0	2	0	0	0	
Unlicensed malting	0	0	0	0	0	0	0	0	
Unlicensed droving	0	0	0	0	0	0	0	0	
Other marketing offences	5	1	0	7	11	4	17	2	
Nuisances	6	0	3	11	11	4	4	3	
Non-payment of excise	0	0	0	0	0	0	0	0	
Miscellaneous	4	2	2	1	1	2	1	2	
Total prosecutions	701	371	769	833	1042	499	415	487	28

1640	1644	1646	1648	1650	1652	1654	1656	1658	1660 −1	1662	1664	1666
19	15	26	11	42	25	7	15	20	23	18	16	6
3	15	13	5	7	14	16	16	14	10	11	19	17
2	0	0	0	1	0	1	1	10	3	2	4	3
1	2	1	2	4	4	6	2	3	1	0	1	0
0	1	0	0	1	0	2	7	2	2	1	5	1
38	58	67	44	56	78	43	65	43	82	81	101	80
54	150	387	0	84	17	4	37	42	15	116	175	30
5	3	5	4	9	11	3	7	10	9	7	6	4
15	92	39	42	70	83	49	56	24	34	11	17	13
1	0	1	0	0	2	3	2	0	0	4	1	0
3	12	16	9	15	18	6	20	3	15	4	5	7
2	2	1	0	0	0	1	1	0	0	0	1	0
0	0	0	0	0	3	0	0	0	0	0	0	0
0	4	0	1	1	5	5	8	3	0	2	1	0
0	1	0	0	3	6	12	0	0	5	0	0	0
0	0	0	1	0	0	0	0	0	0	0	0	0
0	0	0	0	0	0	0	0	0	0	0	0	0
1	0	2	0	5	4	4	8	6	0	2	1	0
0	0	0	0	2	1	4	1	4	4	0	0	0
0	0	0	0	4	4	6	4	2	2	1	0	0
75	95	69	39	19	5	3	18	12	11	41	42	21
0	0	0	0	1	0	4	0	1	0	0	0	0
0	0	0	1	0	0	1	0	0	0	1	0	0
3	1	6	3	2	6	5	19	3	12	11	4	5
2	3	3	6	4	19	7	10	8	19	6	17	3
2	4	21	1	12	11	1	17	16	20	15	10	2
0	0	0	0	0	0	0	0	0	0	0	0	0
0	0	0	0	0	0	0	0	0	0	4	7	0
0	0	0	0	0	0	0	0	0	0	0	0	0
0	0	0	0	0	0	0	0	0	0	0	0	0
7	3	15	1	22	1	1	2	1	10	1	4	0
2	2	5	1	2	4	8	4	4	2	2	2	5
0	0	0	0	0	0	0	0	0	0	0	0	24
0	2	2	1	3	0	1	6	10	0	0	0	2
235	465	679	172	369	321	203	326	241	279	341	439	223

Table 3   *Lancashire petty sessions business, Bolton and Deane division, 1634–8*

	March–August 1634	August 1637–August 1638
Poor children apprenticed	6	0
Vagrants punished	18	57
Harbouring rogues	1	0
Negligent constables	35	0
Unlicensed aleselling	0	11
Alehouses suppressed	0	38

SOURCES: PRO SP 16 265/86, 273/23, 382/81, 397/36.

Table 4   *Lancashire petty sessions business, Rochdale and Middleton division, 1636–8*

	September 1636–August 1637	September 1637–August 1638
Poor children apprenticed	11	0
Vagrants punished	80	83
Harbouring rogues	4	1
Negligent constables	0	2
Negligent watchmen	19	28
Unlicensed aleselling	3	24
Alehouses suppressed	0	2
Allowing tippling	7	0
Tippling	0	21
Drunkenness	3	0
Gaming	1	1

SOURCES: PRO SP 16 351/111, 366/90, 385/15, 397/8.

Table 5 *Essex petty sessions business, Chafford, Barnstable and Becontree division, 1635–9*

	1635–6*	1636–7	1637–8	1638–9
Poor children apprenticed	0	31	46	53
Vagrants punished	87	203	382	303
Unlicensed aleselling	9	15	15	15
Disorderly alehouses	2	10	13	2
Alehouses suppressed	0	12	3	8
Tippling	4	0	20	0
Drunkenness	0	6	0	3
Swearing	0	2	0	0
Church attendance	0	9	0	1
Recusancy	0	0	0	30
Droving on sabbath	3	4	0	0
Masterless men	0	0	6	2
Negligent overseers of poor	0	0	0	1
Refusing to pay poor rate	0	0	4	0

* Years run from July to June inclusive, except for the final year, which runs from July to July.

SOURCES: PRO SP 16 329/48, 364/83, 393/55, 426/67.

Table 6 *Petty sessions business, Oldham division, 1655–7*

| | 1655 | | | 1656 | | 1657 | |
	May	June	August	February	November	January	November
Unlicensed aleselling	3	1	0	10	1	8	0
Allowing tippling	0	0	0	0	2	0	3
Tippling	0	0	0	0	9	0	0
Drunkenness	1	0	3	2	4	1	0
Swearing	0	0	0	1	0	1	0
Working on sabbath	0	0	0	4	0	0	0
Bastardy	0	0	0	3	0	0	0

SOURCES: Lancashire RO QSB/1/1655, 1656, 1657 unsorted.

Table 7 *Petty sessions business, Rochdale and Middleton division, 1653–8*

| | 1653 | 1656 | | 1657 | 1658 | |
	May	June	September	April	August	October
Unlicensed aleselling	7	1	1	1	4	11
Assize of ale	2	0	0	0	0	0
Allowing tippling	0	0	0	1	1	1
Tippling	0	0	0	2	4	2
Drunkenness	0	0	0	0	1	3
Swearing	0	2	1	0	3	0
Bastardy	0	2	1	0	2	0

SOURCES: Lancashire RO QSB/1/1653, 1656, 1657, 1658, unsorted.

Table 8   *Regulation of petty constables 1626–66*

| | South Lancashire | | Essex |
	Orders	Prosecutions	Prosecutions
1626	1	2	13
1628	9	10	16
1629			9
1630	9	2	46
1631			31
1632	8	0	5
1634	11	2	
1634–5			5
1636	16	1	
1636–7			13
1638	13	0	
1639			1
1640	8	1	5
1644			3
1646	33	2	5
1647	65	3	
1648	43	3	4
1649	47	4	
1650	56	36	9
1651	37	17	
1652	28	10	11
1653	22	9	
1654	19	12	3
1656	14	5	7
1658	23	9	10
1660–1			9
1662	29	4	7
1664	12	8	6
1666	19	6	4

SOURCES: Lancashire RO QSR 22–60; Essex RO Q/SR 252–410.

Appendix to Chapter 5 *The accused in the local occupational structure*

There is no occupational census available for the Halifax–Rochdale area in the eighteenth century. However, for the purpose of comparison with the occupational profile of the accused, the Halifax parish marriage registers for 1766–70 can provide a crude guide to the local occupational structure. A distinction must be made here between the urban area of Halifax town, which constituted one township out of twenty-three in the parish, and the rural–industrial out-townships. The occupational structure of Halifax town, the marketing and service centre for the people of the parish and their industries, was markedly different from that of the other townships. The latter, with some variations, tended to resemble each other in occupational structure much more than they resembled Halifax town. In order to compare like with like, the occupational data on the accused (derived from the table on page 199) and the occupational data on bridegrooms (derived from the marriage registers and taken as a guide to the occupational profile of the male population at large) has been divided into two discrete blocs. One juxtaposes the occupational profiles of accused and bridegrooms who were resident in Halifax town. The other juxtaposes the occupational profiles of accused and bridegrooms who were out-township residents. Each column opposite shows the percentages of the group defined in the column heading which fell into the different occupational categories or sub-categories.

Occupational categories	Halifax town		Out-townships	
	accused 1764–73 (15 men)	bridegrooms 1766–70 (277 men)	accused 1764–73 (62 men)	bridegrooms 1766–70 (801 men)
All woollen textiles	27	39	82	73
Piecemakers/clothiers	0	1	29	2
Woolcombers	7	10	10	11
Weavers	14	14	40	52
Tradesmen/craftsmen/ middlemen	73	45	16	16
Innkeepers	46	0.4	3	0
Others	0	16	2	11

SOURCES: West Yorkshire Record Office, D 53/35 and 36; Halifax St John's, Marriages, 1764–9 and 1769–75, and as for the table on page 199 (see note 140, pages 352–3).

NOTE: The occupational profile of bridegrooms from the out-townships is derived from the ten out-townships for which information survives. Three of the eighty accused listed in the table on page 199 were resident outside the boundaries of Halifax parish. Occupational categories are defined as follows:

All woollen textiles All those directly involved in the production or marketing of woollen and worsted cloths. Those weavers with dual occupations, listed under *other occupations* in the table on page 199, are included here in order to avoid in any way underestimating the number of weavers in the out-townships accused column.

Piecemakers / clothiers Stuffmakers / sholloonmakers / kerseymakers / manufacturers. Overwhelmingly the smaller masters.

Tradesmen/craftsmen/middlemen Includes all retailers, artisans and dealers. Inevitably a very broad category, which defies detailed social and economic differentiation, but for a large number of the individuals concerned probably indicates at least small capital.

Others Principally farmers, husbandmen, colliers, quarrymen, labourers, soldiers, professionals and gentry.

Notes and references

Abbreviations

APC	*Acts of the Privy Council*
ASSI	Assize papers, Public Record Office
Br. Lib.	British Library
CSPD	*Calendar of State Papers Domestic*
CSPV	*Calendar of State Papers Venetian*
KB	Court of King's Bench papers, Public Record Office
PRIS	Prison papers, Public Record Office
PRO	Public Record Office
RO	Record Office (names of individual counties are given in full)
SP	State Papers, PRO
T	Treasury Papers, PRO
TS	Treasury Solicitor's papers, PRO
Worcs. Q/S	*Worcestershire County Records, Division 1: Calendar of Quarter Sessions Papers*, ed. J. W. Willis Bund (2 vols., Worcester, 1900), vol. 1: *1591–1643*
WWM	Wentworth Woodhouse Muniments, Sheffield City Library

Introduction

1 Bentham MSS, University College, London, Box 99, p. 178.
2 For some trenchant remarks on this theme see Elizabeth Fox-Genovese and Eugene Genovese, 'The political crisis of social history', *Journal of Social History*, vol. 10, no. 2, pp. 205–20.
3 The best published work on this period using a statistical approach is that of John Beattie, 'The pattern of crime in England, 1600–1800', *Past and Present*, vol. 62 (1974); 'The criminality of women in eighteenth century England', *Journal of Social History*, vol. 8 (1975).

4   Douglas Hay *et al.*, *Albion's Fatal Tree: Crime and Society in Eighteenth-century England* (London, 1975).
5   This is what we take to be the ideology of 'the rule of law'.
6   Edmund S. Morgan, *New York Review of Books*, vol. 25, no. 3 (March 1978), pp. 13–18.
7   D. Hay, 'Property, authority and the criminal law', in Hay *et al.*, *Albion's Fatal Tree*, pp. 32–9.
8   See the important reflections on this subject in E. P. Thompson, 'Eighteenth century English society: class struggle without class', *Social History*, vol. 3, no. 2 (May 1978), pp. 133–65, especially pp. 150–1.
9   The prosecutor's control over the choice of the court, once the decision to take *criminal* proceedings had been made, was very limited. Of course, in the case of assaults, trespasses, etc., the aggrieved party had the option of a remedy in the civil courts.
10   Hay, 'Property, authority and the criminal law', p. 48.

1   Two concepts of order

1   Quoted in F. Aydelotte, *Elizabethan rogues and vagabonds* (Oxford, 1913), p. 489.
2   Lancashire R O Q S B/1/1652 unsorted.
3   'M S S sermons of Christopher Hudson', Lancashire R O D P 353, fo. 55. The 'Homily on Obedience' and Wentworth's speech can be most conveniently found in G. R. Elton (ed.), *The Tudor Constitution* (Cambridge, 1960), pp. 15–16, and J. P. Kenyon (ed.), *The Stuart Constitution* (Cambridge, 1966), pp. 18–19, respectively. For two interesting recent discussions of the concept of order, see E. W. Talbert, *The problem of order* (Chapel Hill, N.C., 1962) and D. Little, *Religion, Order and Law* (Oxford, 1970).
4   John Downame, *A Guide to Godlynesse* (London, 1622), preface.
5   Arthur Dent, *The plaine mans path-way to Heaven* (London, 1601), p. 228. This work went through twenty-five editions up to 1640.
6   M. W. Beresford, 'The common informer, the penal statutes and economic regulation', *Economic History Review*, 2nd series, vol. 10 (1957–8), p. 222; J. R. Kent, 'Attitudes of members of the House of Commons to the regulation of "personal conduct" in late Elizabethan and early Stuart England', *Bulletin of the Institute of Historical Research*, vol. 46 (1973), *passim*; J. B. H.

Jones, 'Puritanism and moral legislation before the civil war' (Unpublished MA thesis, University of Wales, 1954).

7 Hertfordshire RO QSR/7; Lancashire RO QSB/1/70/48.

8 5 & 6 Edw. VI c. 25. Seeal so K. Wrightson, 'Alehouses, order and reformation in rural England 1590–1660', in E. and S. Yeo (eds.), *Class relations and cultural forms: Essays on the working class and leisure* (forthcoming); M. G. Davies, *The Enforcement of English Apprenticeship. A Study in Applied Mercantilism* (Cambridge, Mass., 1956).

9 Dent, *Plaine mans path-way*, pp. 165–6; John Northbrooke, 'To the Christian and Faithful Reader', in *Spiritus est Vicarius Christi in Terra: A treatise wherein dicing, dauncing etc. are reproved* (London, 1579).

10 Davies, *Apprenticeship*, p. 220.

11 H. B. Simpson, 'The office of constable', *English Historical Review*, vol. 10 (1895), *passim*; Davies, *Apprenticeship*, pp. 199–200; Lancashire RO QSR/22. As an increasing number of courts leet ceased to meet in the course of the seventeenth century petty constables came often to be appointed directly by the justices, a practice confirmed in law in 1662.

12 Essex RO Q/SR243/24; Lancashire RO QSR/34, 45.

13 J. Samaha, *Law and Order in Historical Perspective: The case of Elizabethan Essex* (New York and London, 1974), pp. 45–50, 87; M. Campbell, *The English Yeoman under Elizabeth and the early Stuarts* (New Haven, Conn. 1942), pp. 318, 341; Davies, *Apprenticeship*, pp. 168–9, 199; W. G. Hoskins, *The Midland Peasant: The economic and social history of a Leicestershire village* (London, 1957), p. 208.

14 Dalton quoted in Davies, *Apprenticeship*, p. 167; W. J. Hardy (ed.), *Hertford County Records*, vol. 1: *Notes and Extracts from the Sessions Rolls, 1581 to 1698* (Hertford, 1905), p. 149; Campbell, *Yeoman*, p. 324; *Worcs. Q/S*, p. 161; T. Birch (ed.), *A collection of state papers of John Thurloe Esq.* (7 vols., London, 1742), vol. 4, p. 315.

15 The information on the literacy of constables taking the Protestation Oath is drawn from the Literacy File of the Cambridge Group for the History of Population and Social Structure. I wish to express my gratitude to the Cambridge Group and in particular to Dr R. S. Schofield for permission to use this material. The literacy of Terling jurors was determined from signed presentments in Essex RO Q/SR 198–453, *passim*.

16 e.g. in Burnham-on-Crouch, Essex, from 1626 to 1643, one man served three times as constable while three men served twice each. Essex R O D/DGe M 170. Of the forty-two hundredal jurymen from Terling, Essex, 1580–1609, sixteen served once only, eighteen from two to four times and eight on five or more occasions. Essex R O Q/S R 73–185 *passim.*

17 *Worcs. Q/S*, pp. 564–5; Essex R O Q/S R 277/42.

18 Lancashire R O Q S R/29; Essex R O Q/S R 263/18, 247/48.

19 Lancashire R O Q S P/158/25; Hertfordshire R O Q S R/10/984, Q S R/9/830.

20 R. Gough, *The History of Myddle* (Fontwell 1968), p. 89; *Worcs. Q/S.*, p. 544; *R. Parkinson* (ed.), *The Life of Adam Martindale*, Chetham Society, old series, vol. 4, (1875) pp. 46–8.

21 Essex R O Q/S R 267/20; Lancashire R O Q S B/24/27, Q S R/15.

22 *Worcs. Q/S*, pp. 32, 249, 254; Lancashire R O Q S B/1/71/10; Samaha, *Law and Order*, p. 86; Davies, *Apprenticeship*, p. 186.

23 Lancashire R O Q S B/1/78/78, Q S R/33; Essex R O Q S R/230/24; Lancashire R O Q S B/1/123/67.

24 Essex R O Q/S Ba 2/24, Q/S R 352/30, 273/15, 292/21, 276/25; Lancashire R O Q J I/1/1651 unsorted.

25 Essex R O T/A 278, fo. 545.

26 The population estimate for rural Essex, based upon hearth tax returns, is taken from F. Hull, 'Agriculture and rural society in Essex, 1560–1640 (Unpublished PhD thesis, University of London, 1950), p. 121. The Lancashire estimate is based upon hearth tax returns for 1663 and 1666, P R O E 179 250/6, 8, 9. Since the Lancashire returns did not systematically record exempted paupers they have been corrected upwards considerably. The years sampled for the two counties were Essex: 1626, 1628, 1630, 1632, 1634/35, 1636/37, 1639, 1646, 1648, 1650, 1652, 1654, 1656, 1658, 1662, 1664, 1666. Lancashire: 1626, 1628, 1630, 1632, 1634, 1636, 1638, 1646, 1648, 1650, 1652, 1654, 1656, 1658, 1662, 1664, 1666. For the detailed figures see Tables 1 and 2 (pages 300–3). These rates are of course approximate and have been calculated simply as a means of establishing a basis for comparison. If anything, the population estimate for Essex may be rather high and that for south Lancashire rather low. If this is so then the contrast between the counties would be even greater.

27 Essex R O Q/S R 74/50. cf. Q/S R 105/31.

28 Essex R O Q/S R 44/61.

29 Essex RO Q/SR 7–251. Quotation from Q/SR 121/20. cf. 130/17, 134/35.
30 Lancashire RO QSB/1/288/22.
31 Davies, *Apprenticeship*, pp. 230–4. J. S. Cockburn, *A History of English Assizes, 1558–1714* (Cambridge, 1972), p. 116.
32 Lancashire RO QSR/53. The discussion of the regulative drives in Lancashire is based upon comparison of the prosecutions enrolled in Lancashire RO QSR/26–60 with the rolls of indictments and presentments, Lancashire RO QJI/1/7–40.
33 Essex RO Q/SR 264–276, Q/S Ba 5, Q/S Ba 6.
34 The discussion of Burnham-on-Crouch is based upon the following records: N. McNeil O'Farrell (ed.), 'Calendar of Essex assize files in the Public Record Office' (Essex RO typescript); Essex Quarter Sessions, Essex RO Q/SR 160–394, Q/S O 1, Q/S Ba 1/24–39, Q/S Ba 2/1–102, Q/S Ba 6/3/3. Ecclesiastical court records: Archdeacon of Essex, Essex RO D/AEA 35–44, D/AEV 6–7; Bishop of London's Commissary in Essex and Herts., Essex RO D/ABA 1–12; Bishop of London's Consistory Court, Essex RO D/ALV 1–2, Greater London Council RO DL/C/305, 308, 323, 324, 325, 624. Parish Registers of Burnham, 1559–1759, Essex RO D/P 162/1/1; Records of the Manor of Burnham with Mangapp, Essex RO D/DGE M, 158–67, 170, 184, 186, 187; Hearth Tax, 1671, Essex RO Q/R Th 5.
35 Occasional gaps in record survival preclude the assumption that we have a complete record of Burnham business brought to quarter sessions. Nevertheless, record survival is generally so good that one may have some confidence that the broad patterns and chronology of Burnham prosecutions have been accurately established. Had detailed records of the petty sessions meeting in the district from the early 1630s onwards survived, the trend towards increasing regulative activity in the later 1630s, 1640s and 1650s would very possibly be accentuated.
36 These issues are discussed at some length in Wrightson, 'Alehouses, order and reformation'.
37 Essex RO Q/SR 264/103.

2 Grain riots and popular attitudes to the law

1 Quoted in John Gauden, *Three Sermons Preached Upon Severall Publick Occasions* (London, 1642), p. 68.
2 Sir Matthew Hale, *Historica Placitorum Coronae* [1678], ed.

Solomon Emlyn (2 vols., London, 1736), vol. 1, p. 565.

3   Edward Thompson has done most to establish this, for a later period, in his important article, 'The moral economy of the English crowd in the eighteenth century', *Past and Present*, no. 50 (February 1971).

4   John Walter and Keith Wrightson, 'Dearth and the social order in early modern England', *Past and Present*, no. 71 (May 1976), pp. 26–7.

5   S. R. Gardiner, *History of England from the Accession of James I to the Outbreak of the Civil War 1603–1642* (10 vols., London, 1899), vol. 7, p. 84.

6   Essex RO D/B3/3/208, no. 14; Bodleian Library, Oxford, MS Firth, c. 4, p. 501.

7   *Letters from a Lieutenancy Book* OR *The Cloth Trade in Essex, A.D. 1629*, ed. Stephen A. Warner (Braintree, n.d.) thoroughly confuses the two incidents, as does W. A. Hunt, 'The godly and the vulgar: Puritanism and social change in seventeenth century Essex, England' (Unpublished PhD thesis, Harvard University, 1974), pp. 407–9.

8   B. E. Supple, *Commercial Crisis and Change in England, 1600–1642* (Cambridge, 1964), pp. 99–112; see also pages 000–00 of this chapter.

9   *APC, 1628–9*, pp. 309–10. It has not been possible to recover a local grain prices series for Essex in this period, but prices were rising at another regional market, Cambridge, early in the year: J. E. Thorold Rogers, *A History of Agriculture and Prices in England* (7 vols., Oxford, 1887), vol. 6, pp. 40–1. In March, it was reported from Colchester that grain is 'growen to a greate price in our m[ar]kett here', Essex RO, Morant MSS, D/Y 2/7, p. 247.

10   For example, *APC, 1628–9*, p. 170; Essex RO, Morant MSS, D/Y 2/7, p. 247; PRO E 178/5301.

11   PRO SP 16/133/19.i.

12   ibid.

13   *APC, 1628–9*, pp. 309–10.

14   There is no record of any prosecution of the riot at either quarter sessions or assizes (Essex RO Q/SR 266–9; PRO ASSI 35/70/3; 35/71/3).

15   J. S. Cockburn, *A History of the English Assizes 1558–1714* (Cambridge, 1972), pp. 7–8, 58, 181; William Lambarde, *Eirenarcha, or The Office of the Justice of Peace, in foure Bookes*

(London, 1619 ed.), pp. 404–5ff; *William Lambarde and Local Government: His 'Ephemeris' and Twenty-nine Charges to Juries and Commissions*, ed. C. Read (Ithaca, New York, 1962); *The Wiltshire Archaeological and Natural History Magazine*, vol. 14 (Devizes, 1874), pp. 208–16; *Bibliotheca Lindesiana: A Bibliography of Royal Proclamations of the Tudor and Stuart Sovereigns*, ed. R. R. Steele (2 vols., Oxford, 1910); *Tudor Royal Proclamations*, ed. P. L. Hughes and J. F. Larkin (3 vols., New Haven, 1969).

16 Essex R O D/B3/3/215 (file vouchers for payment to messengers bringing proclamations 1629); D/B3/1/19 (Maldon 'Sessions Book 1606–1631': quarter sessions and leet memoranda book); D/B3/3/77; D/B3/1/3, fo. 39v. (market regulations); D/B3/3/423, nos. 9, 10a and 10b (change to special grain jury, 1608); D/B3/3/205, no. 32; /224 unnumbered (dearth orders 1622/3).

17 Essex R O D/B3/1/4, fo. 9v. (Admiralty Record Book 1573–1638); D/B3/3/577, no. 1.

18 Although there are no jury lists for the period proceeding the riots, Thomas Spearman was a member of the jury in 1638 and 1639 (Essex R O D/B3/1/4, fos. 12, 14, 17).

19 N. J. Williams, 'The maritime trade of the East Anglian ports, 1550–1590' (Unpublished D Phil thesis, Oxford, 1952), pp. 2–3, 16, 22, 31–8, 42–3, 82; A. Hassell Smith, *County and Court: Government and Politics in Norfolk, 1558–1603* (Oxford, 1974), pp. 18–19; P R O SP 16/155/54; E 178/5301.

20 While only one licence was issued in January, twenty-six were issued in February and eighteen in March (*APC, 1628–9*, pp. 291–384); no proclamation prohibiting the export of grain was issued until 2 May (*Bibliotheca Lindesiana*, vol. 1, p. 186).

21 Essex R O, Morant M S S, D/Y 2/7, p. 247; for Jacobs, see pages 59–60.

22 Maldon was at the best of times a clearing port for the trade in grain and other foodstuffs from its rural hinterland; for example, the port book for Maldon for 1628–9 shows a considerable shipment of grain to London (P R O E 190/603/4). That little of this trade passed through the hands of Maldon men may have increased local discontent: W. J. Petchey, 'The borough of Maldon, 1500–1688: a study in sixteenth and seventeenth century urban history' (Unpublished PhD thesis, Leicester, 1972), p. 96.

23 Essex R O D/B3/3/208, no. 14 (the words within brackets are

crossed through in the original). Ewers was described in a 1624 note of ships and sailors belonging to Maldon as a 'seafaring man dwelling here age about 53 going to Newcastle' and lived in the same parish as the suspected leader of the riot (Essex RO D/B3/3/405, unnumbered; /167, unnumbered; /202, unnumbered). 'Professional' jealousy may have given an added edge to the complaints of Ewers and the other sailors since few of the ships engaged in the grain trade were from Maldon (Petchey, 'The borough of Maldon', p. 96).

24 Dunkirkers were particularly unpopular on the east coast since their privateering activities seriously disrupted trade with London and the continent (Supple, *Commercial Crisis*, p. 110; Essex RO D/B3/1/19, fo. 269v. [for an example of local hostility in 1629]).

25 Essex RO D/B3/3/208, no. 14. I am indebted to Dr W. J. Petchey for his help in identifying the location of Burrow Hills.

26 Essex RO D/B3/3/208, no. 14 (the words in round brackets are crossed through in the original).

27 This particular expression of a common refrain comes from an earlier crisis (*APC, 1597*, p. 360).

28 Essex RO D/B3/3/208, no. 14 (examination Dorothy Berry).

29 See, for example, the comments of the commissioners appointed to improve the adjacent Tiptree Heath (PRO SP 14/150/7; Bodleian Library, Oxford, MS Firth, c. 4, pp. 489–90).

30 Dr Petchey argues that Maldon did not possess any large wage-earning artisan group and that poor relief was not a special concern of the town's governors ('The borough of Maldon', pp. 35, 43–9).

31 Essex RO D/B3/3/208, nos. 16, 21; D/DQs/134/8. In the 1610 subsidy St Mary's accounted for just under 15 per cent of the town's assessment, the average contribution being between one-third and one-half of that in the other two parishes (D/B3/3/420, unnumbered).

32 Essex RO D/B3/3/208, nos. 14, 20.

33 Essex RO D/B3/1/19, fo. 262; D/B3/3/206, unnumbered; /293, unnumbered; D/B3/1/20, fo. 28.

34 Essex RO D/B3/3/167, unnumbered (Jn. Berry 'newe dweller' October 1623); D/B3/1/19, fos. 216, 260 (shepherd 1626, April 1629), 262v. (labourer May 1629); D/B3/3/198, unnumbered; /206, unnumbered; /381, unnumbered.

35 Essex RO D/P 132/1/1 (parish register St Mary's: marriage

Margaret Boyes, widow, to Geo. Williams [she had formerly married Abraham Boyes in 1612]); D/B3/3/198, unnumbered; /199 unnumbered; D/B3/1/19, fos. 221v., 232v.

36 Essex RO T/R 149/3, fo. 129v.; D/B3/3/393, nos. 9–10; D/B3/1/19, fos. 143, 156v., 178–9, 195–195v., 221–226v.; D/B3/3/167, unnumbered; /392, no. 31.

37 Essex RO D/B3/3/208, no. 32; D/B3/1/19, fos. 244v., 258–258v.

38 Essex RO D/B3/1/34, not fol.; /19, fos. 246v., 248, 250; D/B3/3/208, no. 32 (examination Mary Mansell [that the Carters' servant was pregnant by her fellow servant may of course help to explain the uncertain terms of her employment]); /198, unnumbered; /199, unnumbered; D/B3/1/19, fos. 288v.– 289; D/B3/3/422, no. 7.

39 For example, Essex RO D/B3/3/198, unnumbered (Geo. Williams 'foreigner' trading in town; Jn. Berry keeping hoggs streets town); /167, unnumbered; /381, unnumbered (Jn. Carter unbaited bull and failure scour ditches); /198, unnumbered; /266, unnumbered; /381, unnumbered; (Jn. & Dorothy Berry and Ann Carter forestalling fish); /167, unnumbered; /198, unnumbered; /206, unnumbered (failure work highways: Thos. Spearman 1622, 1623; Jn. Carter 1623, 1630; Geo. Williams 1629, 1630); D/B3/1/19, fo. 216 (Jn. Berry unlawful victualling), fos. 246v., 248, 250 (Jn. Carter alehouse haunting); /20, fo. 28 (Thos. Spearman drunkenness); D/B3/3/167, unnumbered; /198, unnumbered; /393, no. 11 (Absence church Sam. Sturgeon 1621, Ann Carter 1623, Jn. Carter 1629–31).

40 Essex RO D/B3/1/19, fo. 32v.; D/B3/3/474, no. 8; D/B3/1/19, fos. 105, 112, 265; /33, fo. 184v.; D/B3/3/198, unnumbered; /208, no. 27; cf. /177, unnumbered (assault by Jn. & Dorothy Berry in the market 1641).

41 Petchey, 'The borough of Maldon', pp. 170–4, 244–6; Essex RO D/B3/3/397, no. 18; /423, no. 1.

42 None of the rioters' husbands appears in the annual list of freemen entered at the Courts of Election in the period (Essex RO D/B3/1/19 *passim*; all appear in various lists of decenners, one of the qualifications for which was to be 'no freeman', e.g. D/B3/3/167, unnumbered; /198, unnumbered; /206, unnumbered.

43 For the estimate of Maldon's population, see Petchey, 'The borough of Maldon', p. 51.

44 Essex RO D/B3/3/198, unnumbered; /199, no. 6; /208, no. 23;

/298, m. 9 (Chamberlains' accounts 1629, payment for making new stocks St Mary's parish). Dorothy Berry was again in trouble for drunkenness in 1638 (/177, unnumbered).

45   Essex RO D/B3/3/167, unnumbered; D/B3/1/19, fos. 154, 158, 182; D/B3/3/392, no. 31. The sergeant at mace had his revenge: in 1629 he was among those who escorted Ann Carter to her trial and execution (/298, m. 11).

46   Essex RO D/B3/3/198, unnumbered; /206, unnumbered. As if to express their anger neither Ann Carter nor Dorothy Berry appeared at Easter quarter sessions to answer this charge against them (/426, unnumbered).

47   Essex RO D/B3/3/298, mm. 9–10; /407, unnumbered.

48   Essex RO D/B3/3/479, no. 1.

49   Essex RO D/B3/3/298, m. 9.

50   N. S. B. Gras, *The Evolution of the English Corn Market from the Twelfth to the Eighteenth Centuries* (Cambridge, Mass., 1915), pp. 194–5; P. V. McGrath, 'The marketing of food, fodder and livestock in the London area in the seventeenth century' (Unpublished MA thesis, University of London, 1948), p. 124; *CSPD, 1627–8*, p. 50; *CSPD, 1629–31*, p. 203; *APC, 1628–9*, pp. 146–7, 215, 240–1, 246, 328; *APC, 1629–30*, pp. 296, 299, 300.

51   Essex RO D/B3/1/19, fo. 260; D/B3/3/298, m. 10; /426, unnumbered; Q/SR 266.

52   Essex RO D/B3/3/198, unnumbered; /208, no. 14. The inclusion of John Carter is interesting. Since none of the other husbands was required to attend, it perhaps suggests a suspicion on the part of the authorities that he was somehow implicated in the riot. He does not, however, appear among those examined.

53   Essex RO D/B3/3/208, nos. 14–16.

54   Essex RO D/B3/3/208, nos. 19, 20; D/B3/1/19, fos. 262–262v. Samuel Sturgeon's place was taken by Lambert Topliffe, a long-serving member of the corporation and a senior headburgess. However, he also had fallen into debt and was removed from office at the end of 1629, 'being greatlie indebted and whose service the howse the former yere hath altogether wanted' (D/B3/1/19, fos. 1ff, 253v., 255v., 264, 269v.; D/B3/3/198, unnumbered; /217, unnumbered. The co-sureties for all four other husbands were drawn from the ranks of their fellow artisans.

55   Essex RO D/B3/3/208, no. 19; the note of Ann Spearman's

recognizance in the Sessions Book, however, makes no reference to the Privy Council (D/B3/1/19, fo. 262).

56 Essex RO D/B3/1/19, fo. 265.

57 ibid., fos. 265, 267. It is, perhaps, an interesting comment on the immunity that could be enjoyed by members of the early modern crowd that while no action was ultimately taken against Dorothy Berry for her part in the seemingly more serious crime of riot, she had in the midst of these proceedings been stocked for her drunkenness (D/B3/3/208, no. 23).

58 Maldon's magistrates set no more than the usual guard of six men at the annual fair held just two days after the riot (Essex RO D/B3/3/298, m. 9; cf. /297, unnumbered).

59 Thompson, 'Moral economy', p. 116.

60 As, for example, is suggested by Natalie Zemon Davis in her essay, 'Women on top', in N. Z. Davis, *Society and Culture in Early Modern France* (Stanford, Calif., 1975), p. 147.

61 Lambarde, *Eirenarcha*, p. 180; M. Dalton, *The Countrey Justice, Containing the practise of the Justices of the Peace out of their Sessions . . .* (London, 1622 ed.), p. 205.

62 PRO Star Chamber 8/223/7. I hope to deal more fully with the fascinating subject of women and riot elsewhere.

63 In 1631, the justices of Dengie hundred informed the Privy Council that it was customary to send grain to London by sea since it was often difficult to transport it to Maldon by road (Petchey, 'The borough of Maldon', p. 96).

64 *CSPV, 1629–32*, pp. 7–8.

65 Both licences were issued in April, none in May (*APC, 1628–9, 1629–30*).

66 It may be significant that none of Maldon's inhabitants appears to have joined Ann Carter in the second riot and that no grain riots were recorded to have taken place there in later years of distress in the period.

67 Supple, *Commercial Crisis and Change*, pp. 6, 12, 102–9, 158; Gardiner, *History of England*, vol. 7, pp. 82–5; *CSPV, 1629–32*, pp. 7–8; J. E. Pilgrim, 'The rise of the new draperies', *Univ. of Birmingham Hist. Jnl*, vol. 7, no. 1 (1959), pp. 55, 58; F. Hull, 'Agriculture and rural society in Essex, 1560–1640' (Unpublished PhD thesis, University of London, 1950), pp. 79, 471–2, 479–83; Bodleian Library, Oxford, MS Firth, c. 4, pp. 486–7; Essex RO D/DEb/7/1 and 3.

68 Bodleian Library, Oxford, MS Firth, c. 4, pp. 488–91.

69   Essex RO Q/SR 266/120; Bodleian Library, Oxford, MS Firth, c. 4, pp. 486–7, 490.

70   Hull, 'Agriculture and rural society in Essex', pp. 471–2, 479–80; Bodleian Library, Oxford, MS Firth, c. 4, pp. 486–7, 491, 494–5; Essex RO Q/SR 266/121; *CSPV, 1629–32*, p. 7.

71   Essex RO Q/SR 266/121; Bodleian Library, Oxford, MS Firth, c. 4, pp. 484–5.

72   Bodleian Library, Oxford, MS Firth, c. 4, pp. 484–5 (the date of this letter is wrongly transcribed as the 15th: see the original, PRO SP 16/141/1).

73   Bodleian Library, Oxford, MS Firth, c. 4, pp. 489, 490; cf. PRO SP 16/141/16.

74   Bodleian Library, Oxford, MS Firth, c. 4, pp. 485–6.

75   *APC, 1628–9*, p. 416; Bodleian Library, Oxford, MS Firth, c. 4, pp. 493–4; *APC, 1629–30*, pp. 4–5. The minutes of Braintree's remarkably efficient select vestry contain little reference to the provision of employment or extraordinary relief, besides the symbolic assignment of fines (at the overseers' discretion) to the 'poore weavers and keamers' (Essex RO D/P 264/8/3, fo. 58v.). Unfortunately, the accounts of the overseers for the poor do not begin before 1630.

76   *APC, 1629–30*, p. 5.

77   *APC, 1628–9*, p. 416; Bodleian Library, Oxford, MS Firth, c. 4, p. 494; *APC, 1629–30*, p. 4.

78   Bodleian Library, Oxford, MS Firth, c. 4, pp. 494–5.

79   ibid., pp. 495–6.

80   ibid., pp. 499–500; *Bibliotheca Lindesiana*, vol. 1, p. 186.

81   *APC, 1629–30*, p. 23. By contrast, a letter from the minister of Braintree written two days earlier noted, 'the stopp of trade hath bredde much distraction and confusion in our country wch for any course that hitherto hath bin taken is like rather to increase then otherwise' (PRO SP 16/142/113).

82   Although examinations were taken of the rioters – there is a reference in Maldon's records to payment to two men 'for attendinge on the persons examined before his Ma[jest]ies Justices here touching the matter of Ryotts comitted at Burrow hills' (Essex RO D/B3/3/298, m. 11) – these have not survived. The following description of the May riot is drawn from the report of the authorities who suppressed the riot and a later account of the rioters' trial.

83   Bodleian Library, Oxford, MS Firth, c. 4, pp. 501, 503–4;

Essex R O D/B3/3/298, m. 11; /157, unnumbered (references to the charges at Maldon of keeping 'the mutenes peopell that were kept in presion here'). Dr Hunt, 'The godly and the vulgar', p. 487 (and drawn upon by N. Z. Davis, *Society and Culture in Early Modern France*, p. 148), suggests that men dressed as women were present in the crowd. I have found no evidence of this; the reference there cited refers to the March riot and does not suggest the presence of a transvestite element in that particular disorder.

84   F. G. Emmison, *Elizabethan Life: Disorder* (Chelmsford, 1970), pp. 62–4; P R O S P 14/137/13; *APC, 1621–3*, pp. 371–2, 376. It was, for example, reported of Bocking: 'That towne abound[s] with poore, whereof many are very unrulie, and haveinge noe employment will make the place verie hazardous for men of better Ranke to liue amongst them' (Bodleian Library, Oxford, M S Firth, c. 4, p. 490).

85   Bodleian Library, Oxford, M S Firth, c. 4, pp. 494–5, 504–5; Essex R O D/B3/3/298, m. 11.

86   Bodleian Library, Oxford, M S Firth, c. 4, pp. 503–4. The copyist clearly had difficulty in transcribing this letter. He gives the name of the woman as 'Agnes Carke, a woman of Maldon', but other evidence makes it clear that it was in fact Ann Carter, e.g. Essex R O D/B3/3/198, unnumbered.

87   Essex R O D/B3/1/34, not fol. (Ann Carter signs with a mark); John Gardner was a recent freeman who stood surety for Ann Carter after the first riot. He too seems to have fallen on hard times, being later presented as an inmate in 1629, and failed repeatedly to attend the court of election (Essex R O D/B3/1/19, fos. 253v., 271, 285; /20, fo. 5; D/B3/3/198, unnumbered; /208, no. 20).

88   T. Birch, *The Court and Times of Charles the First*, ed. R. F. Williams (2 vols., London, 1848), vol. 1, p. 17. The Maldon authorities had perhaps learnt their lesson: they posted a guard on the bridge leading to Burrow Hills (Essex R O D/B3/3/298, m. 11).

89   Bodleian Library, Oxford, M S Firth, c. 4, pp. 501, 503. The coastal port book for Maldon does in fact contain an entry for 'the Providence of Hull . . . versus Hull' in which a William Gamble had loaded 160 quarters of rye (P R O E 190/603/4, not fol.).

90   Williams, 'The maritime trade of the East Anglian ports',

pp. 2–3, 16, 22, 31, 35; PRO SP 16/155/54 (memorandum on the corruption of officials in the outports). Corruption at the nearby port of Colchester in 1629 was later the subject of an inquiry (PRO E 178/5301).

91 *Bibliotheca Lindesiana*, vol. 1, p. 186; Essex RO D/B3/3/215, unnumbered; /554, unnumbered (vouchers for payment messengers bringing proclamations 'against transportac[i]on of Corne' to Maldon).

92 Walter and Wrightson, 'Dearth and the social order'.

93 Essex RO T/A 465/1, not fol. The evidence available does not suggest the number involved or the precise form their action took. Eleven people were mentioned in the examinations: four men, six women and one boy. They appear to have taken grain off the cart of a Suffolk yeoman as it went through the streets of the town. Two of the women cut the bottom of the sacks and allowed the grain to spill out, probably as the cart ran along the streets. Women and child then seem to have gathered up small amounts of the spilled grain, while several men took sacks of grain off the cart, some of which was then placed in one of the weavers' houses.

94 Bodleian Library, Oxford, MS Firth, c. 4, pp. 495, 499.

95 ibid., p. 509.

96 Walter and Wrightson, 'Dearth and the social order', pp. 36–42.

97 Bodleian Library, Oxford, MS Firth, c. 4, p. 501.

98 PRO ASSI 35/71/3/97. Cousen was ordered to be whipped and sent to the house of correction for a week; a year later he was again in trouble at both quarter sessions and assizes (ASSI 35/73/1/70; Essex RO Q/SR 273/76).

99 For example, Essex RO Q/SR 266/120; cf. Bodleian Library, Oxford, MS Firth, c. 4, p. 505.

100 PRO SP 16/142/113.

101 *APC, 1629–30*, p. 25. Contrast the Venetian ambassador's reference to the disorder made just two days later: 'the poor are in distress from lack of employment, and we hear of some slight riots' (*CSPV, 1629–32*, p. 67).

102 *APC, 1629–30*, pp. 24–5.

103 PRO C/181/4, fo. 1v.

104 Essex RO D/B3/3/208, no. 21; /298, m. 11; Bodleian Library, Oxford, MS Firth, c. 4, pp. 503–4.

105 Bodleian Library, Oxford, MS Firth, c. 4, pp. 503–4. A reference in a list of prisoners in Colchester gaol to one John

Braynwood, committed 'from the last sp[ec]iall sessions', may relate to the trial, but I have been unable to find any further reference to Braynwood that would confirm this (PRO ASSI 35/71/3/97).

106 Bodleian Library, Oxford, MS Firth, c. 4, pp. 503–4; in another report of the trial, Sir George Gresley comments on the severity of the rioters' sentences (Birch, *Court and Times of Charles the First*, p. 17).

107 Bodleian Library, Oxford, MS Firth, c. 4, pp. 503–4 (my italics).

108 Essex RO D/B3/3/208, no. 25. James Brownsward, who was himself several times in trouble with Maldon's authorities in 1629, lived in the same parish as the Carters and was amongst those prosecuted with Ann Carter and Dorothy Berry for earlier forestalling fish, D/B3/3/198, unnumbered; PRO SP 16/92/85. iv.

109 Bodleian Library, Oxford, MS Firth, c. 4, p. 504.

110 ibid., pp. 504–5.

111 ibid., p. 504.

112 ibid., pp. 507, 508; *CSPD, 1629–31*, p. 20.

113 Walter and Wrightson, 'Dearth and the social order', pp. 37–8; PRO SP 16/177/32.

114 Bodleian Library, Oxford, MS Firth, c. 4, p. 504.

115 ibid., pp. 509–11.

116 PRO SP 16/186/62 (I am indebted for this reference – and many other kindnesses – to Mr Arthur Searle, formerly of the Essex RO). The justice, Sir Thomas Barrington, had been a member of the commission that tried the 1629 rioters (PRO C/181/4, fo. 1v.).

117 Essex RO D/Deb/7/1–17.

118 Kent Archives Office, QM/SB 82 (the rioters contented themselves with preventing the grain from leaving the city); P. Clark and P. Slack, *Crisis and Order in English Towns 1500–1700* (London, 1972), pp. 152–3.

119 *The Records of the City of Norwich*, ed. W. Hudson and J. C. Tingey (2 vols., Norwich, 1910), vol. 2, pp. 164–5; F. Blomefield, *An Essay Towards a Topographical History of the County of Norfolk Containing the History of the City of Norwich* (Norwich, 1745), p. 142.

120 Despite the seditious mutterings of individuals, there appears to have been no concerted critique of the law. The political

agitation of the 1640s, however, seems to have had a marked effect on the rhetoric of the poor. A remarkable petition from Wiltshire's poor in 1648, explicitly attacking the self-interest of their governors which prevented them from regulating the market, asked, 'that all p[ar]tiallitie may bee abandoned, whereby equity may take place yt soe wee may not be affamished through Colour of Justice' (Wiltshire RO QS/GR/H 1648, unnumbered).

3 'A set of ungovernable people'

1 Alan Everitt has been especially responsible for drawing attention to these characteristics of forest settlements. See his observations in Joan Thirsk (ed.), *The Agrarian History of England and Wales*, vol. 4: *1500–1640* (Cambridge, 1967), pp. 411–12, 463; A. Everitt, *Change in the Provinces: the Seventeenth Century* (Leicester, 1969), pp. 22–3, 36; and Joan Thirsk (ed.), 'Land, church, and people: essays presented to Professor H. P. R. Finberg', *Agricultural History Review*, supplement to vol. 18 (1970), pp. 188–93. See also Christopher Hill, *The World Turned Upside Down* (London, 1972), ch. 3.

2 E. P. Thompson, *Whigs and Hunters* (London, 1975); Douglas Hay, 'Poaching and the game laws in Cannock Chase', in D. Hay *et al.*, *Albion's Fatal Tree* (London, 1975), pp. 189–253.

3 William West, *A History of the Forest or Chase, known by the Name of Cranborne Chase* (Gillingham, 1816), vol. 6, pp. 122, 131; John Hutchins, *The History and Antiquities of the County of Dorset* (4 vols., London, 1861–70), vol. 3, pp. 411–12.

4 John Collinson, *The History and Antiquities of the County of Somerset* (3 vols., Bath, 1791), vol. 2, p. 194. He noted that more recently 'the cutting down large tracts of wood, establishing small farms, and building the church, have been the means of destroying their haunts, and obliging the possessors to seek subsistence in honest and useful labour'.

5 Arthur Young, *General View of the Agriculture of Oxfordshire* (London, 1813), p. 239.

6 Nehemiah Curnock (ed.), *The Journal of the Rev. John Wesley* (8 vols., London, 1909–16), vol. 2, p. 322.

7 D. G. D. Isaac, 'A study of popular disturbances in Britain 1714–1754' (Unpublished PhD thesis, University of Edinburgh, 1953), pp. 66, 299. I must acknowledge my general indebtedness

to this work and to John Latimer's *The Annals of Bristol in the Eighteenth Century* (Bristol, 1893) for many initial leads on the history of the Kingswood colliers. Although they are seldom referred to in my subsequent notes, both works served as invaluable starting points for much of the research that supports this essay. The locations of the various provincial newspapers which are cited in the notes may be found in the register appended to R. M. Wiles, *Freshest Advices: Early Provincial Newspapers in England* (Ohio State University Press, 1965), pp. 374ff.

8   H. T. Ellacombe, *The History of the Parish of Bitton* (Exeter, 1881), pp. 178ff; Bristol Reference Library, Ellacombe MSS, especially vols. 6, 7, 8, *passim*; and John Latimer, *The Annals of Bristol in the Seventeenth Century* (Bristol, 1900), pp. 59–61, 224, 302–4, 357–8.

9   Ellacombe, *Bitton*, appendix, plates 9, 11; A. Braine, *The History of Kingswood Forest* (London and Bristol, 1891), p. 88.

10   Latimer, *Bristol in the Seventeenth Century*, p. 445; Braine, *Kingswood Forest*, p. 84.

11   Only miscellaneous evidence is available on the organization of the colliery undertakings: see, for instance, Ellacombe, *Bitton*, appendix, plates 9, 11; *Felix Farley's Bristol Journal*, 29 November 1746 (advertisement for the sale of Blacksworth Manor); Gloucestershire R O D 1844/C 10 (letter of 18 November 1706), D 1844/C 11 (letter of 24 August 1713), D 421/E 20 (including plan of 1755), D 1844/E 15.

12   Bristol Ref. Lib., Ellacombe MSS, vol. 6, pp. 131, 173–4; vol. 7, p. 15; 'Survey of Kingswood Chase, 1691', vol. 10; Ellacombe, *Bitton*, appendix, plate 9; Christopher Morris (ed.), *The Journeys of Celia Fiennes* (London, 1949), p. 237.

13   Quoted in Latimer, *Bristol in the Seventeenth Century*, p. 304, and quoted in Romney Sedgwick, *The House of Commons 1715–1754* (2 vols., London, 1970), vol. 1, p. 457.

14   'Survey of 1691', Bristol Ref. Lib., Ellacombe MSS, vol. 10; Latimer, *Bristol in the Seventeenth Century*, p. 462; cf. J. U. Nef in the *Journal of Modern History*, vol. 2 (1930), p. 131.

15   'Survey of 1691', Bristol Ref. Lib., Ellacombe MSS, vol. 10; J. U. Nef, *The Rise of the British Coal Industry* (2 vols., London, 1932), vol. 1, p. 383.

16   John Meredith to Sir John Newton, 18 April 1722, Gloucester-shire R O D 1844/C 12.

17   W. Matthews, *The New History, Survey and Description of the City and Suburbs of Bristol* (Bristol, 1794), p. 44.

18   Ellacombe M SS, vol. 6, pp. 172, 154.

19   Ellacombe M SS, vol. 7, p. 17; Braine, *Kingswood Forest*, p. 85.

20   *The Political State of Great Britain*, vol. 56 (July–December 1738), pp. 143–4.

21   *Bristol Journal*, 7 January and 15 April 1749.

22   *Gloucester Journal*, 31 March 1741; *Bristol Weekly Intelligencer*, 28 April 1750.

23   Ellacombe, *Bitton*, pp. 209ff; Braine, *Kingswood Forest*, pp. 92–4; *Journal of the Life, Labours, and Travels of Thomas Shillitoe* (2 vols., London, 1839), vol. 1, ch. 10 (especially p. 171); Latimer, *Bristol in the Eighteenth Century*, p. 469, and his *The Annals of Bristol in the Nineteenth Century* (Bristol, 1887), pp. 48–9.

24   *Brice's Weekly Journal* (Exeter), 12 September 1729.

25   *Gloucester Journal*, 17 July 1739.

26   *The Bristol Riot* (London, 1714), p. 5, and quoted in D. G. Cooke, *The Story of Temple Colston School, Bristol* (Bristol, 1947), p. 26.

27   P R O SP 35/64, fo. 1.

28   Latimer, *Bristol in the Eighteenth Century*, pp. 78–9; Max Beloff, *Public Order and Popular Disturbances 1660–1714* (London, 1938), p. 68; *Bristol Riot*, pp. 5–8.

29   *Commons Journals*, vol. 20 (1722–7), pp. 769–70, 779, 781, 791.

30   *Farley's Bristol Journal*, 1 July 1727.

31   This account is based on P R O SP 36/1, fo. 56; Bristol Archives Office, 'Common Council Proceedings, 1722 to 1738', p. 131; *Norris's Taunton Journal*, 7 July 1727; *Northampton Mercury*, 3 and 17 July 1727.

32   *Northampton Mercury*, 24 July, 7 and 14 August 1727; *Commons Journals*, vol. 21 (1727–32), pp. 157, 159.

33   *Northampton Mercury*, 9 October 1727; *Commons Journals*, vol. 21 (1727–32), p. 159.

34   *Northampton Mercury*, 3 July 1727.

35   Arthur Young, *Tours in England and Wales (Selected from The Annals of Agriculture)*, London School of Economics and Political Science, Series of Reprints of Scarce Tracts in Economic and Political Science, no. 14 (1932), p. 23.

36 Gloucestershire R O D 15/2; this document is reprinted in full in William Albert, *The Turnpike Road System in England 1663–1840* (Cambridge, 1972), pp. 27–8. In 1770 John Wesley expressed the view that the country gentry could readily raise enough money to repair the roads in their own localities, and thus avoid 'saddling the poor people with the vile imposition of turnpikes for ever' (*Journal of John Wesley*, vol. 5, p. 370).

37 *Commons Journals*, vol. 21 (1727–32), p. 159.

38 Br. Lib. Add. M S 36, 136, fo. 356.

39 *Northampton Mercury*, 31 July and 14 August 1727; Bristol Archives Office, 'Common Council proceedings, 1722 to 1738', p. 18.

40 *Gloucester Journal*, 5 September 1727. During the summer of 1727 there were also some riots against turnpikes on several of the roads running north to Gloucester, erected under other Acts, though little evidence is available on these disturbances and the people involved. Brief references are found in the *Northampton Mercury*, 21 August 1727, and the *Gloucester Journal*, 15 August and 12 September 1727.

41 *Commons Journals*, vol. 21 (1727–32), pp. 157, 159. There was no consistent view of the punishment available at law for turnpike rioters. In April 1728 at the Gloucester assizes two men were convicted for destroying turnpikes, apparently in the Stroud–Dursley region: both were sentenced to death, though one was reprieved for transportation (*Gloucester Journal*, 16 April 1728; *Northampton Mercury*, 22 April 1728).

42 *Commons Journals*, vol. 21 (1727–32), p. 635.

43 *Gloucester Journal*, 6 July 1731; *Northampton Mercury*, 12 and 26 July 1731; P R O SP 36/23, fos. 206–7, 250, and P R O SP 36/25, fos. 257–8.

44 P R O SP 36/25, fo. 257; P R O SP 36/23, fo. 250; P R O SP 36/24, fo. 115.

45 *Commons Journals*, vol. 21 (1727–32), p. 828.

46 Chippenham turnpike trust minutes, Wiltshire R O (meetings of 31 August, 18 September 1732); *Weekly Worcester Journal*, 29 September and 27 October 1732.

47 Sedgwick, *House of Commons 1715–1754*, vol. 2, p. 145.

48 *Commons Journals*, vol. 20 (1722–7), p. 791; vol. 21 (1727–32), pp. 157, 159, 161, 169, 170, 828, 849–50, 881, 925.

49 *London Gazette*, no. 7173, 24–7 February 1732/33; *Read's*

Weekly Journal, 17 February 1733; *Gloucester Journal*, 20 March 1733.

50   Bristol Archives Office, M S 09701, nos. 25, 26.
51   P R O SP 36/35, fos. 170–5, 197; and Br. Lib. Add. M S 32,690, fo. 73.
52   *Commons Journals*, vol. 23 (1737–41), pp. 258–9, 273–4, 330; cf. John Oldmixon, *The History of England, During the Reigns of King William and Queen Mary, Queen Anne, King George I* (London, 1735), p. 804.
53   *Bristol Journal*, 29 July 1749.
54   *Salisbury Journal*, 6 March 1738.
55   Br. Lib. Add. M S 36,136, fo. 356.
56   Oldmixon, *History of England*, p. 804.
57   *Gloucester Journal*, 6 July 1731; P R O SP 36/25, fos. 257–8.
58   Ellacombe M SS, vol. 8, p. 116.
59   Paul Langford, *The Excise Crisis: Society and Politics in the Age of Walpole* (Oxford, 1975), p. 121. For further evidence on these turnpike riots to the north of Bristol, see P R O SP 36/32, fos. 25–9; P R O SP 36/37, fo. 166.
60   *Bristol Riot*, pp. 5–6 and 8; and *Daily Gazetteer*, 9 July 1735 (cf. P R O K B 33/5/3).
61   Sedgwick, *House of Commons 1715–1754*, vol. 1, p. 545.
62   Linda J. Colley, 'The Loyal Brotherhood and the Cocoa Tree: the London organization of the Tory Party, 1727–1760', *Historical Journal*, vol. 20, no. 1 (March 1977), p. 83; see also *Commons Journals*, vol. 21 (1727–32), pp. 823–4, and vol. 22 (1732–7), pp. 11–12.
63   *Commons Journals*, vol. 25 (1745–50), pp. 714, 737.
64   Bristol Archives Office, M S 04379, p. 88.
65   The account in this and the following paragraph is based largely on the following sources: *Bristol Journal*, 29 July and 12 August 1749; *Oracle Country Advertiser* (Bristol), 29 July and 12 August 1749; *Bristol Oracle*, 5 August 1749; *Gloucester Journal*, 8 August 1749; *Cambridge Journal*, 12 August 1749; and P R O SP 36/111, fos. 15 and 39.
66   *Gloucester Journal*, 8 August 1749.
67   *Bristol Oracle*, 5 August 1749.
68   This paragraph is based on the reports in the *Bristol Oracle*, 5 August 1749; *Cambridge Journal*, 12 August 1749; and *Ipswich Journal*, 12 August 1749.
69   *Bristol Journal*, 12 August 1749.

70 *Ipswich Journal*, 26 August 1749.
71 PRO SP 36/111, fos. 15–16; Bristol Archives Office, MS 04379, p. 90.
72 Br. Lib. Add. MS 32,719, fos. 161–2.
73 Br. Lib. Add. MS 32,719, fos. 161–2, 182.
74 *Bristol Oracle*, 2 September 1749; *Northampton Mercury*, 11 September 1749.
75 PRO SP 36/111, fo. 96.
76 *Oracle Country Advertiser*, 29 July 1749.
77 *Northampton Mercury*, 25 September and 2 October 1749.
78 My account of these disturbances is based on the following sources: *Gloucester Journal*, 17 October 1738; *Northampton Mercury*, 23 October 1738; *Political State of Great Britain*, vol. 56 (July–December 1738), p. 542; PRO SP 36/46, fos. 163–6, 175, 179.
79 *Northampton Mercury*, 4 December 1738.
80 *Northampton Mercury*, 13 and 20 November 1738.
81 PRO SP 36/46, fo. 247; *Gloucester Journal*, 10 April 1739.
82 See above, note 28.
83 This statement draws on my own research into the 1740 food riots.
84 This paragraph is based on the following sources: *Northampton Mercury*, 29 September, 6 and 13 October 1740; Col. Francis Leighton to General Wade, 24 September 1740, PRO SP 41/12; PRO SP 36/52, fos. 176–7; and *Gloucester Journal*, 23 December 1740.
85 Thomas Jackson (ed.), *The Journal of the Rev. Charles Wesley* (2 vols., London, 1849), vol. 1, pp. 249–50. For evidence concerning the Methodist preachers' satisfaction with the progress of the early ministry in Kingswood, see ibid., vol. 1, p. 301; William Wale (ed.), *Whitefield's Journals* (London, 1905; reprinted 1969), p. 298; *Journal of John Wesley*, vol. 2, pp. 322–3; John Telford (ed.), *The Letters of the Rev. John Wesley* (8 vols., London, 1931), vol. 2, p. 78 and vol. 3, p. 260.
86 *Salisbury Journal*, 21 May 1753.
87 The account in this and the following paragraph is based on *Felix Farley's Bristol Journal*, 26 May 1753; *Gloucester Journal*, 5 June 1753; PRO SP 36/122, fos. 40–1, 43; Samuel Seyer, *Memoirs Historical and Topographical of Bristol and Its Neighbourhood* (2 vols., Bristol, 1821–3), vol. 2, pp. 596–9.
88 PRO SP 36/122, fo. 43.

89 *Felix Farley's Bristol Journal*, 2 June 1753; PRO SP 36/122, fo. 47.

90 PRO SP 36/122, fos. 52, 58; Br. Lib. Add. MS 32,732, fos. 43, 51; Latimer, *Bristol in the Eighteenth Century*, pp. 304–5.

91 PRO SP 36/122, fos. 52, 110–11; PRO SP 36/124, fos. 48, 194; Isaac, 'Popular disturbances', pp. 306–7 and appendix 63.

92 *Read's Weekly Journal*, 4 August 1753; *Felix Farley's Bristol Journal*, 8 September 1753; Latimer, *Bristol in the Eighteenth Century*, p. 305.

93 PRO SP 36/125, fos. 25, 97; *Felix Farley's Bristol Journal*, 23 March 1754 (cf. issue of 22 December 1753); *Journal of John Wesley*, vol. 4, p. 75.

94 Seyer, *Memoirs of Bristol*, vol. 2, p. 599.

95 *Bonner and Middleton's Bristol Journal*, 16 May 1795.

96 The statement by Walter J. Shelton in *English Hunger and Industrial Disorders: A study of social conflict during the first decade of George III's reign* (London, 1973), p. 142, that 'Bristol colliers were active in regulating food markets in 1766' is incorrect. His source (*Public Advertiser*, 2 October 1766) indicates only that there were rumours that the colliers might riot; there is no evidence that they actually took any action. The Bristol press for this period makes no mention of any disturbances in the area.

97 See, for example, Latimer, *Bristol in the Eighteenth Century*, pp. 323–4, 377–8, 380; *Felix Farley's Bristol Journal*, 27 November 1756 and 4 June 1757.

98 The references to the Kingswood disturbances of the 1790s are as follows: (1) for 1790, J. L. and Barbara Hammond, *The Skilled Labourer 1760–1832* (London, 1919), p. 149, and J. de L. Mann, *The Cloth Industry in the West of England from 1640 to 1880* (Oxford, 1971), p. 128. (2) for 1792, A. Aspinall, *The Early English Trade Unions* (London, 1949), pp. 6–7, and *Felix Farley's Bristol Journal*, 25 August 1792. (3) for 1795, J. Stevenson, 'Food riots in England, 1792–1818', in R. Quinault and J. Stevenson (eds.), *Popular Protest and Public Order: Six Studies in British History 1790–1920* (London, 1974), pp. 46, 60; Latimer, *Bristol in the Eighteenth Century*, p. 516; *Sarah Farley's Bristol Journal*, 21 March and 9 May 1795; *Bristol Gazette*, 26 March and 23 April 1795; *Bristol Mercury*, 30 March 1795; *Bonner and Middleton's Bristol Journal*, 28 March

and 9 May 1795; Gloucestershire RO D 1799/C 170; and PRO HO 42/34, fos. 224, 228, 325, 376, 379.

99 Ellacombe, *Bitton*, p. 222; 'Report from His Majesty's Commissioners for inquiring into the administration and practical operation of the Poor Laws, appendix A, Pt I', *Parliamentary Papers, 1834* (vol. 28), pp. 886–7.

100 Ellacombe, *Bitton*, p. 221; Susan Thomas, *The Bristol Riots* (Bristol Branch of the Historical Association, 1974), pp. 23–4.

101 PRO SP 36/122, fo. 41.

102 Leighton to Wade, 24 September 1740, PRO SP 41/12.

103 *Letters of John Wesley*, vol. 5, p. 121.

104 J. P. Malcolm, *Excursions in the Counties of Kent, Gloucester, Hereford, Monmouth, and Somerset, in the Years 1802, 1803, and 1805* (London, 1814), pp. 211–12; Matthews, *New History of Bristol*, p. 75. cf. George Eayrs, *Wesley and Kingswood and Its Free Churches* (Bristol, 1911), pp. 93–7, and Braine, *Kingswood Forest*, p. 225.

105 *Commons Journals*, vol. 26 (1750/51–4), p. 95; William Barrett, *The History and Antiquities of the City of Bristol* (Bristol, n.d.), pp. 539–40 (written *c*. 1789); Latimer, *Bristol in the Eighteenth Century*, pp. 282–3; and (on the friendly society) Bristol Ref. Lib., Ellacombe MSS, vol. 9, p. 217.

4 The Wilkites and the law, 1763–74

1 Lord Hardwicke, *Parliamentary History* (36 vols., London, 1806–20), vol. 14, col. 20.

2 Characteristic studies include G. S. Veitch, *The Genesis of Parliamentary Reform* (London, 1913); Ian R. Christie, *Wilkes, Wyvill and Reform* (London, 1962); George Rudé, *Wilkes and Liberty. A Social study of 1763–1774* (Oxford, 1962).

3 Ian R. Christie, *Myth and Reality in later-eighteenth-century British Politics* (London, 1970), p. 245.

4 See especially, R. R. Rea, *The English Press in Politics, 1760–1774* (Lincoln, Neb., 1963), for an excellent discussion of this issue.

5 See, for instance, the highwayman who kept detailed notes on crimes so that he could turn evidence if he were apprehended (Peter Linebaugh, 'Tyburn: a study of crime and the labouring poor in London during the first half of the eighteenth century' Unpublished PhD thesis, University of Warwick, 1975).

6 For details of SSBR membership see Br. Lib. Add. MSS 30883 fos. 86–7.

7 *Worcester Journal*, 14 June 1768; *Old Bailey Proceedings*, no. 4, part 3 (1768), pp. 274ff.; *Felix Farley's Bristol Journal*, 16 July 1768.

8 *The Contest* (Newcastle, 1774), p. 10.

9 P. D. G. Thomas, *The House of Commons in the Eighteenth Century* (Oxford, 1971), p. 15; *Worcester Journal*, 22 February, 10 May 1770. cf. D. Duncan to Wilkes, 19 December (1768?), Br. Lib. Add. MSS 30875 fos. 115–16.

10 *North Briton*, no. 179 (1 September 1770); *Extraordinary North Briton*, no. 7.

11 *Worcester Journal*, 28 July, 18 August, 1 September 1768.

12 *Newcastle Journal*, 20 August 1768.

13 Wilkes to Polly Wilkes, 8 August 1768, Br. Lib. Add. MSS 30879 fo. 128; *Worcester Journal*, 11 August 1768.

14 *Newcastle Journal*, 16 August 1768; *Worcester Journal*, 13 August 1768.

15 *Felix Farley's Bristol Journal*, 23 July 1768.

16 Douglas Hay, 'Property, authority and the criminal law', in Douglas Hay *et al.*, *Albion's Fatal Tree* (London, 1976), p. 31.

17 *Newcastle Courant*, 11 March 1769; *Worcester Journal*, 18 August 1768.

18 Hay, 'Property, authority and the criminal law', p. 28.

19 See, for example, the row at the Surrey assize of 1762 over a proposal to drink Lord Bute's health (John Brewer, 'The misfortunes of Lord Bute; a case study in eighteenth-century political argument and public opinion', *Historical Journal*, vol. 16, no. 1 (1973), p. 9).

20 Robert Morris to Wilkes, 6 April 1770, Br. Lib. Add. MSS 30871 fo. 25.

21 J. Wright (ed.), *Sir Henry Cavendish's Debates of the House of Commons, during the Thirteenth Parliament of Great Britain* (2 vols., London, 1841), vol. 2, p. 88; *Parliamentary History*, vol. 16, cols. 1124–7; L. Radzinowicz, *A History of the English criminal law and its administration from 1750* (4 vols., London, 1948–68), vol. 2, pp. 127–8, 132–3, 429–45; Sir William Blackstone, *Commentaries on the Laws of England* (4 vols., Oxford, 1765–9), vol. 4, pp. 9–11.

22 Cavendish. *Debates*, vol. 2, p. 88.

23 *Reflections upon the present dispute between the House of Commons and the Magistrates of London* (London, 1771), p. 25.

24 John Brewer, *Party Ideology and Popular Politics at the Accession of George III* (Cambridge, 1976), p. 180.

25 For these groups and their clubs see my two essays in John Brewer, Neil McKendrick and J. H. Plumb, *The Birth of a Consumer Society: Commercialisation in Eighteenth-Century Britain* (forthcoming).

26 e.g. *Middlesex Journal*, 4, 27, 29 July, 19 August 1769. The number of examples could be considerably extended. Almost every number of the paper had exposés of one kind or another.

27 *Worcester Journal*, 16 March 1769, 15 February 1770; *Leeds Mercury*, 11 April 1769; *Gloucester Journal*, 17 May, 2 July, 5 November 1770; *Middlesex Journal*, 8, 18 April, 13 May 1769.

28 *Worcester Journal*, 7 June 1770.

29 *Gloucester Journal*, 4 November 1771, 15 June 1772; *Felix Farley's Bristol Journal*, 29 February, 13 June 1772; *The Last Journals of Horace Walpole during the Reign of George III from 1771 to 1783*, ed. A. F. Steuart (2 vols., London, 1910), vol. 1, pp. 120–2.

30 The best account of this incident is P. D. G. Thomas, 'John Wilkes and the liberty of the press (1771)', *Bulletin of the Institute of Historical Research*, vol. 33 (1960), pp. 86–98. Most provincial papers carried full details of the incident. Supplementary evidence to that of Thomas can be found in PRO TS 11/603/1972, 'King on Miller v. Whittam'.

31 Thomas, 'Wilkes and liberty of the press', pp. 96–7.

32 For the conditions of parliamentary reporting after 1771 see A. Aspinall, 'Reporting and publishing of the House of Commons debates, 1771–1834', in R. Pares and A. J. P. Taylor (eds.), *Essays Presented to Sir Lewis Namier* (London, 1956), pp. 227–57.

33 Alexander Stephens, *Memoirs of John Horne Tooke, interspersed with original documents* (2 vols., London, 1813), vol. 1, pp. 423–30.

34 *Reflections on the Case of Mr. Wilkes* (London, 1768), pp. 8–9; [Joseph Priestley]. *The Present State of Liberty in Great Britain and her Colonies* (London, 1769), pp. 10–11; *Whisperer*, nos. 29, 30.

35 J. Stephen, *Considerations on Imprisonment for Debt* (London, 1770), p. 68.

36 e.g. John Paul, *The Parish Officer's Guide* (London, 1793), pp. 148–9, 161–2.

37 'An historical account of the trial between John Wilkes Esq. and Halifax', Alnwick Castle, Northumberland MSS.

38 The best discussion of the material in this paragraph is in Rea, *The English Press in Politics*, pp. 59–69.

39 Camden's judgment is in T. B. Howell, *A Complete Collection of State Trials* (34 vols., London, 1809–28), vol. 19, cols. 1044–74.

40 '*Rex* v. *Gillam*', PRO TS 11/920/3213; 'The King against Alexander Murray and others', PRO TS 11/946/3467; 'Papers on St. George's Fields Massacre, prepared for the parliamentary inquiry', East Suffolk RO, Barrington Papers 6cl; PRO SP 44/142/83–7; PRO ASSI 35/208 (Surrey assize, felony, 1768).

41 Stephens, *Memoirs of John Horne Tooke*, vol. 1, p. 103; John Free, *England's Warning Piece* (London, 1769), *passim*; *A Collection of Pieces relative to the inhuman Massacre at St. George's Fields* (London, 1769) esp. 85–7; *Worcester Journal*, 19 May 1768; Wood to Nuthall, 5 July 1768, PRO SP 44/142/163–4.

42 Payne's activities can be followed in the Guildhall sessions files in the Guildhall RO, City of London. cf. *Salisbury Journal*, 2 April 1770.

43 See *Middlesex Journal*, 25 May, 13, 15 June, 22, 24, 31 August, 2 December 1769.

44 *Middlesex Journal*, 26 September 1769.

45 *Middlesex Journal*, 18 September 1769; *Worcester Journal*, 14 June 1768.

46 *North Briton*, no. 69 (8 October 1768).

47 Letter found on London Bridge, quoted in *North Briton Extraordinary*, no. 83.

48 *Thoughts on Capital Punishments, In a Series of Letters* (London, 1770), p. 8.

49 *An Enquiry into the Nature and Legality of Press Warrants* (London, 1770), p. 8.

50 *An Enquiry into the Nature and Legality of Press Warrants*, p. 45. cf. Stephen, *Considerations on Imprisonment for Debt*, p. 2.

51 See, for instance, Robert Holloway to Rochford, 13 June 1772, *Calendar of Home Office Papers*, p. 1331.

52 *Worcester Journal*, 29 September 1768.

53 *Worcester Journal*, 14, 21 June 1768, 12 October 1769.

54 Rea, *The English Press in Politics*, pp. 177–8; *North Briton*, no. 57 (16 July 1768); *Newcastle Courant*, 7 July 1764.

55 *North Briton*, no. 50 (28 May 1768), cf. Junius's attack on Mansfield for bailing a felon (John Cannon [ed.], *The Letters of Junius* [Oxford, 1978], pp. 314, 320–40).

56 *Worcester Journal*, 2 January 1770.

57 Rudé, *Wilkes and Liberty*, pp. 58–61.

58 Stephens, *Memoirs of John Horne Tooke*, vol. 1, pp. 104–5; Ealing Borough Library, Beauchamp Proctor MSS; *Old Bailey Proceedings*, pt 2, sect. 3 (1769), pp. 67–100.

59 *London Gazette*, 7 March 1769.

60 Horace Walpole believed Tatum to be connected with the Duke of Northumberland (Rudé, *Wilkes and Liberty*, 59n).

61 *Old Bailey Proceedings*, pt 3, sect. 2 (1770), p. 125; *Annual Register* (1770), p. 109.

62 J. H. Jesse, *George Selwyn and his Contemporaries* (4 vols., London, 1843–4), pp. 11, 385–90; *British Museum Catalogue of Prints and Drawings, Satires*, vol. 5: *1771–83*, no. 5095.

63 Cannon, *The Letters of Junius*, p. 203.

64 *Worcester Journal*, 17 April 1770; *Freeholders Magazine*, April 1770, pp. 81–95.

65 Stephens, *Memoirs of Horne Tooke*, vol. 1, pp. 103–4, 185–6.

66 Blackstone, *Commentaries*, vol. 4, pp. 308–11; J. H. Baker, 'Criminal courts and procedure at common law, 1550–1800', *Crime in England 1550–1800*, ed. J. S. Cockburn (London, 1977), pp. 17–18.

67 *English Law Reports: King's Bench Division*, vol. 98, p. 471. This case is 5 Burr. 2643.

68 Stephens, *Memoirs of Horne Tooke*, vol. 1, pp. 103–4; *Worcester Journal*, 10, 17, 31 May, 21 June 1770.

69 *Middlesex Journal*, 2, 7 May, 15 June, 27 July, 17 October, 18, 28 November, 2 December 1769, 27 February 1770.

70 *Middlesex Journal*, 25 November 1769.

71 cf. *Middlesex Journal* comments on fees: 11, 15 April 1769; Stephen, *Considerations on Imprisonment for Debt*, pp. 12–14; *The Extraordinary Case of William Penrice* (London, 1768), pp. 1–2.

72 *North Briton*, no. 210.

73 *London Chronicle*, 17 October 1771; *Gloucester Journal*, 28 October 1771.

74 *Worcester Journal*, 23 November 1769.
75 cf. note 69.
76 *Worcester Journal*, 30 June 1768, 23 November 1769, 3 January 1771; *Gloucester Journal*, 29 April 1771; *Felix Farley's Bristol Journal*, 2 September 1769; *Farley's Bristol Journal*, 21 April 1770.
77 See J. R. Hutchinson, *The Press Gang Afloat and Ashore* (London, 1913), pp. 202–32.
78 For a discussion of the literature on this issue see J. S. Bromley (ed.), 'The manning of the Royal Navy: selected public pamphlets, 1693–1873', *Publications of the Naval Records Society*, vol. 119 (1974), pp. xiii–xlvii.
79 *An Enquiry into the Legality of Press Warrants, passim*; *Farley's Bristol Journal*, 15 December 1770; Morris to Wilkes, 27 October 1770, Br. Lib. Add. MSS 30871, fo. 42.
80 *Worcester Journal*, 1 November 1770.
81 *Worcester Journal*, 4, 11, 18 October, 1 November 1770; *Gloucester Journal*, 5 November 1770; *Farley's Bristol Journal*, 13 October, 8 December 1770.
82 *Worcester Journal*, 18, 25 October, 1, 8, 15, 22, 29 November, 6 December 1770; *Gloucester Journal*, 22, 29 November; *Farley's Bristol Journal*, 20 October 1770.
83 *Middlesex Journal*, 29 June 1769.
84 For Stephen and Wilkes see *Felix Farley's Bristol Journal*, 15 February 1772; *London Chronicle*, 19, 21 November 1771, 18 January 1772; *Public Advertiser*, 20 December 1771; *Gloucester Journal*, 27 January 1772.
85 Robert Morris, *A Letter to Sir Richard Aston, Knt. One of the Judges of his Majesty's Court of King's Bench . . . containing a reply to his scandalous Abuse, and some Thoughts on the Modern Doctrine of Libels* (London, 1770), p. 40.
86 *An Enquiry into the Doctrine lately propagated concerning libels, warrants, and the seizure of papers . . . in a letter to Mr. Almon from the Father of Candor* (London, 1764), p. 4.
87 *A Letter to the Jurors of Great Britain* (London, 1771), p. 3.
88 Robert Morris, *A Letter to Sir Richard Aston . . .*, p. 42.
89 *North Briton*, no. 64 (3 September 1768).
90 *North Briton*, no. 176 (11 August 1770).
91 *An Enquiry into the Doctrine concerning libels*, pp. 118–19. cf. the pious platitudes uttered in the parliamentary debate of

November 1770 on *ex officio* informations (Cavendish, *Debates*, vol. 2, pp. 90–100).

92 Walpole, *Last Journals*, vol. 1, pp. 120–2, which includes Glynn's speech to the jury.

93 *The Englishman's Right: A Dialogue between a Barrister at law and a Juryman by Sir John Hawles, Knt., Solicitor General to the late King William* (London, 1764), pp. 5–6; *An Enquiry into the Doctrine concerning libels*, p. 4; *An Enquiry into the Nature and Legality of Press Warrants*, p. 50.

94 *Newcastle Journal*, 3 August 1771; *Felix Farley's Bristol Journal*, 12 December 1772.

95 Br. Lib. Add. MSS 30885, fos. 52–3. cf. ibid., fos. 16, 141–4, 169.

96 Br. Lib. Add. MSS 30885, fo. 20.

97 These speeches also appeared on many Wilkite prints and handbills. See, for instance, *English Liberty Established: or, a mirrour for posterity: John Wilkes esqr the undaunted assertor of the liberty of the press, and the rights of Englishmen* (London, 1768), single sheet.

98 *State Trials*, vol. 19, cols. 1095, 1159.

99 Br. Lib. Add. MSS 30885, fos. 142–3.

100 Anon. to Wilkes, 10 February 1764, Br. Lib. Add. MSS 30868, fo. 35; Cotes to Wilkes, 18 March 1764, ibid., fo. 58.

101 *Worcester Journal*, 26 July 1770; *North Briton*, no. 176. cf. *Newcastle Courant*, 16 July 1763, for jurors in Huckell's case, and *Middlesex Journal*, 12 August 1769, for the special jury for *Wilkes* v. *Halifax*.

102 *Worcester Journal*, 2 August 1770.

103 L. W. Hanson, *Government and the Press, 1695–1763* (Oxford, 1936), pp. 19–20.

104 Quoted in Rea, *The English Press in Politics*, p. 82.

105 Rea, *The English Press in Politics*, p. 83.

106 See, *inter alia, A Letter to the Jurors of Great Britain*, p. 51; Morris, *A Letter to Sir Richard Aston*, p. 42.

107 Rea, *The English Press in Politics*, pp. 180–4.

108 e.g. *Worcester Journal*, 26 July 1770; *Newcastle Journal*, 28 July 1770.

109 Rea, *The English Press in Politics*, p. 184.

110 *Worcester Journal*, 22 November 1770.

111 *North Briton*, nos. 64 (3 September 1768), 176 (11 August 1770); *Whisperer*, no. 24 (28 July 1770); *The Englishman's Right*, p. 32.

112   *North Briton*, no. 50 (28 May 1768).

113   *English Law Reports: King's Bench Division*, vol. 98, p. 467.
This case is 5 Burr. 2798.

114   Cavendish, *Debates*, vol. 2, p. 131; *Worcester Journal*, 5 April,
16 August, 1770; *Gloucester Journal*, 13 August 1770.

115   *North Briton*, no. 64 (3 September 1768).

116   *Worcester Journal*, 16 November 1769; *An Enquiry into the
Nature and Legality of Press Warrants*, pp. 46–7; *Newcastle
Courant*, 28 July 1764.

117   John Campbell, *The Lives of the Chief Justices of England:
From the Norman Conquest to the Death of Lord Mansfield* (2
vols., Philadelphia, 1851), vol. 2, p. 335. cf. the discussion of
Mansfield's career in C. H. S. Fifoot, *Lord Mansfield* (Oxford,
1936).

118   *North Briton*, no. 197 (17 December 1770).

119   See, for instance, *Whisperer*, no. 24 (28 July 1770).

120   For this incident and its background see Stephens, *Memoirs of
Horne Tooke*, vol. 1, pp. 109–14; *Worcester Journal*, 23 November, 14 December 1769; *Genuine Copies of all the letters which
passed between the Right Honourable the Lord Chancellor, and
the Sheriffs of London and Middlesex, and between the Sheriffs
and the Secretary of State, relative to the execution of Doyle and
Valline* (London, 1770).

121   Hay, 'Property, authority and the criminal law', esp. pp.
40–9.

122   e.g. *Middlesex Journal*, 27 May, 17 October, 18, 25 November
1769.

123   J. H. Jesse, *George Selwyn and his Contemporaries* (4 vols.,
London, 1843–4), vol. 2, p. 390.

124   Hay, 'Property, authority and the criminal law', p. 45.

125   [Thomas Percival], *Biographical Memoirs of the late Thomas
Butterworth Bayley Esq., F.R.S. &c. of Hope Hall, nr Manchester* (Manchester, 1802), p. 12.

126   *North Briton*, no. 175 (4 August 1770).

127   On *ex officio* informations see *The Court of Star Chamber, or
the Seat of Oppression* (London, 1768); *An Enquiry into the
Doctrine concerning libels*, pp. 5–9, 19; *North Briton*, no. 64
(3 September 1768); Cavendish, *Debates*, vol. 2, pp. 90–100.

128   J. C. Fox, 'The King v. Almon', *Law Quarterly Review* (1908),
pp. 184–98, 266–371; J. C. Fox, 'The summary process to
punish contempt', *LQR* (1909), pp. 240–78.

129 *The Court of Star Chamber*, pp. 3–6, 8–11; *A Letter to the Jurors of Great Britain*, pp. 26, 28–9; *North Briton*, nos. 64 (3 September 1768), 75 (12 November 1768).

130 Fox, 'The King v. Almon', p. 184.

131 *North Briton*, nos. 52 (13 June 1768), 63 (27 August 1768), 75 (12 November 1768), 191 (18 February 1769); *Worcester Journal*, 10 November 1768, 23 February 1769.

132 *North Briton*, no. 91 (18 February 1769); *Worcester Journal*, 19 January, 9 February, 1769, 5 April 1770; *Felix Farley's Bristol Journal*, 11 March 1769.

133 *Gloucester Journal*, 29 April 1771; *Farley's Bristol Journal*, 14 March 1772; *North Briton*, nos. 64 (3 September 1768), 91 (18 February 1769); *Hampshire Chronicle*, 17 January 1774; *An Enquiry into the Doctrine concerning libels*, pp. 6–7.

134 Rudé, *Wilkes and Liberty*, chs. 3, 4, 6; Brewer, *Party Ideology*, pp. 245–57.

135 Rudé, *Wilkes and Liberty*, pp. 52–3, 90–104; 'A List of the several persons presented, and now under prosecution for riots in Middlesex and Surrey, 1768', PRO TS 11/443/1408; 'King agst Alexander Murray Esq & others', PRO TS 11/946/3467; 'Rex v. Gillam', PRO TS 11/920/3213.

136 *North Briton*, nos. 91 (18 February 1769), and 92 (21 February 1769). cf. *Salisbury Journal*, 8, 15 January 1770.

137 For attacks on trading justices see *Middlesex Journal*, 24 August, 26 September 1769; *Worcester Journal*, 23 November 1769; *Felix Farley's Bristol Journal*, 24 October 1772; Cavendish, *Debates*, vol. 1, pp. 102–5.

138 Wood to Barrington, 10 June 1768, SP Domestic Entry Book, PRO SP 44/142/139.

139 *Worcester Journal*, 19 October 1769.

140 See note 120 and *Middlesex Journal*, 14, 19 October, 21 November 1769.

141 For the conduct of the sheriffs see *Felix Farley's Bristol Journal*, 3 October 1772; *London Chronicle*, 17 October, 19 December 1771, 22 February 1772; *Public Advertiser*, 21 December 1771; Walpole, *Last Journals*, vol. 1, pp. 79–80.

142 See the statements of Wilkes, Lewes and Bull in 1772, *Felix Farley's Bristol Journal*, 11 July, 3 October 1772.

143 Guildhall Sessions Files, September 1771.

144 *Worcester Journal*, 15 November 1770.

145 See, for instance, [T. B. Bayley], *Thoughts occasioned by the*

alarming increase of Justiciary Trials at Glasgow (Glasgow, 1788), pp. 4–5.

146   *Middlesex Journal*, 27 April, 27 May, 17 June, 12 August 1769; *Farley's Bristol Journal*, 15 June 1771; *Felix Farley's Bristol Journal*, 7 March, 7 September 1772.

147   *Worcester Journal*, 9 June 1768.

148   *Middlesex Journal*, 19, 22, 24 July 1769.

149   ibid., 21 December 1769.

5   'Our traitorous money makers'

1   C. Jenkinson, first Earl of Liverpool, *A Treatise on the Coin of the Realm* (London, 1805), p. 229.

2   *Leeds Intelligencer*, 27 July 1773.

3   See D. Defoe, *The Complete English Tradesman* (2 vols., London, 1727), vol. 1, pp. 304–5, 307, 315.

4   Quoted in Jenkinson, *Treatise on the Coin*, p. 145.

5   Sir J. Craig, *The Mint* (London, 1953), pp. 193 and 214.

6   T. S. Ashton, *An Economic History of England: the Eighteenth Century* (London, 1955), pp. 169, 171.

7   Craig, *The Mint*, p. 215.

8   Jenkinson, *Treatise on the Coin*, p. 144.

9   Rogers Ruding, *Annals of the Coinage of Great Britain* (3 vols., London, 1840), vol. 2, p. 81.

10   Ashton, *Economic History*, p. 177.

11   Craig, *The Mint*, p. 212. Variations in the weight of coins produced at the Mint actually increased with the introduction of machine stamping in 1662 (Craig, *The Mint*, p. 167).

12   Br. Lib., Egerton MSS 257, fo. 166 (Cavendish's Parliamentary Debates, Mr Halcom's evidence to the Parliamentary Committee on the State of the Gold Coinage, 9 May 1774); Craig, *The Mint*, 243.

13   Jenkinson, *Treatise on the Coin*, p. 143.

14   Quoted in Craig, *The Mint*, p. 242.

15   See, for example, 'Animadversions' by 'T' in the *Leeds Intelligencer*, 8 February 1774.

16   Ashton, *Economic History*, pp. 167–8 and 176; Craig, *The Mint*, ch. 8.

17   The Mint price for gold was progressively reduced in 1696, 1699 and 1717, but for the rest of the eighteenth century the Mint prices for both gold and silver remained unchanged. The

reduction of 6 d. in the value of the guinea in 1717 caused bitter resentment in the country and in Parliament; Craig, *The Mint*, pp. 218–19.

18 Sir A. Feavearyear, *The Pound Sterling* (1931; 2nd ed. rev. by E. V. Morgan, Oxford, 1963), pp. 148–9; Ashton, *Economic History*, 176; Br. Lib., Egerton MSS 257, fo. 170 (Lord North's statement to the 1774 Parliamentary Committee on the Coinage). North commented, with regard to the relative Mint values of gold and silver, that the latter was still the standard and that any alteration should be made in the Mint price for gold. But he emphasized that no such alteration was contemplated. Nevertheless, his proposal for a gold recoinage, unaccompanied by a corresponding recoinage of silver, merely confirmed the status of gold as, for all practical purposes, the British standard.

19 A correspondent in the *Leeds Intelligencer*, 12 December 1773, compared English practice unfavourably with that in France, where, he claimed, general recoinages were undertaken at the start of each reign.

20 See Craig, *The Mint*, ch. 11.

21 ibid., p. 239.

22 A. Smith, *The Wealth of Nations* (1776), ed. R. H. Campbell and A. S. Skinner (2 vols., Oxford, 1976), vol. 2, p. 551.

23 *Leeds Intelligencer*, 3 August 1773 (letter from 'an old merchant').

24 Quoted in Craig, *The Mint*, p. 240. 'Moidore' was an English corruption of the Portuguese *moeda*.

25 ibid., p. 241.

26 ibid., p. 253.

27 ibid., p. 253.

28 Quoted in ibid., p. 253.

29 PRO Mint 1/11, fo. 40 (Mint Record Book, 1747–64); PRO HO 42/5, fo. 18 (Home Office in-letters: printed notice concerning bad coppers at Manchester, dated 31 October 1783).

30 11 Geo. III c. 40.

31 By 15 Geo. II c. 28.

32 Craig, *The Mint*, p. 253; PRO HO 42/5, fo. 18; A. P. Wadsworth and J. de L. Mann, *The Cotton Trade and Industrial Lancashire* (Manchester, 1931), p. 400.

33 Sir L. Radzinowicz, *A History of English Criminal Law and its*

Administration from 1750 (4 vols., London, 1948–68), vol. 1 (1948), p. 707, *n.* 56.

34 Depriving the coin of part of its metal content by clipping, filing or sweating (physical or chemical abrasion).

35 See below, page 182.

36 The following account of Lightowller's activities is based on the Mint Solicitor's accounts for 1756 and 1757 (PRO Mint 1/11, fos. 77–116), and on John Hewitt, *The Proceedings of J. Hewitt, Alderman . . . in the year 1756 . . . Being a particular account of the gang of coiners, apprehended in the counties of Oxford, Warwick and Stafford, pursued by the author . . . the extraordinary adventures of . . . Thomas Lightowller . . .* (Birmingham, 1783).

37 Hewitt, *Proceedings*, p. 9.

38 ibid., p. 55. Lightowller went to Austria to produce metal dies and rolling presses, but did not fulfil the hopes placed in him by the Austrian authorities; see Gustav Otruba, *Die Wirtschaftspolitik Maria Theresias* (Vienna, 1963), p. 35, and Mr Langlois to the Earl of Rochford, 23 May 1769, PRO SP 80/206 (State Papers Foreign, Germany [Empire], 1769). I am indebted to Dr Derek Beales of Sidney Sussex College, Cambridge for these references, which confirm and amplify Hewitt's account of Lightowller's activities in Austria.

39 Hewitt, *Proceedings*, pp. 9, 10, 12; PRO Mint 1/11, fos. 77–116. In addition, the Mint Solicitor's account for 1746 refers to a Timothy Lightholder who was an active counterfeiter in the Kingswood area (PRO AO 3/703 [Audit Office, Mint Solicitors' papers, Mint Solicitor s account for 1746]).

40 PRO Mint 1/11, fos. 95 and 105.

41 Hewitt, *Proceedings*, p. 50.

42 ibid., p. 11. Pinchbeck was a copper-zinc alloy resembling gold, used in clock-making and cheap jewellery. It was named after its inventor, Christopher Pinchbeck, a London watch and toy maker (died 1732).

43 Hewitt, *Proceedings*, p. 45.

44 ibid., pp. 23, 39–40 (note).

45 ibid., p. 21.

46 By 1750, some gold coin in circulation was so deficient in weight that the Bank of England and the excise office were anxious to obtain the authority to refuse those guineas deficient by more than one shilling's worth of gold. Government, how-

ever, refused to provide such authority (Ruding, *Annals of the Coinage*, vol. 2, p. 79).

47 Entered in PRO Mint 1/11, fos. 3–10.

48 PRO Mint 1/11, fo. 4.

49 Diminishing the gold coin had caused some complaint in the 1730s, but had only affected coins minted in particular years when the inscription was struck unnecessarily far from the edge (Craig, *The Mint*, p. 241). The Mint Solicitor reported that the practice of diminishing greatly increased during the late 1740s; Fountaine Cooke to the Treasury, 1 November 1751, PRO SP 36/117, fo. 283 (State Papers Domestic, George II). The following account of Joseph Wood's activities is based on William Chamberlayne's evidence before the 1774 Parliamentary Committee on the Coinage (Br. Lib., Egerton MSS 257, fos. 151–3) and his accounts as Mint Solicitor for 1757–8 (PRO Mint 1/11, fos. 101–16).

50 Br. Lib., Egerton MSS 257, fo. 166 (Mr Halcom's evidence).

51 Br. Lib., Egerton MSS 257, fo. 152 (William Chamberlayne's evidence).

52 PRO Mint 1/11, fo. 112.

53 PRO Mint 1/11, fo. 95 (Lightowller), fo. 164 (Wrag); see also fo. 94 (John Pickering case at Warwick summer assizes, 1756).

54 Of those tried on a capital coinage charge, between 1732 and 1769, for which evidence survives in Mint Solicitors' accounts, 59 per cent were convicted (see PRO T 54/32–4 [Treasury warrants not relating to money, 1732–48], AO 3/703, Mint 1/10–12 [Mint Record Books, 1739–76]). Of those tried for capital offences against property in Surrey between 1736 and 1753, only 33 per cent were convicted on the capital charge (J. M. Beattie, 'Crime and the courts in Surrey, 1736–1753', in J. S. Cockburn [ed.], *Crime in England, 1550–1800* [London, 1977], p. 176). In the cases of another 29 per cent of those accused of capital offences against property in Surrey, the jury exercised its right to find the offender guilty, not of the capital offence, but of non-capital theft. This was an option not available to juries in capital coinage cases. Yet it is striking that the proportion of guilty verdicts in capital coinage cases was only slightly below the porportion of *all* convinctions (capital or otherwise) on capital property indictments in Surrey. It should be noted, however, that in the years 1755–69, when William Chamberlayne was Mint Solicitor, the con-

viction rate in capital coinage cases was only 41 per cent.

55   Principally by 25 Edw. III c. 2 (counterfeiting), 8 & 9 Will. III c. 26, and 15 & 16 Geo. II c. 28 (gilding), 5 Eliz. c. 11 (clipping English coin), 18 Eliz. c. 11 (clipping current foreign coin), 8 & 9 Will. III c. 26 (edging), 8 & 9 Will. III c. 26 (coining tools).

56   By 6 & 7 Will. III c. 17, and 15 & 16 Geo. II c. 28.

57   6 & 7 Will. III c. 17.

58   By 14 Eliz. c. 3.

59   J. H. Baker, 'Criminal courts and procedure at common law, 1550–1800', in J. S. Cockburn (ed.), *Crime in England, 1550–1800*, p. 40. Trials for coinage treasons were conducted according to common law procedure (see Sir Matthew Hale, *History of the Pleas of the Crown*, rev. G. Wilson [2 vols., London, 1800], vol. 1, p. 214).

60   PRO Mint 1/11, fo. 81.

61   PRO Mint 1/11, fo. 80.

62   Robert Cockerill to J. E. Blackett, 24 February 1773, Northumberland RO ZBL 230 (Blackett of Matton MSS).

63   Craig, *The Mint*, pp. 205–6.

64   PRO AO 3/703 (Statement by the Mint Solicitor of the duties and emoluments of his office, 1798).

65   By 7 Anne c. 28.

66   15 Geo. II c. 24.

67   Memorial to the Lords Commissioners of the Treasury from Fountain Cooke, late Mint Solicitor, 12 January 1764, Br. Lib., Add. MSS 38421, fos. 28–9 (Liverpool MSS); PRO Mint 1/12, fo. 191.

68   PRO Mint 1/11 and 1/12 *passim* (Mint Solicitor's accounts, 1756–69).

69   PRO Mint 1/12, fos. 39, 135–6.

70   Marquis of Rockingham to Lord Weymouth, 1 December 1769, PRO SP 37/7 (State Papers Domestic, George III).

71   Hewitt, *Proceedings*, pp. 49, and 54.

72   PRO Mint 1/11, fo. 105.

73   PRO Mint 1/12, fo. 351.

74   Dr Pye to J. E. Blackett, 12 March 1773, Northumberland RO ZBL 230.

75   R. Burn, *The Justice of the Peace and Parish Officer* (1755; regularly reprinted); M. Dalton, *The Countrey Justice* (1618; regularly reprinted).

76 It is difficult to produce a definitive execution rate from the Mint Solicitors' accounts. Although it was the custom of successive Solicitors to record the outcome of the cases they financed, they often indicated only that a convicted offender had been 'left for execution', with no record of any subsequent pardon, reprieve or execution. However, in other instances, the Solicitor would record that the offender actually was executed. Where it has proved possible to check these latter cases in the local press, the Solicitor's statement has always proved accurate. On this basis it is possible to compute that *at least* 65 per cent of those known from the Solicitors' accounts to have been convicted of a capital coinage offence were executed in the period 1732–69 (PRO T 54/32–4, AO 3/703, Mint 1/10–12). The proportion executed of those capitally convicted of crimes against property (overwhelmingly theft) in Surrey between 1736 and 1753 was 49 per cent (Beattie, 'Crime and the courts in Surrey', p. 180).

77 Br. Lib., Egerton MSS 257, fo. 153 (William Chamberlayne's evidence).

78 Since the mid nineteenth century, these operations have been the subject of several historical accounts and fictional reconstructions by local authors. The best concise account is T. W. Hanson, 'Cragg coiners', *Transactions of the Halifax Antiquarian Society* (1909), pp. 85–106. H. L. Roth, *The Yorkshire Coiners, 1767–1783* (Halifax, 1906), provides extensive transcriptions of relevant documents from the Calderdale Metropolitan Borough Archives (HAS: 1400/1 [Coiners' papers], and PRO SP 37). I have followed Roth in describing the practitioners of clipping and coining in the Halifax–Rochdale area as the 'Yorkshire coiners', although their activities were not restricted to coining and extended across the county boundary into Lancashire. For a detailed discussion of the extent of the clipping and coining district, see below, page 205.

79 Enclosure by Samuel Lister, attorney, in Richard Wilson to Lord Rochford, 30 June 1774, PRO SP 37/10.

80 Edward Bacon to Bacon Frank, 19 July 1773, Sheffield City Library, BFM 1327/25 (Frank of Campsall MSS). For another instance of this usage, see Thomas Grimston to John Grimston, n.d. (?1770), Humberside RO DDGR 42/33 (Grimston MSS).

81 Br. Lib., Egerton MSS 257, fo. 154 (William Chamberlayne's evidence).

82   *Leeds Intelligencer*, 23 February 1768 (letter signed 'Philo Patriae'); 29 August 1769 (letter signed 'E.C.').

83   William Chamberlayne, appointed Mint Solicitor late in 1755, conducted the prosecutions of Lightowller and his associates in 1756 and 1757. He later stated that he did not encounter the practice of diminishing the gold coin until the Wood case in 1757 (Br. Lib., Egerton MSS 257, fo. 151). This, and the evidence that Lightowller's associates elsewhere coined in mixed or base metals, suggests that coining in the West Riding during the 1750s was not associated with clipping.

84   The *silver* coin was clipped in the Halifax area during the 1680s and 1690s, before and during the silver recoinage of 1696–8; see, for example, PRO ASSI 45/15/2/50, ASSI 45/15/3/62 and 115, ASSI 45/16/3/20 and ASSI 45/17/2/135. However, at that period clipping was widespread throughout the country. Within the West Riding, it was confined neither to Halifax parish, nor to the textile district.

85   Yorkshire Archaeological Society MSS, MS 385 (Prosecution Brief in the case against Robert Thomas, Matthew Normanton and William Folds for murder, Yorkshire assizes, 4 August 1770).

86   *Leeds Intelligencer*, 18 July 1769 (letter signed 'A.R.').

87   PRO SP 37/27 (William Chamberlayne's comments on Messrs. Garbutts' report on the state of the Mint).

88   Br. Lib., Egerton, MSS 257, fo. 155 (William Chamberlayne's evidence).

89   D. Defoe, *A Tour thro' the whole Island of Great Britain* (1727; 2 vols., London, 1928), vol. 2, p. 603.

90   See H. Heaton, *The Yorkshire Woollen and Worsted Industries from the earliest times up to the Industrial Revolution* (Oxford, 1965), pp. 267–71, 286–7, and R. Wilson, *Gentlemen Merchants: The Merchant Community in Leeds, 1700–1830* (Manchester, 1971), 54–5.

91   J. James, *History of the Worsted Manufacture in England* (1858), p. 285. I follow James in treating the woollen and worsted manufactures of east and north-east Lancashire as part of the West Riding industry.

92   Thomas Woolrich, a Leeds merchant, collected production figures for the West Riding woollen and worsted industry in 1772. He estimated that between Easter 1771 and Easter 1772 72 per cent of total production of woollens and worsteds in the

West Riding was exported. Deane's figures for national production suggest that the proportion of all English woollen and worsted output exported rose from 40 per cent in 1695 to only 67 per cent in 1800. Woolrich specified that 90 per cent of West Riding-produced kersies were exported in 1771–2, and 75 per cent of its worsteds. However, the area's worsted output, at £1.4 million in value, was over twelve times that of kersies (see Wilson, *Gentlemen Merchants*, pp. 42–3, and P. Deane, 'The output of the British woollen industry in the eighteenth century', *Journal of Economic History*, vol. 17 [1957], p. 221).

93 Wilson, *Gentlemen Merchants*, pp. 47–8.

94 *York Courant*, 31 December 1765 (letter from 'A Manufacturer').

95 T. S. Ashton, *Economic Fluctuations in England, 1700–1800* (Oxford, 1959), pp. 150–4. The following discussion of Anglo-American trade in the early 1760s is also based on M. Engal, 'The economic development of the thirteen continental colonies, 1720–1775', *William and Mary Quarterly*, 3rd series, vol. 32 (1975), pp. 191–222, and J. A. Ernst, *Money and Politics in America, 1755–1775* (Chapel Hill, North Carolina, 1973), *qassim*.

96 Memorial of the Magistrates, Merchants and Principal Manufacturers of Halifax, 21 October 1765, P R O T 1/443 (Treasury in-letters).

97 The shortage of cash in the Halifax locality did not pass without complaint at this stage. A June 1765 memorial to the Treasury from the tradesmen of Halifax stressed the inconvenience arising 'from all the Land Tax money of the county being in the hands of the receivers at Leeds' (P R O T 29/37, fo. 25 [Treasury Board Minutes, 12 June 1765]).

98 See, for examples of the use of such nicknames, *A brief Account of the leading Transactions of the Lives of Thomas Spencer and Mark Sattonstall* (1783), single sheet in Calderdale Metropolitan Borough Reference Library, Horsfall Turner Collection, P 343, and P R O ASSI 45/29 (information of Matthew Normanton, 20 November 1769).

99 In formulating this approach to the analysis of criminal organization, I have drawn on Mary McIntosh, *The Organisation of Crime* (1975), particularly pp. 9–17, and A. K. Cohen, 'The concept of criminal organisation', *The British Journal of Criminology*, vol. 17 (1977), no. 2, pp. 97–111.

100   PRO ASSI 45/29 (Assizes, Northern Circuit Depositions, 1768–70: deposition of Jonas Tillotson, 19 December 1769).

101   Br. Lib., Egerton MSS 257, fo. 157.

102   PRO ASSI 45/29 (deposition of Joseph Broadbent, 1 May 1769).

103   PRO ASSI 45/29 (deposition of John Kitson, 1 January 1770).

104   PRO ASSI 45/29 (deposition of Joseph Shaw, 3 February 1770).

105   Br. Lib., Egerton MSS 257, fo. 155.

106   Br. Lib., Egerton MSS 257, fo. 155 (William Chamberlayne's evidence). For an account of such a transaction, see PRO ASSI 45/29 (deposition of Joseph Shaw, 9 October 1769).

107   PRO SP 37/27 (Chamberlayne's comments on Garbutt's report).

108   Br. Lib., Egerton MSS 257, fo. 157 (William Chamberlayne's evidence).

109   Arthur Young reported that seven shillings was an average week's earnings for a weaver at Leeds in the late 1760s (A. Young, *A Six Months Tour through the North of England* [4 vols., London, 1770], vol. 1, p. 152).

110   PRO ASSI 45/29 (deposition of Samuel Magson, 25 December 1769).

111   PRO ASSI 45/29 (deposition of Adam Liley, 5 February 1770).

112   PRO ASSI 45/29 (depositions of Samuel Magson, 25 December 1769, and Brian Dempsey, 27 December 1769).

113   Richard Townley to Rockingham, 12 January 1770, Sheffield City Library, WWM R 11/28; Rockingham MSS).

114   See below, page 211.

115   Rockingham to Weymouth, 1 December 1769, PRO SP 37/7.

116   Yorkshire Archaeological Society MSS, MS 385 (prosecution brief).

117   PRO ASSI 45/29 (deposition of Robert Iredale, 1 January 1770).

118   Rockingham to Weymouth, 1 December 1769, PRO SP 37/7.

119   PRO ASSI 45/29 (deposition of John Kitson, 1 January 1770).

120   Br. Lib., Egerton MSS 257, fos. 157–8 (William Chamberlayne's evidence).

121   B. Loomes, *Yorkshire Clockmakers* (Clapham, North Yorkshire, 1972), p. 21.

122   Calderdale Archives, HAS:1400/1, fo. 27 (information of John

Bates, n.d. [winter 1769/70]). At Christmas 1768 Sunderland left Halifax to work as a painter and decorator for Edwin Lascelles, Esq., Member of Parliament for Yorkshire, at Harwood House, north of Leeds (see Loomes, *Yorkshire Clockmakers*, p. 161, and PRO ASSI 45/29 [depositions of Thomas Varley, 4 January 1770, and Thomas Sunderland, 3 January 1770]).

123 PRO ASSI 45/29 (deposition of James Shaw, 10 January 1770).

124 PRO ASSI 45/29 (deposition of Samuel Magson, 25 December 1769).

125 PRO ASSI 45/29 (deposition of Thomas Varley, 4 January 1770); Calderdale Archives, HAS:1400/1, fo. 27 (information of John Bates, n.d.).

126 Calderdale Archives, HAS:1400/1, fo. 27 (information of John Bates, n.d.).

127 PRO ASSI 45/29 (deposition of William Varley, 4 January 1770).

128 See for example, PRO ASSI 45/29 (deposition of James Crabtree, 7 September 1769).

129 PRO ASSI 45/29 (deposition of Adam Liley, 5 February 1770).

130 See, for example, PRO ASSI 45/29 (deposition of Joseph Broadbent, 1 May 1769).

131 See Richard Townley, John Chadwick and Robert Entwisle to the Treasury, 16 February 1770, PRO T 1/476.

132 Roth, *The Yorkshire Coiners*, p. 13*n*. In the light of the evidence referred to on pp. 193–4, demonstrating the close association of some Halifax merchants with leading coiners, I consider Roth's scepticism concerning the assertions by nineteenth-century local historians to be misplaced.

133 *Leeds Intelligencer*, 18 July 1769 (letter signed 'A.R.').

134 *Leeds Intelligencer*, 29 August 1769 (letter signed 'E.C.').

135 PRO ASSI 45/28–31 (Assizes, Northern Circuit Depositions, 1765–74); PL 27/4–5 (Palatinate of Lancaster, Assize Depositions, 1761–80); Calderdale Archives, HAS:1400/1.

136 PRO ASSI 45/29 includes a bundle of fifty-two depositions relating to clipping and coining in Yorkshire, 1769–70. Thirty-three of these carry numbers 18 to 50 in an eighteenth-century hand. Numbers 1 to 17 appear to be missing, as the remaining nineteen are not numbered.

137 Wilson, *Gentlemen Merchants*, p. 58.

138 E. M. Sigsworth, 'William Greenwood and Robert Heaton; two eighteenth-century worsted manufacturers', *Bradford Textile Society Journal* (1951–2), p. 72.

139 Calculated, as below, on the basis of the figures provided in 1774 by Thomas Woolrich, the Leeds merchant, and John Sutcliffe, a stuffmaker at Holdsworth, in Halifax parish (James, *Worsted Manufacture*, pp. 281, 284, 285). One pound of combed wool had an average value, when manufactured into cloth, of 4 s. Heaton's average annual production of £900's worth of cloth therefore required approximately 4500 lbs of combed wool. One comber produced, on average, 36 lbs of combed wool per week. Hence Heaton required 2·5 combers, working constantly, to sustain his average annual output. One comber kept 14 spinners and 3·5 weavers employed. Heaton required, therefore, at least 35 spinners and 9 weavers to sustain his level of production. In fact, these figures are almost certainly an underestimate of the actual number of Heaton's employees, as they fail to include other processes, such as wool sorting, and assume continuous working, which was unusual. Hence the number of combers and weavers has been rounded upwards. I have preferred, as a basis for calculation, Yorkshire figures, dating from approximately the same period as Heaton's business activities and the yellow trade, to the strikingly different figures, from a pamphlet published in the 1720s, quoted in James, *Worsted Manufacture*, p. 217, *n.* 2. A calculation based on the latter would produce roughly double the number of employees.

140 I have taken into account all those accused of the capital offences of clipping, coining, or possession of coining tools, for whom occupational information is available. I have disregarded those seventeen individuals, for whom occupational information is available, who stood accused of uttering counterfeits, uttering clipped coin, supplying coin for clipping, or soliciting coin at a premium. These offences appear to have concerned the examining magistrates less than the principal capital offences, and the small numbers accused of each cannot, therefore, be assumed to be representative of the occupational profile of all those involved in these activities. However, the overall occupational profile does not change significantly if these seventeen are added to the eighty accused of the capital offences. Sources are principally P R O A S S I 45/28–31; A S S I 44/80–88

(Assizes, Northern Circuit Indictments [includes recognizances], 1765–73); P L 27/4–5; P L 28/3 (Palatinate of Lancaster, Assize Minute Books [Series one], 1766–96); P L 28/11 (Palatinate of Lancaster, Assize Minute Books [Series two], 1766–7); Calderdale Archives, H A S:1400/1; York Minster Library, Hailstone MSS LL 1 (Yorkshire Assize Crown Calendars, 1765–73); *Leeds Mercury*, 1767–73; *Leeds Intelligencer*, 1765–73. I have ignored the descriptions of occupation provided by indictments because they employed only a limited range of stereotyped occupational designations.

141 The occupational profile does not change significantly if those accused of clipping are separated from those accused of coining and of possession of coining tools. However, an even higher proportion of men of small capital emerges if one isolates those fifty among the accused against whom evidence for the three principal capital offences was considered strong enough to merit commencing criminal proceedings (by committal or recognizance) or, in the case of those who fled justice, to prompt the advertising of rewards.

142 *Leeds Mercury*, 19 September 1769.

143 Richard Townley to Lord [Weymouth], 10 January 1770, P R O T 1/476.

144 T. W. Hanson, 'Cragg coiners', p. 100; J. Fawcett, *An Account of the Life, Ministry and Writings of the late Rev. John Fawcett, D.D.* (London, 1818), p. 124.

145 *Manchester Mercury*, 15 May 1770.

146 Joseph Hanson, deputy constable of Halifax town (see *Leeds Mercury*, 26 December 1769). James and Joseph Shaw, bailiffs (see P R O ASSI 45/29, deposition of Thomas Sunderland, 3 January 1770).

147 The worsted industry continued in a depressed state during the late 1760s; see *Leeds Intelligencer*, 12 January 1768, and 18 July 1769 (letter signed 'A.R.').

148 Samuel Magson, former merchant (see P R O ASSI 45/29, deposition of Joshua Stancliffe, 24 December 1769). Robert Iredale, master woolcomber (see P R O ASSI 45/29, deposition of Robert Iredale, 31 December 1769). Jonas Tillotson, shalloonmaker (see Calderdale Archives, H A S:1400/1, fo. 27, information of John Bates, n.d.). James Oldfield, stuffmaker (see P R O ASSI 45/29, deposition of Samuel Magson, 25 December 1769). The two prisoners for debt continued to clip

and to teach others to clip while in the debtors' prisons at Halifax and York.

149 PRO ASSI 45/29 (deposition of Robert Iredale, 31 December 1769).

150 See for example, *Leeds Mercury*, 17 October 1769.

151 PRO SP 37/8 (information of Joseph Broadbent, 19 September 1771).

152 Calderdale Archives, HAS:1400/1, fo. 27 (information of John Bates, n.d.). Bates also claimed that 'Lightoulers made David Hartley's coining irons'. There is no doubt that Thomas Lightowller was resident in the West Riding during the late 1760s, although by spring 1768 he had departed for Austria (see Hewitt, *Proceedings*, pp. 54–5; and Mr Langlois, Vienna, to Rochford, 23 May 1769, PRO SP 80/206). Though he appears to have been involved in counterfeiting in Yorkshire, the precise nature of his contribution to the yellow trade remains obscure. The trade was very different in character and organization from Lightowller's counterfeiting activities during the previous decade, but it would have made similar demands on his particular skills as a die sinker. If David Hartley did learn his counterfeiting while absent from his native county in Birmingham, it is not unlikely that he became acquainted there with Lightowller, who enjoyed a considerable reputation in the town as a counterfeiter (Hewitt, *Proceedings*, p. 26).

153 See, for example, Calderdale Archives, HAS:1400/1, fo. 27 (information of John Bates, n.d.); PRO ASSI 45/29 (deposition of Joshua Stancliffe, 24 December 1769, and deposition of James Shaw, 10 January 1770).

154 This list consists of all those accused of any involvement in the yellow trade, between 1765 and 1773, who lived within the area covered by the map and whose place of residence can be identified precisely. The place of residence of two informers is also indicated.

Eighty-four of all those accused of clipping, coining, or possession of coining tools in the Halifax–Rochdale area, 1765–73, can be identified by township of residence. Of these, twenty-two lived in the three townships of Erringden, Sowerby and Wadsworth and precise residence is known for fourteen of that twenty-two. Twenty-eight others, identified by township of residence, were accused of a variety of other kinds of participation in the yellow trade, from soliciting coin for clipping to

murdering William Deighton, the Halifax exciseman. Eighteen
of these lived in the three townships and precise residence is
known for ten of that eighteen. Forty-four others, identified by
township of residence, were listed for the authorities by one
Ely Hoyle as 'coiners, etc.' (Calderdale Archives, HAS:1400/1/
13). Twenty-six of these lived in the three townships and precise
residence is known for ten of that twenty-six. For the principal
sources, see note 142 above.

155 PRO ASSI 45/29 (deposition of Matthew Normanton, 20
November 1769, and deposition of Robert Thomas, 20 November 1769); 'Brief Account . . . of the Lives of Thomas Spencer
and Mark Sattonstall', Calderdale Libraries, Horsfall Turner
Collection, P 343.

156 *Leeds Intelligencer*, 29 August 1769 (letter signed 'E.C.').

157 For King David see, for example, *Leeds Mercury*, 17 October
1769; for Duke of York, *Leeds Mercury*, 25 March 1770; for
Duke of Edinburgh, *Leeds Mercury*, 2 January 1770; for Royal
Clayton, Calderdale Archives, HAS:1400/1, fo. 33 (information
of Joshua Sharp, 9 December 1772).

158 *Leeds Intelligencer*, 29 August 1769 (letter signed 'E.C.').

159 For evidence of coinage offences at William Varley's, see
Calderdale Archives, HAS:1400/1, f. 27 (information of John
Bates, n.d.), and PRO ASSI 45/29 (depositions of John Kitson,
1 January 1770, Robert Iredale, 1 January 1770; George Rams-
den, 3 January 1770; Daniel Greene, 3 January 1770; Thomas
Varley, 4 January 1770; William Varley, 4 January 1770). For
evidence of coinage offences at Isaac Dewhirst's, see Calderdale
Archives, HAS:1400/1, fo. 27 (information of John Bates,
n.d.), and PRO ASSI 45/29 (depositions of Daniel Greenwood,
21 December 1769; Jonathan Barrowclough, 3 February 1770;
Joseph Shaw, 10 September 1769, 14 September 1769, 27
November 1769 and 3 February 1770).

160 PRO ASSI 45/29 (depositions of Jonas Tillotson, 19 December 1769; John Cockroft, 20 December 1769; Thomas Wilson,
22 December 1769; Jonathan Barrowclough, 3 February 1770;
Thomas Varley, 4 January 1770).

161 PRO ASSI 45/29 (depositions of James Shaw, 10 January
1770; Jonathan Barrowclough, 3 February 1770; Joseph Shaw,
3 February 1770).

162 See PRO ASSI 45/29 (depositions of Samuel Magson, 25
December 1769, and Joshua Stancliffe, 24 December 1769).

163   Calderdale Archives, HAS:1400/1, fo. 27 (information of John Bates, n.d.).
164   *Leeds Intelligencer*, 29 August 1769 (letter signed 'E.C.').
165   *Leeds Intelligencer*, 23 February 1768 (letter signed 'Philo Patriae').
166   Calderdale Archives, HAS:1400/1, fo. 27 (information of John Bates, n.d.).
167   PRO ASSI 45/29 (depositions of James Crabtree, 10 August 1769, and William Haley, 8 September 1769).
168   PRO Mint 1/12, fo. 144; Br. Lib., Egerton MSS 257, fo. 154 (William Chamberlayne's evidence).
169   See above, page 183.
170   See above, page 195.
171   John Crabtree, *Concise History of the Parish and Vicarage of Halifax* (London, 1836), pp. 311, 313.
172   See Archbishop of York to Sir Robert Walpole, 2 January 1731, quoted in C. Collyer, 'The Yorkshire election of 1734', *Proceedings of the Leeds Philosophical and Literary Society (Literary and Historical Section)*, vol. 7, pt 2 (1953), p. 59.
173   *Leeds Intelligencer*, 9 December 1766.
174   It is not my intention here to argue that Halifax parish was a 'dark corner' in the mould of Kingswood (see Chapter 3 above) or certain extra-parochial areas. Despite the absence of resident gentry, the population was by no means socially homogeneous. Nor was this a lawless area, where warrants could not be served and taxes could not be collected. It sent a regular complement of theft and assault cases to quarter sessions and assizes, and was well supplied with attorneys. Indeed, it was precisely because an area of this sort, comprising a large urban centre and a densely settled rural–industrial hinterland, generated so much law business that local men in the Commission of the Peace were so reluctant to take out their dedimus and act.
175   Br. Lib., Egerton MSS 257, fo. 154 (William Chamberlayne's evidence).
176   For the magistrates' reluctance to issue search warrants in theft cases see *Leeds Intelligencer*, 6 December 1774.
177   *Leeds Intelligencer*, 29 August 1769 (letter signed 'E.C.'). The letter added, probably facetiously, that 'with the assistance of their Privey Council', the coining monarchs had 'lately come to a resolution of presenting Mr WILKES with 45 moidores, and a large gold medal, with this motto, *Wilkes nobis haec otia fecit*

[From Wilkes it is that comes this rest from toil], as a testimony of their gratitude to that worthy patriot' (the Latin motto was a play on a quotation from Vergil, *Eclogues*, I, 6). There is no doubt that it was considered to have been a common practice among magistrates to issue general search warrants in criminal cases, although one that was condemned by the best authorities; see Burn, *Justice of the Peace*, 2nd edition (2 vols., London, 1756), vol. 2, p. 383. The scale of the celebrations at Halifax on the occasion of Wilkes's release from the King's Bench prison, in April 1770, suggests the town was a particularly enthusiastic local centre of Wilkite support (*Leeds Intelligencer*, 3 April 1770 and 24 April 1770).

178   Rockingham to Weymouth, 1 December 1769, PRO SP 37/7 (and see above, page 184); also see PRO T 29/37, fo. 373 (Treasury Board Minutes, 6 March 1766), PRO SP 82/85 (State Papers Foreign, Hamburgh, 1767), fos. 165–293 *passim*, and SP 82/86 (1768), fo. 23.

179   *Leeds Intelligencer*, 18 July 1769 (letter signed 'A.R.').

180   Richard Townley to Lord [Weymouth], 10 January 1770, PRO T 1/476.

181   *Leeds Intelligencer*, 18 July 1769 (letter signed 'A.R.').

182   *Leeds Mercury*, 9 August 1774.

183   Rev. J. Crosley, *God's Indignation against Sin* (Halifax, 1770).

184   ibid., p. 36.

185   ibid., p. 39.

186   See D. Hay, 'Poaching and the game laws on Cannock Chase', in D. Hay *et al.*, *Albion's Fatal Tree* (London, 1975), pp. 207–8.

187   Calderdale Archives, HAS:1400/1, fo. 13 (handbill, dated Halifax, 14 December 1769). John Bates, a Halifax innkeeper, claimed that Isaac Dewhirst 'told me he could make or diminish or coin gold, and said it was no sin and he would let me see how to do it, and I, not thinking it treason, agreed he should' (Calderdale Archives, HAS:1400/1, fo. 27 [evidence of John Bates, n.d.]).

188   PRO Mint 1/11 and 1/12 (Mint Solicitor's accounts), *passim*.

189   The provisions of 9 & 10 Will. III, c. 21 were interpreted as extending merely to the silver coin; see PRO T 29/40, fo. 160 (Treasury Board Minutes, 2 January 1770); T 29/42, fos. 96–7 (Treasury Board Minutes, 2 June 1772); T 29/43, fo. 75 (Treasury Board Minutes, 3 June 1773). Also see above, note 46.

190   Richard Townley to Lord [Weymouth], 10 January 1770, PRO T 1/476.

191   Calderdale Archives, HAS:1400/1, fo. 27 (evidence of John Bates, n.d.).

192   *Leeds Intelligencer*, 29 August 1769 (letter signed 'E.C.').

193   *Leeds Intelligencer*, 29 August 1769 (letter signed 'E.C.').

194   See, for example, G. Cressner to C. Jenkinson, 30 August 1772, Br. Lib., Add. MSS 38207, fo. 156.

195   'Two Letters, one sent by Richard and Thomas Boys to their Parents at Coln, the other from a Gentleman at York to a Gentleman in Halifax' (n.d. [1767]), single sheet in Calderdale Library, Horsfall Turner Collection, P 343.

196   Richard Townley to Rockingham, 12 January 1770, Sheffield City Library, WWM R 11/28.

197   *Leeds Intelligencer*, 18 August 1769 (letter signed 'E.C.').

198   Officially only the collector himself should have been involved in taking payment of the tax; see E. Hughes, *Studies in Administration and Finance, 1558–1825* (Manchester, 1934), p. 161. However, in the Halifax locality it appears to have been the practice for the Supervisor to assist; Yorkshire Archaeological Society MSS, MS 385 (prosecution brief).

199   Yorkshire Archaeological Society MSS, MS 385 (prosecution brief). Perhaps Deighton's singular zeal in a cause that was not his official responsibility was also prompted by an anxiety to re-establish his standing in the excise service, through a display of especial merit. In 1758, when stationed elsewhere, he had committed a professional misdemeanour, for which he suffered temporary demotion. The Halifax post was his first advancement after that setback. For Deighton's career in the excise service see PRO Customs 47/175–269 (Excise Establishment and Minutes, 1741–69).

200   PRO Mint 1/12, fos. 139–40, 143–4. Also see above, page 205.

201   PRO ASSI 45/29 (deposition of Joshua Stancliffe, 24 December 1769).

202   PRO ASSI 45/29 (deposition of William Haley, 10 August 1769).

203   See *Leeds Intelligencer*, 12 June 1764.

204   See York Minster Library, Hailstone MSS, Box 5.29 (parcel of correspondence and papers on the fraudulent winding of wool, 1752), and H. F. Killick, 'Notes on the early history of

the Leeds and Liverpool canal', *Bradford Antiquary*, N.S., vol. 1 (1900), p. 178.

205 Killick, 'Leeds and Liverpool canal', pp. 181, 184. John Hustler, a Bradford woolstapler, was the leader of the manufacturers' campaign against the yellow trade and also one of the leading projectors of the canal.

206 *Leeds Intelligencer*, 12 June 1764; PRO ASSI 45/29 (deposition of William Haley, 10 August 1769).

207 Narrative signed by Samuel Lister (of Manningham, attorney) and John Hustler, 2 December 1769, in John Hustler to the Marquis of Rockingham, 2 December 1769, PRO SP 37/7.

208 Enclosure by Samuel Lister (attorney) in Richard Wilson to Lord Rochford, 30 June 1774, PRO SP 37/10.

209 It is unclear whether Deighton and the manufacturers knew of each other's activities at this stage.

210 Joseph Broadbent and James Broadbent (see Calderdale Archives, HAS:1400/1, fo. 9: information of James Broadbent, 13 November 1769).

211 Enclosure by Samuel Lister (attorney) in Wilson to Rochford, 30 June 1774, PRO SP 37/10.

212 YML, Hailstone MSS LL1 (Yorkshire Assize Crown Calendar, Lent 1770).

213 See advertisement of absconders, *Leeds Intelligencer*, 20 November 1769. Royal Clayton certainly remained in hiding in the locality, as he was present there in November 1769 (PRO SP 37/10: information of Thomas Clayton, 2 May 1774). Other absconders went further afield – John Cockcroft, master woolcomber, to Darlington (a minor centre of the worsted industry) and others as far as Ireland (*Leeds Mercury*, 19 December 1769; Richard Townley to Lord [Weymouth], 10 January 1770, PRO T 1/476).

214 PRO ASSI 45/29 (depositions of Joseph Shaw, 10 September 1769 and 14 September 1769 [provided additional depositions 12 October 1769, 27 November 1769 and 3 February 1770]).

215 Thomas Wade and John Barker (YML, Hailstone MSS LL 1 Yorkshire Assize Calendar, Lent 1770). The only evidence in the surviving depositions laid against them before their committals was that of Shaw.

216 *Leeds Mercury*, 19 September 1769.

217 'Coiners committed to York Castle on Suspicion of Chipping [*sic*], Filing, Edging and Diminishing the Gold Coin of this

Kingdom', single sheet in Calderdale Library, Horsfall Turner Collection, P 343, dated 16 September 1769.

218 *Leeds Intelligencer*, 3 October 1769.

219 Leeds City Archives, DB 250 (Ledger book of John Eagle of Bradford, attorney, 1768–77), fos. 138–9. Eagle was not only attorney to the association, but also to the Leeds and Liverpool canal.

220 Calderdale Archives, HAS:1400/1, fo. 9 (information of James Broadbent, 13 November 1769).

221 *Leeds Intelligencer*, 17 October 1769.

222 YML, Hailstone MSS LL 1 (Yorkshire Assize Calendar, Lent 1770).

223 PRO SP 37/7 (narrative signed by Samuel Lister (attorney) and John Hustler, 2 December 1769). The information referred to was probably Stephen Morton's of 5 September 1769, in PRO ASSI 45/29. How the coiners were able to breach, so easily, the secrecy surrounding the employment of the inspectors is unclear. Perhaps their links with minor local law officers were important here, although Deighton undoubtedly used his own hired men in apprehending suspects, rather than law officers, in order to ensure secrecy. The coiners' access to information about plans to apprehend suspects may explain the ability of a large number of offenders to evade capture and abscond.

224 For the authorities' continuing ignorance of the evidential requirements of the courts, see below, page 228.

225 Yorkshire Archaeological Society MSS, MS 385 (prosecution brief).

226 The following account is based principally on Calderdale Archives, HAS:1400/1, fo. 9 (information of James Broadbent, 13 November 1769).

227 Yorkshire Archaeological Society MSS, MS 385 (prosecution brief).

228 ibid.

229 PRO SP 37/10 (information of Robert Thomas, 3 May 1774).

230 *Leeds Intelligencer*, 16 August 1774 (confession of Robert Tommis [Thomas]); PRO SP 37/8 (information of Joseph Broadbent, 19 September 1771).

231 The two killers both had special reason to wish Deighton dead, beyond the attractive reward and a concern to protect the yellow trade. Thomas was Royal Clayton's brother-in-law and

Normanton his neighbour and occasional employee. Both were anxious to secure Clayton from prosecution and the financial ruin which threatened Clayton's family as long as he had to remain in hiding; see Calderdale Archives, HAS:1400/1, fo. 10 (information of Robert Thomas, 20 November 1769).

232 Calderdale Archives, HAS:1400/1, fo. 43 (confession of Robert Tommis [Thomas] to the Rev. William Dade, 5 August 1774).

233 See John Royds to Rockingham, 24 November 1769, Sheffield City Library, WWM R 11/1, and Weymouth to Rockingham, 14 November 1769, PRO SP 44/142, fo. 222 (Domestic Entry Book, George III, 1769). It is not implausible that local notables, threatened with violence, should have contemplated deserting the area. During the 1757 grain riots in Wensleydale, in the North Riding, several of the substantial inhabitants actually fled to Richmond 'for their greater safety'; PRO ASSI 45/26 (Assizes, Northern Circuit depositions, 1757–62: deposition of George Metcalf and George Dinsdale, 12 March 1759).

234 However, sympathy and intimidation at Halifax did not prevent an inquest jury, with several large manufacturers on it, from bringing in a murder verdict.

235 See John Royds to Rockingham, 24 November 1769, Sheffield City Library, WWM R 11/1.

236 PRO ASSI 45/29, deposition of James Broadbent, 20 November 1769. That Broadbent knew the identity of the two murderers suggests that it was fairly common knowledge in the upper hand country and that popular solidarity shielded them until Broadbent succumbed to the temptation of the large reward.

237 Edward Leedes to My Lord [Barrington], 21 November 1769, PRO WO 1/990 (War Office, miscellaneous in-letters, 1769–72). It was pointed out locally that foot soldiers would be more useful in a hilly area than horse, but the justice requested the latter. The nearest infantry detachment, at Derby, would 'not be so proper to be sent', as it was enlisted in the Halifax area, where popular sympathies were with the coiners; John Royds to Rockingham, 24 November 1769, Sheffield City Library, WWMR 11/1.

238 Leeds City Archives, DB 250 (Eagle Ledger Book, 1768–70), fos. 138–9; and see, for example, *Leeds Intelligencer*, 28 November 1769. Another subscription list was later opened at Wakefield.

239 Weymouth to Rockingham, 14 November 1769, PRO SP

44/142; WO 5/56, fo. 329 (War Office, Marching Orders, 23 November 1769). Since 1765, the government had been repeatedly unco-operative when approached on the subject of coinage offences in the West Riding. The secretary of state's office, loth to enter the highly technical and contentious field of coinage policy (for which it had no direct responsibility), had refused to become involved. Correspondence on the subject had been passed on to the consistently unresponsive Mint Solicitor.

240   R. J. S. Hoffman, *The Marquis, a Study of Lord Rockingham, 1730–82* (New York, 1973), pp. 219–38.

241   Which were not very onerous. The great magnates who held the posts of lord lieutenant and *Custos* (by the second half of the eighteenth century usually simultaneously) tended to intervene in county affairs only spasmodically in their official capacity (except for nominating men to the Commissions of the Peace and organizing the militia); see S. and B. Webb, *English Local Government from the Revolution to the Municipal Corporations Act: The Parish and the County* (London, 1924), p. 353.

242   See P. Langford, 'The Marquis of Rockingham', in H. van Thal (ed.), *The Prime Ministers* (2 vols., London, 1974), vol. 1, p. 130.

243   See Edmund Burke's complaint from Beaconsfield about Rockingham's preoccupations in Yorkshire, 5 December 1769, in T. W. Copeland *et al.* (eds.), *The Correspondence of Edmund Burke* (9 vols., Cambridge, 1958–70), vol. 2, p. 114.

244   By courtesy of his political alliance with his close friend Sir George Savile; see C. Collyer, 'The Rockinghams and Yorkshire politics, 1742–1761', *Thoresby Society Miscellany*, vol. 12, pt 4 (1953), pp. 373–4.

245   See Jeremy Dixon to Rockingham, 26 December 1769, Sheffield City Library, WWM R 1/1255.

246   Rockingham to Royds, 25 November 1769, Sheffield City Library, WWM R 11/2.

247   ibid. The support that Rockingham gave to a local suggestion that Deighton's widow and children should be made objects of public and private charity illustrates his concern both to terrorize the yellow traders and to encourage informing. He argued that 'over and above its being a truely charitable act, it is also equally right in point of policy and would have the effect of showing that the town of Halifax will equally be alert to assist

and reward those who support the laws, as well as to punish those who break them'. Rockingham himself donated £50 and he was instrumental in securing a royal pension for the family.

248   See J. W. Houseman, 'Notes and comments on the Halifax churchwardens' accounts, 1714 to 1800', *Transactions of the Halifax Antiquarian Society (THAS)* (1926), pp. 123–4, and J. W. Houseman, 'Further notes and comments on the Halifax churchwardens' accounts, 1714 to 1832', *THAS* (1927), p. 91. I have assumed that sums paid to ringers (which fluctuated considerably) varied according to the duration of the peal.

249   Resolutions of and those present at a meeting at the Talbot in Halifax, 28 November 1769, P R O S P 37/7. Of the forty-three men who attended, seventeen were in the West Riding Commission of the Peace and two were acting magistrates.

250   Rockingham to Royds, 25 November 1769, Sheffield City Library, W W M R 11/2.

251   Rockingham to Weymouth, 1 December 1769, P R O S P 37/7; Halifax gentlemen and townsmen to Rockingham, 6 January 1770, Sheffield City Library, W W M R 11/26.

252   Rockingham to Royds, 25 November 1769, Sheffield City Library, W W M R 11/2; Sir George Savile to Rockingham, n.d. [2 December 1769] R 1/1249; Rockingham to ?, 28 December 1769, R 11/10.

253   Rockingham to Weymouth, 1 December 1769, P R O S P 37/7.

254   Rockingham to Royds, 25 November 1769, Sheffield City Library, W W M R 11/2.

255   P R O C 193/45 (Crown Office Dedimus Book, 1746–89). Five other men in the Commission of the Peace, who were reported to have pledged themselves to act, failed to do so (*Leeds Mercury*, 19 December 1769). Although there survives no evidence as to why they chose not to act, their decision may indicate that the enthusiasm of local gentlemen was less thoroughgoing than Rockingham's eulogies might suggest.

256   Rockingham argued that as the crimes were 'of the most public nature . . . the expence of prosecuting, etc seems properly to be a public expence' (Rockingham to Weymouth, 1 December 1769, P R O S P 37/7).

257   Chamberlayne was to spend at least £1450 on Yorkshire cases alone during 1769 and 1770 (P R O Mint 1/12, fo. 165; T 1/483 [Mint Solicitor's account for 1770]). His *total* prosecution expenses for the year 1770 were £1737, £1137 over the £600

Mint prosecution allowance. Payment of the excess had to be authorized by a special clause in an Act of Parliament (PRO T 29/41, fo. 239 [Treasury Board Minutes, 23 July 1771]).

258 Br. Lib., Egerton MSS 257, fo. 155 (William Chamberlayne's evidence).

259 PRO Mint 1/12, fo. 165; Royds to Rockingham, 20 December 1769, Sheffield City Library, WWM R 11/3.

260 YML, Hailstone MSS LL 1 (Yorkshire Assize Calendar, Lent 1770). Chamberlayne arrived in Halifax on 13 December 1769 (Royds to Rockingham, 13 December 1769, Sheffield City Library, WWM R 11/7).

261 YML, Hailstone MSS LL 1 (Yorkshire Assize Calendar, Lent 1770).

262 For Yorkshire assizes 1770, see PRO ASSI 44/85 (Yorkshire Assize Rolls, 1770) and ASSI 42/8 (Northern Curcuit Gaol Book, 1762–74). For Lancashire assizes 1770, see PRO PL 28/11. For executions, *Leeds Mercury*, 1 May 1770. For the pardon, PRO SP 44/89 (Criminal Entry Book, 1766–70, fo. 364).

263 See, for example, Calderdale Archives, HAS: 1400/1, fo. 29 (prosecution brief in the case of the King against David Greenwood, for high treason and misprison of treason, at York Assizes, 4 August 1770). This was the only capital coinage indictment presented at the Yorkshire Lammas assizes, 1770. It was founded on a malicious information by the deceased David Hartley's relatives and was dismissed by the grand jury.

264 *Leeds Intelligencer*, 8 January 1771; also see *Leeds Intelligencer*, 16 June 1772 and 29 June 1773 for other comment on the persistence of the yellow trade.

265 Thomas Ramsden to Charles Jenkinson, 4 January 1773, Br. Lib., Add. MSS 38207, fos. 208–9. To prevent informing, another murder was perpetrated in 1771, although not of an official (*Leeds Intelligencer*, 8 January 1771).

266 See YML, Hailstone MSS LL 1 (Yorkshire Assize Calendars, 1771–4); PRO ASSI 44/86–9 (Yorkshire Assize Rolls, 1771–4); PRO PL 28/3 (Palatinate of Lancaster, Assize Minute Book series one, 1766–96); PRO Mint 1/12 (Mint Solicitor's accounts, 1771–4), *passim*.

267 Yorkshire Archaeological Society MSS, MS 385 (prosecution brief).

268 Br. Lib., Egerton MSS 257, fo. 155.

269 William Chamberlayne to Treasury Board, 16 December 1769, PRO T 1/472. The magistrates had persisted in these misconceptions despite the early involvement in the campaign of a leading barrister (Stanhope had died in September 1769) and the continuing participation of prominent (and much respected) local attornies.

270 Richard Townley to My Lord [? Weymouth], 10 January 1770, PRO T 1/476.

271 PRO T 1/483 (Mint Solicitor's account for 1770).

272 Such blandishments also provided the coiners with access to details of the evidence to be offered by the prosecution in particular cases (enclosure by Samuel Lister (attorney) in Wilson to Rochford, 30 June 1774, PRO SP 37/10). This information may have been used to render intimidation or bribery of witnesses particularly effective. However, the availability to the yellow traders of this information also opens up the possibility that they may have deliberately contrived the tangled web of accusation and counter-accusation, which characterizes the surviving depositions and which so dismayed the Mint Solicitor. Many counter-accusations may have been deliberate falsifications, intended to compromise the acceptability in court of the evidence of a particular witness.

273 See, for example, Rockingham to Lord ?, 28 December 1769, PRO SP 37/7.

274 There is clear evidence of intimidation of the witnesses against King David (anonymous threatening letter to Joshua Stancliffe, 19 April 1770, PRO SP 37/7). Nevertheless Hartley was convicted and hanged.

275 Indictments against David Hartley (4), James Oldfield and William and Thomas Varley, PRO ASSI 44/85 (Yorkshire Lent Assize Roll, 1770). The trial juries were drawn from parts of Yorkshire (the largest English county) distant from Halifax.

276 Sir George Savile to Rockingham, n.d. [2/12/1769], Sheffield City Libraries, WWM R 1/1249.

277 Although the extent to which large scale base- and mixed-metal counterfeiting operations enjoyed the sympathy of the 'lowest orders' is almost impossible to judge, it is unlikely that counterfeiting of this kind was actively endorsed by men of 'fair and unquestionable' character, in any numbers. Moreover, such counterfeiting operations, though they might involve large networks of dealers, did not depend upon the willing partici-

pation of an extensive public. Indeed, they were manifestly injurious to those who were unwittingly passed near-worthless counterfeits.

278   *Manchester Mercury*, 15 May 1770.

279   Br. Lib., Egerton MSS 257, fo. 159 (William Chamberlayne's evidence).

280   But the gradual discovery of the social realities of the trade must have added to the authorities' existing doubts about securing effective witnesses and convictions, in the face of the solidarities and blandishments which defended the yellow traders. Rockingham's belief in the ability of 'the exertion and support of the civil power' successfully to counteract intimidation and popular solidarity had been based on his experience of policing the grain and militia riots at Sheffield in 1756 and 1757 (see above, page 223). Yet during those riots, he had been of the opinion that a concerted display of resolve by local gentlemen and magistrates, to assert their authority and to apply the law, could only succeed in overcoming popular solidarity and intimidation, if popular hostility to the law in a locality was limited; see Rockingham to Newcastle, 3 October 1757, Br. Lib. Add. MSS 32834, fos. 421–3 (Newcastle MSS). As the true extent of support for the yellow trade became apparent, his confidence in the local magistrates' capacity to provide convictions must have further declined.

281   Br. Lib., Egerton MSS 257, fo. 159 (William Chamberlayne's evidence). The same opinion was expressed in a report from Halifax in the *Leeds Intelligencer*, 8 March 1774.

282   See Hay, 'Property, authority and the criminal law', pp. 48–52. Even if a large number of convictions had been available, the conventions of eighteenth-century punishment made mass executions of previously 'respectable' offenders inconceivable.

283   Hay, 'Property, authority and the criminal law', p. 51.

284   PRO T 1/483 (Mint Solicitor's account for 1770).

285   PRO Mint 1/11, fos. 77–116 (Mint Solicitor's accounts, 1756 and 1757).

286   Four indictments against David Hartley, PRO ASSI 44/85 (Yorkshire Lent Assize Roll, 1770).

287   PRO ASSI 41/6 (Northern Circuit Rough Minute Book, 1769–75: Yorkshire Lent Assizes 1770). Hartley was the last to be tried of the four Halifax coinage defendants.

288   Lord Weymouth to Mr Justice Gould, 16 April 1770 (PRO SP

44/89, fo. 356), refers to a plea of mercy from Rockingham and others for James Oldfield, who was, nevertheless, hanged. I assume that the pardon for William Varley was not granted without Rockingham's acquiescence.

289 Calderdale Archives, HAS:1400/1, fo. 5 (affidavit to put off the trials of James Broadbent, Robert Thomas, Matthew Normanton and William Folds, n.d. [1770]). It was probably to extract additional evidence that some of the offenders who had absconded during the winter of 1769–70 were outlawed, and those coinage offenders, against whom prosecutions were dropped at the Lent assizes 1770, bound over to reappear at the Lammas assizes (where they were merely discharged).

290 See above, page 227.

291 The third acquitted man, William Folds, was known by the prosecution to have been wrongfully accused (Yorkshire Archaeological Society MSS MS 385 [prosecution brief]).

292 Richard Townley to Robert Parker, 12 April 1775, Calderdale Archives, HAS:1400/1, fo. 45.

293 *Leeds Mercury*, 9 August 1774.

294 William Chamberlayne to Treasury Board, 16 December 1769, PRO T 1/472. In the absence of a reformation of the gold coinage, or the possibility of making the terrors of the law bear effectively against offenders, the authorities were rendered impotent. The multitude of small transactions that comprised the yellow trade could hardly be confronted by troops, in the manner of a riot or a smuggling party carrying contraband.

295 Gentlemen of Halifax to Rockingham, 6 January 1770, Sheffield City Library, WWM R 11/26.

296 William Chamberlayne to Treasury Board, 16 December 1769, PRO T 1/472.

297 Richard Townley, John Chadwick and Robert Entwisle to the Treasury, 16 February 1770, PRO T 1/476.

298 PRO T 29/40, fo. 160 (Treasury Board Minutes, 2 January 1770).

299 See above, pages 210–11.

300 All these features, especially unwelcome in the fraught political climate of 1770, were to accompany the recoinage of 1773–6. That recoinage awaits its historian. For a concise account, see Craig, *The Mint*, pp. 242–6.

301 PRO T 29/42, fo. 90 (Treasury Board Minutes, 27 May 1772); fos. 96–7 (2 June 1772); fo. 433 (12 March 1773).

302   Br. Lib., Egerton MSS 251, fo. 29 (Cavendish's Parliamentary
      Debates: Lord North's speech in the debate on the gold
      coinage, 13 January 1774). For other comment on the careful
      and time-consuming deliberations that preceded the bill, see
      Gloucester Journal, 2 August 1773.

303   Br. Lib., Egerton MSS 257, fos. 184–5 (Lord North's statement
      to the Parliamentary Committee on the coin, 9 May 1774).

304   Hence confirming the worst fears of the large worsted manu-
      facturers concerning the value of their holdings of diminished
      coin; see above, page 215.

305   See, for examples, *Leeds Intelligencer*, 27 July 1773, 3 August
      1773, 10 August 1773, 17 August 1773; Br. Lib., Egerton MSS
      251, fos. 24–7 (speech of Mr Prescott in the debate on the gold
      coinage, 13 January 1774).

306   13 Geo. III c. 11.

307   Br. Lib., Egerton MSS 257, fos. 178–9 (Lord North's state-
      ment).

308   Craig, *The Mint*, p. 244; the loss is calculated from the esti-
      mates given in Br. Lib., Egerton MSS 257, fo. 162 (evidence of
      Mr Samuel Etheridge to the Parliamentary Committee on the
      coin, 9 May 1774).

309   Under these later measures, compensation was offered to those
      who held the deficient coin, at an eventual cost of £317,314
      (PRO T 1/499 [Draft summary of expenses connected with the
      recoinage, 1773–6]). As long as the deficient guineas were
      handed in to appointed receivers before stated dates, they were
      exchanged for the new, full-weight guineas. These were being
      produced in large quantities, out of the diminished coins cut
      and withdrawn from circulation, under the 1773 Act. Compen-
      sation, it was argued rather tenuously by Lord North, was justi-
      fied under the 1774 and 1776 measures, because the weight
      thresholds established in 1773 had been taken on trust by the
      public as a guide to which coin was to be above suspicion there-
      after (Br. Lib., Egerton MSS 257, fo. 187 [Lord North's state-
      ment]). It also served to assuage public and parliamentary ill-
      feeling.

310   PRO T 1/499 (Draft summary of expenses connected with the
      recoinage, 1773–7).

311   Craig, *The Mint*, p. 245, and see above, page 174.

312   PRO T 29/43, fo. 115 (Treasury Board Minutes, 22 July
      1773).

313 *Leeds Mercury*, 28 September 1773 and 4 January 1774.

314 P R O T 29/44, fo. 36 (Treasury Board Minutes, 3 August 1774).

315 Ashton, *Economic Fluctuations*, pp. 156–60.

316 *Leeds Intelligencer*, 10 August 1773.

317 *Leeds Intelligencer*, 10 August 1773, 8 February 1774 and 6 December 1774.

318 See, for example, *Leeds Intelligencer*, 26 July 1774, 21 February 1775; *Leeds Mercury*, 12 March 1776, 9 June 1776, 13 August 1776.

319 P R O A S S I 44/89–97 (Yorkshire Assize indictments, 1774–82).

320 Perhaps the greatest ingenuity in applying their skills in a novel manner was displayed by those among the former yellow traders who took up the (legal) counterfeiting of the valuable Roman silver pieces which were discovered in a field near Keighley in 1775 (*Etherington's York Chronicle*, 1 April 1775 and 12 May 1775). This was the occasion of the reference to the coiners as 'our traitorous money makers'.

321 Five of the eight men tried at York for coining offences committed between 1774 and 1782 were found guilty.

322 In four cases in particular, material evidence of this sort was especially strong (Calderdale Archives, H A S:1400/1, fo. 49 [examination of William Hirst and others, 7 October 1778]; fo. 57 [prosecution brief against John Cockroft, 1782]; P R O A S S I 45/34 [Northern Circuit Assize Depositions, 1780–3; depositions of J. Ramsden and others, 13 June 1782]). However, the relative ease with which the authorities laid their hands on evidence of this kind (on one occasion surprising a coiner at work) may itself indicate a breakdown of those solidarities which formerly provided the practitioners of the yellow trade with some advance warning of detection.

323 'Brief Account . . . of the lives of Thomas Spencer and Mark Sattonstall', Calderdale Library, Horsfall Turner Collection, P 343.

324 See, for example, J. Beattie, 'The pattern of crime in England, 1660–1800', *Past and Present*, no. 62 (1974), pp. 47–95. A similar approach has been adopted for the sixteenth and seventeenth centuries in J. S. Cockburn, 'The nature and incidence of Crime in England, 1559–1625', in Cockburn (ed.), *Crime in England 1550–1800*.

325 See, in particular, E. P. Thompson, *Whigs and Hunters* (London: Allen Lane, 1975).

326   For an elaboration of these criticisms, see J. A. Styles, 'Criminal records', *Historical Journal*, vol. 20, no. 4 (1967), pp. 977–81. I am not, of course, suggesting here that the study of the social origins and uses of the criminal law is not of vital importance to the history of crime. Crime is not a given, ahistorical category. I am concerned merely to point to some of the limitations of an approach which has focused on *extensions* in the legal definition of crime during the eighteenth century.

327   See, for example, H. Mannheim, *Social Aspects of Crime in England between the Wars* (London: Allen & Unwin, 1940), especially ch. 5.

328   See, for an example of criticism of the utility of the modern statistics, S. Box, *Deviance, Reality and Society* (London: Holt, Rinehart & Winston, 1971), ch. 3.

329   I have aired these issues at greater length in an unpublished paper entitled 'English criminal records', delivered to the Social History Society Conference at Birmingham in January 1977. For an outline of the argument see *Social History Society Newsletter*, vol. 2, no. 1 (spring 1977).

330   See above, note 75.

331   See Cohen, 'The concept of criminal organisation', p. 98.

332   D. Hay, 'Property, authority and the criminal law', in Hay *et al.* (eds.), *Albion's Fatal Tree*, especially pp. 40–56, 61–3.

333   ibid., p. 48.

334   The manner in which the campaign against the trade was abandoned is clearly an instance of what Douglas Hay has identified as the conspiratorial manipulation of the law by authority to conceal weakness and to sustain the illusion of power (ibid., p. 52). In this instance, the effectiveness of such sleight of hand is extremely doubtful. Not only did the yellow trade continue to flourish after 1770, but the most notorious offenders brought to trial, Deighton's murderers, were acquitted.

335   See E. J. Hobsbawm, 'Social criminality', *Bulletin of the Society for the Study of Labour History*, no. 25 (1972), p. 5, and E. P. Thompson, 'Eighteenth century crime, popular movements and social control', *Bulletin of the Society for the Study of Labour History*, no. 25 (1972), p. 9.

336   Thompson, 'Eighteenth century crime', p. 11, and Hay *et al.*, *Albion's Fatal Tree*, p. 14.

337   Br. Lib., Egerton MSS 257, fo. 212 (Governor Johnson's

speech to the Parliamentary Committee on the coin, 9 May 1774).

6   The King's Bench prison in the later eighteenth century

1   The best textbook account of the credit network in the eighteenth century is in T. S. Ashton, *An Economic History of England: The Eighteenth Century* (London, 1955). Among recent articles, B. L. Anderson, 'Money and the structure of credit', *Buisness History*, vol. 12, no. 2 (1970), and B. A. Holderness, 'Credit in a rural community 1660–1800', *Midland History*, vol. 3, no. 2 (1975), are worthy of note. Several histories of particular industries contain extended discussions of the role of credit in production, e.g. A. P. Wadsworth and J. de L. Mann, *The Cotton Industry and Industrial Lancashire* (Manchester, 1931) and M. B. Rowlands, *Masters and Men in the West Midland Metalware Trades before the Industrial Revolution* (Manchester, 1975). Consumer credit is discussed in D. Davis, *A History of Shopping* (London, 1965).

2   The early history of the English debt law, with particular regard to the practice of imprisonment for debt, is discussed in Abraham L. Freedman, 'Imprisonment for debt', *Temple Law Quarterly 2* (1928), and in R. Pugh, *Imprisonment in Medieval England* (Cambridge, 1968), pp. 5–8, 45–6. For a learned (and critical) eighteenth-century account of the evolution of the eighteenth-century law, see [T. Delamayne], *The Rise and Practice of Imprisonment in Personal Actions Examined* (London, 1772). This pamphlet was composed in response to the controversy discussed on pages 290–8.

3   A meticulous account of the legal process is provided by Ian P. H. Duffy in his unpublished DPhil thesis, 'Bankruptcy and insolvency in London in the late eighteenth and early nineteenth centuries' (Oxford University, 1973), pp. 62–5. See also P. J. Lineham, 'The campaign to abolish imprisonment for debt in England 1750–1840' (Unpublished MA thesis, University of Canterbury, New Zealand, 1974), pp. 5–8. I am indebted to both these theses for their clear and careful accounts of the state of the law of debt in the later eighteenth century.

4   There has yet to be a scholarly study of the manner in which eighteenth-century creditors actually employed the powers they enjoyed under the law. Mr Paul Haagen, of Princeton Univer-

sity, is currently at work on a Ph D thesis on the subject of imprisonment for debt in eighteenth-century England. It is possible that his researches will throw some light on this neglected topic. The account which follows is a highly conjectural but plausible reconstruction, based on a wide reading of the many polemical pamphlets published on the subject of imprisonment for debt in the course of the eighteenth century. It draws also upon the report of a parliamentary committee set up in 1791 to investigate the law and practice of imprisonment for debt; the committee's report, which confines itself to the London area, is printed in *Commons Journals*, vol. 47, pp. 640–73. There have been several suggestive accounts of the practice of imprisonment for debt as it has been carried on in recent years; see e.g. Paul Rock, *Making People Pay* (London, 1973), and Richard Ford, 'Imprisonment for debt,' *Michigan Law Review*, vol, 25 (1926–7).

5   *Commons Journals*, vol. 47, p. 645.

6   ibid., p. 647.

7   The entire set of prison books for the King's Bench prison for the period 1760–1800 is preserved at PRO PRIS 4. Careful analysis of these books would yield *some* information about the practices of creditors. Unfortunately, however, the record in the books is purely formal: what actions creditors took at law are recorded, but how much if any money changed hands at any stage of the process is nowhere indicated. The same limitations inevitably characterize all formal records of the legal process.

8   For the writ of supersedeas, see 'An Old Practitioner', *The Debtor's Pocket Guide in cases of Arrest* (London, 1776).

9   Numerous technical guides to those portions of the law of debt of potential interest and advantage to debtors were published in the eighteenth and early nineteenth century. Two outstandingly informative examples are the *Debtor's Pocket Guide* (1776) and Richard Dorset Neale, *The Prisoner's Guide; Every Debtor his own Lawyer*, 3rd ed. (London, 1813).

10 A friendly action could be dropped at any time, of course. When John Howard toured the prisons of England and Wales in the 1770s and 1780s he was told by a number of gaolers of the significant proportion of their prisoners who moved in and out of prison apparently at their own convenience. See, for example, John Howard, *Account of the principal lazarettos* (Warrington, 1789), p. 186.

11 Lineham, 'The campaign to abolish imprisonment for debt', p. 31. The act in question is 1 Geo. III c. 17. The compulsive clause was repealed 2 Geo. III c. 2.

12 The mode of obtaining both the 'day rules' and the privilege of the Rules in the early nineteenth century is discussed in *Parliamentary Papers*, no. 152 (1814–15) vol. 4, pp. 537, 635. Eighteenth-century practice was the same. 'Day rules' – formal permission to make a trip out of the prison – were available only during the legal terms. In 1790, the court of King's Bench ruled that prisoners should only be allowed three day rules a term and that the extent of the rules should be narrowed. See *The Debtor and Creditor's Assistant* (London, 1793), pp. 9–10. See also note 34.

13 See e.g. PRO KB 1/17 Bundle Hilary 1768, unnumbered (petition of King's Bench prisoners).

14 PRO KB 1/21 Bundle Trinity 1779, 68 (affidavit of Thomas Phillips), notes the especial desire of distressed tradesmen to obtain the liberty of the Rules.

15 See note 9.

16 For a hostile account of gaol lawyers, see *A Companion for Debtors and Prisoners, and advice to Creditors, in Ten Letters* (London, 1699), pp. 31–7. The name 'gaol lawyer' was usually a term of opprobrium. Richard Dorset Neale, author of the early nineteenth century *Prisoner's Guide*, however, announced that he had 'attained the summit of his ambition . . . in being instrumental to the release of many worthy, but unhappy debtors'. He was, he said,' content to bear the appellation of "the Gaol Lawyer"' (*Prisoner's Guide*, pp. iii–iv).

17 The 'debtor ethos' is expressed in many of the written productions of debtors. Thus, for a histrionic account of the debtor as victim, see Maria Barrell, *The Captive* (London, 1790). In pro-creditor accounts, the adoption by debtors of a hostile attitude to the law of debt, and to those who made use of it, is described as the 'corrupting' effect of a gaol.

18 Sympathy for the imprisoned debtor is evident in many eighteenth-century newspaper reports, and also in such novels as Henry Fielding's *Amelia*. As Peter Lineham remarks in his thesis (p. 77), the hero of an eighteenth-century novel is much more likely to suffer imprisonment for debt than the villain.

19 The biblical injunction to visit those in prison was commonly

invoked in the eighteenth century in favour of debtors, rarely in favour of criminal prisoners.

20   For the 'Thatched House Society' see especially [James Nield], *An Account of the Rise, Progress and Present State of the Society for the Discharge and Relief of Persons Imprisoned for Small Debts throughout England* (London, 1796), and Lineham, 'The campaign to abolish imprisonment for debt', pp. 81–101, 110, 140.

21   The earliest relief legislation for debtors is discussed in Philip Shaw, 'The position of Thomas Dekker in Jacobean prison literature', *Publications of the Modern Language Association of America*, vol. 62, no. 2 (1947) pp. 372–3*n*. Interregnum measures are discussed in the several histories of interregnum law reform, e.g. Donald Veall, *The Popular Movement for Law Reform* (Oxford, 1970), pp. 146–51.

22   The first post-restoration Insolvency Act was in 1670. In the later eighteenth century, Insolvency Acts were passed in 1755, 1761, 1765, 1769, 1772, 1774, 1776, 1778, 1781, 1794, 1795 and 1797.

23   After 1711, debtors seeking release under Insolvency Acts were required to publish their names in the *London Gazette* in order to avert their creditors. Not *all* debtors who sought release were released; none the less, these lists provide the most easily accessible indication of numbers making use of the Acts. Lists of those actually discharged were drawn up by the quarter sessions justices. Some such lists of King's Bench prisoners are preserved in the Surrey County Record Office, Q S 3/2.

24   Lineham, 'Campaign to abolish imprisonment for debt', pp. 112–15.

25   *Commons Journals*, vol. 39–47; *Lords Journals*, vol. 37. The journals are indexed at this period, so the fate of insolvency legislation is easily traced.

26   Lineham, 'Campaign to abolish imprisonment for debt', pp. 142–54.

27   For a detailed account of an early petitioning campaign, see Moses Pitt, *The Cry of the Oppressed* (London, 1691). Petitions from debtors in the later eighteenth century may be traced in the indexes of the Commons Journals.

28   For the jurisdiction of the court of King's Bench, see William Blackstone, *Commentaries on the Laws of England* (Oxford,

1768) pp. 41–3. The court had the power to commit to any prison in the land, but prisoners who actually appeared before the court were usually committed to the King's Bench prison. Debtors arrested in the country were usually committed to the nearest local gaol until their suits came to trial; they could choose to transfer to the London prison even at the mesne process stage of the proceedings, however. The instrument for effecting such a transfer was the writ of habeas corpus.

29 Duffy, 'Bankruptcy and insolvency', Table 2.2, gives annual commitment totals, derived from the prison books.

30 *Commons Journals*, vol. 47, p. 647. John Howard, in *State of the Prisons* (Warrington, 1777), p. 198, gives a slightly more detailed picture. According to him, the 395 prisoners in the prison at one point in 1776 had between them 279 wives and 725 children, a total of 1004 dependents, of whom he estimated approximately two-thirds lived within the walls.

   Sources for the table of prison population on page 263 are as follows: PRO KB 1/17 Bundle Hilary 1768 (petition of King's Bench prisoners); Howard, *State of the Prisons*, 3rd ed. (Warrington, 1784), p. 243, and *Account of the principal lazarettos* (Warrington, 1789), p. 130; *Commons Journals*, vol. 47, p. 651. For other accounts and estimates, see PRO TS 11/73/228; PRO KB 1/17 Bundle Hilary 1769, unnumbered item (petition of William Bingley); Guidhall Library, London, MS 659.1, 'Copy of a letter sent to the Right Honourable Lord Mansfield December 26 1775. . . .': PRO KB 1/24 Bundle Trinity 1785, 65 (petition of prisoners), and PRO 30/8/149, fo. 183. It is notable that the prisoners, on one or two occasions, estimated their numbers as in the 770 to 800 range – unfortunately with no greater degree of precision. It is possible therefore that the variations in the number of prisoners were somewhat greater than this table might suggest.

31 Chatham Papers, PRO 30/8/149, fos. 182–3.

32 Howard, *State of the Prisons*, appendix, p. 283.

33 Several prison reformers wrote generally critical accounts of the prison as a physical environment. See William Smith, *State of the Gaols in London, Westminster and the borough of Southwark* (London, 1776), pp. 43–61; Howard, *State of the Prisons*, pp. 196–201; and *Report of the subcommittee (of the society for giving effect to His Majesty's proclamation against vice and immorality) respecting the improvements which have lately*

been made in the prisons and houses of correction of England and Wales (London, 1790) p. 19. The last report did not note that any marked improvements had been made. See also the later editions of Howard. On the other hand, for a highly enthusiastic description of the prison see *The Debtor and Creditor's Assistant*, pp. 1–55.

34   The Rules of the King's Bench prison were generously defined in the early eighteenth century: see *A Report from the Committee appointed to enquire into the State of the Goals* (sic) *of this kingdom. Relating to the King's Bench Prison* (London, 1730), p. 8. In 1790 the court of King's Bench redefined them more narrowly, and ruled all taverns out of bounds. The rule of court is reproduced in *Commons Journals*, vol. 47, p. 665.

35   For the investigations which led to a parliamentary vote to finance the reconstruction of the prison, and for the early plans, see *Commons Journals*, vol. 26, pp. 437, 505–13, 680, 764, 921.

36   The table of fees drawn up by the court of King's Bench in 1760, which pertained for the rest of the century, is reproduced in *Parliamentary Papers*, no. 152 (1814–15), vol. 4, p. 775.

37   M. Dorothy George, *London Life in the Eighteenth Century* (Harmondsworth, 1966), p. 100.

38   On overcrowding, see e.g. PRO KB 1/17 Bundle Hilary 1768 unnumbered (petition of King's Bench prisoners), and *St. James' Chroncile*, 21 February 1769.

39   e.g. *Public Advertiser*, 13 June 1785.

40   *Parliamentary Papers*, no. 152 (1814–15), vol. 4, p. 592.

41   PRO KB 21/38 fos. 225–6, rule 1 (1759).

42   PRO KB 1/25 Bundle Michaelmas 1783, 38 (affidavit of T. C. F. Noel *et al.*).

43   *Commons Journals*, vol. 47, p. 660.

44   On the absenteeism of prison officers, see ibid., p. 655; PRO KB 1/27 Bundle Easter 1792, 34 (affidavit of Hill and Young), and KB 1/44 Bundle Michaelmas 1821, 1 (affidavit of William Jones).

45   The account of the prison government presented here is compiled from a mass of small pieces of information, contained mainly in the affidavit files of the court of King's Bench (PRO KB 1). There are some observations on the workings of prison government in *The Debtor and Creditor's Assistant*, but there is no extended eighteenth-century account. The report of the

committee appointed in 1815 to look into the state of the London debtors' prisons (*Parliamentary Papers* [1814–15], vol. 4) contains much useful information but must be employed with care when an earlier period is under consideration: the character of the prison government did change in some respects between 1800 and 1815.

46 On conflicts between the marshal and junior officers, see especially *Middlesex Journal*, 18 November 1769; PRO KB 1/20 Bundle Hilary 1776, 6 (affidavit of R. Curtis), and KB 1/27 Bundle Easter 1792, 34 (affidavit of Hill and Young).

47 For the scale of fees see note 36. It is not easy to determine the incomes of prison officers. The marshal's income is probably to be reckoned in the thousands of pounds. He reported the sources of his income to a parliamentary committee in 1791 (*Commons Journals*, vol. 47, p. 657) but gave no overall figure. In 1750, according to an itemized estimate drawn up by some hostile prisoners, the marshal was drawing an income of some £3752 from a population of 200 prisoners – a figure that did not include the profits of the day rules (Guidhall Library, London, MS 659.1 ['Original affadavits complaining of the marshal's treattment'], p. 16). The marshal himself in 1815 reported that his gross income for the past few years had averaged £6192 *per annum*, and his net income, £4462 (see *Parliamentary Papers*, no. 152 [1814–15], vol. 4, p. 778, and John Wade, a *A Treatise of the Police and Crimes of the Metropolis* [1829; reprinted New York, 1972], p. 264). It is probable that the general trend in the marshal's income was upwards, since certainly the number of prisoners was increasing. As for the other officers, when, in the 1790s, the marshal began to pay salaries to his turnkeys he paid them at the rate of one guinea a week (Guildhall MS 659.1: 'An account of all the fees &c. 1791'); it is probable, however, that the turnkeys' income was augmented by other perquisites. In 1815, the marshal estimated the profits of the clerk of the papers as £600–£700 p.a. At the same time, the deputy marshal reported his profits as £350–£400 p.a. (*Parliamentary Papers*, no. 152 [1814–15,] vol. 4, p. 779.

48 See, for example, *Sone* v. *Ashton* (1762) 3 Burr. 1287, in *English Law Reports*, vol. 97.

49 Pugh, *Imprisonment in Medieval England*, pp. 242–3.

50 In 1815, the warden of the Fleet prison, a prison very similar to

the King's Bench, told a parliamentary committee that he only bothered to contest at law claims of £200 or more (*Parliamentary Papers*, no. 152 [1814–15], vol. 4).

51   On the bonds furnished as sureties for junior officers, see e.g. [William Penrice], *The Extraordinary Case of William Penrice* (London, 1768), p. 13, and PRO KB 1/27 Bundle Easter 1792 59 (affidavit of William Milward).

52   The laxity of the prison's security precautions was most fully revealed by the inquiries of the 1815 parliamentary committee, whose members were prompted to probe into the subject by an incident which marked their visit to the prison: they learnt from conversation with the prisoners of the escape of a particularly notorious prisoner (the radical politician Lord Cochrane, imprisoned on charges of fraud) of which the prison officers proved to be unaware (*Parliamentary Papers*, no. 152 [1814–15], vol. 4 *passim*, especially p. 542).

53   e.g. *Public Advertiser*, 18 June 1779.

54   *Commons Journals*, vol. 47, col. 657.

55   This seems to be indicated by *Sone* v. *Ashton* (1762) 3 Burr. 1287.

56   See e.g. for the marshal Benjamin Thomas PRO ASSI 31/12 (Surrey Summer Assizes 1779, Grand Jury list), and 31 Geo. III c. 23.

57   Guildhall MS 659.1 ('An account of all the fees &c. 1791').

58   [Penrice], *The Extraordinary Case*, p. 9.

59   *Parliamentary Papers*, no. 152 (1814–15), vol. 4, p. 609.

60   ibid., p. 589.

61   For turnkeys rising from the ranks of prisoners, see e.g. [Penrice], *The Extraordinary Case*, pp. 5–6. A large proportion of all the turnkeys appointed in the later eighteenth century first entered the prison as prisoners. Not uncommonly, they were appointed even before their debts were discharged.

62   Until the mid eighteenth century, the position of the prison officers had been much more financially precarious; from the early seventeenth century, the right to make appointments to all offices in the prison had lain in the hands of mortgagees, who had rack-rented the offices at stiff rates. The suspicion that financial pressure on the officers led them to engage in various corrupt and exploitative practices prompted parliamentary inquiries in 1696 and 1729. In 1753, Parliament had voted to compel the mortgagees to surrender their rights, in return for

£10,500, provided from public funds (*Commons Journals*, vol. 26, pp. 505–13, 680–94, 764).

63 For 1771, see *Gentleman's Magazine*, 4 May 1771, and pages 294–5 of this essay. For other incidents, see PRO KB 1/23 Bundle Easter 1782, 29, 38; Bundle Michaelmas 1783, 23, 38; *Commons Journals*, vol. 47, p. 655.

64 *Parliamentary Papers*, no. 152 (1814–15), vol. 4, p. 545. The marshal's disciplinary powers were defined by rules of court in 1729, reprinted in ibid., p. 774.

65 All legal charges brought against prisoners were noted in the prison books (PRO PRIS 4).

66 *Parliamentary Papers* (1814–15), vol. 4, pp. 573–4, 592. For an interesting account by an ex-turnkey of the problems of preserving order in the prison, see [Penrice], *The Extraordinary Case*, p. 6.

67 *Parliamentary Papers*, no. 152 (1814–15), vol. 4, pp. 575–6.

68 *Morning Chronicle*, 21 June 1779; *London Chronicle*, 22 June 1779.

69 For troubles in the prison arising from the prisoners' wariness of tyrannical excess, see PRO KB 1/27 Bundle Easter 1791, 122, and for general comment, James Pearce, *A Treatise on the Abuses of the Laws, particularly in actions by arrest* (London, 1814), p. 108.

70 The report of the 1791 troubles carried in the *Public Advertiser*, 28–31 May 1791, provides an exceptionally detailed and informative account of a prison riot, of the difficulties prison officers experienced in putting down unrest, and of the various expedients they adopted. See also pages 295–8.

71 The judges' powers over the prison, and their right to exercise them or not as they saw fit, were discussed in a series of cases in 1703; see Sutton's case, 6 Mod. 91, in *English Law Reports*, vol. 87, and at 2 Ld Raym 1005 in ibid., vol. 92. It is because the judges did claim and exercise judicial powers over their prisoners that so many affidavits relating to upsets in the prison are preserved in the court's affidavit files (PRO KB 1). Sentences imposed by the judges are recorded in the court rule book; see e.g. KB 21/43 (entries for Saturday after fifteen days after Easter, Thursday after three weeks after Easter and Saturday after the morrow of Ascension 1782). When prisoners were removed to other gaols, a note was also made in the prison commitment book; see, for example, for occasions in 1785 and

1791, when prisoners tried to blow up the prison wall with gunpowder, PRIS 4/10, fo. 1672 and PRIS 4/12, fo. 296.

72 See A. Jessopp (ed.), *The Oeconomy of the Fleete,* Camden Society Publication, N.S. 25 (Westminster, 1879), pp. 168–71.

73 2 Geo. II c. 22 and 32 Geo. II c. 28. These Acts substantially repeated the provisions of seventeenth-century legislation: see C. H. Firth and R. S. Rait (eds.), *Acts and Ordinances of the Interregnum 1642–60* (London, 1911), pp. 753–64 (especially pp. 756–7) and 22–3 Chas. II c. 20. The function of legislation in these instances seems to have been essentially hortatory: Parliament was not creating any new responsibilities but merely urging the judges on to discharge their duties. For rules the judges drew up in the eighteenth century, see pages 280, 287 and 288 of this essay. The Acts did provide specific monetary penalties for prison officers failing to comply with court orders. Even before thus specifically empowered to punish, however, the judges had claimed a general disciplinary power over prison officers as over all other servants of the court.

74 *Commons Journals,* vol. 47, p. 662. Only two written records of reports made by visitors over this period have survived: see PRO KB 21/40 (entry for Monday after three weeks after Trinity 1771), and KB 1/29 Bundle Michaelmas 1796, 96 (Templer's report of the state of the prison).

75 *Commons Journals,* vol. 47, p. 661.

76 Petitions of prisoners are preserved in the affidavit files of the court of King's Bench (PRO KB 1). They are most easily traced through the affidavit index (KB 39), a notebook kept by clerks as a record of the fees they received for filing documents, in which all documents in the affidavits files are chronologically listed. Guildhall MS 659.1, a miscellaneous collection of documents relating to the prison, also contains some letters and petitions of prisoners. Letters and petitions are frequently annotated with remarks on the action taken by the court.

77 For a suggestive account of the prison visitor at work, see PRO KB 1/24 Bundle Trinity 1784, 51, 52.

78 See pages 286–98 below.

79 *The Debtor and Creditor's Assistant,* p. 43.

80 The account of the 'prison economy' provided here draws upon *The Debtor and Creditor's Assistant;* the 1815 parliamentary report, *King's Bench, Fleet, Marshalsea &c. (Parliamentary*

Papers, vol. 152, no. 152); and miscellaneous information in the affidavit files (PRO KB 1).

81 For the account of a prisoner doctor, see *Commons Journals,* vol. 47, p. 660. For a prisoner lawyer, see the testimony relating to Paul Patrician Carne in the collection of documents headed 'Original affidavits of the prisoners complaining of the marshal's treatment 24 July 1750', Guildhall MS 659.1. An Act of 1729 (2 Geo. II c. 23) forbade attorneys in prison to sue out writs or prosecute suits on pain of being struck off the roll; legal knowledge was, however, at a premium in the prison, and was a highly marketable commodity. See also note 16.

82 *Parliamentary Papers,* no. 152 (1814–15), vol. 4, p. 595.

83 William Bingley, petitioning the court in 1769, suggested that it was the responsibility of those running the prison to facilitate his carrying on his business as a bookseller and stationer, either by making a large room available to him, or by giving him the liberty of the Rules: PRO KB 1/17 Bundle Hilary 1769, unnumbered, and KB 1/18 Bundle Michaelmas 1769, unnumbered (affidavits of William Bingley). For Bingley see pages 135, 145, 162–3 above.

84 The remarks on the prison market in rooms in the 1815 report are *not* a reliable guide to practice in the earlier period, as is indeed suggested by the report: see, for example, *Parliamentary Papers,* no. 152 (1814–15), vol. 4, pp. 567–8. For the late eighteenth-century practice see especially PRO KB 1/21 Bundle Trinity 1779, 79.

85 *Commons Journals,* vol. 47, col. 652.

86 On gambling and smuggling, see notes 67–8. For 'whistling shops' see *Debtor and Creditor's Assistant,* p. 50. On coining in prisons, see John Styles, 'Our traitorous money makers', *n.* 148, pages 353–4 above.

87 *Debtor and Creditor's Assistant,* p. 42.

88 Some prison charities (those whose payment was in arrears) are listed in [Penrice], *The Extraordinary Case,* p. 43.

89 *Commons Journals,* vol. 47, p. 657.

90 *Parliamentary Papers* (1814–15), vol. 4, p. 539. For numbers of poor prisoners earlier, see their various petitions, e.g. KB 1/20 Bundle Trinity 1775, 56.

91 *Debtor and Creditor's Assistant,* pp. 47–8.

92 *Parliamentary Papers,* vol. 152, col. 60.

93 'The lower sort of prisoners' is a phrase which crops up fre-

quently in all accounts of the prison: see *The Debtor and Creditor's Assistant*, p. 48 and PRO KB 1/24 Bundle Trinity 1784, 51 (affidavit of James Spragg).

94   John Lane, *Masonic Records* (London, 1895), pp. 32, 33, 62.

95   Smith, *State of the Gaols*, p. 61. On charitable dealings between prisoners see, for example, *Commons Journals*, vol. 47, pp. 657, 660.

96   e.g. *Public Advertiser*, 14 August 1783; *Middlesex Journal*, 17 June 1769.

97   e.g. for an entertainment sponsored by John Wilkes, on his release from the King's Bench prison: *London Chronicle*, 19 April 1770.

98   For early accounts of prisoner self-government, see Clifford Dobb, 'Life and conditions in London prisons, 1553–1643, with special reference to contemporary literature' (Unpublished BLitt. thesis, Oxford University, 1952), pp. 192–201, 216, 277–83. W. J. Sheehan discusses eighteenth-century prisoner self-government in Newgate briefly in his essay, 'Finding solace in eighteenth century Newgate', in J. S. Cockburn (ed.), *Crime in England 1550–1800* (London, 1977), pp. 233–4. His account is marred, however, by his failure to distinguish between debtors and felons: he runs together, in a misleading way, accounts of their very different experiences and activities.

99   This account of the commonside corporation is based mainly on affidavits and petitions in PRO KB 1; especially for this period KB 1/19 Bundle Hilary 1774, 74. The richest documentation of the affairs of commonside prisoners dates from the first half of the century, especially from the period 1727–34: a period marked by strife and contention and giving rise to an extraordinary number of affidavits and petitions.

100   These rules are reprinted in summary form in *Parliamentary Papers*, no. 152 (1814–15), vol. 4, p. 774, and in full in *The Debtor's Pocket Guide*, pp. 45–9.

101   For documents relating to the appointment of stewards see PRO KB 1/20 Bundle Trinity 1775, 24 (petititon of poor prisoners); Bundle Easter 1776, 20 (election and approbation of steward).

102   Rule 14 (see note 100).

103   'S.S.', author of *The Prisoner's Complaint to the King's Most Excellent Majestie or the Cries of the King's Bench*, a pamphlet published in London in 1673, describes himself as 'a Fellow of

King's College in Southwark'. It seems likely, however, that the college was already old at that time. Use of the term 'college' in this context calls for some brief comment: it was apparently a common joke to speak of prisons as 'colleges' at this time (see *1811 Dictionary of the Vulgar Tongue* [Illinois, 1971], entries 'college' and 'Whittington's College'). In the King's Bench prison, however, something more than a joke was involved, even if the name sometimes had overtones of parody. For contemporary applications of the term 'college' to workhouses and even small factories, illustrating the very wide range of its possible meanings, see, for example, Michael Laithwaite, 'The buildings of Burford', in Alan Everitt (ed.), *Perspectives in English Urban History* (London, 1973), p. 88, and James Hall, *A History of the town of Nantwich* (Nantwich, 1883), p. 270.

The account of the college provided here is based in part on surviving college rule books, of which there are three in the Guildhall Library, London (one at Pam 5339, two bound in MS 659.1), and on affidavits and petitions in PRO KB 1, especially KB 1/21 Bundle Trinity 1779, 68, 79; KB 1/23 Bundle Easter 1782, 29, 38; and KB 1/24 Bundle Trinity 1785, 45. For a brief notice of a very similar kind of organization existing in the Fleet prison, another London debtors' prison, see Howard, *State of the Prisons* (1777), p. 164.

104 See Guildhall MS 659.1 (affidavits of Joseph Wingrave *et al.*, 28 November 1750).

105 e.g. PRO KB 1/21 Bundle Trinity 1779, 79 (affidavit of Thomas Phillips).

106 Guidhall MS 659.1, 'Rules to be obeyed and observed by every member of this college', *c.* 1782, pp. 1–2. Compare the declaration in the eighteenth-century *Lawbook of the Crowley Ironworks*, ed. M. W. Flinn (London, 1951), p. 8. This book affords several interesting contrasts and comparisons with the material presented here. See also, for example, ibid., p. 159.

107 See PRO KB 1/23 Bundle Easter 1782, 29; KB 1/24 Bundle Trinity 1785, 45.

108 On the work of leet and manorial courts in the eighteenth century, see Sidney and Beatrice Webb, *The Manor and the Borough* (London, 1908), *passim*. The part which petty courts and informal arbitration played and were perceived to play

in late eighteenth-century English society deserves historical attention. Governmental paraphernalia and ritual were also frequently adopted by artisanal associations, and experience of self-government in such groups as these may well have provided another source for prisoners' practices. See for this Iorwerth Prothero, *Artisans and Politics* (Folkestone, Kent, 1979), pp. 34–5, and R. A. Leeson, *Travelling Brothers* (London, 1979), pp. 143–4. In the latter the use of the term 'garnish' among the hatters is noted. See also Ned Ward, *A compleat and humorous account of all the remarkable clubs and societies in the cities of London and Westminster*, 7th ed. (London, 1756), p. 2.

109   Guidhall MS 659.1, 'Rules to be obeyed and observed by every member of this college', *c.* 1779, rule 37.

110   e.g. PRO KB 1/19 Bundle Easter 1774, 42.

111   Viz. Captain Phillips, Captain Campbell, Sir Alexander Hay, Philip Dormer Stanhope Esq. etc. The affidavits collected at PRO KB 1/23 Bundle Easter 1782, 29 and 38, suggest very strongly that office in the prison, as in society, was a function of rank.

112   PRO KB 1/21 Bundle Trinity 1779, 68 (petition of 300 plus prisoners).

113   See especially PRO KB 1/24 Bundle Trinity 1785, 45.

114   See Affidavits headed 'Original affidavits of prisoners complaining of the marshal's treatment', Guildhall MS 659.1; PRO KB 1/21 Bundle Trinity 1779, 68, 79; and documents in Guildhall MS 659.1 relating to the troubles of 1779.

115   For an example of formal co-operation between the prison officers and the college see PRO KB 1/21 Bundle Trinity 1779, 79 (affidavit of Thomas Phillips).

116   *Annual Register 1779*, 18 June, 22 June; PRO KB 1/23 Bundle Easter 1782, 78.

117   See especially the rules of court of 1759 (PRO KB 21/38, fos. 225–6, summarized in *Parliamentary Papers*, no. 152 [1814–15], vol. 4, p. 775.

118   For the rule, see *Parliamentary Papers* (1814–15), vol. 4, p. 777. For subsequent admission of its ineffectiveness, see PRO KB 1/39 Bundle Trinity 1816, 69.

119   PRO KB 1/23 Bundle Easter 1782, 29, 38.

120   *King's Bench, Fleet, Marshalsea &c.* (*Parliamentary Papers*, no. 152 [1814–15], vol. 4), *passim*. Howard, noting the existence

of the college for the first time in the 1784 edition of *State of the Prisons* (p. 284), remarked that the college rules were in many cases 'arbitrary and improper'. 'But', he added, 'they are now abolished.' He also announced the suppression of the prisoners' laws in the Fleet at this time.

121 See the account of the mock election held in the King's Bench prison in 1827: *Explanation of the picture of chairing the members, a scene in the mock election which took place at the King's Bench prison* (London, 1828), Guildhall Library, London, Pam 3949.

122 Smith, *State of the Gaols*, p. 59.

123 PRO KB 1/23 Bundle Michaelmas 1783, 23, 38.

124 Only events of 1770–1 are discussed here. For other disturbances in the King's Bench associated with the notion that imprisonment for debt was unconstitutional, see especially PRO KB 1/24 Bundle Trinity 1784, 51, 52; *London Chronicle*, 12–14 August 1784; KB 1/24 Bundle Michaelmas 1785, 69, 71, 72; *Gentleman's Magazine*, 10 February 1786; *London Chronicle*, 11 February 1786; *The King against Burgh*, PRO TS 11/2506/ 780; KB 1/27 Bundle Hilary 1793, 80; *Annual Register*, 26 November 1792. For the cessation of the Insolvency Acts in 1780s to 1790s, see above, page 260.

125 James Stephen, *Considerations on Imprisonment for Debt* (London, 1770). For comparable later pamphlets, see Edward Farley, *Imprisonment for Debt Unconstitutional and Oppressive* (London, 1788), and *The Trial of P. W. Duffin and Thomas Lloyd* (London, 1793), reprinted in ed. T. J. Howell, *A Complete Collection of State Trials* (London, 1817), vol. 22, pp. 317–48. Both Stephen and Duffin and Lloyd were prisoners at the time their pamphlets were published; Edward Farley had been a prisoner for debt in the King's Bench in 1785 (see PRO PRIS 4/10, fo. 1881).

126 [Delamayne], *The Rise and Practice of Imprisonment*, is a sympathetic but critical response by a professional lawyer to these radical claims. Delamayne was a prisoner for debt in the King's Bench from November 1767 to January 1769 (see PRO PRIS 4/4 fos. 124–5).

127 For the campaign of James Stephen, and the troubles he precipitated, see especially Stephen's own account in *Considerations on Imprisonment; Middlesex Journal*, 22 November 1770; PRO KB 1/18 Bundle Michaelmas 1770, 21, and Bundle

Trinity 1771, 42, 51; and the account provided by Stephen's son (Merle M. Bevington, [ed.], *The Memoirs of James Stephen* [London, 1954], pp. 93–106). For the campaign which Stephen conducted even after his release, see *London Chronicle*, November 1770–February 1771 *passim*.

128 *Middlesex Journal*, 7, 9 August 1770. I have not been able to find a copy of the original pamphlet. It is advertised, however, in *London Chronicle*, 4 August 1770.

129 Br. Lib. Add. MS 30871, fo. 96.

130 For Stephen's friends, see Bevington, *The Memoirs*, pp. 89–90 and notes; Frank Luther Mott, *American Journalism* (New York, 1962), pp. 79–80; Lucyle Werkmeister, *The London Daily Press 1772–1792* (Lincoln, Neb., 1962), pp. 80–2; *Complete Baronetage*, vol. 5: *1707–1800* (Exeter, 1906), pp. 35–7.

131 For indications that Stephen used the formal machinery of the college to organize his campaign see Stephen, *Considerations on Imprisonment*, pp. 5–20; PRO KB 1/18 Bundle Trinity 1771, 42 (affidavit of Thomas Fletcher).

132 PRO KB 1/18 Bundle Michaelmas 1770, 21; [Stephen], *The Memoirs*, pp. 97–8.

133 PRO KB 1/18 Bundle Michaelmas 1770, 21.

134 PRO KB 11/47, 20, and Bevington, *The Memoirs*, p. 101. The statement of Stephen's son that the prisoners indicted the marshal on this occasion seems to arise from a confusion with a later incident.

135 PRO KB 1/18 Bundle Trinity 1771, 42 (affidavit of Thomas Fletcher).

136 For Stephen's transfer to the Fleet prison, see PRO PRIS 4/4, fo. 260; PRIS 2/21. For disturbances there, *London Chronicle*, 23 November 1770, 12, 14 March, 2 April 1771.

137 *Farley's Bristol Journal*, 18 May 1771.

138 PRO KB 1/18 Bundle Trinity 1771, 42, 51; *London Chronicle*, 2 May 1771; *Farley's Bristol Journal*, 1 June 1771.

139 PRO KB 1/18 Bundle Trinity 1771, 42 (affidavit of Thomas Watson).

140 PRO KB 21/40 (entry for Monday after three weeks after Trinity 1771). There is also a copy of the report in Guildhall MS 659.1.

141 PRO ASSI 31/10 (Surrey Summer Assizes 1771).

142 PRO KB 1/18 Bundle Michaelmas 1771, unnumbered (memorial of King's Bench prisoners). There is no indication

in the *Commons Journals* that they made anything other than the ordinary application for an insolvency act (vol. 33, p. 447).

143   See PRO PRIS 4/4, under names of individual prisoners, and *London Gazette* (1772) *passim.*

Index